YOUR VITALITY PERSONALITY

Decode the Real You
and Hack Into Happiness

CANDICE THOMAS

Desert Sky Press
Tucson, Arizona, USA

Copyright © 2024 Candice Thomas

All rights reserved. This book may not be reproduced in whole or in part, stored in a retrieval system, or transmitted in any form or by any means electronic, mechanical, or other without written permission from the publisher, except by a reviewer, who may quote brief passages in a review.

Desert Sky Press

Published by Desert Sky Press
Tucson, Arizona, USA
desertsky.press

Library of Congress Cataloging-in-Publication Data
Thomas, Candice, 1972-
Your Vitality Personality: Decode the Real You and Hack Into Happiness / Candice Thomas

ISBN: 979-8-9908088-0-5 paperback
ISBN: 979-8-9908088-1-2 hardback

DEDICATION

Thank you Sandy.
You were magnificent.

CONTENTS

Acknowledgements — i

Introduction — iii

CHAPTER ONE
Happiness is Being Who You Really Are — 1

CHAPTER TWO
Personality Type 1: The Architect | The Judge — 9

CHAPTER THREE
Personality Type 2: The Altruist | The Victim — 35

CHAPTER FOUR
Personality Type 3: The Luminary | The Pretender — 61

CHAPTER FIVE
Personality Type 4: The Creative | The Diva — 89

CHAPTER SIX
Personality Type 5: The Sage | The Miser — 123

CHAPTER SEVEN
Personality Type 6: The Guardian | The Alarmist — 155

CHAPTER EIGHT
Personality Type 7: The Uplifter | The Hedonist — 187

CHAPTER NINE
Personality Type 8: The Leader | The Bully — 221

CHAPTER TEN
Personality Type 9: The Healer | The Submissive — 253

CHAPTER ELEVEN
Integration — 281

CHAPTER TWELVE
The Real You Methods — 287

About the Author — 297

ACKNOWLEDGMENTS

First and foremost, I want to thank my mom, Verna Zaydel, for being my lifelong champion. During my childhood she prioritized education and developing skills, and that turned out to be the most empowering thing she could have done for me. Teaching me early that I can learn how to do anything made me feel fearless and helped me trust my own intelligence. I can't think of a more amazing gift. I am so grateful for her love, praise, encouragement and support.

Deep thanks and gratitude to my spiritual mastermind partner and friend Ken Alexander. Who knew, all those years ago, what deciding to study the Enneagram and Law of Attraction together would do for us? Since then we have taken a most amazing journey together exploring metaphysics, quantum science, sacred geometry, and spiritual alchemy. He was my primary beta reader and consultant, and this book is definitely better for it. It has been so meaningful and uplifting to have such an amazing Purpose Partner.

Thank you to coach and mentor Sandy Hogan, who introduced me to the Enneagram and changed my life. She is always loved, and never forgotten.

Heartfelt gratitude to Developmental Editor Ivri Turner, for her masterful guidance. She challenged me to create my own system for teaching the Enneagram, and recommended I develop a graphic as the model. It launched me on a most enormous and inspiring labor of love that just keeps expanding. It was an incredible collaborative experience. I learned so much.

Thank you to Georgia Jean and the Circle of Light, for the years of enlightened education. profound energy healings and activations, and most helpful tools for integration. Their Love and Acceptance technique informed the Charged Energy Clearing technique seen here. I am very grateful for their combined mentorship and healing.

I would like to acknowledge a woman I have never met, named Cindy Farries. Her YouTube channels, Lady of the Forest 444 and Out of This World, were very important companions to me as I completed this book.

Thank you to J Clark, the highest-vibration human I have ever personally met, who taught me a most miraculous method for self-healing, which was adapted to become the Real You Method known as the Integration Exercise. She just mentioned it in passing, but it has become the single most powerful healing exercise I have ever encountered. My patients, clients, friends and I have all benefited enormously. I'm excited for more people to learn of it.

Many thanks to Jack Canfield, who gave me the encouragement and mentorship I needed to inspire me to give this project the time and space it required to be done right.

And finally, thank you so much to my tribe of patients and clients who gave me their trust and loyalty, allowing us to take a most extraordinary journey of healing, love and expansion together. To see them improve and blossom has been my greatest joy.

INTRODUCTION

I was first introduced to the Enneagram in 2009 while I was in acupuncture school. I was fortunate enough to take a class there called Self-Actualization for the Practitioner, taught by the extraordinary angelic being, Sandy Hogan.

Sandy was the executive life coach for a Fortune 500 company who oversaw the personal development of the employees they flagged as the "High Potentials." She groomed a generation of exceptional leaders, and it was my great privilege to have her as my mentor, coach, teacher, patient, officemate, and champion for over a decade. I was at her bedside when she crossed over in 2019.

This experience was life-changing to say the least. Not only did Sandy train me in the ways of the Enneagram, Non-Violent Communication, Christ Consciousness, and the Law of Attraction, but she herself radiated unconditional love. Being in her presence was like being bathed in light.

Having a role model who embodied kindness, love, acceptance, generosity, and patience was the most profound education of all. I had never seen anything like it, and I knew I was nowhere close to it, but I discovered a deep desire to get myself there. Thus launched a most extraordinary spiritual journey happening for me personally, at the same time that I launched my acupuncture practice in Tucson, AZ.

Right from the beginning, I had every new patient take the Enneagram personality type quiz at the first appointment. I didn't know how I intended to use the information, but I just had the feeling it could prove to be important. Little did I know it would open my mind and rock my world.

First of all, what an icebreaker! The process of correctly identifying my patient's Personality Type became an unexpectedly direct route to developing intimacy and trust with a stranger. By the end of the first appointment, they felt seen and heard, and I felt clarity and compassion. This created an unanticipated extra dynamic in my acupuncture practice – nobody left.

I have had the extraordinarily good fortune to work continuously with many of my original patients for over ten years, which gave me a most remarkable view of the Personality Types over a long period of time. I became consumed with this work - it was utterly fascinating. In 2016 I became certified as an Enneagram teacher and began teaching what I was learning in the field.

I saw how people's behavior changed as good and bad times came on in their lives. I saw their coping mechanisms and choices. I saw how the perspective of the Personality Type was at the dead center of all of it – their health, their relationships, their career, their money, and their sense of purpose.

The connection between the perspective of the Personality Type and the nature of the health ailment became immediately obvious. There were clear Sabotage Patterns per Type. I could see it was the beliefs they held, the way they thought about things, and the feelings they swam in that were in the way of change or progress. (The results of the study on health pattern by Personality Type are in Book Three).

Meanwhile, in my private life, my study, meditation, shadow work, journaling, and intentional living were all starting to change me in amazing ways. I began experiencing clairvoyance, clairaudience, clairsentience, and claircognizance. I began to communicate with my guides and Higher Self. I began to remember past lives. I began to discover my true power.

Now, I am very clear about who I am and why I'm here. And this book series is a big part of it.

As I continued learning and growing, I experimented with how I talked with my patients, venturing onto new topics. I gave the same counsel about how to shift perspective to all, but only some were receptive.

And actually that became even more fascinating. I ended up having two test groups of sorts – the ones who were resistant and the ones who were open.

Sure enough, the distance between these two groups became great. Ultimately those who were not interested in self-awareness or change generally remained in a cycle of stress and deterioration. And the ones who became curious about themselves and launched themselves upon their own journey of self-discovery began to blossom and thrive.

Serious health issues reversed and resolved. Miraculous repairs in relationships occurred. Unexpected promotions happened at work. People went off their anxiety meds and antidepressants. Many let go of their addictions. Some started having their own intuitive abilities begin to come online.

I began receiving thank-you letters and gifts. I began receiving referrals from all over the country. I began winning awards. I began speaking at conferences and being invited on podcasts. It took on a life of its own.

When I decided to write a book to collect these teachings into something coherent, I realized I had my own approach and observations that went well beyond the traditional scope of the Enneagram. I wanted to somehow include all of the wisest and most helpful teachings I had encountered over 30 years of education, plus my clinical observations, plus my intuitive insights. I wanted there to be a way to boil it all down into a single system that can be easily taught and understood.

Thus I created Your Vitality Personality, an entirely new and different approach to personal development.

This book is for people who feel stuck and frustrated in their life. It might be in the area of health, or relationships, or money, or career, or a sense of meaning, or most of these. This is for people who want things to change, but can't see how to go about it.

This book is also for people who want to be their best self and activate their happiest life. If you are starting to suspect that you are built for something important, then you are in the right place. The Universal principles and powerful methods for healing and advancement that you learn here will take you to the next level.

Your Vitality Personality offers you a clear, simple blueprint – a map that depicts exactly how to extricate yourself from the limitations of your unconscious programming, and activate your access to your Higher Consciousness.

This approach revolutionizes your relationship with yourself and your reality. It gives you the opportunity to dramatically elevate your quality of life in a short amount of time. It is my joy to share this with you, and pass on the healing keys that I received, so that you may finally unlock yourself.

Sending you so much love and light,

Candice Thomas

CHAPTER ONE
HAPPINESS IS BEING WHO YOU REALLY ARE

As you may have noticed, times are changing rapidly. We perhaps cannot recall another time in our history that had quite this much volatility and upheaval. The old paradigms don't seem to work anymore, and the new ones haven't been invented yet. Even the old version of yourself probably doesn't really fit you anymore, yet you're not quite sure how to evolve into the new, upleveled version you really want to be.

Start with learning about your Personality Type. It has so much more to do with your personal quality of life and your ability to influence your world than you ever would have guessed.

Your Personality Type has much to do with holding your mind inside a pattern of beliefs and thoughts that are generated from a platform of scarcity and survival. You can think of it as your default hardwiring. It always runs in the same circuit, creating the same old dynamics in your life that lead to unhappiness.

This is not The Real You. It is The Programmed You. The Programmed You actually blocks you from connecting deeply with The Real You, and this creates so many unwanted dynamics in your life.

The yearning that you feel to live differently – to have more freedom, more stability, more insight, more health, more money, more love, more peace, and more joy – these are all in actuality the yearning to be released from the programmed constraints inside your unconscious mind. These constraints are patterned by your Personality Type. To gain mastery over your Personality Type is to gain mastery over your unconscious mind, and therefore your entire reality.

Many of us have been students of the Law of Attraction, trying so hard to "raise our vibration" and "manifest our dreams," but most haven't seen the kinds of results we were hoping for. This is because the mental preoccupation of the Personality Type is having a totally different, unconscious, conversation with the Universe -- that you don't even know about. It is sabotaging you every step of the way.

In order to manifest the life of your dreams, you must become willing to go inward. You must discover how to love yourself anyway, despite the way your mind is wired to make you feel disconnected. You must learn about your shadow and how to integrate it, so you may finally shine your brightest light. That is when you will finally get to start living your life as The Real You.

This book is a guide out of the unconscious state, bringing to light the key things you need to watch out for that have been holding you back, and the precise changes to make in order to embrace your happiest, healthiest life. It is the blueprint you have always longed for, that allows you to finally make sense of yourself, love yourself, and have the life you always wanted.

Even though the map is clear, the road is not easy. Self-awareness is not for everyone. It is not terribly fun to learn all about your shadow and drag it out into the light. That's why there is so much conflict in the world – so many of us are too afraid to really look in the mirror, and take responsibility for what we find there. It takes love, willingness and maturity to get you through.

Yet the rewards for this inner work are really quite beyond imagination. Once you know The Real You you will find yourself in uncharted levels of joy and deep satisfaction. Your self-esteem, your relationships, your money, your work, your health, and your sense of purpose will all transform! And here you are, taking the next step on this journey.

Decoding your secret inner programming – and releasing self-sabotage – is what allows you to discover the most potent and mighty aspects of yourself. It allows you to consciously see what has previously been hidden within your unconscious – power, love, genius.

Gaining access to this wisdom will deepen and expand you in ways you cannot currently fathom. You have launched yourself on a path towards your happiest, healthiest, most fulfilling life.

So let's get started on this journey.

We'll begin with some of the basics first. This way, you will be ready to learn about how you are wired, and how to thrive.

*** If you don't know your Personality Type yet, please go online to take the free quiz.

> This is available at **www.YourVitalityPersonality.com**.

What is a Personality Type?

Your personality and your **Personality Type** are not at all the same thing.

Your personality includes things like your favorite color, your love for turtles and motorcycles, your preference for shoes with a square toe, your utter loathing for mushrooms. They are the personal quirks and traits that evolve out of your life experiences.

Your Personality Type is something deeper than that. It is likely encoded into your DNA (studies are just beginning to reveal this), and serves as a framework for your unconscious mind. It is an archetype – a template for your psychology. It creates within you drives and desires. You were born with it, and you can never change it... But you can evolve it.

This does not have to feel like a life sentence! Rather than feeling condemned or fated to be a certain way, think of your Personality Type as a tool. *When used properly, it gives you an enormous advantage.*

There are 9 Personality Types. Each Type is encoded with a very particular set of talents and abilities – ones most other people do not have. When you take advantage of these special talents and abilities, this is living as **Your Vitality Personality.**

When you embrace these most powerful assets you can create exactly the life you desire, while serving the Greatest Good at the same time. If you could live your life as this magnificent person – all day, every day – you would be your happiest, healthiest self, and the world would be a better place.

BUT . . . there is also a default mechanism encoded within you that takes over and drives whenever you're not paying attention. It is your survival mechanism – often called the Ego – and you really don't want to let it be in charge of your life.

Living in a permanent state of survival mode leads you to make reactive choices, with no consideration for the long-term consequences. A survival strategy is not a thrival strategy. The longer you remain unaware of this, the more difficult it becomes to bring forth a life that serves The Real You.

This default survival mechanism is called **Your Primal Persona**, and it actually blocks and suppresses The Real You. In the coming pages you will learn all about the specific programming of Your Primal Persona, which is the first step to gaining mastery over it and having the freedom to step into Your Vitality Personality.

Crack the Code of You

How can you tell whether you have been living as Your Vitality Personality or Your Primal Persona? The answer is quite simple: If your relationships, your finances, your work, your health, and your sense of purpose are all fully thriving – then you are clearly embodying Vitality! You are living as Your Vitality Personality.

But, if your life feels unpleasant and chaotic – if your relationships are troubled, or your finances are dire, or your work is unfulfilling, or you're living with chronic pain or disease, or you're struggling to find any joy in life – this is showing you that Your Primal Persona has been driving your thoughts, feelings and behaviors. The natural and unavoidable outcome of living as Your Primal Persona is self-sabotage and erosion of your Vitality.

Even though behaving as Your Primal Persona is automatic and default, you are not stuck or trapped. It is entirely within your power to guide yourself towards an awakened mind, a healthy body, and a limitless spirit -- my definition of Vitality!

This requires you to crack your own code. The architecture of the encoding of your Personality Type is spelled out in a simple yet powerful graphic, called your **Mandala**.

The Mandala: Key Concepts

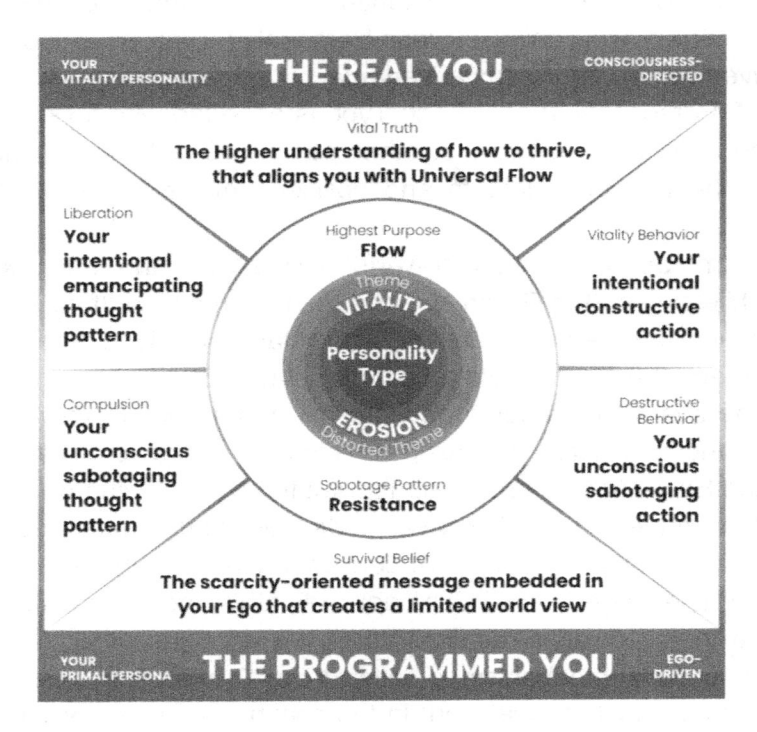

YOUR VITALITY PERSONALITY — **THE REAL YOU** — **CONSCIOUSNESS-DIRECTED**

- Vital Truth: The Higher understanding of how to thrive, that aligns you with Universal Flow
- Liberation — Your intentional emancipating thought pattern
- Highest Purpose: **Flow**
- Vitality Behavior — Your intentional constructive action
- Theme: **VITALITY** — Personality Type — **EROSION** Distorted Theme
- Compulsion — Your unconscious sabotaging thought pattern
- Sabotage Pattern: **Resistance**
- Destructive Behavior — Your unconscious sabotaging action
- Survival Belief: The scarcity-oriented message embedded in your Ego that creates a limited world view

YOUR PRIMAL PERSONA — **THE PROGRAMMED YOU** — **EGO-DRIVEN**

This is a Mandala. It is the blueprint that maps out the coding of your Personality Type. The bottom half depicts the dynamics of the Primal Persona hardwiring. The upper half depicts the dynamics of the Vitality Personality. Each of the 9 Personality Types has its own Mandala, and we will be exploring them in great detail.

Take a look at this general Mandala now so that you can see some of the vocabulary that we will be using. But don't get too attached at the moment, there is much to uncover here and we'll do it step-by-step.

But before we dig in, I need to let you in on *the* key to understanding what powers all of this...

Inside your secret internal code there exists two halves: Your **Higher Consciousness** - which directs Your Vitality Personality - and your **Ego** - which drives Your Primal Persona. It is necessary for you to learn how to integrate your Ego, rather than ignore it or fight against it, in order to gain access to your Higher Consciousness – the endless source of your true power.

Your Higher Consciousness: The Real You

Your Higher Consciousness is **The Real You**. It is pure energy – a stream of Consciousness made entirely of love and light. It is eternal, limitless, and cannot be destroyed.

Higher Consciousness is infinite and contains all of the Personality Types. But when your Higher Consciousness condensed Its energy into your physical mind and body (in order to become human) It chose to express Itself through the lens of a particular Personality Type. At the time you became human your Higher Consciousness simultaneously activated the programming of your specific Personality Type.

The human expression of your Higher Consciousness is what we call Your Vitality Personality. Its dynamics are the Power Paradigm described in the upper half of your Mandala.

Your Vitality Personality is the highest, most enlightened version of your Personality Type, because it has so much Higher Consciousness influencing it. Living this way, in communion with your Higher Consciousness, as Your Vitality Personality, is called being **Consciousness-Directed.**

Flow & Vitality

Not only are *you* made up of energy – *everything* is. All the physical things of your reality are made up of energy, and all the non-physical aspects of the Universe are made of energy. All energy operates according to the fundamental principles of the Universe. This dynamic state of energetic harmony is called the **Flow of the Universe.**

When you stay connected with The Real You – Your Higher Consciousness – and live out your day as Your Vitality Personality, you move yourself into this Flow.

Really experiencing The Flow for the first time can be rather shocking. You literally ask yourself if you've just stepped into an alternate reality, because you can't believe how smoothly and easily your life Flows.

In one single day you might finally find your missing watch, get all green lights in traffic, receive a compliment from a stranger, get a call to cancel the thing you were totally dreading, discover a surprise check in the mail, see a hummingbird hover for a full minute directly in front of you, and receive an affectionate love-pat from your honey. It's like your whole life is suddenly a fluid glide along an escalator.

Being willing to let go of the attachment to the Ego-mind energy and engaging the heart energy is the first step that ultimately launches you out of struggle and into the Flow of the Universe. The natural outcome is **Vitality.**

Vitality is more than just good health, although that is certainly part of it. Vitality is when all of you – the visible parts and the invisible parts – are alert, energized, joyful, and in harmony with each other and All That Is. **Vitality is the joyful expression of an awakened mind, healthy body, and limitless spirit.**

So, when you live as Your Vitality Personality you are naturally cultivating Vitality. Your Vitality is essential to creating the life you want. But it must be nurtured to avoid the pitfalls ahead . . .

Your Ego: The Programmed You

There is a whole other half of you… and yet you may actually be unaware when it is operating. It is called your **Ego**, and it is in charge of the functioning of your **unconscious.**

Your Ego is *not* The Real You. It is the "programmed" you. Your Ego is the operating system of your mind (according to your Personality Type), and behaves according to its programming.

The Ego's purpose is to keep you alive - survival in extreme circumstances. Unfortunately, its Survival Programming can be overzealous to the max. If allowed to operate unchecked, it keeps you unnecessarily inside a permanent state of scarcity and survival. It is not at all advocating for your highest outcomes. It is not promoting grace and ease. It does not operate from an abundance perspective. Although it is needed, and at times valuable, make sure it is only being employed when absolutely necessary.

The human expression of your Ego is what we call Your Primal Persona. It is what is described in the lower half of your Mandala. It is a programmed expression of you without much of your Higher Consciousness shining through.

Living as Your Primal Persona is automatic and default. When you blindly act on the instructions of your Ego, unaware that you are essentially sleep-walking, this is called being **Ego-Driven**. This means you will always operate as your Ego drives you to, unless you make a conscious, intentional choice to do something different.

Ego-Driven thoughts, feelings, and actions are entirely brutal, destructive and self-serving. (Even when you think you are giving and kind, this can actually be a manipulative strategy for survival). You believe these thoughts and feelings – you buy into them – and this leads you to make sabotaging choices and take destructive actions. This is how you end up living as Your Primal Persona.

The reason you can think of your Ego as the "programmed you" is because **your Ego contains all your Survival Programming.** Your Survival Programming is an established architecture for the working of your unconscious. **While it is meant to protect you in times when your safety is threatened, in truth, this program operates whenever you are not self-aware** – which for most people is nearly all the time. It's trying to help you survive but, sadly, it profoundly inhibits your ability to thrive.

Resistance & Erosion

When you are unconscious to The Real You and are Ego-Driven, **resistance** is the mainstay of your life. The Survival Programming of your Ego keeps you hyper-focused on *only* some aspects of life, and very resistant to the rest. Resistance shows up in many ways, but think of it as resistance to "what is." This keeps you limited and out-of-balance. It is the fundamental source of your own **self-sabotage**.

Resistance places you squarely in opposition to the Flow of the Universe. The Flow shows you what direction is best for you, but you resolutely refuse to heed the guidance, insisting your way is best.

Resistance is directly responsible for your ultimate decline. Resisting treating your body with respect, resisting feeling love and compassion, resisting acknowledging your real feelings and needs… these all erode your well-being over time. Rather than Vitality, resistance leads to the **erosion** of Vitality: a despairing mind, a failing body, and a smothered spirit.

♦♦♦

So that was a lot of potentially uncomfortable stuff. But remember, you are not doomed to be stuck in this muck. You can actually evolve from Your Primal Persona into Your Vitality Personality. This takes maturity and willingness.

Let's dive deep into your Mandala now, so that you may see how this whole encoded system operates within you.

YOUR VITALITY PERSONALITY

CHAPTER TWO
PERSONALITY TYPE 1
THE ARCHITECT | THE JUDGE

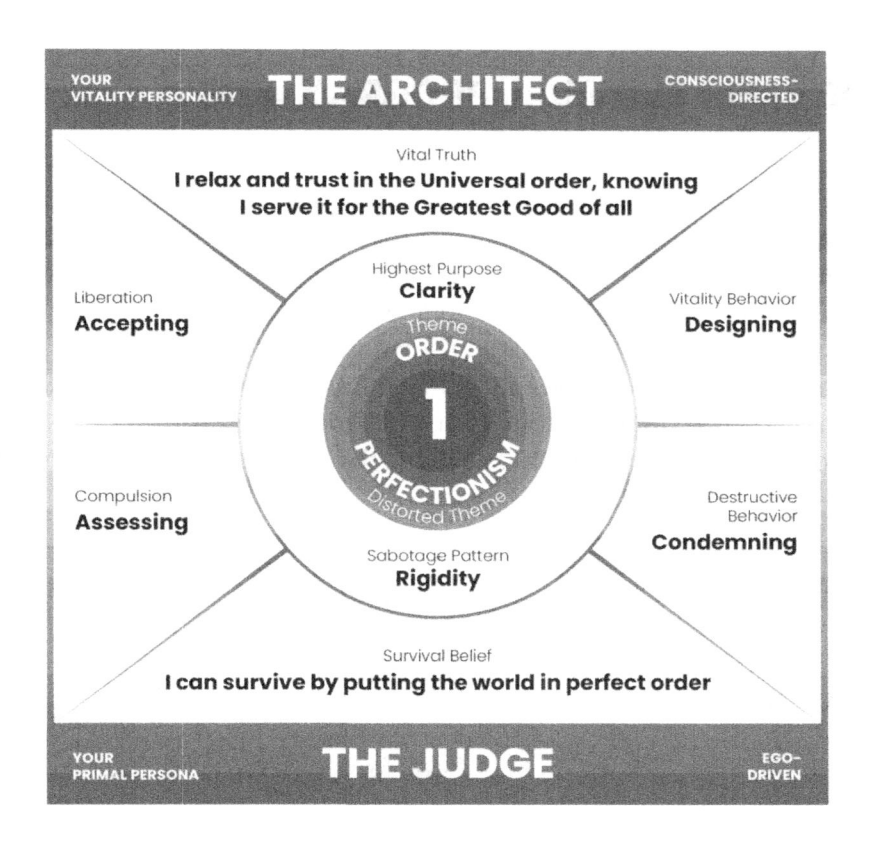

YOUR VITALITY PERSONALITY — THE ARCHITECT — CONSCIOUSNESS-DIRECTED

Vital Truth
I relax and trust in the Universal order, knowing I serve it for the Greatest Good of all

Highest Purpose
Clarity

Liberation
Accepting

Vitality Behavior
Designing

Theme
ORDER

1

PERFECTIONISM
Distorted Theme

Compulsion
Assessing

Destructive Behavior
Condemning

Sabotage Pattern
Rigidity

Survival Belief
I can survive by putting the world in perfect order

YOUR PRIMAL PERSONA — THE JUDGE — EGO-DRIVEN

Hello Type 1, and welcome. Interestingly, your inner coding makes you especially open to this sort of teaching… but resistant to acknowledging the truth of your shadow. You love self-improvement and reaching for your best self, but your default programming leads you to consider your judgment to be superior, making it difficult for you to face how deeply entrenched your Ego really is.

If you have been led here, then it is because you are ready to take a quantum leap ahead of your other Type 1 peers. The wisdom and insight you will gain here will propel you into an awareness far more advanced than most. This will benefit the entire world, for you are the one capable of designing a future world of balance and harmony – Utopia.

This chapter focuses on the dual nature of your Personality Type 1, and the primary factors that hinder or help your ability to thrive. You will totally love the descriptions about your highest potential and purpose… but you will totally not love reading about your dark side, called Your Primal Persona.

Hang in there! We intentionally go through the Primal Persona stuff first, so that you can finish on a high note – the magnificence that is Your Vitality Personality.

Give yourself permission to surrender to this process, and you will see how it takes you on a journey, getting richer and richer the further it goes. The part of you that is wired for Clarity will quickly come to see the massive value and advancement you will receive from this higher understanding.

DECODE YOUR SURVIVAL PROGRAMMING

As we just learned, Your Primal Persona is the version of you that exists when you allow your Ego to unconsciously drive your thoughts, feelings and actions. It is the operating system of your survival-oriented mind, limiting you from tapping into the love and light that is your Higher Consciousness.

In this state, you are closed off from your sense of love for yourself or others. And the actions you take from this place only serve to fulfill the Survival Programming of the small, fearful you. This can be really uncomfortable to face, but it is critical to see clearly so that you can gain freedom from this dark influence.

The bottom half of your Mandala spells out the dynamics of Your Primal Persona and its Ego-Driven Survival Programming:

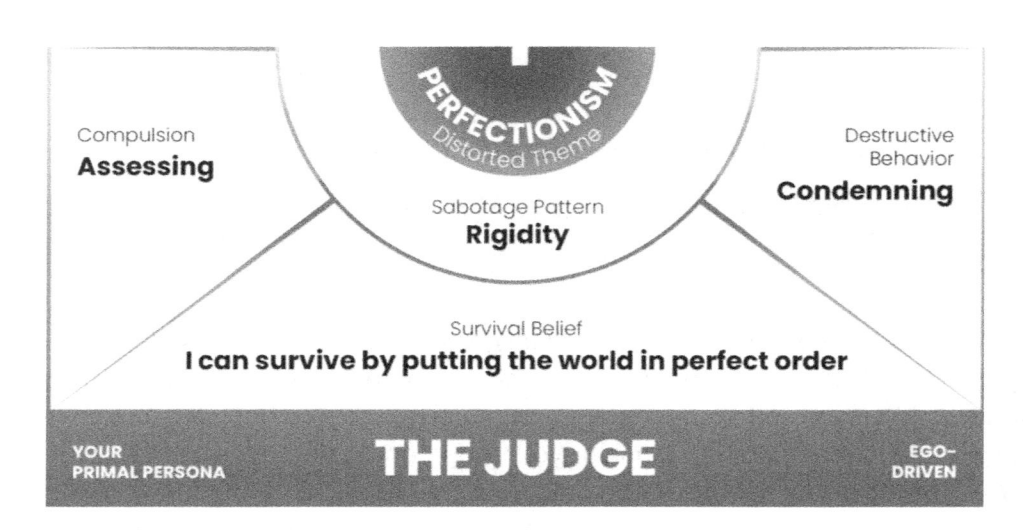

Distorted Theme: **PERFECTIONISM**

Compulsion
Assessing

Destructive Behavior
Condemning

Sabotage Pattern
Rigidity

Survival Belief
I can survive by putting the world in perfect order

YOUR PRIMAL PERSONA — **THE JUDGE** — EGO-DRIVEN

Your Primal Persona: The Judge

As a Type 1,

> - Your Primal Persona is known as **The Judge.**

This is your Ego's version of "playing small," even though its programming is all about being perfectly good and right. But, as we will now explore, being good and right and being correctly aligned with the Flow of the Universe are not at all the same thing.

In *Fig. 2A*, see a brief summary of your Ego-Driven Survival Programming (we will dig deeper into it in just a moment). It is characterized by resistance, eroding your Vitality and degrading your life.

These are some painful truths. But you must forgive yourself for your Survival Programming. Have compassion for yourself, for it was the pain in your life which led you to feel that you couldn't survive without this perspective. Without self-awareness, you had no choice but to behave this way.

And this is true for everyone else, as well. We all deserve forgiveness for the way we act when we are asleep to ourselves -- we are totally unaware this is what we are doing and how much it hurts ourselves and those we love.

Even once you are aware of your Survival Programming, it can be quite challenging to take command over it. Yet every degree of progress you make in this direction brings you enormous reward. You will be joyfully inspired to continue the work.

Let's dive just a little bit deeper into what these dynamics of your Survival Programming really mean, so that you may begin the most rewarding journey of integrating yourself.

Fig. 2A **PERSONALITY TYPE 1 SURVIVAL PROGRAMMING**
Your Primal Persona: THE JUDGE
The Programmed You; The limited and diminished version of yourself that you default to when you are Ego-Driven
Distorted Theme: PERFECTIONISM
Your Ego's warped and downgraded interpretation of your true Theme
Survival Belief: I CAN SURVIVE BY PUTTING THE WORLD IN PERFECT ORDER
The scarcity-oriented message embedded in your Ego that creates your world view
Compulsion: ASSESSING
The repetitive internal process you instantly launch as a way of discharging the emotional tension caused by your Survival Belief
Destructive Behavior: CONDEMNING
The ruinous actions you regularly engage in when you operate according to your Survival Belief
Sabotage Pattern: RIGIDITY
The totality of all your Survival Programming combined into an overall template for self-destruction

Your Distorted Theme

Each of the 9 Personality Types orient around a particular **Theme**. The whole point of you being here, at this time and in this place, is because you wanted to explore this Theme. This is the thing you are encoded to care about the most.

> Your Theme is **Order.**

We will fully explore the true meaning of Order in the next section (about Your Vitality Personality), when we discuss the Consciousness-Directed understanding of your Theme.

But right now, we are discussing your Survival Programming, and how your Ego *degrades* your understanding of your Theme of Order.

Unfortunately, when Your Primal Persona interprets this Theme**, it becomes contorted – a warped, downgraded version of your highest potential.** This is called the **Distorted Theme.**

> Your Distorted Theme is **Perfectionism.**

Perfectionism is about perpetually finding fault or flaw and correcting it. Things which are disorderly or flawed cause you internal tension and stress, and the sense of relief at having perfected them is a balm that washes over you. Unfortunately, there is always another something that needs improving. Much like addiction, the thirst for Perfecting remains unquenched, no matter how often you try to satisfy it.

Even though the desire to reach for perfection serves a higher purpose, it is quite important to realize that you are not the authority on what is perfect – the Universe is. If it exists, then the Universe designed it to be that way, and it is not for you to decide that you know better. Your impulse to hold yourself as the highest authority of what is perfect takes you down an Ego-Driven road that does not lead anywhere beneficial.

Additionally, the Ego-Driven understanding of Perfection is rather limited. Perfection is not a fixed, permanent state which must not ever be allowed to change. In the Universe, everything is in motion, in flux, rotating, expanding, collapsing. While there might be a moment in time, a golden era, a peak of the rise, it cannot stay that way. Everything moves and changes, and it is not realistic to expect what you perfected to actually stay that way.

The Ego is content to trap you inside this loop for all of your life: forever trying to make things better, but never experiencing a lasting sense of peace or satisfaction.

Rather than accepting that all of life is in process, your Ego prompts you to insist on a final, static state called perfection. As you will soon see, Perfectionism does not connect you to a sense of higher Order… it blocks you from it.

In the hands of Your Primal Persona, you spend all your time assessing and condemning, believing you are creating Order by improving things, but instead are introducing factors which degrade:

- Relying solely on logic and intellect, you close down your heart and smother your emotions, blocking your access to your Higher Consciousness – the true source of wisdom
- Regarding your own abilities of discernment to be the highest, you find your own opinion to be the most valid, fostering resentment rather than cooperation, and limiting your own growth
- Highly invested in thinking of yourself as good and right, it is nearly impossible for you to admit fault or apologize, creating hostility and distance in your relationships
- When you do realize you were incorrect or inappropriate or otherwise imperfect, you become obsessed with it, unable to forgive yourself and filled with self-loathing -- destroying your sense of wellbeing
- Believing in impossibly high standards, you become controlling, micro-managing, and perpetually frustrated in your efforts to adhere to them
- With ever more needing perfecting, you find it difficult to relax, be present, or enjoy yourself, eroding any pleasure in your life

Although Perfectionism makes you feel certain of your own goodness and rightness, this is only your Ego rewarding you for so fully surrendering control of your mind. Because even though it has you thinking you are always correct, it is exactly this belief which causes things to go horribly wrong.

This is no fun at all to read about. It's a bummer to realize your default, unconscious wiring is a sadly small version of who you could really be – who you actually are. The Real You is full of radiance and love and light, taking pleasure in the Now moment while serving its highest potential. You are on your way to discovering how to access this Higher aspect of yourself.

Your Survival Belief

Your **Survival Belief** is the **scarcity-oriented message embedded in your Ego that creates your world view.** It is the secret programming in the basement of your unconscious which drives all your thoughts, feelings, and actions without you ever realizing it.

> Your Survival Belief is **I can survive by putting the world in perfect order.**

This belief is fundamental to you, even though you never knew it was there. It defines your understanding of how the world works.

Typically, this Survival Belief is activated within you at a young age.

As a child you likely experienced an element of chaos in your life – perhaps an unreliable authority figure. This would have triggered in you a mistrust for authority figures, preferring to be in charge of everything yourself, and a desire to smooth out the wildness in your environment by not being a cause for upset in any way. Taking control of yourself and your environment seemed like the best strategy for survival, and it's never occurred to you to re-examine it as an adult.

You may read your Survival Belief and think to yourself, *Well yes, of course! What's wrong with making everything perfect? It's the ideal way to be!*

Unfortunately, this simple sentence is a template for destruction! Let's unpack all the ways in which this Survival Belief sets you up for problems, rather than the solutions you think it does.

Idealism: The Shoulds

Your Survival Belief that you must always put the world in perfect order creates an immediate dissatisfaction with how things are *right now*, and that is quite in opposition to the Flow of the Universe.

In the Universe, there is no such thing as time – even time is merely a construct of the Ego. The truth is, there is only ever Right Now.

In order to live in the Flow and create Vitality, you must become able to love and accept what exists Right Now. Whenever you are not in a state of love and acceptance, you resist the Flow of the Universe, creating obstruction and illness in your life.

Your Ego, of course, is wired to keep you out of this Flow. Rather than prompting you to love and accept what you see before you, your Ego prompts you to identify how what is before you is not right, and to determine how it *should be* instead.

The Ego-Driven Type 1 creates an entire lifestyle around living according to The Shoulds, and cannot comprehend why everyone else does not also live this way. According to The Judge, everyone who does not live as they *should* is bad and wrong.

This world view creates joylessness – believing you should never honor what your heart wants or the body needs, and only obey The Shoulds of the mind. Joylessness is quite the opposite of living in the Flow, which is full of love, joy, and abundance.

Superiority Complex

Holding a Survival Belief that you must put the world in perfect order prompts you to consider your judgment as superior to other people's. If you are the decider of what perfection looks like, then you must obviously be smarter and better than everyone else. That's why they are not already perfect, but you are.

Obviously when you look at this rationally you can see this is not true in lots of ways. But the Ego has absolutely nothing to do with being rational – it is always a skewed perspective. It's rather amusing to consider how the Ego, which can only ever offer an unenlightened view, convinces the Type 1 to consider themself so much more enlightened than everybody else.

Type 1s tend to be a major presence in both the spiritual and legal arenas, because they are attracted to positions which allow them to demonstrate their moral and judicial prowess. This would be heaven if these individuals actually were enlightened, because they would produce outcomes of the highest order. But, unfortunately, they are far more likely to be lacking humility and compassion, producing outcomes which are far from ideal.

Misunderstanding Hierarchy

Because your unconscious is wired to believe in perfect order, your mind naturally likes to create hierarchy.

Hierarchy is indeed used to create order in the Universe. When the Universe creates a hierarchy, it is a hierarchy of *function* – from a subatomic particle to an overarching structure, all pieces of the puzzle have their specific function to perform, and are therefore equally important.

When the Type 1 Ego takes hold of this concept, however, it gets downgraded into a belief that the hierarchy indicates a ladder of *value* – where the subatomic particle is considered lowly and insignificant, and the overarching structure holds the highest status.

This assigning value to people and things based on how "high" they are in the hierarchy creates a world of polarity: best and worst, right and wrong, desirable and disgusting, accepted and condemned.

All of the Universe exists as a spectrum of Consciousness – which is made of love and light. No matter how small the piece of Consciousness, it holds the exact same value as any other. In the Universe, there is no such thing as good and bad, and right and wrong. It is all loved and accepted exactly how it is, because that's how it was designed.

◆◆◆

As you can see, your Survival Belief that you must make everything perfect is at the heart of much difficulty and self-sabotage for you. It is this belief which launches a cascade of repetitive thoughts and behaviors, that ultimately lead to your unhappiness. Learning about these, and how to take hold of them, is fundamental to becoming able to create a life you love.

If you have read this far, you are doing so well! Thank you for hanging in there, this stuff is definitely not fun to face. Remember, we are in the thick of the section about the Ego's Survival Programming. But then we will move ahead to discuss Type 1 at your highest and best.

We just finished discussing your Type 1 Survival Belief, which was activated somewhere in your childhood. It is the primary driver behind all of your unconscious thoughts and behaviors.

Now, we will look at the most common thought, feeling and behavior patterns that emerge as a result of holding your Survival Belief.

Your Compulsion

Your Compulsion is the repetitive internal process you instantly launch as a way of discharging the emotional tension caused by your Survival Belief.

> Your Compulsion is **Assessing.**

This Compulsion is much like a guilty addiction – you know you should give it up, but don't want to... because you privately love it.

And even if you decide *That's it, I'm through with this*... you will still find it very difficult to stop, until you become able to embrace your Vital Truth (see the upper half of your Mandala), rather than your Survival Belief.

Assessing refers to the way you scan whatever is in your purview and privately decide what you like and don't like, what you approve or disapprove of, what is acceptable and what requires improvement. It is the process of taking in information and deciding what you think about it.

Type 1s believe this is the normal way to be, and that everyone does it. You may be shocked to learn that not everyone has a constant stream of judgmental mental chatter going on! Although all Egos do prompt negative mental chatter, the Type 1 is the only one who is wired to be preoccupied with constantly Assessing whether things are good, right, and correct.

Assessing is an entirely mental activity. Type 1s spend an enormous amount of time in their minds, and are extremely attached to using logic and reason in all circumstances. In fact this is their primary means of feeling safe and in control. For this reason they intensely dislike things which are nebulous, murky, and confusing – it upsets their sense of order and disturbs their peace.

Unfortunately, relying on orderly thought to make sense of your world is not as certain a practice as you think it is. The mind is controlled by the Ego, which means you are wired to have internal preferences and biases which are not logical, and which you are entirely unconscious of.

Feelings are Guidance

Rather than analyzing and assessing, it is possible to *feel a knowingness*, a certainty which has been communicated to you through the heart, by your Higher Consciousness. There is actually a way to live that is well beyond mere mental control.

It occurs through living through the heart, rather than the mind. Instead of being guided by logic, which may be faulty, you may be guided by your feelings, which are always your personal Truth.

Your Higher Consciousness speaks to you through your heart – aka your feelings. This is problematic for you, because you don't really *do* feelings. In fact, you spend an inordinate amount of energy trying to smother and deny them.

Whenever you feel "positive" emotions – feelings that are pleasant to experience, such as love, joy, excitement, peace – this is encouragement from your Higher

Consciousness to continue in that direction. You're being told that whatever idea or action you're in the middle of is beneficial to you, and leading somewhere constructive.

You may or may not heed this advice, depending on whether you approve of what is exciting or attracting you. You may talk yourself out of it, telling yourself you must hold yourself to a higher standard.

Whenever you feel "negative" emotions – feelings that you dislike experiencing, like anger, resentment, jealousy, or shame – your Higher Consciousness is sending you a warning that whatever thought or action you are in the middle of is *not* serving your highest interest.

Your inclination as a Type 1 is to reject or deny feelings which you do not approve of. You don't approve of resentment, so you don't admit you feel it. You don't approve of jealousy, so you don't admit you feel it. You use your energy to try to hold these feelings away from yourself – a truly exhausting endeavor which depletes your health.

Rather than denying your feelings, take in the guidance you are receiving. You are being shown that your thoughts are not accurate, because they cause you to feel harmed. Any thought which causes you a feeling of upset is a cautionary cue to question your thoughts. You will know when you are on the right track when you think thoughts that cause you to relax and feel at ease.

In this way, you have an internal Truth barometer which is never wrong. You can always trust that the decisions you make while in a positive state of mind are for the Greatest Good, and will turn out well. There is no need for mental Assessing once you understand the deeper way to *know*.

Your Destructive Behavior

Your Survival Belief – that you must always put the world in perfect order – also prompts your actions and behaviors. When you are Ego-Driven, and therefore **not questioning your inherent attitudes and beliefs, you will repeatedly behave this way.** This is called your **Destructive Behavior.**

You may be entirely unaware of it, or you may be doing it on purpose in the utter certainty it's the best way to be. Either way, this behavior is never for the Greatest Good of all, and therefore is destructive.

As an Ego-Driven Type 1 who believes you are the judge of what is perfect and what is flawed . . .

> ➢ Your Destructive Behavior is **Condemning.**

Condemning means judging someone or something to be unworthy of love. It is the withdrawing of attention, affection, or support out of a feeling of contempt, loathing, or disgust. It is the rejection or exclusion from society because of unacceptable fault.

There are several Ego-Driven factors at play here which lead the Type 1 to believe

Condemning is the correct and appropriate way to behave when faced with imperfection. These must be reconciled in order to move into the Flow.

Conditional Love Isn't Love

The Flow of the Universe is the astonishing rush of unconditional love. All of the Universe operates according to this principle. In order to thrive, we must align ourselves with this loving Flow.

Only being willing to love yourself or others when they behave perfectly turns your love conditional – you only feel love when your conditions have been met. This is not really love. Real love is abundant and available at all times. Anything which is not that, is Ego distortion. The Ego does not nourish – it destroys. The Ego version of love does not create Vitality – it kills it.

Experiencing your conditional love is very painful for your relationships. They only get to receive your love (the thing that builds them up) occasionally – the rest of the time they feel your Condemnation (the thing that tears them down).

The thing for you to come to understand is that everyone is on a journey of discovering love for themselves. People who struggle with emotional and physical problems, who feel disengaged or apathetic… these are people who have not found love for themselves yet. Which means they are lost. They need your compassion, your love and acceptance. Not your Condemnation.

It is possible to love and accept people even as you see the aspects of them which need improving. It is ok that there are parts of them (or you) which still have room for growth. That is normal and appropriate. You can love them (and yourself) anyway. This is what unconditional love looks like, the fabric of the Universe.

No Expectations

Type 1s have lots of extremely high expectations – of themselves, of other people, and of the world at large. Not only do they believe they should be reaching for perfection… they think everyone else should be, too. As we discussed previously, Type 1s are very attached to The Shoulds.

This does not align with Universal principles. The Universal law of free will requires that every being be allowed to find its own way without interference. This means that people are allowed to believe and behave however they see fit. Their own karma will deliver their lessons – it has nothing to do with you.

Furthermore, whatever "shoulds" you have deemed the correct ones, are based on your personal understanding of reality.

The reality that you experience is singular to you – you have past lives, old karma, psychic wounds, soul contracts, intuitive abilities, latent talents, learned skills, programmed DNA and so much more which make your perception of reality very specific to you.

And knowing this exists differently for every person, is it reasonable to hold a paradigm of expectations for someone else, who has an entirely different quantum history than you? How could you possibly know what are appropriate expectations for someone else, when you do not have access to their soul's blueprint?

Your reality isn't "right." It isn't "correct." It's just your reality, and there are almost 8 billion other realities also occurring on the planet. You have to let everyone have their own journey, their own reality. This is the Flow. When you embrace this, your impulse to Condemn will disappear.

Infinite Shades of Gray

Condemning happens as the result of black-or-white thinking. Type 1s want everything to be organized and orderly, with clear labels and predictable, measured behavior. It's like insisting that life behave like a circuit board when really it's more like a lava lamp.

Again, this is the danger of letting that Survival Belief of perfection lead you to a false idealism. There is no point in telling yourself that life is supposed to be clear, organized and tidy – when it totally isn't.

Black and white are extremes, the far ends of the poles. All of life is happening along the grayscale in between. It is confusing, it is messy. It can be scary and painful and unpredictable. You must allow this to exist, because this is how it was designed by a Consciousness far more enlightened than yours. You must trust that the messy grays of life are there for a divine purpose, and see the beauty in that.

Your Sabotage Pattern

As we have discussed, your Personality Type has much Survival Programming built in. Your Survival Belief, Compulsion, and Destructive Behavior are undeniable impulses within you that all drive your well-being into the ground.

In other words, these all combine into an overall template for self-destruction. This is called your **Sabotage Pattern – the way you repeatedly behave throughout your lifetime which leads directly to the destruction of your health and happiness.**

> ➢ Your Sabotage Pattern is **Rigidity.**

Rigidity is a lack of flexibility, an unyieldingness, a state of tension. This unwillingness to soften or adapt is the ultimate source of sabotage for the Ego-Driven Type 1.

Rigidity of the Mind

In the mind, Rigidity is the result of an over-attachment to being right, to believing that your way is the best and only way. It is believing in and upholding The Shoulds. It is resisting new ideas and outside opinions. It creates a world of judgment – of good and bad, right and wrong, insiders and outsiders.

As we have discussed, your Type 1 Ego mind is compulsively Assessing, seeking to make the world seem orderly by giving everything a label and a rank. This makes you feel safe and in control, but limits your capacity for understanding and connection. There is much subtlety and nuance happening outside the lines.

The Rigidity of the Ego-Driven type 1 mind leads to conditional love – only being willing to find someone or something lovable once it meets your approval. Not only do you do this to others – you are quite ruthless with yourself.

As we will discuss shortly, shifting to an attitude of acceptance will allow your mind to soften. Letting go of the need to judge will free you up enormously. When you no longer feel responsible for monitoring for perfection, you will find you are much more able to relax and enjoy yourself.

Rigidity of the Body

In the body, Rigidity is expressed as physical tension, the clenching down on the flow of energy. Holding the breath and clenching the jaw lead to stiffness throughout the upper torso, tightness in the hips, knees and ankles, and chronic constipation. It is inflexibility, and a lack of resilience.

The tension in the body is happening because of the control you are trying to have over your thoughts and feelings. You are closely monitoring yourself and your behavior, trying not to let "inappropriate" feelings show, trying to perform at your very best. As you resist allowing yourself full expression, the body tightens and clenches.

You will find the Real You Method called The Sway to be extremely beneficial. It helps you shake out and loosen the tension in your hips, back, jaw, neck and shoulders. It will cause your diaphragm to open, so that you may breathe deeply down into your belly.

The body and mind are connected – softening and relaxing your body will soften and relax your mind. If you find yourself feeling tense and locked into a negative mental loop, use swaying or other forms of free easy movement to shift your entire energetic signature.

Rigidity and the Heart

In the heart, Rigidity is demonstrated as a lack of compassion, an unwillingness to nurture. It is intolerance and rejection. It is the withholding of love until conditions are met – even for yourself.

In truth, these are all machinations of the mind, not the heart. The heart is ready, willing and able to love at all times, but the mind has locked it down tight.

The key to unlocking your heart portal, so that you may gain access to the entirely loving being that is The Real You, is allowing yourself to feel appreciation and joy.

Start with the innocent. Babies, puppies, kittens, foals. You get the idea. There is nothing about them to judge, they are all so easy to love. Just watching footage of them on social media brings a smile to your heart.

It is this smile in the heart that you want to reach for, all day every day. It is love for its own sake, the joy of being alive in such a beautiful magical place as Earth.

Not everything needs to be so serious, Type 1. You need play and laughter and fun. This world is here for your pleasure and enjoyment – it's not the cage your Ego mind encourages you to believe. Your belief in following rules and making yourself perfect has turned the world grim and bleak for you. You must let the sunshine in.

This sense of happy playfulness will unlock your access to an entirely different world of love and light, where you get to be the Architect of systems that Flow, rather than restrict.

♦♦♦

As you can see, rather than creating the Utopia you imagine, Rigidity sabotages it. Your relationships, your health, and your sense of well-being will not thrive as long as Rigidity is the main pattern of your life.

By now you are probably feeling battered and bruised – horrified to discover all these shadows inside your unconscious. Remember, Rigidity is only the Survival Programming of Your Primal Persona – it is *not* who you really are. The Real You is loving, compassionate, generous, and kind.

Learning how to release your Sabotage Pattern does not require more control, more tension, more strict self-monitoring. No, you do not need to smother your Sabotage Pattern – you need to love and accept it.

Your Primal Persona was triggered in you at a young age. As a child, you saw the world as a dangerously confusing and chaotic place. This launched within you a deep desire for order and safety, and thus your inherent Survival Programming. You must have compassion for your inner child, who still believes that Rigidity is the only way to survive.

As you learn to love yourself and let go of expectations, you will naturally begin to experience ease. You will start to have more open thoughts, a more relaxed body, a more generous heart. You won't have to force yourself to soften and flex – it will happen organically on its own.

It is not too late to reconnect with The Real You. You will find the road vulnerable and scary... and you will also find love, peace, satisfaction and a deep sense of serenity. It is a journey worth taking. The guidance on how to do this is coming up next.

♦♦♦

Now that you have opened your eyes to the destructive inner workings of your own Ego, operating as Your Primal Persona, do not despair. It is certainly within your capacity to transform these behaviors and patterns of your Survival Programming.

If you have made it this far, CONGRATULATIONS. We lost many along the trail – not everybody is ready for the journey that is Getting Real! This book is really only interesting to people who are about to make an enormous advancement in their consciousness.

We made it through the hardest part. Now, let's explore how you can be, act and live differently. There is an entirely different kind of life available to you, filled with love and connection and joy. And it is mapped out in the top half of your Type 1 Mandala.

ACTIVATE YOUR POWER PARADIGM

In Chapter One we revealed the meaning of Your Vitality Personality. Let's recap now.

Your Vitality Personality is the version of you that exists when you allow your Higher Consciousness to guide your thoughts, feelings, and actions. It is the opening of your heart, and allowing the loving intelligence found there to Flow through you. This infuses you with insight, wisdom, love and compassion, and the actions you take from this place always serve the Greatest Good.

Let's take a look now at the top half of your Mandala which spells out the dynamics of The Real You - Your Vitality Personality - and all its wondrous gifts and talents

Your Vitality Personality: The Architect

As a Type 1,

> Your Vitality Personality is known as **The Architect.**

This is the truth of who you really are. You have always felt a call to improve things, to make things better, to fulfill the highest potential. Your mind has always seemed especially clear and sharp, quick to identify the source of the problem and envision its solution. You have always derived great satisfaction in creating order out of chaos.

The Real You is a visionary, inspired to upgrade humanity though creating

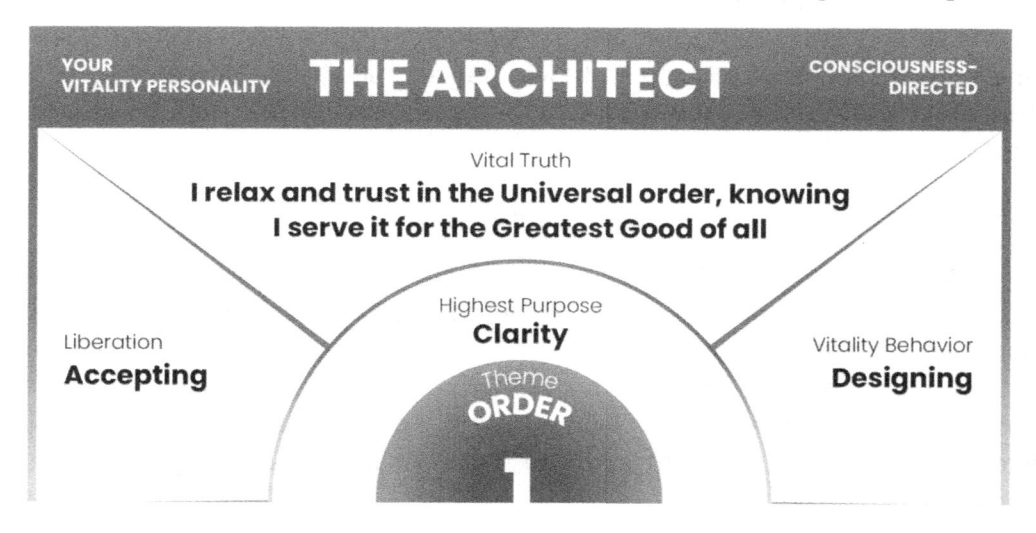

YOUR VITALITY PERSONALITY — **THE ARCHITECT** — **CONSCIOUSNESS-DIRECTED**

Vital Truth
I relax and trust in the Universal order, knowing I serve it for the Greatest Good of all

Highest Purpose
Clarity

Theme
ORDER
1

Liberation
Accepting

Vitality Behavior
Designing

effective and efficient structures and processes. You are the one who elevates Consciousness through designing elegant upgrades to our systems. You help us all function at a higher capacity, creating a better world.

In *Fig 2B*, see a brief summary of the Consciousness-Directed half of your Mandala, identifying how to use your Personality Type to bring into your life a sense of completeness, fulfillment, joy and love.

When you embody all these natural gifts, you are a dazzling light, inspiring all who know you. It is so exciting to think you are just on the precipice of launching a new life of love, acceptance, and Vitality for yourself! It might have required some serious deep-breathing to get here, but the effort is so well worth it.

Let's explore these dynamics of your POWER PARADIGM, so that you may begin to fully comprehend just how open, uplifting, happy and healthy your life could really be.

Fig. 2B PERSONALITY TYPE 1 POWER PARADIGM	
Your Vitality Personality: **THE ARCHITECT**	The Real You; The most magnificent version of yourself you joyfully embody when you heed the guidance of your Higher Consciousness
Theme: ORDER	The dynamic realm of Life your Higher Consciousness wants to explore to the fullest
Vital Truth: I RELAX AND TRUST IN THE UNIVERSAL ORDER, KNOWING I SERVE IT FOR THE GREATEST GOOD OF ALL	A higher understanding of how to thrive, that aligns you with the Flow of the Universe
Liberation: ACCEPTING	The emancipating philosophy you freely embrace to enhance your connection to the Flow
Vitality Behavior: DESIGNING	The empowering and uplifting actions you intentionally choose to create your best life
Highest Purpose: CLARITY	How you serve the Greatest Good through embracing your encoded genius, and the source of your Vitality

Your Theme

As was mentioned earlier,

> Your Theme is **Order**.

When you pursue the highest form of this Theme – Order – you are truly aligned with Source, and therefore always serving the Greatest Good.

Order is the organizing and refining of elements into an inspired, harmonious system. It is a most profound and divine aspect of the Universe – it is the creation of the Universe out of the Void.

As a Type 1, you can inherently sense this. You have always felt a deep pull towards continually refining yourself, making yourself more and more effective and wise. You are the living breathing example of the Universal desire for Order.

Because your Higher Consciousness was delighted to explore this Theme in big and small ways, your mind was wired to be particularly sharp and astute, with a natural desire to solve problems. You are encoded to be the designer of divine solutions.

The reason you know this is true is because you feel giddy and high when you create and execute a plan which successfully improves something. You can feel the rightness of it in your bones. That is not something to be laughed at or dismissed – it is an authentic connection to Higher Consciousness. It is true – you actually do feel high when you connect to the Flow of the Universe.

This is why Your Vitality Personality is named The Architect. You are the one who builds a brighter future through continually creating inspired improvements to function and form.

The thing which is key for you to remember is that solutions are only divinely inspired if they include Love. Order created only with the mind is merely the Perfectionism of the Ego. True Order which aligns with the Flow involves systems created out of compassion, acceptance, joyfulness and love.

In the hands of Your Vitality Personality, you apply your fully heart-centered Self towards efforts which serve the Greatest Good, making you an inspired and revered Architect:

- Embracing the beauty of Now, accepting limitations and flaws
- Pleased at progress, without expectation
- Feeling relaxed and easy-going, embracing all emotions as they arise
- Enjoying a sense of love and freedom in your daily life
- Offering love and empathy, rather than criticism
- Experiencing fulfillment in being able to meaningfully contribute to Life through designing inspired solutions and systems

Most people feel muddled in their mind. They feel overwhelmed by all the factors at play, the confusion of their feelings, and their doubt about their own capabilities. They know they are in trouble and need to make changes but they can't see how to get there.

You are the one who is built to serve the world by engaging your natural abilities to design inspired solutions that clarify how to realize the highest potential.

Once you are able to love and accept all of yourself, you will begin to find it much easier to love and accept other people. If you are in this relaxed state when unnecessary mistakes occur and impractical choices happen, you are in the best position to offer guidance that truly meets the need.

When you are Consciousness-Directed, it is your joy to be able to make a difference in the world with your designing mind and open heart. You don't need to feel bothered by how much Ego-Driven behavior you see going on around you – feel satisfied in knowing you are leading the way towards making the world a better place.

Your Vital Truth

Your **Vital Truth** is the **Higher understanding of how to thrive by aligning with Universal principles.** It is the escape hatch your Ego doesn't want you to know about, because **it unlocks all of its Survival Programming, and connects you to your Higher Consciousness – The Real You.**

> Your Vital Truth is **I relax and trust in the Universal order, knowing I serve it for the Greatest Good of all.**

This is a direct contradiction to what your Survival Belief encourages you to believe. Your Survival Belief prompts you to think that everything is dangerously chaotic, so you'd better make yourself and your world perfect in order to survive.

Coming to replace your Survival Belief with this Vital Truth takes time. It is a gradual process of accepting by degrees. But every degree of progress is experienced as a huge upgrade in your quality of life.

Although this Vital Truth is a brief, simple statement, it is dense with meaning. Let's take a moment to unpack this.

Relaxing

Type 1s hold an enormous amount of tension in the body, because they hold their breath and grit their teeth, and they suppress their anger.

Holding your breath and gritting your teeth happens because you're trying to frantically get all your Shoulds done today, and it's an impossible list in a dysfunctional world.

This closes your diaphragm, blocking energy from descending into the belly, and making the jaw, neck and shoulders dense and hard.

The smothered anger and resentment that the world is so naughty and selfish translates into heat in the Gallbladder channel, which runs from the top of the head all the way down the sides of the body – traveling through jaw, shoulder, hip, knee and foot. The heat of the emotions dries out the fascia, making it tighten and become brittle. You experience this as a sense of tightness throughout your body.

Tension in the body creates resistance against the Flow. It is blocking you from letting more love and light into your body, which would empower you.

It is essential that you develop a daily relaxation practice for yourself, where you intentionally allow yourself to breathe deeply and soften, while also processing your true feelings.

All you need to do is drop your attention out of your mind into the center of your chest, and say to your heart *I love and accept the part of me who is angry. I love and accept the part of me who is frustrated. I love myself. I accept myself.* Pull these feelings into your heart and imagine the emotional charge being washed off and neutralized.

You are allowed to experience all the human emotions, Type 1. It's perfectly normal and acceptable to feel feelings deeply, and it's okay to admit to them. Rather than judging them and holding them back, let them come up and out. This allows you to release the feelings, rather than hold them in your body.

The sense of freedom and openness this brings you is amazing. Now you are able to put yourself fully in receiving mode, where you rest quietly and let your Higher Self in.

Over time you will see what holding more of your Higher Self in your body does for your quality of life. You will feel more relaxed, clearer, more creative, and generally in a better mood.

Trusting the Universe

Your Ego mind puts all its muscle behind convincing you that you know best. It urges you to think that you can use rational thought and willpower to control and organize all of Life.

The Ego does not have the capacity to really grasp the vastness of the intelligence and power of the Universe, and cannot see the higher Order which is already in place.

It is not possible, inside the limited framework of the Ego-mind, to comprehend the true "big picture" of how things are meant to go. That was designed by a genius far greater than yours. You must trust that there is a Higher plan already in place, whether you can make sense of it or not, and allow it to be revealed at its appropriate time.

Even though agreeing to let go of control and trust in the Universe sounds slightly terrifying, you will discover it brings you an enormous sense of elation to be free of the burdens you were carrying.

As you can see, all the advice you are receiving here in your Vital Truth has to do with softening that Rigidity which is your Sabotage Pattern. Surrendering to the Universe and trusting is your pathway to Vitality.

Knowingness

As a Type 1, you have been gifted with a special sort of intuition – you can *feel* when you have aligned with the Universal Order. Although your Ego prompts you to sort, arrange, reconfigure, and redesign all that you see before you… you are not ready to do so until you can feel this internal *knowingness* of what is the most appropriate next step.

Knowingness occurs when the heart, mind and body are in harmony. This is the state of being Consciousness-Directed.

Normally, in the Ego-Driven state, the heart, mind and body are all out of whack. For the Type 1, the heart is closed, the mind is in zealous control, and the body is tense.

In order to become Consciousness-Directed, you must fully open the heart, silence the Ego-mind, and relax the body. This is the state of Flow, where the vital life force and intelligence of the Universe moves through you. (These are advanced teachings we learn in our private membership at **YourVitalityPersonality.com**.)

When you are in a place of physical, mental, and emotional stillness, you are in the receiving state. This is when all the answers to your questions drop in. This is where the sudden genius ideas arrive. This is when the unconsidered solution magically appears. This is true knowingness – it is deep and true and lasting in a way that intellect alone can't touch.

This experience of receiving guidance from your Higher Consciousness provides you with the feeling of rightness you were always chasing in your perfectionism. The spiritual high you wanted is not in the outside world – it's inside of you.

It takes practice to develop the ability to reside in this aligned state. However, once there, your ability to design truly inspired solutions and refinements radiates and shines. It is what you were made for – there is no one more talented at it than you.

Serving the Greatest Good

This is deeply meaningful for you. You have always felt called to serve something greater than yourself. This is because it is part of your Purpose.

Whenever you design or decide anything from a place of being Consciousness-Directed, you can trust that it serves the Greatest Good for all. However, there is another important aspect of serving the Greatest Good which must be acknowledged in order to fully embrace your Vital Truth: you must be *invited* to do so.

The Universal law of free will must always be honored. Part of serving the divine Order means waiting to be brought in at the appropriate time. This is what it means to *go with the Flow*.

Even though you are eager to be of service, you must always watch out for that Ego who likes to demonstrate its superiority. Inserting yourself into other people's reality because you've decided they really need your help is a straight-up Ego move. Unsolicited advice is a great big Universal no-no.

Rather, you will find you are asked for help when it is time for you to make your contribution.

When you make a practice of balancing your heart, mind and body, and living in a relaxed, happy way… you become extremely noticeable to other people. With your natural inclination to improve and organize yourself – now with a newly acquired smile on your face and spring in your step – you will stand out as the one with wisdom. Don't worry, your Consciousness-Directed advice will be in high demand.

Your Liberation

Your **Liberation** is the **emancipating philosophy you freely embrace**. This is a powerful shift, out of the Survival Programming of the mind, and into the Flow of the Universe through the heart. Rather than being owned by a chronic Compulsion, you are now *intentionally choosing* this Liberation.

> Your Liberation is **Accepting.**

Type 1, if you can get a handle on Accepting rather than Assessing, your whole life will radically change for the better. It sounds so simple, and yet Accepting goes against all your Ego programming. At first you will find it hard to do. But then... you will totally love it.

Accepting means that, rather than taking in information and giving it a value judgment, you simply take in the information.

So for example, rather than angrily deciding that because your son regularly makes you 15 minutes late, he is obviously selfish and lazy, you Accept that there is a problem with your expectation, and remain neutral. This allows you to investigate why this is happening, and perhaps discover that your son has a dread of going to school because he's being bullied. It's not that he's selfish and lazy, he's troubled. Now you can help design a solution that meets everyone's needs.

As we have discussed, the Type 1 encoding includes a propensity for having lots of expectations, lots of attachment to how things "should" be. But when you really think about it, this has been the primary source of your unhappiness in life. You could be upset ten times a day because every day ten of your expectations did not go as you wanted them to!

Accepting is the answer. It releases all your expectations and attachments. It's giving everyone permission to be who they are and make their own choices, and just focus on yourself instead. You just won't believe how much more you'll like your life when you begin Accepting the world (and yourself) the way that they are.

You came here, to this time and place, in order to explore and expand yourself. You are not here to monitor other people, and you are not in charge of how the world should be. What a relief it is to realize you may simply give your time to your own joy! Make Accepting your policy, and you move yourself into the easy Flow of the Universe, where Abundance, Love and Vitality await you!

Letting Go of The Shoulds

As a Type 1 you have been ruled by that loud inner critic, always harping about how you should be, how others should be, how the world should be. It gives you no peace and creates a harsh world view. Wouldn't it be so lovely to learn how to let go of The Shoulds?

The Shoulds are an idea, an ideal. They look at "what is" and pronounce it to be not right, not good enough. It is entirely a mental activity, and the Ego runs the mind.

The key to Accepting is dropping out of the mind and into the heart, and letting yourself feel love and compassion as you take in the environment around you.

Your heart is the portal for your Higher Consciousness to come through. The Real You does not speak to you in your mind, It speaks to you in the heart.

When you are seated in your heart, your perspective shifts. That homeless person is not a lazy bum, it's somebody who is struggling to be functional, likely due to a history of pain you know nothing about.

That tardy person is not irresponsible and flaky, they are overwhelmed and ungrounded and could probably use a friend.

You are not fat and despicable, you are tired and disheartened. You don't need more scolding and contempt, you need a vacation and some kindness.

There is no such thing as Bad and Wrong in Universal terms. We are all here exploring stories -- of success and hardship, of joy and pain, of love and loss. They are all worthwhile explorations.

All experiences offer insight and learning and expansion. None of them are bad and wrong. They are all acceptable.

When you are able to Accept your reality without Assessing it, you are finally able to make the positive impact you desire. Now you can see, from a clear and neutral perspective, how to design solutions that will actually meet needs and effect change.

Your Vitality Behavior

Vitality Behavior is the **empowering and uplifting actions you intentionally choose when you are Consciousness-Directed,** rather than the Destructive Behavior your Ego drives you to act out.

> Your Vitality Behavior is **Designing.**

This is sooo much lovelier than your previous go-to – Condemning! This is where you really shift out of Your Primal Persona, The Judge, and into Your Vitality Personality, The Architect.

As The Judge, you were assessing everyone and everything for their value, deciding if they measure up to your expectations, feeling resentful about how inadequate they all are, and condemning them as unacceptable. But now, as The Architect, you love and accept what you see before you, even as you begin Designing the upgrade. When Ego-Driven, you were more about breaking defective things down, but now that you are Consciousness-Directed, you're all about building things up!

Your natural talent, Type 1, is your fabulous ability to create structure. You have the rather amazing ability to build something out of nothing, to take etheric things like ideas, questions, and desires, and design the framework which brings them into physical existence. This is why we all need you so much – you help us create our reality.

Remember to hold love in your heart as you envision your new creation. As The Architect, you design the world the rest of us live in. You are in the position of elevating mass consciousness through your Consciousness-Directed design.

For example, the American legal system is currently a model of how Ego-Driven perfectionism breaks down society, rather than raising it up (to be fair, the model was established far earlier than the U.S.). There is literally a judge, who condemns people as bad and wrong and sends them to prison, a bleak and loveless place, where they will be punished and demeaned for being so defective.

What if the prison system were Designed by a Consciousness-Directed Architect, who is gifted with higher insight about how to uplevel consciousness through loving and accepting? Punishment would perhaps no longer be seen as appropriate, perhaps rehabilitation would become the focus. Rather than condemning for not knowing how to be a functional member of society, education, support, and advocacy could become the plan.

As a Designer, your focus is on "How can I guide them to help themselves? Where are they struggling and what can be done to stabilize and improve? What would meet their needs the best, and in what order should it be presented? What can be done to accommodate where they are now, while fostering their growth?"

Our judicial system, education system, political system... these were all fashioned from a place of Ego, with rigid unrealistic expectations and false beliefs, and they are all now collapsing. Wouldn't it be amazing if enlightened Architects stepped in and raised Consciousness through Designing systems and solutions which allow and foster change and growth? What if we were not all forced to live in boxes with limiting labels? What if there were room for us all to be nebulous and expansive the way we really are?

In daily life, Designing rather than Condemning means not being upset when things don't go as expected, staying focused on finding the best solution. In Condemning mode, you tend to be angry at what you find faulty – you are offended by the imperfection.

In Designing mode, that all disappears, and you can see the beauty there. You feel compassion for the scars and the sharp edges, the frailties and the shortcomings. And you can calmly see that your expectations were misplaced, based on impractical ideals, and begin fashioning a better situation which would realistically meet everyone's needs.

Your Highest Purpose

You chose to be here, in this time and place, because you wanted to contribute something. You came here for a reason, and you chose your Personality Type because it was the one that would help you accomplish it. **Your Personality Type has a special set of talents and abilities, and you wanted to use them to make a contribution.** This is your **Highest Purpose**.

➢ Your Highest Purpose is **Clarity.**

Clarity is the knowingness that happens when your mind is quiet, your heart is open, and your body is relaxed. You are in the Flow state, when divinely-inspired understanding and solutions drop into your awareness.

There is no denying you are built to be of service. You have always felt the call to improve and fix things, and not only for your own pleasure, but because it would benefit everyone. You are best able to serve the Greatest Good with your rare access to Clarity.

Clarity and the Mind

Type 1s are inclined to analysis and rationality and logic. In the Ego-Driven state, these are hailed as the highest form of mind.

Actually, knowingness is higher. Knowingness does not require analysis. There is nothing to figure out or think through. You just *know*. It is a sense of certainty, and it is not derived in the mind. It arrives through the heart, and is experienced in the body.

Therefore, when Consciousness-Directed, it is not logical thought that brings Clarity, it is the absence of it. A still, quiet mind is what allows the Clarity of Higher guidance to come through. Rather than the chatter of the Ego mind, this gains you access to the Higher Mind – when you allow the wisdom of the heart to direct your thoughts.

Clarity and the Body

Energetically speaking, you have a mental body, an emotional body, and a physical body. Your thoughts are electric, and your emotions are magnetic – and these combine to create the electromagnetic field which emanates from your physical body.

Your electromagnetic biofield can be measured as sound waves. This is the "vibration" you emit out into the Universe, and by the Law of Attraction, you call into your life everything which is a match for that vibration.

The Clarity of your biofield refers to how muddled or clear the sound waves are. The clearer the waves, the more love energy is able to pass through your body. This is the ultimate state of Vitality.

Feelings like love, joy, gratitude and peace are exponentially more powerful than ones such as anger, frustration, resentment, and contempt. The more powerful the emotion, the clearer the signal.

These energetically weak feelings don't have enough power to send out clear rolling waves. Instead, they create choppy, murky, muddled distortions in the biofield. This eventually becomes physical illness and all the other examples of powerlessness and disharmony such as money issues, interpersonal conflict, and despair.

In order to bring Clarity to your electromagnetic biofield which brings vital health to your body, you must learn how to harmonize it.

Harmonizing

Harmonizing basically means fully processing your feelings so that they can smooth out in your biofield. Type 1s typically suppress many of their emotions, trying not to feel them. This keeps the energy in knots. In order to have a smooth easy Flow of energy, you must learn to let all feelings come, and let them all go.

(These are the kinds of advanced teachings we are able to do together in our private membership, the Vitality Voyagers. Check out **yourvitalitypersonality.com/membership**.)

Additionally you can play Solfeggio Frequencies as background music throughout your day. These frequencies are the clear sound waves which promote vitality. Your biofield harmonizes itself to these clear tones.

Clarity and the Heart

The Clarity that you want in your heart is the open communication between you and your Higher Consciousness.

Again, this requires your willingness to feel love and compassion. Instead of your Sabotage Pattern of Rigidity, you want to be soft and fluid in your heart. Adaptable, malleable, resilient.

Rather than seeking in your mind for what is "right" and then using this to try to force everyone and everything to align to your ideal – turn inward, to your humble heart.

Let everyone be who they are, and love them for all their quirky traits. Instead of emitting outwards toward others your expectations of them, let yourself receive them, just as they are.

Even if they use inappropriate language and haven't bathed in days, even if they believe in things you don't, even if they aren't providing obvious value to society… let other people into your heart anyway. They all deserve love and compassion.

Your willingness to love and accept your world is what creates a clear open line of communication between you and your Higher Self. The more you can embrace these, the more you are capable of embodying The Real You, a being of immense love and light.

◆◆◆

Even though your Highest Purpose of Clarity primes you to be of service to others and help them solve their problems, do not worry that this means you are fated to a life of sacrifice. It will not at all feel like sacrifice.

The secret that you may not know is that it feels ecstatically wonderful to deliver your Highest Purpose. Even though you are giving out, you are receiving even more. Opening your mind, body and heart to Higher Consciousness and placing yourself directly in the Flow brings you a rush of love and energy that floods your nervous system with joy.

Whenever you deliver your Highest Purpose, you feel as uplifted and happy as you possibly could. Share your compassionate Clarity with the world, and you will love your life.

◆◆◆

Well, Type 1, you've been given quite a lot of information about yourself to digest. But hopefully by now you've come to see that even though you are wired to act out Your Primal Persona, it is possible for you to be someone so much more magnificent than that – Your Vitality Personality.

Now is the time to decide who you want to be in this world. If you are ready to step into the full power of who you really are, and seize your best life… then your next step is **Integration.** See Chapter Eleven.

YOUR VITALITY PERSONALITY

CHAPTER THREE
PERSONALITY TYPE 2
THE ALTRUIST | THE VICTIM

THE ALTRUIST — YOUR VITALITY PERSONALITY — CONSCIOUSNESS-DIRECTED

- **Vital Truth:** I give to myself first because my life is a precious gift to me from the Universe
- **Highest Purpose:** Self-Love
- **Theme:** GIVING
- **Distorted Theme:** SELF-ENSLAVEMENT
- **Liberation:** Introspecting
- **Vitality Behavior:** Honoring Myself
- **Compulsion:** Ingratiating
- **Destructive Behavior:** Chasing
- **Sabotage Pattern:** Self-Neglect
- **Survival Belief:** I can survive by giving to the people in power

THE VICTIM — YOUR PRIMAL PERSONA — EGO-DRIVEN

Hello, Type 2, you are most welcome. You are likely here because you have become unhappy enough in your current situation that you are willing to learn about what you could be doing differently.

The tricky part for you will be actually making the changes required. You are all about showing up for other people, but not at all inclined to show up for yourself. We will be exploring what it looks like to put yourself first, and this will probably make you feel a little uncomfortable. It will be challenging for you to actually apply the teachings you will learn here... but you'll quickly agree it's worth the effort.

If you have been led here, then it is because you are ready to take a quantum leap ahead of your other Type 2 peers. The wisdom and insight you will gain here will propel you into an awareness far more advanced than most. This will bring you and your world into balance, creating a ripple effect reaching much further than you would ever suspect.

This chapter focuses on the dual nature of your Personality Type 2, and the primary factors that hinder or help your ability to thrive. You will totally love the descriptions about your highest potential and purpose... but you will totally not love reading about your dark side, called Your Primal Persona.

Hang in there! You, more than anyone, are way tougher than you think. We will go through the Primal Persona stuff first, so that you can finish on a high note – the magnificence that is Your Vitality Personality.

Give yourself permission to surrender to this process, and you will see how it takes you on a journey, getting richer and richer the further it goes. The part of you that is wired for Self-Love will quickly come to see the massive value and advancement you will receive from this higher understanding.

DECODE YOUR SURVIVAL PROGRAMMING

As we just learned, **Your Primal Persona is the version of you that exists when you allow your Ego to unconsciously drive your thoughts, feelings and actions.** It is the operating system of your survival-oriented mind, limiting you from tapping into the love and light that is your Higher Consciousness.

In this state, you are closed off from your sense of love for yourself or others. And the actions you take from this place only serve to fulfill the Survival Programming of the small, fearful you. This can be really uncomfortable to face, but it is critical to see clearly so that you can gain freedom from this dark influence.

The bottom half of your Mandala spells out the dynamics of Your Primal Persona and its Ego-Driven Survival Programming:

SELF-ENSLAVEMENT
Distorted Theme

Compulsion
Ingratiating

Destructive Behavior
Chasing

Sabotage Pattern
Self-Neglect

Survival Belief
I can survive by giving to the people in power

YOUR PRIMAL PERSONA — **THE VICTIM** — EGO-DRIVEN

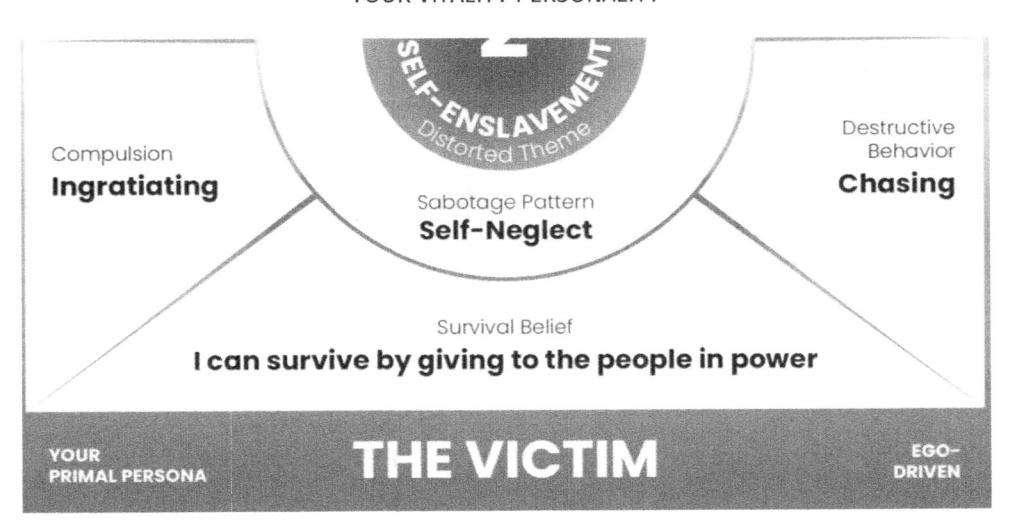

Your Primal Persona: The Victim

As a Type 2,

> Your Primal Persona is known as **The Victim.**

This is your Ego's version of "playing small," even though its programming is all about being a good person through service. But, as we will now explore, serving others while neglecting yourself does not align with the Principles of the Universe and holds you in resistance to the Flow.

See *Fig. 3A* for a brief summary of your Ego-Driven Survival Programming (we will dig deeper into it in just a moment). It is characterized by resistance, eroding your Vitality and degrading your life.

These are some painful truths. But you must forgive yourself for your Survival Programming. Have compassion for yourself, for it was the instability in your life which led you to feel that you couldn't survive without this perspective. Without self-awareness, you had no choice but to behave this way.

And this is true for everyone else, as well. We all deserve forgiveness for the way we act when we are asleep to ourselves -- we are totally unaware this is what we are doing and how destructive it is.

Even once you are aware of your Survival Programming, it can be quite challenging to take command over it. Yet every degree of progress you make in this direction brings you enormous reward. You will be joyfully inspired to continue the work.

Let's dive just a little bit deeper into what these dynamics of your Survival Programming really mean, so that you may begin the most rewarding journey of integrating yourself.

Your Distorted Theme

Each of the 9 Personality Types orient around a particular **Theme.** The whole point of you being here, at this time and in this place, is because you wanted to explore this Theme. This is the thing you are encoded to care about the most.

> Your Theme is **Giving.**

We will fully explore the true meaning of Giving in the next section (about Your Vitality Personality), when we discuss the Consciousness-Directed understanding of your Theme.

But right now, we are discussing your Survival Programming, and how your Ego degrades your understanding of your Theme of Giving.

Unfortunately, when Your Primal Persona interprets this Theme, it **becomes contorted – a warped, downgraded version of your highest potential.** This is called the **Distorted Theme.**

> Your Distorted Theme is **Self-Enslavement.**

Self-Enslavement is about assigning yourself the role of perpetual servant. You are wired to believe deeply in being a giver... but this does not mean you must turn yourself into a slave. Self-Enslavement and Giving are not at all the same thing.

You are totally unaware that you do this to yourself. You believe you are doing the right thing, being a good person. But forever putting yourself last, ignoring your own feelings and needs, and smothering your own voice are definitely not required in order to be a good person.

Self-Enslavement has to do with thinking of yourself as less important than everyone else. You believe it is your duty to serve them, to help them have what they

Fig. 3A **PERSONALITY TYPE 2 SURVIVAL PROGRAMMING**
Your Primal Persona: THE VICTIM
The Programmed You; The limited and diminished version of yourself that you default to when you are Ego-Driven
Distorted Theme: SELF-ENSLAVEMENT
Your Ego's warped and downgraded interpretation of your true Theme
Survival Belief: I CAN SURVIVE BY GIVING TO THE PEOPLE IN POWER
The scarcity-oriented message embedded in your Ego that creates your world view
Compulsion: INGRATIATING
The repetitive internal process you instantly launch as a way of discharging the emotional tension caused by your Survival Belief
Destructive Behavior: CHASING
The ruinous actions you regularly engage in when you operate according to your Survival Belief
Sabotage Pattern: SELF-NEGLECT
The totality of all your Survival Programming combined into an overall template for self-destruction

want and need, while you go without. Unbeknownst to you, there is a hidden belief within you that you are not inherently lovable, and constantly serving others is actually a strategy for trying to earn love.

Your impulse towards Self-Enslavement makes you feel that you can never say No. This is a really big problem area for you – you can't tolerate the feeling of guilt you experience at the thought of refusing. Even if you totally don't want to do what you are being invited to do, you agree because you believe you must. Much like an addiction, you feel compelled to give yourself away, even though this lifestyle makes you desperately unhappy.

The Ego is content to trap you inside this loop for all of your life: forever chasing love through making yourself indispensable, but never experiencing a lasting sense of value and security. As you will soon see, Self-Enslavement does not bring you love and appreciation… it blocks you from it.

In the hands of Your Primal Persona, you spend all your time ingratiating and chasing, believing you are serving the Greatest Good, but actually you are creating dynamics which are far out of balance:

- Wanting to demonstrate your value, you offer to do other people's work for them, overexerting yourself while blocking them from becoming self-sufficient
- Seeking to become the favorite, you go out of your way to give thoughtful gifts and do special favors, secretly feeling entitled to special treatment in return – which you may or may not ever receive
- Regarding yourself as less important, you give what you could not really afford to spare, leaving yourself in perilous circumstances
- Telling yourself what a good person you are by being so generous, you privately keep score of every act of generosity and whether it was appropriately appreciated and repaid, appointing unspoken obligations to your gifts
- Attaching yourself to troubled and damaged people who forever need your help, you set yourself up for a life of one-sided relationships, always the giver but never the receiver
- Feeling guilt for ever attending to your own needs or giving yourself special care, you create pain and illness in your own life

Although Self-Enslavement makes you feel pleased with yourself for being so self-sacrificing, this is only your Ego rewarding you for so fully surrendering control of your mind. Because even though it makes you think you are generous and kind, it is your cruelty to yourself and your enabling bad behavior in others which causes things to go horribly wrong.

This is no fun at all to read about. It's a bummer to realize your default, unconscious wiring is a sadly small version of who you could really be – who you actually are. The Real You is full of radiance and love and light, taking pleasure in treating yourself with love, generosity, and respect. You are on your way to discovering how to access this higher aspect of yourself.

Your Survival Belief

Your **Survival Belief** is the **scarcity-oriented message embedded in your Ego that creates your world view.** It is the secret programming in the basement of your unconscious which drives all your thoughts, feelings, and actions without you ever realizing it.

> Your Survival Belief is **I can survive by giving to the people in power.**

This belief is fundamental to you, even though you never knew it was there. It defines your understanding of how the world works.

Typically, this Survival Belief is activated within you at a young age.

As a child you likely experienced volatility in your life. Perhaps a parent figure had unstable emotions or lack of capabilities which left you feeling unsafe. This would have triggered in you a desire to appease or stabilize them, inventing ways to please them or doing their work for them. Making yourself into the one they can count on seemed like the best strategy for survival, and it's never occurred to you to re-examine it as an adult.

This Survival Belief has several important parts to examine:

Giving

It's true, having a mindset of giving wherever possible is a high-vibration way to live. However, this is only true as long as you yourself are stable and peaceful as you offer it, and you're offering out of a heartfelt desire, not a compulsive sense of obligation.

In the Ego-Driven state, giving is mandatory, whether you can afford to or not. It is not a free-will choice made in the heart. It's self-sacrifice, resentfully given.

Self-sacrifice does not align with the principles of Flow. You are a deeply loved expression of Source, and the Universe does not want any harm to come to you. Giving is only beneficial when it harmonizes and balances the energy dynamics on both sides.

Also, all human beings have access to their own assistance through communicating with their own Higher Consciousness. It is not your job to rescue people. This is doing other people's karmic work for them, which blocks them from learning their own lessons and discovering their own power.

Aligning with Powerful People

It probably surprised you to see that your Survival Belief mentions specifically that you are programmed to align yourself with other people who hold power. The reason this is true is because you falsely believe that you yourself are not powerful. You regard pretty much anyone other than yourself to be one who has more power.

This is so beyond incorrect. You are immensely powerful. Your Higher Consciousness – The Real You – has access to all of the Flow of the Universe. There is nothing beyond your reach. The problem is that as long as you focus on the outer, physical world, and never venture inward to where your true power resides, you will never discover this.

Ego-Driven Type 2s are not trying to have their own power, because they don't think they're worthy or capable of it. They're trying to become the right-hand-man to the person in power, believing that then they will be taken care of in return.

This does not turn out well for you. Others are also Ego-Driven, answering to their own programming, and if they are not a Type 2 then they are not wired to give a hoot about you. They're obsessing about other things entirely. The reciprocation you were counting on will likely never happen.

In particular, you wrongly ascribe power to the members of your nuclear family, such as your spouse/partner and your children. In truth, you hold equal status to your partner. Yet you defer to them as if you are quite inferior, smothering your own voice and neglecting your own needs.

The same is true with your children. Making your children into little royals is a terrible idea. They become tyrants with major entitlement issues, and they will never respect you. Lots of Type 2 parents who spoiled their children wonder why as adults they can't get so much as a return phone call. They are not grateful to you as you had envisioned – they have contempt for you and treat you like you're invisible (if they're also Ego-Driven, which is likely).

As you can see, your insistence that you are less important creates really unbalanced power dynamics in your life. This is why your Ego-Driven name is called The Victim.

Needing to be Needed

When you are Ego-Driven and answering to your Survival Belief, being needed is the primary cue you're looking for to signal that others see your value. This creates enormous problems because it is so profoundly out of alignment with the Flow of the Universe.

Being of service is lovely, but needing to be needed means you actually don't want other people to feel powerful and self-sufficient in their own right. If they were totally balanced and healthy, then they wouldn't need you anymore. Their autonomy is a threat. Helping people stay incompetent and deficient is not helpful at all.

You only feel the need to be needed when you won't admit your own true worth to yourself. As you raise yourself into Consciousness-Directedness, where you can feel your own power and value, you will no longer feel the need to be needed.

◆◆◆

As you can see, your Survival Belief that you must serve others is at the heart of much difficulty and self-sabotage for you. It is this belief which launches a cascade of repetitive thoughts and behaviors, that ultimately lead to your unhappiness. Learning about these, and how to take hold of them, is fundamental to becoming able to create a life you love.

If you have read this far, you are doing so well! Thank you for hanging in there, this stuff is definitely not fun to face. Remember, we are in the thick of the section about the Ego's Survival Programming. But then we will move ahead to discuss Type 2 at your highest and best.

We just finished discussing your Type 2 Survival Belief, which was activated somewhere in your early childhood. It is the primary driver behind all of your unconscious thoughts and behaviors.

Now, we will look at the most common thought, feeling and behavior patterns that emerge as a result of holding your Survival Belief.

Your Compulsion

Your **Compulsion** is the **repetitive internal process you instantly launch as a way of discharging the emotional tension caused by your Survival Belief.**

➢ Your Compulsion is **Ingratiating.**

This Compulsion is much like a guilty addiction – you know you should give it up, but don't want to… because you privately love it.

And even if you decide *That's it, I'm through with this…* you will still find it very difficult to stop, until you become able to embrace your Vital Truth (see the upper half of your Mandala), rather than your Survival Belief.

Ingratiating refers to all the ways in which you offer yourself up to other people. You are constantly striving to stay connected to your existing relationships, or to establish new ones. Although these may seem to you like spontaneously generous gestures, they are in fact predictable and calculated, because when you are Ego-Driven you feel compelled to act on your Survival Belief – that you must always be in service to others or else you might die.

Ingratiating means trying to "get in good" with other people, and there are several strategies you may employ to accomplish this:

Offering to Help

Well, this is classic Type 2. As soon as you hear about what's going on for one of your relationships, you offer to insert yourself as the solution to their problem. And boy, does it work, because we are all so overwhelmed in our lives that we are happy to accept any offer to make it better.

So there you are, driving people to the airport, picking up their kids from aftercare, making them meals when they're sick, helping them move, loaning them money (you'll probably never get it back btw), and ten billion other examples of how you help out.

But what about you? Aren't you also overwhelmed in your life? If you are Ego-Driven, then the answer is Yes. But you're pretending that you aren't, and so you ignore your own feelings and needs, and make yourself available to do even more.

However, if you were hoping to bask in the glow of their eternal appreciation (which you totally were), you will be sorely disappointed. Takers take, especially when you insist your help comes for free (it totally doesn't). If you tell them your gifts have no strings attached, then they take them… and move on to their next personal drama without another thought.

This leaves you feeling frustrated, depleted, and resentful, all of which you smother.

The lesson here is only to offer help when you genuinely want to and are fully able – not because you're trying to seduce others into adoration and loyalty.

Giving Gifts

Another strategy for Ingratiating yourself to others is giving them random gifts. Not for their birthday, not for Christmas, these are gifts "just because."

Flowers from your garden, fruit from your tree, you baked a special something… You certainly are amazing at demonstrating your thoughtfulness.

Again, that's really beautiful if there isn't an Ego-Driven agenda behind it – but there is. You feel compelled to do these things, congratulating yourself all along the way about what a good person you are. Congratulating yourself for being owned by your Ego is profound self-sabotage.

The way to identify if you are doing this is if you feel disappointment for not receiving a thank you note or a heartfelt phone call. If you feel sad that your gift didn't seem to be appreciated, this is showing you that you never gave it for the joy of giving – you gave it in hopes of receiving appreciation. This is called "giving to get," and it is most certainly an Ego-Driven impulse.

Flattery

Flattery is another strategy for Ingratiating yourself with other people. Telling people what they want to hear, steering conversations to be all about them, expressing outrage on their behalf... this is all flattery.

Although you may be telling yourself that this is what it means to be a friend, if you don't feel free to speak your truth or talk about yourself in their presence, then this is just another one-sided friendship, where they are the important one and you aren't.

It's one thing to say "You look nice today," but it's quite another to become a permanent Yes Man. If it's your perpetual role to be the flatterer in the relationship, you can know that you are Ego-Driven and thus far away from the Flow.

◆◆◆

Geez, who knew that going out of your way to be nice was such a terrible thing to do? You're probably feeling pretty defeated right about now.

You are not required to stop being nice to people and giving love. You just need to become very present first, and make sure you are acting authentically, as The

Real You. You have always intended to come here and be a source of love and help – but only on terms that feel healthy and balanced.

Your Destructive Behavior

Your Survival Belief – that you must always serve the ones with power in order to get by – also prompts your actions and behaviors. When you are Ego-Driven, and **therefore not questioning your inherent attitudes and beliefs, you will repeatedly behave this way.** This is called your **Destructive Behavior.**

You may be entirely unaware of it, or you may be doing it on purpose in the utter certainty it's the best way to be. Either way, this behavior is never for the Greatest Good of all, and therefore is destructive.

As an Ego-Driven Type 2 who believes you are not capable of survival on your own . . .

> ➢ Your Destructive Behavior is **Chasing.**

For as much effort as you put in every day to being good to everybody, it is completely shocking and devastating to you if someone ends their relationship with you.

This prompts panicked desperation, and you will begin Chasing after them, doing whatever it takes to get them back. Texts apologizing, phone calls begging, extravagant gift-giving, surrendering whatever boundaries and self-respect you were hoping to keep… you are not above groveling in order to keep other people in your life.

This brings up a fundamental problem area for the Ego-Driven Type 2: Holding healthy boundaries.

Holding Healthy Boundaries

Boundaries delineate a person's limits. They are the lines a person is unwilling to cross; this protects their own integrity. It is normal and healthy to have boundaries, and they vary according to each individual. Honoring your own boundaries and other people's is what it means to show respect.

The Ego-Driven Type 2 has big problems with boundaries, in both directions: they don't assert their own, and they don't want other people to assert theirs.

The reason you don't want to assert your own boundaries is because that might be off-putting to someone else.

What if you say No? What if you insist on being treated with respect? These could lead to rejection, and you are not willing to risk that. And if perchance you dared to take the risk and actually did get rejected, then you Chase after them, taking back whatever boundaries you attempted to assert, promising not to ever uphold them again.

The reason you don't want other people to hold boundaries is because you will likely end up outside of them, and that also feels like rejection when you are Ego-Driven. You are trying to feel safe by being the ultra-insider.

This often leads you to violate other people's boundaries without realizing it. Their privacy, their desire to attend to their own needs, their need to retreat when they feel wounded or unwell... These all offend you, because they leave you out. You tell yourself that you know better than they do what they need. Even if you're right, they will not appreciate you infringing upon their free will.

When you trespass upon other people's boundaries out of insecurity and neediness, it is likely you will be rejected. Again, this is your personal nightmare, and you frantically try to find a way to get back into their good graces. This is Chasing.

In the coming sections, you will learn that honoring yours and others' boundaries is the natural outcome of Self-Love. When you love and respect yourself, you will not allow your boundaries to be violated. This generates healthy relationships, not one-sided toxic ones. And also you will not violate other people's boundaries anymore, because you will no longer feel needy and desperate.

It is possible to feel totally complete within yourself. In this state, relationships become only about love and joyfulness, with no hidden agendas and no codependency. Loving yourself heals all the imbalances in your life.

Your Sabotage Pattern

As we have discussed, your Personality Type has much Survival Programming built in. Your Survival Belief, Compulsion, and Destructive Behavior are undeniable impulses within you that all drive your well-being into the ground.

In other words, these all combine into an overall template for self-destruction. This is called your **Sabotage Pattern – the way you repeatedly behave throughout your lifetime which leads directly to the destruction of your health and happiness.**

> Your Sabotage Pattern is **Self-Neglect.**

Your Survival Programming is all about serving others. Not only do you believe it is good and right to be totally others-centric... but you believe it is bad and wrong to attend to yourself.

Type 2s feel enormous guilt at the thought of making time for themselves and attending to their own feelings and needs. So much so, that they train themselves at an early age not to even acknowledge them.

This can lead you very far away from The Real You, because feelings and needs are the way your Higher Consciousness is communicating Its guidance to you. Shutting down your feelings and needs means cutting off communion with who you really are. This is self-sabotage of the first order.

Neglecting Your Mind

Neglecting your mind has to do with failing to check in with yourself.

You have been so conditioned to live in service, to let someone else be in charge, that it's possible you let outsiders shape what you think and value as well.

Do you make the time to go inward? Do you know what your true beliefs are? Do you know what to do with the resentful chatter going on in your mind?

It takes quiet and privacy to be able to pay attention to yourself and get to know your own mind. You tend to keep yourself too busy for this. Are you willing to adjust your lifestyle to make room for being alone with you?

Slowing down and treating your own company as interesting and important will be an enormous help in shifting your power back to yourself.

Neglecting Your Body

Oh dear Type 2, you take notoriously horrible care of yourself!

Your health really tells the story of how you have put everyone else first, and treated yourself as unimportant.

Most Type 2s are sugar and alcohol oriented, using these as the easiest escape from sadness. They are also not terribly exercise oriented as adults, because that would take up time that should be applied to other people. And finally, Type 2s don't prioritize rest, staying on their feet for long hours. These combine to create serious and unpleasant health outcomes.

Self-Neglect seriously harms your body because you will not honor its needs. Your body needs rest and rhythms, it needs healthy food. Your body needs healing. It needs attention. If you ignore all these, breakdown is the only thing possible.

As we will discuss shortly, your life was a special gift meant just for you. Your body was created with enormous love and care, so that it could serve you however you need. When you treat your body with respect, you honor the spirit of love it carries.

Neglecting Your Heart

Self-Neglect sabotages your connection to your Higher Self, because It communicates with you through the heart – through your feelings. Feelings are guidance from your Higher Consciousness. If you suppress and ignore these you are literally cutting yourself off from your true self. Instead you live as some kind of miserable zombie, going through the motions of life but finding no joy in it.

Type 2s are notoriously disconnected from their own feelings and needs. When we are in an appointment together, I give them a cue card where they can read through a list of feelings and needs to identify what theirs are. This is how it is possible for you to make choices against your own interest – you aren't listening to your inner guidance.

As you learn to love and honor yourself, your life will begin to shift and change. Treating yourself as special will bring a much higher quality of relationships into your life, with people who entirely agree that you are spectacularly special. You won't have to chase a thing – love, appreciation and respect will all arrive without effort.

It is not too late to reconnect with The Real You. You will find the road vulnerable and scary... and you will also find love, peace, satisfaction and a deep sense of serenity. It is a journey worth taking. The guidance on how to do this is coming up next.

✦✦✦

Now that you have opened your eyes to the destructive inner workings of Your Primal Persona, do not despair. It is certainly within your capacity to transform these behaviors and patterns of your Survival Programming.

Let's explore how you can be, act and live differently. There is an entirely different kind of life available to you, filled with love and connection and joy. And it is mapped out in the top half of your Type 2 Mandala.

ACTIVATE YOUR POWER PARADIGM

In Chapter One we revealed the meaning of Your Vitality Personality. Let's recap now.

Your Vitality Personality is the version of you that exists when you allow your Higher Consciousness to guide your thoughts, feelings, and actions. It is the opening of your heart, and allowing the loving intelligence found there to Flow through you. This infuses you with insight, wisdom, love and compassion, and the actions you take from this place always serve the Greatest Good.

Let's take a look now at the top half of your Mandala which spells out the dynamics of The Real You - Your Vitality Personality - and all its wondrous gifts and talents:

YOUR VITALITY PERSONALITY — **THE ALTRUIST** — CONSCIOUSNESS-DIRECTED

Vital Truth
I give to myself first because my life is a precious gift to me from the Universe

Liberation
Introspecting

Highest Purpose
Self-Love

Theme
GIVING
2

Vitality Behavior
Honoring Myself

Your Vitality Personality: The Altruist

As a Type 2,

> Your Vitality Personality is known as **The Altruist**.

This is the truth of who you really are. You have always felt a call to help, to give, to be of service. You have always had a heart as big as a whale, with easy access to love and compassion.

The Real You is a beacon of love and generosity. You are the one who is the soft place to land, the generous listener, the kind friend. You are the one who elevates Consciousness through emanating love – beginning with love for yourself. You help us all feel connected, seen and heard.

See *Fig 3B* for a brief summary of the Consciousness-Directed half of your Mandala, identifying how to use your Personality Type to bring into your life a sense of completeness, fulfillment, joy and love.

It may surprise you to see that much of this Vitality Paradigm is about how to be good to yourself, rather than a bigger picture perspective. The reason for this is because if you are depleted and unhappy, you will be unable to contribute in a bigger picture way. This is the paradigm that will support you, so that you can go out there and support others. When you embody all these natural gifts, you are a dazzling light, inspiring all who know you. It is so exciting to think you are just on the precipice of launching a new life of love, acceptance, and Vitality for yourself! It might have required some serious deep-breathing to get here, but the effort is so well worth it.

Fig. 3B **PERSONALITY TYPE 2** **POWER PARADIGM**
Your Vitality Personality: **THE ALTRUIST**
The Real You; The most magnificent version of yourself you joyfully embody when you heed the guidance of your Higher Consciousness
Theme: GIVING
The dynamic realm of Life your Higher Consciousness wants to explore to the fullest
Vital Truth: I GIVE TO MYSELF FIRST BECAUSE MY LIFE IS A PRECIOUS GIFT TO ME FROM THE UNIVERSE
A higher understanding of how to thrive, that aligns you with the Flow of the Universe
Liberation: INTROSPECTING
The emancipating philosophy you freely embrace to enhance your connection to the Flow
Vitality Behavior: **HONORING MYSELF**
The empowering and uplifting actions you intentionally choose to create your best life
Highest Purpose: SELF-LOVE
How you serve the Greatest Good through embracing your encoded genius, and the source of your Vitality

Let's explore these dynamics of your Power Paradigm, so that you may begin to fully comprehend just how open, uplifting, happy and healthy your life could really be.

Your Theme

As was mentioned earlier,

> ➢ Your Theme is **Giving.**

When you pursue the Highest form of this Theme – Giving – you are truly aligned with Source, and therefore always serving the Greatest Good.

Giving is the contributing of resources for the benefit of others. It is sharing your riches – riches of love, of talent, of time, and of money. Whatever abundance you have in your possession, Giving means you are delighted to impart it to others who lack it. As a Type 2, you can inherently sense this. You are the living breathing example of the Universal celebration of love and abundance.

Because your Higher Consciousness was delighted to explore this Theme in big and small ways, you were wired to notice people and how they are doing. You are encoded to be the generous giver of loving attention and help… beginning with yourself. This is why Your Vitality Personality is named The Altruist.

You know this is true because of how much joy and peace you feel when you are in balance – giving yourself the love and support you need empowers you to be authentically loving and supportive to others. You feel so much happier and healthier when you get to be your own priority, too.

In the hands of Your Vitality Personality, you embrace your power and strength, so that you are fully capable of being of service to others, making you a glowing, angelic Altruist:

- Offering to give when you truly want to do so and are capable of it, while never allowing yourself to come to harm
- Offering help or gifts which are for the Greatest Good
- Lovingly holding boundaries, and kindly saying No
- Cultivating your own personal growth
- Treating yourself as your most beloved relationship
- Vital health derived from being mindful of your thoughts, respectful of your body, and connected to your own spirit

Most people are Ego-Driven, with closed hearts and judgmental minds. They believe in scarcity and survival, unwilling to demonstrate concern and care because they believe it will deplete them in some way. They can't bring themselves to see beyond their own personal affairs.

You are the one who is built to serve the world by engaging your natural abilities to deliver love, help and care to all… including yourself.

Once you are able to treat yourself with love and kindness, you will greatly increase your own energy and strength. In this newly empowered state, you are in the best position to offer help while never harming or weakening yourself.

When you are Consciousness-Directed, it is your joy to feel healthy and powerful, and to see others feel that way, too. You no longer need to sublimate yourself, and you no longer need to feel that other people's autonomy is a threat. You love for *all* to be in a stable position to fully celebrate Life.

Your Vital Truth

Your **Vital Truth** is the **Higher understanding of how to thrive by aligning with Universal principles.** It is the escape hatch your Ego doesn't want you to know about, because it unlocks all of its Survival Programming, and connects you to your Higher Consciousness – The Real You.

> Your Vital Truth is **I give to myself first because my life is a precious gift to me from the Universe.**

This Vital Truth is the contradiction of your Survival Belief. Whereas endorsing your Survival Belief leads you directly to resistance, self-sabotage and erosion, embracing your Vital Truth places you in the Flow of the Universe. This leads you directly towards your happiest, healthiest life – Vitality!

However, your unconscious is encoded to automatically revert to the Survival Belief. To replace this with the Vital Truth takes conscious intention and daily practice.

Although this Vital Truth is a brief, simple statement, it is dense with meaning. Let's take a moment to unpack this.

Giving to Yourself First

Just this snippet alone probably makes you feel really uncomfortable. This seems so selfish!

This is not a suggestion that you suddenly begin acting like a diva, expecting to be treated like royalty. It's really just meant to remind you that you are not inferior to or less than anyone else, and you must not treat yourself as if you don't matter.

So sure, give the older lady on the bus your seat, unless you yourself should really be the one sitting. Yes, agree to take the grandkids for the weekend when you feel delighted to do so, but not when you are tired, depleted, or resentful. Yes, gift your struggling friend some money, but only if it doesn't end up leaving you short.

It is natural for you to want to be a giver, but not all the time. Sometimes you will need to refrain or decline, in order to make sure you are not harmed or destabilized. Your tendency has been to live far out of balance, and adopting an attitude of prioritizing yourself will bring this back to center.

Your Life is a Precious Gift

The amount of love, planning and guidance that went into creating this lifetime here and now for you is quite beyond our human understanding. But please be assured, this life was given to you with the intention that it be meaningful and important to YOU. This lifetime is meant to serve you, and no one else.

Even though your Higher Consciousness chose your Personality Type on purpose because It wanted to help support humanity, that does not mean you *only* came here to be of service to others. Each lifetime you live is for *your* learning, *your* growth, *your* expansion.

You are here to give, and you are here to receive. You are here to learn, and you are here to teach. As much as everybody would love for you to be their permanent helper who never has any needs or interests of their own, you did not come here for them. You came here for yourself, to have the experiences that are interesting and exciting to you.

So don't give yourself away in a way that dishonors you, and don't let yourself be lured away from a life that serves The Real You. The Universe loves you very much, and wants to see you treated well.

Upsetting the Applecart

It's possible that you now find yourself in a quandary. You understand and see the value in treating yourself as a top priority… but you don't know how to extract yourself from the long-established one-sided dynamics that currently exist in most of your relationships.

Type 2s can be worriers, and you may feel concerned about how to actually bring up a conversation where you ask for new dynamics in the relationship.

Try starting with something along the lines of *My needs have changed.* When you stay focused on discussing your own feelings and needs, there is nothing upsetting or offensive in it. It will not cause anyone to be angry. Inconvenienced, possibly, but that is not the same thing,

So for example you might say something like, *I have to talk to you about something, because my needs have changed. I'm finding I'm just not able to keep up the pace that I was. I need to reduce the number of days I pick up your kids after school.*

Can you see how this is a perfectly reasonable request? You won't be a bad guy. Most people will be glad to see you treating yourself better. Healthy relationships are the ones where people are happy to see you uplevel your quality of life, and treat yourself as special as they have always known you to be.

It's possible that taking back the power you've always given away for free may upset certain people… but really only the ones who have been happy to take advantage of you. Heads up: those are *toxic* relationships. You might get pushback from these folks, but that is your blaring signal to let these relationships go if they are not willing to make room for your beautiful growth.

It is totally possible to have one hundred percent healthy relationships... just as soon as you decide to have a healthy relationship with yourself.

This may sound scary and overwhelming to you, to upset the applecart to such a big degree. Don't worry. In our private membership called the Vitality Voyagers, you will meet your circle of like-minded friends, who would be delighted to become your new support system as you move to embrace The Real You. You will see that you are not alone, and that you are loved.

> Check out **www.yourvitalitypersonality.com/membership**

If you have made it this far in the reading, then your Higher Consciousness has led you here because you are ready. You can do this. It is time for you to celebrate yourself, and step into your true power. An extremely beautiful future is waiting for you, just around the bend, where you feel important, appreciated, and loved.

Your Liberation

Your **Liberation** is **the emancipating philosophy you freely embrace.** This is a powerful shift, out of the Survival Programming of the mind, and into the Flow of the Universe through the heart. Rather than being owned by a chronic Compulsion, you are now intentionally choosing this Liberation.

> Your Liberation is **Introspecting**

Introspecting means exploring your own inner terrain. It means checking in with your own feelings and needs.

This impulse is generally missing for the Type 2, and it can cause you to end up living very far away from the life you desire. Your feelings and needs are communication from your Higher Consciousness, trying to guide you. They are your connection to The Real You.

You will need to intentionally practice Introspecting. Your hardwiring normally leads you to compulsively Ingratiate yourself to other people – focusing on their needs, their feelings and their desires... and not your own. Now it is time to take command over this compulsion to focus outward, and bring your focus inward.

You came here to be The Altruist – the one who delivers transformative, healing love and support while never harming themself. In order to embody this, you must commit to making time for connecting with yourself, alone, in silence, and stillness.

Can you do that?

Your normal lifestyle has you busy every second of the day, meeting other people's expectations or even going above and beyond. You may actually feel a bit of anxiety come up at this request that you become quiet and present with yourself. It's ok. You really, really need this. It will make you feel so much better. Just give it a try once, and see.

I recommend you begin with giving minutes every evening to Introspecting.

Shut the door, and put your phone to Do Not Disturb. If you're in a loud house maybe you need to go sit in your car or go to a coffeehouse. I really want you to treat this like it's important, not something you're doing halfheartedly.

Introspecting Exercise

This exercise is for you to start identifying how you really feel and what you really need -- and then releasing all attachment to it. This is how you let feelings come, and let them go.

This is a safe space for you to be really honest with yourself. You have spent many years saying Yes when you wanted to say No, to the point you don't totally know yourself anymore. The Real You is calling out for your deep introspection.

Feelings

Type 2s typically have a really hard time identifying what their true feelings are. In private coaching sessions, it has been very useful to give them a handout which lists out common feelings, so that they can see which feeling leaps out at them.

Even though we humans enjoy a flamboyant vocabulary, most human feelings can be boiled down to a handful of words. Here are some suggestions to help you explore how you have been feeling lately.

Afraid	Frustrated	Lonely
Angry	Grateful	Peaceful
Anxious	Happy	Relaxed
Bored	Hurt	Resentful
Concerned	Inspired	Sad
Excited	Jealous	Safe

Which of these feelings holds a charge for you?

Once you have identified it, close your eyes, and breathe deeply in through your nose, all the way down into your belly, letting the belly expand. Hold, and on the exhale, imagine you are breathing out of your chest as you exhale out of your mouth. Pretend you can exhale through the mouth and chest at the same time. Do this 3 times – it quiets down your nervous system.

Now, let that feeling waft up to you, out of the chest. Let yourself fully feel it. We are not at all going to delve into the story associated with it. No mental chatter – that is the Ego trying to take control. Just feel the feeling.

Let yourself cry or rage if that's what comes up. Don't judge it and don't hold back. Let it run its course, it won't last long. It is very good to discharge the energy.

Imagine there is a sun in your chest, golden and radiant. As if it has gravitational pull, pull all of your feelings, and all of the story connected to these feelings, into this fiery orb. Pull it all inward, and hold it in the chest, and say to yourself 3 times: *I love and accept the part of me who feels {feeling}*.

This perspective aligns you with your Higher Consciousness. You are with the bigger aspect of yourself, neutrally observing the smaller part of you having this experience. There is no judgment, just love and acceptance.

As you pull this energy inward, you are integrating it back into your biofield, smoothing it out into harmony. It's as if you are washing the charge off the emotion, returning it to neutrality. You will see how this makes you feel calm and peaceful.

Needs

You also have a whole bunch of needs you haven't given much attention to! Now it is time to focus on what parts of you feel incomplete. These are your needs.

Even though most of us are under the impression that we are meant to meet each other's needs, once you become an adult, you are capable of meeting your own needs – even needs for love and companionship. It is possible to feel entirely complete when you know you are experiencing your life alongside your Higher Consciousness, your truest friend and deepest love.

Here are some suggestions of needs you might be experiencing lately.

Abundance	Happiness	Purpose
Affection	Harmony	Relaxation
Autonomy	Healing	Respect
Creativity	Love	Safety
Freedom	Order	Self-expression
Friendship	Peace	Trust
Fun	Pleasure	Understanding

Identify the word that holds the most charge for you. Close your eyes and breathe deeply again, centering yourself in your chest and lighting up the golden orb.

Let yourself imagine having the thing you feel you need. Imagine yourself living that lifestyle where your needs are met. Let yourself feel the sense of completion, of relaxation, of happiness and peacefulness that comes with having everything you need. Just sit with the feeling, as if you already have everything you need.

Inside, say to your heart 3 times: *I am this. Bring me more of this.*

This is how you speak directly to the Universe. You are sending out a powerful vibration of satisfaction and completion, and the Flow will bring more and more ot if back to you, bringing your life out of scarcity and lack and into abundance,

Then, once again, pull the whole scene into the fiery orb in your chest, and hold it there. Imagine the power of this vision seeping into your body, spreading out in every direction. This uplevels the amount of energy your body can access to thrive more fully.

◆◆◆

Going inward connects you to The Real You, and all your power. It keeps your mind calm and your emotions stable. It brings you a sense of certainty, of capability, of self-trust. It is from this state that you can manifest whatever sort of life you desire. Becoming adept at Introspecting will radically improve your reality.

Your Vitality Behavior

Vitality Behavior is the **empowering and uplifting actions you intentionally choose when you are Consciousness-Directed,** rather than the Destructive Behavior your Ego drives you to act out.

> Your Vitality Behavior is **Honoring Myself.**

This is sooo much lovelier than your previous go-to – Chasing! This is where you really shift out of Your Primal Persona, The Victim, and into Your Vitality Personality, The Altruist.

As The Victim, you found it nearly impossible to say No. You allowed your boundaries to be violated again and again. And you lost your mind at the thought of losing a relationship, toxic though it may be.

But now, as The Altruist, all of that misery disappears, to be replaced with the elation of knowing your true worth and never being willing to sell yourself short.

In intentionally choosing to Honor Yourself, you only participate in actions which are for your Greatest Good. And you can trust that, when you do this, it also serves the Greatest Good of all.

So for example, when you are asked to give of yourself in a way that feels wrong to you, you can kindly refuse. Do NOT weaken your position by inventing fake reasons for saying No. Speak your truth, because this teaches everyone else what Honoring Yourself looks like.

At work, common scenarios might be being asked to work late, work on your day off, or do someone else's work for them. If this interferes with your plans for yourself, do not buckle to your Ego's pressure to abandon them in favor of meeting other people's needs. Simply say something like, "Unfortunately, I'm not available to do that because I have commitments elsewhere." There is nothing rude or mean in this – it is completely reasonable.

At home, if you're asked to babysit your friend's kids for free for the millionth time, but you actually don't want to, decline in a way that makes it clear that it's time for these unfair expectations to shift. You can say something like, "I know in the past I implied that I was available for that, but I'm actually finding that it's blocking me from taking care of other things I need to attend to. Unfortunately I think you're going to have to find another solution."

Many Type 2s have confessed that, when they tried this for the first few times, their heart was racing and they broke out into a sweat. It's really scary to do this when you've never done this before. But once they discovered there were actually no negative consequences (because what you've said is entirely legitimate and understandable, so there was nothing to argue about) ... they felt totally elated and set free.

Just imagine a world in which you have the time and energy to do what you want to do – even if that means do absolutely nothing at all! It's your business, and it's your life, and you get to do whatever would please you!

Get a massage! Take a nap! Read a book! Go to a movie! Pamper yourself, and treat yourself as your own best friend. Your time is your own, and you deserve to be happy. And meanwhile, you are teaching other people how to be respectful and fair.

Feelings are Guidance

The main reason you were not able to Honor Yourself when you were Ego-Driven is because you had learned to smother your feelings and needs. Many Type 2s, if asked, wouldn't even be able to identify their genuine feelings and needs, because they'd become so disconnected from them.

The extremely important thing to understand is that your Higher Consciousness communicates to you through your feelings. If you want to align with the Flow of the Universe and develop your Vitality, then you must begin paying attention to your feelings.

If you are being asked to do something that you don't want to do, you will feel an immediate pulse of displeasure. Normally, you would override this and agree anyway. However, this is your Higher Consciousness communicating caution to you. Since you are a very agreeable and kind person, if you feel resistance to giving, it's surely for a good reason.

Maybe you're committed elsewhere. Maybe you're in a one-sided relationship. Maybe you're really tired and need to rest. Your Higher Consciousness is trying to take excellent care of you, and is telling you this request is not a good idea for you through the feeling of displeasure. Do not ignore this, because every time that you do, you destroy your Vitality a little bit more.

Honoring Yourself means becoming willing to heed the guidance of your Higher Consciousness, which exists in a constant state of love, joy, and peace. If the feelings you are experiencing are not these, then you are not in alignment with the Flow, which means you are sabotaging your wellness. In order to cultivate your happiness, you must only give when it feels good and right to do so. Listen to your feelings, they are always trying to show the way to Vitality.

Your Highest Purpose

You chose to be here, in this time and place, because you wanted to contribute something. You came here for a reason, and you chose your Personality Type because it was the one that would help you accomplish it. **Your Personality Type has a special set of talents and abilities, and you wanted to use them to make a contribution.** This is your **Highest Purpose**.

> Your Highest Purpose is **Self-Love**.

You might be surprised to learn that your Highest Purpose is about loving yourself. You may have thought that a Highest Purpose would be all about how you contribute to the world at large. It certainly would make sense to you if your Highest Purpose was to bring Love to the world, because that feels natural and easy for you.

But the thing you probably have never realized before is that you are actually only capable of loving others at the capacity with which you love yourself. If you don't love yourself, then you are a greatly diminished and out-of-balance being, and are not fully capable of offering genuinely unconditional love to anyone!

It is only when you are Consciousness-Directed that you are able to love unconditionally with no expectations, judgments, or attachments. When you are Ego-Driven, your love is always conditional, meaning you only offer it sporadically when you approve of someone. And as long as you never approve of and love yourself, you will never be able to offer genuine unconditional love to anyone else!

So actually, learning to love yourself unconditionally is the key that unlocks your nourishing and healing love for us all!

Yes, it's true, your Personality Type is the archetype which teaches us all how to love ourselves, and this is the only way we can heal our world and uplevel our reality! You thought I was kidding when I said you were important! You are so very precious, and we all depend upon you learning how to love yourself.

As an example, just think about the role a mother plays in the legacy of an entire family line.

If the mother is Ego-Driven and does not love and honor herself, she very likely marries a man who also does not love and honor her, such as an addict, a narcissist, or an abuser. Then she births children into this dynamic, who are raised to witness their mother never taking any action which fixes anything, continually allowing herself to be emotionally, psychologically or physically abused. Having no role modeling for self-respect or self-love, they internalize the patterns of the home, and play them out for themselves in their adult lives. They either become the abuser or the abused, and they model this for their children. As you can imagine, this becomes the fixed reality for every generation thereafter, populating hundreds of damaged and dysfunctional people over time.

However, if the mother completely loves and honors herself, she will only marry a man who reveres and adores her. He protects her, he encourages her, he helps her. The children they bear are raised in a household where self-esteem and talents are fostered and supported. Those children go out into the world, modeling to their friends and co-workers what wholeness looks like. They attract much attention because of their bright light – their influence is far-reaching. Not only do they choose healthy relationships, but so do the people whose lives they have touched. Now, not only is it the generations within a single family that thrive, but the generations of the families of all they helped guide. Imagine how quickly this dynamic multiplies. Imagine the thousands of people who would be positively impacted over time.

This is how your singular effort to simply love yourself raises up the whole world. The ripple effect you are capable of initiating is quite beyond comprehension. And meanwhile, you will come to enjoy your life in a way you never imagined was possible.

Self-Love in the Mind

How do you think of yourself? What is your self-talk?

Chances are you have spent a lifetime calling yourself very mean things.

It is so very important for you to understand how powerful your self-talk is. For your body, it is as if God has spoken.

Imagine that the voice in your mind is like that of a mama duck, and every cell in your body are her baby ducks.

When you say to all your babies "*You're stupid, you're ugly, you're worthless*, they hear you, and they feel sad. Your energy starts to wane, and health issues start creeping in.

It is time to become much more attentive to what your inner chatter is saying.

Every time you notice your mind saying unkind things to you, take a moment to reset yourself.

Pull all of this mental chatter, like streaks of light, into your heart, imagining it is washing off the emotional charge these words bring up in you. Say to your heart *I love and accept the part of me who thinks I'm stupid. I love and accept the part of me who thinks I'm ugly. I love and accept the part of me that is genius. I love and accept the part of me who is beautiful. I love myself. I accept myself.*

Become a loving protector of yourself, and do not let your Ego mind abuse you. Take hold of the chatter and neutralize it, shifting to loving thoughts instead.

Loving Your Body

In the past, the punishing way you treated yourself caused you to crave more sweetness in your life. This usually becomes a penchant for sugary sweets, creamy carbs, and alcohol. As much as you wanted them to make you feel better, these are habits which end up making you feel much worse.

Now as you actively cultivate your love for yourself, you will notice that you start to feel more internally fulfilled. This is an important, inspiring shift.

Love for yourself, happiness with yourself, contentment with yourself – these make you feel strong and complete.

As your self-love increases, your cravings will dissipate. You will become more inclined to start choosing to eat food which enlivens you, and getting rid of the ones which weaken you.

You will also start to honor your body's needs more.

You will let yourself rest, because you've learned to say No.

You will let yourself receive care, because you've learned how to ask for help.

You will start to feel delighted to take care of your body, the magnificent vessel you were gifted so that you could have this physical life.

Loving Your Heart – The Real You

Your heart is the doorway to The Real You – the eternal light being you have always been. This is your Higher Consciousness, who has been choosing your lifetimes and stories, knowing how challenging they would be. There is no judgment there, only understanding.

Self-Love means coming to love and accept ALL parts of yourself – even your shadow. This is a process, and takes practice and effort. Are you willing to make time for this in your life? You will need private alone time, so that you can feel safe and free enough to give yourself the attention you need and deserve.

Learning how to love your whole self requires quiet contemplation during such activities as meditation, journaling, and creative endeavors. There is much guidance available to you in our private membership, the Vitality Voyagers. These practices are where you will find your strength.

As a result, you will start to remember what is so magical and special about yourself. Instead of feeling like you must physically *do* things in order to earn love from other people, you need to discover who you already *are*... and fall madly in love with that person.

Here are some examples of who you are as a Type 2 that makes you so wonderfully lovable, and surely there are so many other things to list that are specific only to you:

- You are highly intuitive, able to read body language and sense energy, allowing you to have a special kind of *knowing* about the truth of people that others lack
- You have a rare warmth that is communicated through a sparkle in your eyes, an openly friendly smile, and easy laughter, signaling without words that you are kind and safe
- You are trustworthy, naturally honest and desiring to do right by other people
- You have a willingness and eagerness about you, making you able to be happily present and focused on the task at hand
- You are deeply compassionate, able to offer love to all the ones the rest of society would turn their back on in judgment
- You are steadfastly loyal, willing to be a source of help and encouragement when others fall on hard times
- You are stupendously generous, quick to offer whatever support and assistance you can
- You are intelligent, with a rare astuteness that allows you to take in quite a lot of information about what is going on around you which most people miss
- You are excellent at nurturing the vulnerable ones, making you the valuable caretaker of animals, plants, children, the elderly, and anyone else with special needs

Can you understand now how you are so completely worthy of love, appreciation and respect, without ever having to lift a finger to earn it? You are so incredibly important to this world. Just by embracing who you already are, you create a safe, nurturing environment for the rest of us to thrive in. In Loving Yourself, you make Vitality easily accessible to us all.

◆◆◆

Well, Type 2, you've been given quite a lot of information about yourself to digest.

But hopefully by now you've come to see that even though you are wired to act out Your Primal Persona, it is possible for you to be someone so much more magnificent than that – Your Vitality Personality.

Now is the time to decide who you want to be in this world. If you are ready to step into the full power of who you really are, and seize your best life... then your next step is **Integration.** See Chapter Eleven.

CHAPTER FOUR
PERSONALITY TYPE 3
THE LUMINARY | THE PRETENDER

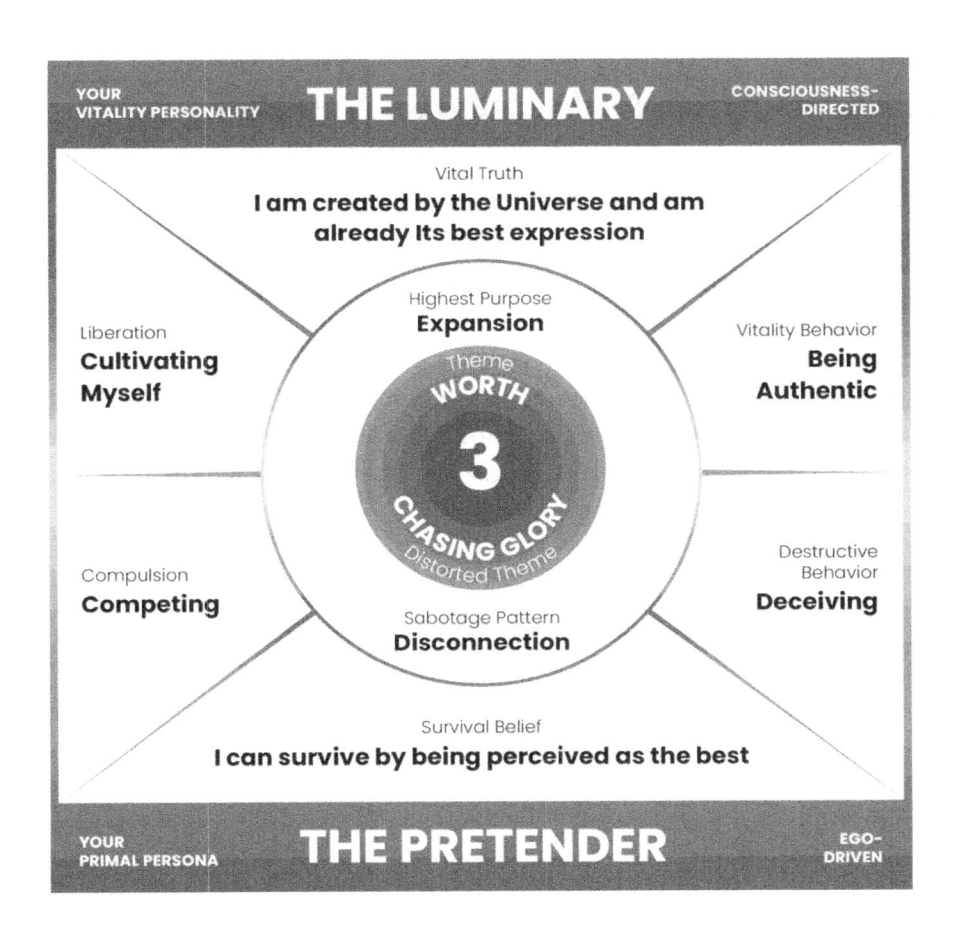

THE LUMINARY — YOUR VITALITY PERSONALITY — CONSCIOUSNESS-DIRECTED

- **Vital Truth:** I am created by the Universe and am already Its best expression
- **Highest Purpose:** Expansion
- **Theme:** WORTH
- **Distorted Theme:** CHASING GLORY
- **Liberation:** Cultivating Myself
- **Vitality Behavior:** Being Authentic
- **Compulsion:** Competing
- **Destructive Behavior:** Deceiving
- **Sabotage Pattern:** Disconnection
- **Survival Belief:** I can survive by being perceived as the best

THE PRETENDER — YOUR PRIMAL PERSONA — EGO-DRIVEN

Well hello there, Type 3. It's quite exciting that you're here, because it's rather rare. Your inner coding typically would make you more disinclined to pursue this sort of teaching. Between an attachment to being productive, and a tendency to focus on the external material world, it is unusual to give your time and attention to something so introspective.

If you have been led here, then it is because you are ready to take a quantum leap ahead of your other Type 3 peers. The wisdom and insight you will gain here will propel you into an awareness far more advanced than most. You will finally understand why you feel so compelled to achieve, and how you can use this high energy to serve the Greatest Good.

This chapter focuses on the dual nature of your Personality Type 3, and the primary factors that hinder or help your ability to thrive. You will totally love the descriptions about your highest potential and purpose… but you will totally not love reading about your dark side, called Your Primal Persona.

Hang in there! We intentionally go through the Primal Persona stuff first, so that you can finish on a high note – the magnificence that is Your Vitality Personality.

Give yourself permission to surrender to this process, and you will see how it takes you on a journey, getting richer and richer the further it goes. The part of you that is wired for Expansion will quickly come to see the massive value and advancement you will receive from the experience.

DECODE YOUR SURVIVAL PROGRAMMING

As we just learned, **Your Primal Persona is the version of you that exists when you allow your Ego to unconsciously drive your thoughts, feelings and actions.** It is the operating system of your survival-oriented mind, limiting you from tapping into the love and light that is your Higher Consciousness.

In this state, you are closed off from your sense of love for yourself or others. And the actions you take from this place only serve to fulfill the Survival Programming of the small, fearful you. This can be really uncomfortable to face, but it is critical to see clearly so that you can gain freedom from this dark influence.

The bottom half of your Mandala spells out the dynamics of Your Primal Persona and its Ego-Driven Survival Programming:

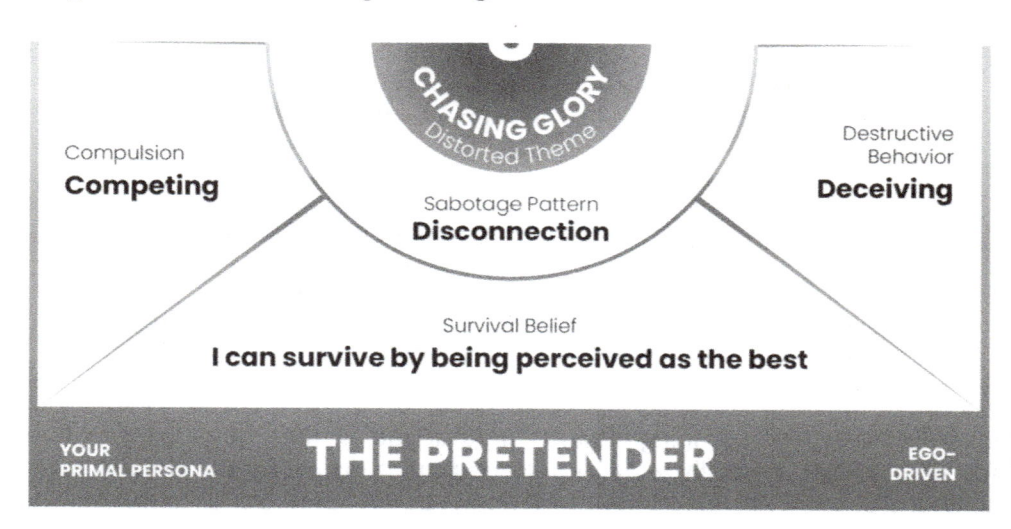

Distorted Theme: **CHASING GLORY**

Compulsion: **Competing**

Sabotage Pattern: **Disconnection**

Destructive Behavior: **Deceiving**

Survival Belief: **I can survive by being perceived as the best**

YOUR PRIMAL PERSONA — **THE PRETENDER** — EGO-DRIVEN

Your Primal Persona: The Pretender

As a Type 3,

- Your Primal Persona is known as **The Pretender**.

This is your Ego's version of "playing small," even though its programming is all about seeming big. But, as we will now explore, seeming big and being authentically expansive are not at all the same thing.

See *Fig. 4A* for a brief summary of your Ego-Driven Survival Programming (we will dig deeper into it in just a moment). It is characterized by resistance, eroding your Vitality and degrading your life.

These are some painful truths. But you must forgive yourself for your Survival Programming. Have compassion for yourself, for it was the pain in your life which led you to feel that you couldn't survive without this perspective. Without self-awareness, you had no choice but to behave this way.

And this is true for everyone else, as well. We all deserve forgiveness for the way we act when we are asleep to ourselves -- we are totally unaware this is what we are doing and how much it hurts those we love.

Even once you are aware of your Survival Programming, it can be quite challenging to take command over it. Yet every degree of progress you make in this direction brings you enormous reward. You will be joyfully inspired to continue the work.

Let's dive just a little bit deeper into what these dynamics of your Survival Programming really mean, so that you may begin the most rewarding journey of integrating yourself.

Your Distorted Theme

Each of the 9 Personality Types orient around a particular **Theme**. The whole point of you being here, at this time and in this place, is because you wanted to explore this Theme. This is the thing you are encoded to care about the most.

- Your Theme is **Worth**.

We will fully explore the true meaning of Worth in the next section (about Your Vitality Personality), when we discuss the Consciousness-Directed understanding of your Theme.

But right now, we are discussing your Survival Programming, and how your Ego *degrades* your understanding of your Theme of Worth.

Unfortunately, when Your Primal Persona interprets this Theme, **it becomes contorted – a warped, downgraded version of your highest potential. This is called the Distorted Theme.**

- Your Distorted Theme is **Chasing Glory**.

Chasing Glory is about perpetually pursuing a specific feeling – the feeling of being the best, the winner, the impressive one. The high, when you accomplish this, is like no other. Yet it is fleeting, and leaves you craving more. Much like addiction, the thirst for Chasing Glory remains unquenched, no matter how often you try to satisfy it.

Chasing Glory keeps you focused on achieving in the external world, without ever going inward, and checking in with The Real You. It has you trying to construct an identity as a winner, from the outside in. It keeps you perpetually on the hunt, rather than bringing you a sense of fulfillment and peace.

The Ego is content to trap you inside this loop for all of your life: forever chasing proof of your greatness, but never experiencing a lasting sense of Worth.

Rather than feeling an internal "knowingness" about your own value, your Ego prompts you to seek validation outside of yourself. As you will soon see, Chasing Glory does not lead you to feel a deeper sense of Worth... it actually destroys it.

In the hands of Your Primal Persona, you spend all your time building up the external evidence of your Worth:

- Feeling dismayed at an internal sense of lack, you seek to appear as someone others would admire
- Believing that the world is a competitive ruthless place, you make sure you are the one that wins
- Securing relationships with people who you feel make you look good or could be useful to you
- Pursuing work which provides high status, wealth and prestige, rather than something that fulfills the heart

Fig. 4A **PERSONALITY TYPE 3** **SURVIVAL PROGRAMMING**	
Your Primal Persona: **THE PRETENDER**	The Programmed You; The limited and diminished version of yourself that you default to when you are Ego-Driven
Distorted Theme: CHASING GLORY	Your Ego's warped and downgraded interpretation of your true Theme
Survival Belief: I CAN SURVIVE BY BEING PERCEIVED AS THE BEST	The scarcity-oriented message embedded in your Ego that creates your world view
Compulsion: COMPETING	The repetitive internal process you instantly launch as a way of discharging the emotional tension caused by your Survival Belief
Destructive Behavior: DECEIVING	The ruinous actions you regularly engage in when you operate according to your Survival Belief
Sabotage Pattern: **DISCONNECTION**	The totality of all your Survival Programming combined into an overall template for self-destruction

- Pushing your body far beyond its limits if that is what it takes to achieve the goal, rather than trusting the Universe to easily deliver your dreams to your door
- Regularly disconnecting from feelings of inadequacy, insincerity, shame, and a lack of meaning, rather than integrating them

Although Chasing Glory makes you feel like the best in the moment, this is only your Ego rewarding you for so fully surrendering control over your mind. Because even though it has you thinking you are getting ahead, it is exactly this behavior that leads to your downfall.

This is no fun at all to read about. It's a bummer to realize your default, unconscious wiring is a sadly small version of who you could really be – who you actually are. The Real You is full of radiance and love, with a desire to express Its full potential. You are on your way to discovering how to access this higher aspect of yourself.

Your Survival Belief

Your **Survival Belief** is the **scarcity-oriented message embedded in your Ego that creates your world view.** It is the secret programming in the basement of your unconscious which drives all your thoughts, feelings, and actions without you ever realizing it.

> Your Survival Belief is **I can survive by being perceived as the best.**

This belief is fundamental to you, even though you never knew it was there. It defines your understanding of how the world works. Or, in Type 3 language, it defines how the game is played.

This Survival Belief has several important parts to examine:

Image-Consciousness

Your Survival Belief does *not* say: I can survive by being the best. It says: I can survive by *being perceived as* the best. You are wired specifically to care about how you appear to other people. This is called being image-conscious, a major Ego-Driven concern for the Type 3.

Being image-conscious is destructive to your happiness in very fundamental ways, because:
- It disempowers you from feeling satisfied with yourself – you need to seem admirable to somebody else in order to feel good about yourself
- It makes you feel like all eyes are on you, creating enormous pressure to be perfect and leaving no room for human frailty
- It ties your life choices to other people's opinions, prompting you to choose for outward appearances rather than inner truth

Note:

It is possible a certain demographic within the Type 3s would not necessarily relate to this "being perceived as" piece. They would say they only care about actually being the best and not what other people think about it. If this is you, you likely have a Self-Oriented Connection Style, which shifts your general focus away from what other people think, and toward what you think about yourself. However, as a Type 3 you do still embody image-consciousness – it's just a lot subtler. You can find out more about your Connection Style in Book Two.

Being the Best

Your Survival Belief programs you to believe that life is about always being or having "the best." This is a primal survival strategy straight out of the caveman days, promising that you will never be ousted from the tribe as long as you continually demonstrate your value. This drive runs very deep.

A fundamental belief in being The Best means that you regard life as a competition, made up of winners and losers. There's The Best, and then everyone else has to be less than that. It sets up a polarizing expectation of having to defeat other people, which requires you to disconnect from your compassion for them.

It also blocks you from intimacy, because it feels extremely dangerous to allow anyone to know anything vulnerable about you, which would certainly lead to their seeing past the facade you so artfully designed.

Even though you have been buying into your Survival Belief all these years, and have even had experiences confirming that it is indeed unsafe to lower your guard and reveal your true self… your Survival Belief is sabotaging you. For your true self – The Real You – is the one with all the power and the glory… and absolutely nothing to prove.

Scarcity-Orientation

Your Survival Belief that *I can survive by being perceived as the best* is fundamentally scarcity-oriented. This means that deep down, you believe you will have to claw and fight for what you want. It signals to you that it's a dog-eat-dog world out there, a world of stiff competition, and that you will have to "do what it takes" to emerge on top.

As a Type 3 you are likely extremely proud of your work ethic and your willingness to put in long hours in order to get what you want. Unfortunately this actually all stems from your scarcity mentality.

The truth is that the belief that you have to work extra-hard to become somebody important is the utter opposite of going with the Flow of the Universe. The Universe is made of Love and Abundance, not scarcity and competition. It doesn't take more outer work to get what you want or become important. It takes more *inner* work, to connect with The Real You – who is already important.

In the world of quantum energy – the fabric of the Universe – you are the Creator of your reality. What you believe is what you experience. As long as you agree that it's a harsh world and you have to fight and compromise yourself in order to get ahead, that will absolutely be your experience.

This is profound self-sabotage – unnecessarily turning your life into a battle when it could have been a beautiful ride. You will learn in the coming sections how to release yourself from this losing programming, and embrace ease and abundance instead.

◆◆◆

As you can see, your Survival Belief that you must always look like a winner is at the heart of much difficulty and self-sabotage for you. It is this belief which launches a cascade of repetitive thoughts and behaviors, that ultimately lead to your unhappiness. Learning about these, and how to take hold of them, is fundamental to becoming able to create a life you love.

If you have read this far, you are doing so well! Thank you for hanging in there, this stuff is definitely not fun to face. Remember, we are in the thick of the section about the Ego's Survival Programming. But then we will move ahead to discuss Type 3 at your highest and best.

We just finished discussing your Type 3 Survival Belief, which was activated somewhere in your childhood. It is the primary driver behind all of your unconscious thoughts and behaviors.

Now, we will look at the most common thought, feeling and behavior patterns that emerge as a result of holding your Survival Belief.

Your Compulsion

Your **Compulsion** is the **repetitive internal process you instantly launch as a way of discharging the emotional tension caused by your Survival Belief.**

> Your Compulsion is **Competing.**

This Compulsion is much like a guilty addiction – you know you should give it up, but don't want to… because you privately love it.

And even if you decide, that's it, you're through with this… you will still find it very difficult to stop until you become able to embrace your Vital Truth (see the upper half of your Mandala), rather than your Survival Belief.

Competing is how you monitor your status as The Best. How else would you know how you rank? You constantly feel this impulse to assess your own status, and therefore want to "beat" other people.

Competition is Not a Thing

Although Competing seems like your true nature, that is just your Ego tricking you. Your Higher Consciousness is your true nature, and in Universal Consciousness there is no such thing as competition – only Love. The Real You is not competitive – It is loving.

This may have just been a totally mind-blowing concept for you... *What? No such thing as competition? Huh?*

Consider nature, which always exists in harmony with the Flow of the Universe. For example, which tree wins – the ash or the birch? Which ocean is the best? Which blade of grass is better than all the rest? The elemental life forms on the planet show us how to thrive, free of Ego. They are examples of wholeness, and there is no single best example of wholeness.

But what about the animal kingdom? you may ask. *What about survival-of-the-fittest? Doesn't that prove the need for competition?*

There are certainly examples in the animal kingdom of predators and prey, who are permanently operating inside a reality of scarcity and survival. This is because they also are wired with an Ego. Their primal impulse for survival is the same as yours.

You, however, are a human being with spectacularly unique DNA, which provides you access to Higher Consciousness and the Flow of the Universe. You have the ability to question, and learn, to observe yourself and expand yourself in ways no other member of the animal kingdom can. You have the ability to consciously use your intention.

You are miraculously special and rare because you have the ability to awaken yourself to a higher way of living, beyond survival, beyond Ego, using the combined power of your heart and mind.

You are in the fabulously privileged position of getting to choose which worldview you prefer: one of violence and menace and fear and survival, or one of energy, intention, Love and Flow. Which kingdom do you choose for yourself?

If you could release yourself from the limitations of your Ego, you would see that there is no winner, and there is no loser. Those are constructs of the Ego, which tricks you into forgetting your true quantum nature.

Life is not a competition – it is the ability to navigate the Flow of the Universe. Competing is not a part of the Flow of the Universe – it is created out of Ego-Driven polarity, and therefore it is a destructive impulse.

As we will discuss in the upcoming Your Vitality Personality section, this is where you must shift your focus to Cultivating Yourself, Type 3, rather than Competing. In shifting your attention away from what other people are doing, or what they think about what you are doing, you become completely free to be who you really are. You will get to know yourself in a much deeper way, and fall in love with The Real You.

Your Destructive Behavior

Your Survival Belief – that you must always be seen as the best – also prompts your actions and behaviors. **When you are Ego-Driven, and therefore not questioning**

your inherent attitudes and beliefs, you will repeatedly behave this way. This is called your Destructive Behavior.

You may be entirely unaware of it, or you may be doing it on purpose in the utter certainty it's the best way to be. Either way, this behavior is never for the Greatest Good of all, and therefore is destructive.

As an Ego-Driven Type 3 who believes you must always appear to have it all together . . .

> Your Destructive Behavior is **Deceiving**.

Your Ego has convinced you that image is everything, that your only chance of survival is to seem a certain way, whether that's really who you are or not. Your obvious and natural go-to behavior, then, is Deceiving.

This impulse to deceive – to reframe the truth so that you seem more attractive – is so instinctive in you, so primal, that it is likely you don't always realize you are doing it. In fact, if you are a Type 3, then it is quite likely that there are fundamental ways in which you have been deceiving yourself.

Deceiving Yourself

Facing this deep-rooted aspect of yourself is not easy and not fun. However, it is at the heart of why you can't totally feel your life. There is a numbness, a wall, that has secretly pervaded your heart, and this self-deception is the reason for it. All of your life is disconnected when you can't feel your truth.

Here are some typical examples of how Ego-Driven Type 3's deceive themselves and therefore deny their inner truth:

- I may have experienced pain or hardship in the past, but I am totally fine and certainly don't need to talk about it with anyone
- My opinions and tastes are my truth and not just something I've adopted to fit in
- It doesn't bother me when I learn of someone's disapproval or rejection of me, I'm unfazed
- Being productive is the best way to be and highly necessary – and isn't really my favorite excuse for avoiding intimacy
- When I make lifestyle choices they're totally for me and I don't consider how these will make me look to other people
- I have healthy relationships and am fully capable of being there for other people
- I don't evaluate people by their usefulness to me, I'm genuinely invested in them
- I feel my feelings just as deeply as everyone else, and don't sometimes pretend to feel them
- I am excellent and have no flaws or problem areas I should be working on

As you can see, it is likely that you have been deceiving yourself about some very important aspects of yourself. And as long as this remains the case, you cannot help but to deceive others, encouraging them to believe the same untruths you've been telling yourself.

Deceiving Others

As we just discussed, sometimes your deception of others is accidental, because you don't realize you're deceiving yourself. But now that we're being totally honest, the truth is, sometimes you also just straight-up lie.

Lying is a major get-ahead strategy for the Type 3. The main way that they can feel ok about this is by telling themselves that "everyone does it" or "this is what it takes."

This takes us back to that concept of a scarcity mentality – the belief that it's a dog-eat-dog world and you have to do what you must to survive. Which in your case means doing whatever it takes to continue to appear as the best. As long as you embrace this as your world view, it makes it possible for you to commit all kinds of deceptions in the name of survival.

While there now might be a list of people who would feel hurt or angry if you came clean about how you deceived them, the person who pays the biggest price of all for this Destructive Behavior is you.

It is a constant dull ache, to feel like the life you're living has almost nothing to do with who you really are. It is painful and lonely when there is no one in your life who you can be yourself with, who you can trust to love you anyway, despite the pain and fears and flaws you were hiding. It leaves you with an emptiness inside that you can't shake.

Even though it feels scary to let someone know the raw truth about you, that is the way to build relationships that are authentic and deep. People don't love you less when you admit that you really aren't all that perfect... they love you more. Because they are flawed too, and now can feel safe enough to show you their vulnerability in return.

Forgiveness

So here you are, after many years of living unknowingly as The Pretender, ready to work on yourself and grow, and now you've just received an unexpectedly painful glimpse in the mirror in harsh lighting. Right about now is when most Type 3s run for the hills.

It is normal to feel some grief at seeing yourself so nakedly. But there is something you can do right now, in this moment, that will allow you to stick with this growth journey, while also coming to feel much better. You can forgive yourself, and you can apologize energetically.

Instead of feeling shame or disgust for your past self and the deceptions you committed, you must forgive yourself. Remember that this is how your unconscious Survival Programming is encoded, and that is why Deceiving seemed like the best strategy at the time. Have compassion for yourself – who was afraid to let anyone down, who was afraid to be seen as lacking, who couldn't find a Higher way to be. Give yourself love and acceptance.

And if you are feeling pain and remorse over a past deception, but are afraid to expose it now because of the damage it will cause, don't worry. There is another way to move forward. You can apologize energetically, from your Higher Self to another's.

Create an opportunity to have total privacy and quiet. Turn off your phone. Close your eyes, and breathe deeply in through your nose, all the way down into your belly, letting the belly expand. Hold, and on the exhale, imagine you are breathing out of your chest as you exhale out of your mouth. Pretend you can exhale through the mouth and chest at the same time. Do this 3 times – it quiets down your nervous system.

In your mind's eye, call up the face of the person you wish you could come clean to. Give a totally sincere, heartfelt apology to their Higher Consciousness. Do not couch it and protect your Ego, because Higher Consciousness knows the truth. Let it be raw and meaningful – you are healing yourself with the release of these deep feelings. Let it crack open your heart and grip you by the guts. Let yourself cry. Here is an example:

J, please forgive me for cheating on you. Even though I had reasons at the time that I thought were justified, now I feel sadness and guilt that I did that. I was unhappy and didn't feel safe enough to talk to you about it. I think maybe I cheat when I need to feel better about myself, when I need admiration and praise. Now I wish I had found a better way to deal with my feelings. I am so sorry. I commit now to finding out how to feel safe being The Real Me in front of other people.

The person's Higher Consciousness that you are speaking to will indeed receive that message, and the genuine remorse and concern you demonstrate. In time it may help your person feel more complete without ever understanding why. There may even come a day when it is possible to have that conversation face to face.

The thing to understand is, you are forgiven. From the perspective of Higher Consciousness, there is nothing to forgive. We have been perpetuating these pains on each other over and over again, lifetime after lifetime, so that we may experience all of Life as fully as possible – the good, the bad, and the ugly.

Nobody in the Higher realms of Consciousness is shocked or appalled by human Ego-Driven behavior. That's how it's supposed to go until eventually you end up exactly here – learning how to elevate yourself through connecting with your own love and light.

This is an incredibly cleansing and healing exercise you can do, without ripping your world apart. The most important reckoning is with yourself. When you apologize sincerely for something that was really weighing heavily on you, it shifts your energy. It makes you feel lighter, freer, and stronger.

This shift will be felt by others. Your relationships will benefit and change, as you become more and more willing to be your vulnerable, authentic self.

Your Sabotage Pattern

As we have discussed, your Personality Type has much Survival Programming built in. Your Survival Belief, Compulsion, and Destructive Behavior are undeniable impulses within you that all drive your well-being into the ground.

In other words, these all combine into an overall template for self-destruction. This is called your **Sabotage Pattern – the way you repeatedly behave throughout your lifetime which leads directly to the destruction of your health and happiness.**

> Your Sabotage Pattern is **Disconnection.**

Disconnection refers to the technique the Type 3 develops at a young age of turning off their feelings. They learn to detach from their heart when vulnerability reveals itself to be unsafe.

There seems to be a common history among the 3's of having once been an emotional, sensitive child, but then receiving signaling early on that this was unacceptable. They burned with shame and sadness to have been teased or scolded or shunned, and found the trick to turning off the thing that had led them astray.

This experience or something like it would have acted as the trigger of all your Survival Programming – your wellbeing was threatened by seeming rejection from the tribe, and your Survival Belief that you must always look like the best kicked in. Apparently looking like the best means never, ever appearing to have vulnerabilities.

This childhood shift fundamentally changed you. You no longer trusted the messages of the heart, and so you put your faith squarely into the material, external world, and let it guide you instead. You unconsciously developed a deep mistrust of your inner voice, and thus a lifestyle of never consulting it. This was the process of Disconnecting from The Real You.

Instead, you began making all your life choices based on how they would look, not how they would feel. You thought about the connections these life choices would provide, the status, the money, the reputation – surely these are the things you can trust to make you happy. In seeking to become a successful winner in the world, you likely lost touch with that child you were, who just wants to be loved as they are.

Now, all these years later, you are likely wondering why your beautiful, picture-perfect life doesn't fulfill you like you thought it would. You find yourself wondering if there is a way to fill the hollowness you sense inside. You wonder if you are really capable of deep love, and you wonder if you really know anything about yourself.

These questions are right on time. You are exactly where you are supposed to be. The answer is Yes – there is still plenty of time for you to become your most favorite person and live a life that you can feel all the way to your soul. It starts right here, examining the Sabotage Pattern that was in the way the whole time.

Disconnection from the Heart

This is really the crux of the matter – you can't feel your feelings. Somewhere in childhood they got turned off and now you don't know how to fully access them anymore.

Many Type 3s will privately admit that they don't really mind the vague numbness they experience. They like being able to be productive even when under high stress, so this trick of walling everything off at times seems invaluable.

The reason it is so important to feel your feelings is because feelings are Guidance from your Higher Consciousness. They are your tether to The Real You, and disconnecting from them was how you came to lose a solid sense of Self.

Disconnection from the Body

Actually Type 3s are generally quite physical people. Many are sporty. Many are sexual. All like to be busy.

The Disconnection from the body is more about refusing to acknowledge its limitations and needs.

Intense workaholics, hyper-aware of their physical appearance, highly competitive, and uncomfortable with down time, Type 3s stay busy far beyond what is healthy. They will deny fatigue, hunger, and pain in order to stay focused on their external goals.

Disconnection from the Higher Mind

Logic, analysis, statistics, research... these are still only aspects of the Ego mind. Your true wisdom is in the heart. Rather than trying to think things through and figure things out with the limited Ego mind, you can access your deep *knowingness* through the Higher Mind.

The Higher Mind is a "room" in your mind where you and your Higher Consciousness merge. Access to the Higher Mind is only available when your body is relaxed, the chatter of the Ego mind is quiet, and the heart is open (see Chapter Twelve).

This is an elevated form of thought, where solutions come to you fluidly and without effort. You are capable of new insights and seeing new possibilities. When you are Ego-Driven, believing in competition and chasing glory, the Higher Mind is inactive.

◆◆◆

As you can see the overall Type 3 Sabotage Pattern of Disconnection limits you immensely. It blocks you from the wisdom of your body, your Guidance from your Higher Consciousness, and your access to your Higher Mind.

This leaves you doing everything the hard way, making you feel that you always have to be working at something. Whereas opening your heart and connecting to your Higher Consciousness would bring you ease, fulfillment, and joy.

◆◆◆

Now that you have opened your eyes to the destructive inner workings of your own Ego, operating as Your Primal Persona, do not despair. It is certainly within your capacity to transform these behaviors and patterns of your Survival Programming.

If you have made it this far, CONGRATULATIONS. We lost many along the trail – not everybody is ready for the journey that is Getting Real! This book is really only interesting to people who are about to make an enormous advancement in their consciousness.

We made it through the hardest part. Now, let's explore how you can be, act and live differently. There is an entirely different kind of life available to you, filled with love and connection and joy. And it is mapped out in the top half of your Type 3 Mandala.

ACTIVATE YOUR POWER PARADIGM

In Chapter One we revealed the meaning of Your Vitality Personality. Let's recap now.

Your Vitality Personality is the version of you that exists when you allow your Higher Consciousness to guide your thoughts, feelings, and actions. It is the opening of your heart, and allowing the loving intelligence found there to Flow through you. This infuses you with insight, wisdom, love and compassion, and the actions you take from this place always serve the Greatest Good.

Let's take a look now at the top half of your Mandala which spells out the dynamics of The Real You - Your Vitality Personality - and all its wondrous gifts and talents:

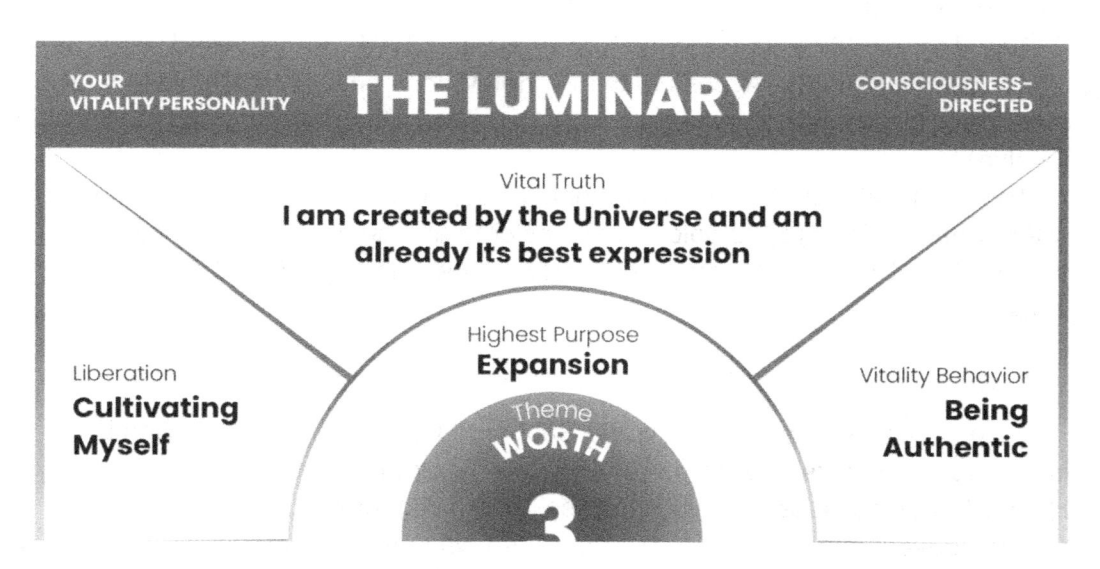

YOUR VITALITY PERSONALITY — **THE LUMINARY** — CONSCIOUSNESS-DIRECTED

Vital Truth
I am created by the Universe and am already Its best expression

Highest Purpose
Expansion

Liberation
Cultivating Myself

Vitality Behavior
Being Authentic

Theme
WORTH

3

Your Vitality Personality: The Luminary

As a Type 3,

> Your Vitality Personality is known as **The Luminary**.

This is the truth of who you really are. You have always felt a light inside of yourself, a sense of bigness, of having something special to offer. You felt a desire to explore your own potential and see how far you can go. In applying your electric energy toward projects which hold genuine meaning and excitement for you, The Real You has the capacity to show the entire world how to contribute to the Greatest Good on an epic scale.

See *Fig. 4B* for a brief summary of the Consciousness-Directed half of your Mandala, identifying how to use your Personality Type to bring into your life a sense of completeness, fulfillment, joy and love.

When you embody all these natural gifts, you are a dazzling light, inspiring all who know you. It is so exciting to think you are just on the precipice of launching a new life of love, acceptance, and Vitality for yourself! It might have required some serious deep-breathing to get here, but the effort is so well worth it.

Let's explore these dynamics of your Power Paradigm, so that you may begin to fully comprehend just how open, uplifting, happy and healthy your life could really be.

Fig. 4B **PERSONALITY TYPE 3 POWER PARADIGM**
Your Vitality Personality: THE LUMINARY
The Real You; The most magnificent version of yourself you joyfully embody when you heed the guidance of your Higher Consciousness
Theme: WORTH
The dynamic realm of Life your Higher Consciousness wants to explore to the fullest
Vital Truth: I AM CREATED BY THE UNIVERSE AND AM ALREADY ITS BEST EXPRESSION
A higher understanding of how to thrive, that aligns you with the Flow of the Universe
Liberation: CULTIVATING MYSELF
The emancipating philosophy you freely embrace to enhance your connection to the Flow
Vitality Behavior: BEING AUTHENTIC
The empowering and uplifting actions you intentionally choose to create your best life
Highest Purpose: EXPANSION
How you serve the Greatest Good through embracing your encoded genius, and the source of your Vitality

Your Theme

As was mentioned earlier,

> Your Theme is **Worth**.

When you pursue the highest form of this Theme – Worth – you are truly aligned with Source, and therefore always serving the Greatest Good.

Worth means a sense of value, of importance, of greatness. You came here to explore what this means to you.

You have always had Worth, because you are a joyful expression of Source. You don't have to prove your value to anyone, because you are already rare and valuable beyond measure.

Therefore, your life is not about chasing a sense of Worth outside of yourself, but expressing out into the world the magnificence you are inside. You are a light who loves to burn ever brighter, and this inspires others around you to do the same.

In the hands of Your Vitality Personality, you apply your fully heart-centered Self towards efforts which serve the Greatest Good, making you an exciting and inspiring Luminary:

- Joyfully pursuing experiences which help you expand your own sense of Self
- Focusing on enjoying the journey, unconcerned with winning or losing
- Making quality time for relationships where everyone feels seen and valued, and everyone feels safe to reveal their hopes and fears
- Having the confidence to publicly be who you really are, regardless of the opinions of others
- Feeling connected to your own internal wisdom -- your Higher Consciousness

Most people are afraid to believe in their own greatness. They don't believe they are capable of creating a life that delights them. They believe it will require more hard work than they can handle. They collapse at the first hint of an obstacle. They feel heavy and tired and burdened by their stories of pain and limitation.

You are the one who is built to serve as a shining example of what it means to embrace your own talents, abilities, and interests, and express them outward in an impactful and authentic way. This is actually demonstrating Self-Love, and in its current shabby state the world needs to see living examples of how to light itself up *from the inside.*

You will inspire the world with your joyful love of the journey, rather than the destination. When you are Consciousness-Directed, you don't ever need to prove your Worth, to yourself or anyone else. You simply feel it inside of you, nourishing and exciting you, and the joy of expressing this uplifts and inspires you.

Your Vital Truth

Your Vital Truth is the Higher understanding of how to thrive by aligning with Universal principles. It is the escape hatch your Ego doesn't want you to know about, because it unlocks all of its Survival Programming, and connects you to your Higher Consciousness – The Real You.

> Your Vital Truth is **I am created by the Universe and am already Its best expression**

This is a direct contradiction to what your Survival Belief encourages you to believe. Your Survival Belief prompts you to think that you need to repeatedly demonstrate your high value in order to earn a place of status and security within the tribe. But that is a scarcity mentality, and not at all how the Universe actually works.

Let's unpack this Vital Truth statement, so that you can see that you have always been magnificent, with absolutely nothing to prove.

Created by the Universe

Do you realize you are actually made of energy? You are a being of light, and you are eternal. You were created with love, excitement, and intention, because your unique perspective would be so special.

This may be an elusive concept to grasp, because as a Type 3 your focus is very much rooted in the physical world. In general you like things you can see, touch, count and measure. You like practical action steps. Esoteric spiritual chats are probably not really your thing.

Nevertheless, the sooner that you recognize your energetic nature, the sooner you will finally access your true power. For one who likes great success so much, you've hardly tapped your full potential. It is when you learn how to wield energy like a boss that you will understand what you've always been capable of.

Don't turn your back on your quantum nature. It is the truth of you and the heart of you. Yes you came here in a state of forgetting, and so bought into the 3D beliefs about scarcity and survival and competing and winning. But now you are ready to awaken to a much vaster understanding of who you really are and why you're really here.

Your life is a spiritual journey – whether you want it to be or not – because you are a spirit having a physical experience. It is the journey of exploring and expanding yourself, becoming ever wiser. As you shift into this perspective – of awe, and gratitude, and magic – your sense of connection to the Universe will become greatly enhanced. And from there you will discover that you are limitless.

Already Its Best Expression

You were created by an unfathomable Source of love and light. You were created in joy, already perfect in your uniqueness. There is not another being like you in all of Creation. You are magnificent, and there is no need for you to prove your value or strive to earn status. As a spark of Source, you already hold divine status.

Embracing this Vital Truth brings you an enormous sense of freedom. Can you even imagine what it would be like to *not* feel driven to push yourself ever harder?

If you were already your most successful, your most wealthy, and your most beautiful... how would you spend your day? If you had absolutely nothing to earn and nothing to prove, what would you be doing differently?

Think about it. With nothing left to prove, you only have your interests, your pleasures, your loves to concern yourself with. These are the things you actually care about. These are the things that connect you to The Real You.

And yet, thus far, those are probably the things that get the least amount of time and attention in your life. Instead, you're putting all your efforts and energies into things which *do not* align with The Real You.

Every time you choose to explore and express your authentic self with joy, you are expanding into an ever-greater version of yourself. Engaging in activities you love, rather than the ones you believe are "productive," is the fastest and easiest pathway to becoming your best self. When you release yourself from your scarcity mentality, you are able to see how life could be relaxed and easy.

So for example, instead of playing golf in order to network with bigshots, play golf because you love the outdoors, spending time with your friends and expanding your skill. Instead of working out because you want to appear skinny and fit, exercise because you love to feel vibrant and strong. Instead of putting in long hours to get ahead, spend 20 minutes connecting with love and gratitude in your heart and attract what you desire without effort.

Excitingly, when you release your belief that you must chase after success, opportunities and synchronicities Flow to you instead. The Flow is really rather astonishing in how It provides uplifting and meaningful experiences you never even dreamed of! If you could embrace your inherent greatness, you could stop Chasing Glory, and finally live your best life– one of ease, abundance, authenticity and love.

Your Liberation

Your **Liberation** is the **emancipating philosophy you freely embrace**. This is a powerful shift, out of the Survival Programming of the mind, and into the Flow of the Universe through the heart. Rather than being owned by a chronic Compulsion, you are now *intentionally choosing* this Liberation.

> Your Liberation is **Cultivating Myself.**

Cultivating Yourself is the opposite of Competing, which has always been your Compulsion. Cultivating Yourself means engaging in activities which expand your delight and love for yourself – rather than hoping to impress enough in order to earn these from others.

To some others this would sound easy, but for the Type 3s awakening from the unconscious Ego state this is actually quite challenging. The entire Primal Persona for the Type 3 is oriented around Disconnecting from yourself, and instead making choices that *look* good, rather than *feel* good. At this point it's likely you don't totally know what delights you.

You may not have any hobbies, because all your attention went towards career goals. You may not really know what you might desire outside of material possessions. You may not really understand what it means to cultivate something which will not lead to a payoff, or why you would bother.

Try thinking of it this way: Committing to making a lifestyle of going inward and connecting with The Real You will bring you payoffs your Ego mind can't currently fathom. The more time you spend *not* grinding-it-out, the better your relationships, health, career, wealth and sense of purpose will become.

The reason this is so important is because Cultivating a strong sense of self will help you make choices and attract opportunities that uplift and fulfill you and make you feel proud of yourself. That make you feel peaceful and complete. This has been missing for you – this is that sense of Worth you've always been chasing.

In the past, there always seemed to be another mountain to climb, another challenge to be faced, before you could finally feel peaceful and happy about yourself. No matter what money, promotions, accomplishments or accolades you earned, you never could feel satisfied and complete for long.

This is because you were looking for a feeling of Worth outside of yourself. You were trying to earn it. Instead you need to go inward, and discover you already have it.

Of all the fields on your Mandala, this Liberation needs to be your primary focus in order to shift out of living as The Pretender and into The Luminary and a life of abundant thriving. I invite you to consider a new lifestyle of giving one hour a day to going inward.

Here are some examples of activities which foster your connection to The Real You:

Meditation

Most Type 3s will say they "can't" meditate. They're too busy, their mind is too distracted with the to-do list, it doesn't serve their obsession with productivity.

But that is the argument of the disconnected, status-chasing, living-at-a-superficial level Pretender. Once you've decided to invest in your genuine power and substance, you can see what flimsy excuses these really are. Now you are ready to sit quietly and take hold of the Universe.

If you are a beginner I recommend guided meditations – meaning someone else is talking you through the experience. Begin with 3-5 minutes, building to 20 or 30 minutes. I offer several on **YouTube.com/@yourvitalitypersonality** which all focus on centering your energy in your heart.

I will not bother citing all the research advising how meditation benefits your well-being. You already know meditation is "good for you." This is generally never a strong enough motivator to get us to do something new and different.

Rather, I encourage you to think of meditation as the times when you are opening up your heart and mind, and allowing much more of your Higher Consciousness in. It is the brief pitstop where you take yourself off the racetrack, and allow yourself to be repaired, tuned, and upgraded to go back out there at ever-increasing levels of performance.

Journaling

This journal is for introspection and self-discovery. Again, typically a Type 3 would regard this as an insignificant exercise and not worthy of the time it "costs" you. But now that you understand that the most important thing you can do for your success is get to know and love yourself better, you are now willing to give yourself the gift of your own time and attention. Here are some prompts:

- Who are you grateful for and why? Write them a letter, telling them what they did for you, and how much it means to you, and how grateful you are. Really feel this in your heart as you write. Even if they never see this, even if they have already crossed over, their Higher Self will receive this message. Meanwhile, you are getting into your heart and experiencing the feeling of deep love and gratitude. These high-voltage emotions build you and amplify your energetic power and reach, while making you feel uplifted and fulfilled at the same time.

- How old were you when you began learning that it wasn't safe to reveal or experience vulnerable feelings? What needs did you have that went unmet? How did you adapt – what parts of yourself did you start to shut down? This child aspect of you is still there, in trauma, in need. Imagine you are face to face with them now. Write a letter to yourself at that age. Ask them how they are doing, what do they need? Write down what you imagine you hear them say. Tell them you are sorry they felt lost and unprotected, but you are with them now, and you will be their safe space. Tell them how much you love them. To end this exercise, imagine kissing their face, and hugging them so hard that they begin to melt into you. Pull them all the way in, into your heart, and hold them there.

- Separate from earning money or status, what experiences give you a feeling of meaning and joy? At first this question may be a stumper, which in itself is revealing. It is perhaps important to realize if you do not actually know what feels uplifting outside of Chasing Glory. The experiences I want you to identify have to do with the high that happens when you have delivered your purpose. As a Type 3 this will likely have to do with the feedback you received about how you helped someone else. You are a natural mentor, coach, and catalyst. The point of this exercise is for you to begin identifying where your true source of real joy derives from. How can you give more of your day to these experiences?

Creativity

Creativity is the expression of the inner self. Normally you would not have been willing to give this much attention unless it was a potential source of income or status. Now it is time to explore this, simply because it is your joy to connect with yourself.

Please understand that creativity has a much broader meaning than just artistry. By no means are all people artistic. That is only one example. Creativity is really anything that captures your imagination and brings you positive feelings like peacefulness, excitement, fun, relaxation or contentment. It is the joy of putting your own personal stamp on something.

This may actually be a confusing one for you, unless you have a Type 4 "wing". (Wings are the Personality Types on either side of yours which you may share traits with. We will go into this in-depth in Book Two.) Type 4s are highly creative, so if you share traits with them, then this is an easier reach for you.

But otherwise, you may be drawing a blank on how to suddenly enjoy being creative when you've never really done that before. Actually, there's probably a way to connect your creativity to your interests.

For example, if you are a physical, sporty sort, perhaps you could spend some time designing a totally new exercise regimen that feels more playful or fun. Maybe you could just let yourself freeform dance in the living room.

Or maybe you could make yourself a few new music playlists with different vibes. Make sure that one of them is your favorite music from high school – this is one of the greatest ways to reconnect with yourself and the early experiences that shaped you.

Or maybe now is the time to finally take a class on that topic that intrigues you. Perhaps learning a new language or how to cook.

The point is, make time for things which light you up, that have nothing to do with productivity or proving yourself. This is your free time *away* from all that, where you give yourself permission to silence outer expectations and obligations, and just putter away doing whatever pleases you.

◆◆◆

Cultivating Yourself is called your Liberation because it is the escape hatch out of the loop of your Survival Programming.

In the past, you would adapt yourself to external standards, changing how you outwardly seemed in order to gain favor and acceptance. This ultimately required you to become someone other than The Real You.

Now you free yourself from these constraints, and give yourself permission to connect with and express who you really are. This brings you a sense of peacefulness and certainty, and an unshakable sense of self.

Your Vitality Behavior

Vitality Behavior is the empowering and uplifting actions you intentionally choose when you are Consciousness-Directed, rather than the Destructive Behavior your Ego drives you to act out.

> Your Vitality Behavior is **Being Authentic.**

This is sooo much lovelier than your previous go-to – Deceiving!

Being Authentic means being truthful with yourself and others. This takes courage and trust: courage to boldly reveal how you are different and unique from what society dictates, and trust that you will be loved and accepted for who you really are. It requires vulnerability, and this is not necessarily comfortable at first.

In fact it can be slightly terrifying. All of your hardwiring tells you that it is not safe to reveal who you really are. What you need to understand is that your old dynamic of Deceiving wasn't really serving you anyway.

Although you thought that projecting an image of success and competence would make people love you more – it was actually sabotaging your ability to connect with them. Other people know all about their own flaws and limitations, but in the company of your falsely perfect persona they would not have felt safe revealing themselves. It was actually you who created a dynamic of distance and falseness in your relationships.

In choosing now to Be Authentic, by revealing you are less conventional or perfect than you previously indicated, you clear the way towards having relationships based on deeper understanding and real connection. In disclosing that you have experienced pain, and fear, and loneliness, and despair… you will be astonished at the rush of love and compassion you receive in return.

Revealing your humanity simultaneously releases you from the pressure of having to maintain a false front, while attracting to you relationships which are deep, and true, and therefore incredibly valuable.

Everybody finds vulnerability uncomfortable, but only some have the courage to be vulnerable anyway… and receive the astounding gift of unconditional Love that comes in return. You must be willing to "go first" – to put yourself out there with no promise of safety – in order to receive the healing and nourishing embrace of the Flow of the Universe.

This is when you really start stepping into your potential to be a great Luminary. The glory you were always chasing will just emanate forth from within you instead. Because you, Type 3, have always had a glorious light inside you, and in Being Authentic you finally let it shine.

Being Authentic with Yourself

When Ego-Driven, Type 3s don't really check in with themselves. They just tell themselves "I'm fine" and keep on moving.

Now that you are aligning with your Higher Consciousness – which is *inside* of you – you are going to have to develop a new lifestyle which supports this. This has to do with checking in with The Real You on a regular basis, and integrating whatever you find there.

Feelings & Needs

Please check out the Personality Type 2 section about their Liberation, called *Introspecting*. There is an Introspecting Exercise described there that is important for you as well. It will give you lists of words to help you identify how you are feeling and what you need.

The reason you need help finding the words for your feelings and needs is because you have numbed yourself to them for a very long time. You've been telling yourself *I'm fine*, which is a deception.

This was of course an unconscious impulse, but even when you look at it in the light of day, your Type 3ness might still prefer to skip the feelings-and-needs thing so you can keep on being productive. The attachment to productivity is an enormous obstacle to your emotional development.

Everything you really want in life – love, abundance, health, meaning – exists energetically in the same place as your feelings and needs. To feel complete in one area means to feel complete in all of them. You must open yourself and do the inner work.

Your fear of your own feelings far outweighs the intensity of the feelings themselves. Feelings are just energy. When you resist them you create friction and obstruction. When you let them flow, they come and go without much of a charge. You want your life to flow, so you must commit to letting go of your resistance.

Values & Actions

Part of Deceiving yourself had to do with fooling yourself about the real reasons for why you're doing what you're doing.

What are the true values of your heart? Don't just say the conventional things or what you think others expect to hear. This is just between you and you.

If you found out you had a terminal illness with two years left to live, how would you live differently? At the end of your life, would you look back and say *If only I had worked longer hours*? Or would you say *If only I could have my kids' childhood back*?

Most Type 3s *say* they value family and friends, but do their actions align with these? Usually they work far longer hours than most people. Again, you can see how the attachment to productivity is in the way.

So you're going to have to start Getting Real with yourself about how much time you're giving to your Ego's values rather than those of The Real You.

The good news is, as you become more adept at releasing your resistance to regularly checking in with your feelings and needs, you are placing yourself into the Flow of the Universe, where life becomes magically easy.

Good luck, good ideas, synchronicities and new opportunities will all start showing up unexpectedly. You will see for yourself how the Universe rewards you for your commitment to Being Authentic.

You will be able to let go more and more of your attachment to productivity in favor of letting the Universe handle things for you. Life will get easier and freer, and you will bring your true values and your actions into alignment.

Being Authentic with Others

In order to live a fulfilling life that really suits you, you will need to advocate for your authentic feelings, needs, and desires. For a Type 3 this is easier said than done.

Although Type 3s are assertive, they are not always straightforward communicators – the fear of rejection and need for approval and admiration get in the way.

So typically, rather than telling the bald truth, like *I'm not really enjoying this*, you'll offer an alternative, less offensive story, like *Oh gosh, I just got called in to work, I have to run.*

While this may seem like a harmless white lie, if they're happening all the time, then you are slowly weaving a falseness into your relationships. Over time, there becomes a widening divide between who you really are and the life you're actually living.

Self-Love Makes All Things Possible

These small or big deceptions were your attempt to control your world. They are born out of that primal fear of rejection, of being banished from the tribe. This fear reveals an even deeper problem: you don't find yourself inherently lovable.

As always, our lack of self-love is the ultimate inhibitor of our ability to prosper and thrive. If you believed yourself to be lovable the way you are, you wouldn't be afraid to let others see you, warts-and-all.

It works like this: If you really and truly understood yourself to be a being of light – who is eternal, and can create any reality you desire – you would never fear what might happen. You would know with certainty that you are able to use the Flow of the Universe to navigate it successfully.

This attitude makes you willing to let the chips fall where they may.

These varying degrees of deception, as you can see now, were attempts to manipulate other people. You wanted to control the image they had of you, so that they would not have cause to reject you.

If you found yourself lovable and you trusted in your own ability to always manifest a great life for yourself, you would feel free to speak your truth.

You don't have to be harsh and mean – there's always a gentle way to be direct. If you stick with explaining your feelings and needs, people can hear what you need to say.

But now you're giving them the chance to know The Real You, and letting them decide if this relationship works for them based on the truth.

And even if they say, *I'm sorry, that doesn't work for me*, you can hold fast in the knowledge that it is not a reflection upon your worth. Everybody has different styles and preferences, and we're not all going to be an ideal match with each other.

But there will be plenty who will align with you. Because people usually do align themselves with intelligent, talented, mature people they find trustworthy. When you speak up for your feelings and needs, you honor other people's need for respect and trust. That's actually quite likable.

◆◆◆

Allowing the world to see you – The Real You – takes trust and love in yourself, and in the Universe. It gives you a sense of exhilarating freedom, when you are rid of the need to please and impress. You have finally given yourself permission to live the life you truly desire.

Your Highest Purpose

You chose to be here, in this time and place, because you wanted to contribute something. You came here for a reason, and you chose your Personality Type because it was the one that would help you accomplish it. **Your Personality Type has a special set of talents and abilities, and you wanted to use them to make a contribution.** This is your **Highest Purpose**.

> Your Highest Purpose is **Expansion**.

You have always been someone who wanted *more*. You wanted to go further, go bigger, to get better, to push the limits. You want to go all the way. That is no accident, Type 3. It's exactly what you were built for. For you are the one who is meant to strive for Expansion, a fundamental principle of the Flow of the Universe.

The Universe is always Expanding. Further and further, it grows. This is Life, emerging. This is Vitality, thriving. This is Source, exploring. You are meant to be the living example of this Universal truth.

This orientation makes you quite different from other people. Most people crumble at the first hint of an obstacle. Most people have tantrums and implosions that sabotage their progress. Most people can't touch your degree of steadfastness, persistence and endurance. You are the rare person who identifies your desire, and is unwavering in your intention until it is fully manifested.

This is what empowers you to emerge as The Luminary, out ahead of the rest, lighting the way for all of us towards our collective future.

Expansion of Yourself

In the past, your Ego distorted your understanding of Expansion, and turned it into Chasing Glory. This led you to seek out inflation instead – making yourself seem bigger and better on the outside, but with little substance on the inside.

Expansion begins on the inside, at the core of you. It is your own inner light which burns brighter and brighter and radiates further and further outward, as you cultivate the feeling of love for yourself.

Expansion of Your Body

Many Type 3s are naturally athletic and enjoy being physical beings. However, they also take many shortcuts to health. Expansion of the body means cultivating physical power, from cell function outward. This requires love and attention of the body.

Honor your body's need for rhythm, especially sleep. Your body needs around 7 hours of sleep or more, and this is something you cut short on the most. Let your new lifestyle of Flow include easily allowing for your full rest.

Honor your body's need for whole foods. Not protein powders and a fistful of supplements. Real, fresh food from the earth, which you sit down and consume at a leisurely pace. Enjoy your meal, be present, relax.

Expansion of Your Mind

When functioning according to their Survival Programming, Type 3s are not always open to new thought. They allow convention to dictate how they live, wanting to stay popular and relevant.

In other words, they don't advocate for change of a bad system, they search for shortcuts, loopholes and winning strategies within the tried-and-true matrix. They are trying to be the best within the paradigm that already exists.

When you become Consciousness-Directed, now you move into Expanding out into the new and innovative. You are willing to trust your attraction and excitement as cues from your Higher Self that you are on the right track as you strive to do something that's never been done before. You step forward as a leader, venturing out into uncharted territory.

As you develop your ability to be heart-based, this opens up a new room in the mind, called the Higher Mind. This is where your thoughts merge with that of your Higher Consciousness. This is where new ideas, new insights, and new solutions arrive. Opening your heart Expands your mind.

Gaining access to this Higher way of thinking is an upgraded way of being the calm, even-tempered person you prefer to be, yet no longer aloof. Even while feeling your compassion and concern for others, your mind is still peaceful and clear. This empowers you to make decisions and take actions which serve the Greatest Good for all.

Expansion of Your Heart

The heart is so much more than an organ. It is a portal -- the nexus point where the enormous eternal light being that you are converges with the body that is encoded to be the *you* that you are in this lifetime.

Expansion of your heart means opening this portal door wide. This allows you to freely connect with The Real You and be steeped in authenticity.

Opening the portal in your heart means agreeing to feel all of your feelings, for that is the language your Higher Consciousness uses to communicate with you.

Feelings of happiness, excitement, love, certainty – these are all cues from your Higher Self that you are on track. Uplifting feelings mean Yes.

Feelings of anger, fear, shame, doubt – these are alarm bells from your Higher Self that more awareness is required here. What Ego messages are disturbing your peace? You must notice these and process them, rather than pretending they don't exist. Is the No that you're feeling coming from a legitimate concern, or self-destructive impulses?

Expanding your connection to your heart expands your self-awareness, and it also does something else very important: it fires up your ability to give and receive love.

In the past, your Compulsion towards Competing kept your heart closed. It's not really possible to feel love and compassion for the person you want to beat.

Now you are ready to let that go, and just be yourself, with nothing to prove. This softens you. It makes you more present, more patient, more empathetic. It Expands your capacity to love.

The biggest shift of all for you though, Type 3, is when you Expand your capacity to *receive* love.

All your life you've been on the move, swinging in and making an early exit out. You gave all your time to making yourself appear more attractive, more impressive, more accomplished – all so you could prove yourself worthy of love.

And yet when the love comes, you haven't been able to really receive it. All this time, underneath all the striving and the earning, you have felt inherently unlovable. You felt that, if people knew The Real You, they would reject you.

But now that you are committing to living authentically as The Real You, you will see this inspires more and more love for you. Your feelings, your needs, your wins and your losses, your pains and your joys – your humanity inspires much love in others. And, because your heart is finally open and connected, it will fill you to the brim.

Expansion of Others

As you expand yourself through a steady stream of self-love, acceptance and joyfulness, other people will notice. They will start asking you for your insight and advice. You attract them all with your light.

No need for bragging. No need for false filters. No need for competing. You attract just by being you.

You can be an enormous source of information, encouragement and support to others who struggle with self-sabotage. You can teach them your attitudes, your methods, your wisdom, and they will grow exponentially under your mentorship.

This is how you serve your Highest Purpose of Expansion. Because you have learned how to Expand yourself, you are the way-shower for others. Just by being your authentic self, having a lovely day and offering heart-based guidance when asked, you serve the Greatest Good for all.

Expansion of the Collective

Your impact has the potential to be very far-reaching indeed Type 3. You like to go as big as you can, so it's possible you could even influence the culture of the country or the world.

Your Higher Consciousness chose a Personality Type with star quality on purpose. Yes you must remain humble, for the front man is no more important than the drummer in the back. But don't deny your capacity for greatness, when deep down you know you were built for something big.

Remember you are an influencer everywhere you go, and that brings with it a higher level of responsibility. As a noticeable, visible person with your inner light shining brightly, people will want to hear what you have to say.

So let your message be one of love, of acceptance, of authenticity, of gratitude, of excitement. Let yourself be The Real You in front of them all. No false advertising, no chasing glory. Just your desire to give love and be of service. This is enough to light up the whole world, you Luminary, you.

♦♦♦

Well, Type 3, you've been given quite a lot of information about yourself to digest. But hopefully by now you've come to see that even though you are wired to act out Your Primal Persona, it is possible for you to be someone so much more magnificent than that – Your Vitality Personality.

Now is the time to decide who you want to be in this world. If you are ready to step into the full power of who you really are, and seize your best life… then your next step is **Integration.** See Chapter Eleven.

CHAPTER FIVE
PERSONALITY TYPE 4
THE CREATIVE | THE DIVA

THE CREATIVE

YOUR VITALITY PERSONALITY — CONSCIOUSNESS-DIRECTED

Vital Truth
I adore my unique Self, and thank the Universe for my special place in it

Highest Purpose
Insight

Liberation
Gratitude

Vitality Behavior
Self-Appreciating

Theme
SPECIALNESS

4

Distorted Theme
DISAPPOINTMENT

Compulsion
Comparing

Destructive Behavior
Self-Obsessing

Sabotage Pattern
Melancholy

Survival Belief
I can survive by being regarded as special

THE DIVA

YOUR PRIMAL PERSONA — EGO-DRIVEN

Hello Type 4, and welcome. It is excellent that you are here. You find yourself rather confusing, and will be glad to gain insight into how to make sense of yourself.

In particular the teachings here about what emotions really are, and how to navigate them, will be enormously helpful for you. Your over-attachment to your feelings is the primary way you get off-track.... but you will learn self-mastery here.

YOUR VITALITY PERSONALITY

If you have been led here, then it is because you are ready to take a quantum leap in the advancement of your consciousness. The understanding you will gain will propel you into an awareness far more elevated than most, and a newfound willingness to expand yourself. This will benefit the entire world, for you are the one capable of inspiring us all towards greater awareness, compassion, and beauty.

This chapter focuses on the dual nature of your Personality Type 4, and the primary factors that hinder or help your ability to thrive. You will totally love the descriptions about your highest potential and purpose… but you will totally not love reading about your dark side, called Your Primal Persona.

Hang in there! We intentionally go through the Primal Persona stuff first, so that you can finish on a high note – the magnificence that is Your Vitality Personality.

Give yourself permission to surrender to this process, and you will see how it takes you on a journey, getting richer and richer the further it goes. The part of you that is wired for Insight will quickly come to see how applying this wisdom will get you there, and the rest of us as well.

DECODE YOUR SURVIVAL PROGRAMMING

As we just learned, **Your Primal Persona is the version of you that exists when you allow your Ego to unconsciously drive your thoughts, feelings and actions.** It is the operating system of your survival-oriented mind, limiting you from tapping into the love and light that is your Higher Consciousness.

In this state, you are closed off from your sense of love for yourself or others. And the actions you take from this place only serve to fulfill the Survival Programming of the small, fearful you. This can be really uncomfortable to face, but it is critical to see clearly so that you can gain freedom from this dark influence.

The bottom half of your Mandala spells out the dynamics of Your Primal Persona and its Ego-Driven Survival Programming:

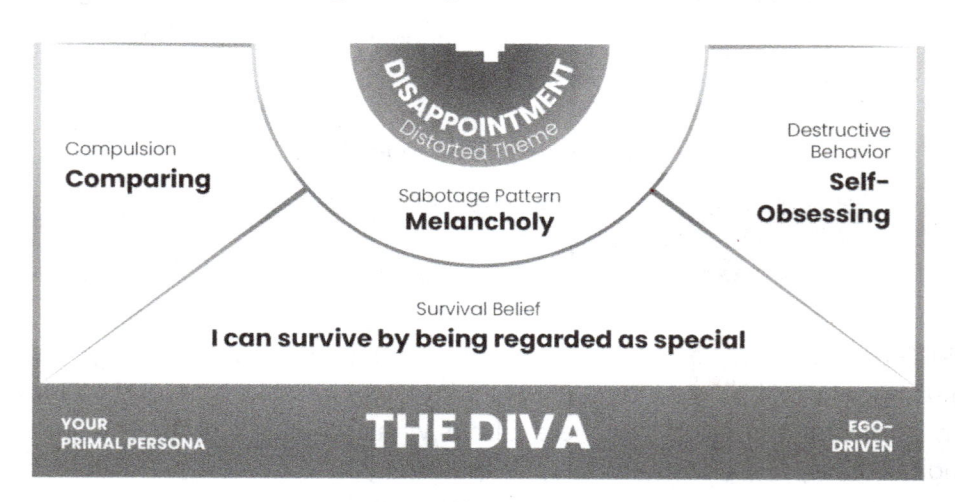

Distorted Theme: **DISAPPOINTMENT**

Compulsion: **Comparing**

Sabotage Pattern: **Melancholy**

Destructive Behavior: **Self-Obsessing**

Survival Belief: **I can survive by being regarded as special**

YOUR PRIMAL PERSONA: **THE DIVA** — EGO-DRIVEN

Your Primal Persona: The Diva

As a Type 4,

> Your Primal Persona is known as **The Diva**.

This is your Ego's version of "playing small," even though its programming is all about seeming special. But, as we will now explore, self-indulgence and self-love are not at all the same thing.

See *Fig 5A* for a brief summary of your Ego-Driven Survival Programming (we will dig deeper into it in just a moment). It is characterized by resistance, eroding your Vitality and degrading your life.

These are some painful truths. But you must forgive yourself for your Survival Programming. Have compassion for yourself, for it was the pain in your life which led you to feel that you couldn't survive without this perspective. Without self-awareness, you had no choice but to behave this way.

And this is true for everyone else, as well. We all deserve forgiveness for the way we act when we are asleep to ourselves -- we are totally unaware this is what we are doing and how much it hurts ourselves and those we love.

Even once you are aware of your Survival Programming, it can be quite challenging to take command over it. Yet every degree of progress you make in this direction brings you enormous reward. You will be joyfully inspired to continue the work.

Let's dive just a little bit deeper into what these dynamics of your Survival Programming really mean, so that you may begin the most rewarding journey of integrating yourself.

Fig. 5A PERSONALITY TYPE 4 SURVIVAL PROGRAMMING
Your Primal Persona: THE DIVA
The Programmed You; The limited and diminished version of yourself that you default to when you are Ego-Driven
Distorted Theme: DISAPPOINTMENT
Your Ego's warped and downgraded interpretation of your true Theme
Survival Belief: I CAN SURVIVE BY BEING REGARDED AS SPECIAL
The scarcity-oriented message embedded in your Ego that creates your world view
Compulsion: COMPARING
The repetitive internal process you instantly launch as a way of discharging the emotional tension caused by your Survival Belief
Destructive Behavior: SELF-OBSESSING
The ruinous actions you regularly engage in when you operate according to your Survival Belief
Sabotage Pattern: MELANCHOLY
The totality of all your Survival Programming combined into an overall template for self-destruction

Your Distorted Theme

Each of the 9 Personality Types orient around a particular **Theme**. The whole point of you being here, at this time and in this place, is because you wanted to explore this Theme. This is the thing you are encoded to care about the most.

> Your Theme is **Specialness**.

We will fully explore the true meaning of Specialness in the next section (about Your Vitality Personality), when we discuss the Consciousness-Directed understanding of your Theme.

But right now, we are discussing your Survival Programming, and how your Ego *degrades* your understanding of your Theme of Specialness.

Unfortunately, when Your Primal Persona interprets this Theme, **it becomes contorted – a warped, downgraded version of your highest potential**. This is called the **Distorted Theme**.

> Your Distorted Theme is **Disappointment**.

Disappointment is feeling sad that things didn't go a certain way. It is the sense of dissatisfaction about *what is*.

As we will explore, the Type 4 lifestyle is a dreamy one. They are sensitive, emotional people who spend much time in their mind, imagining and wishing for their ideal life. However, they are frequently dismayed at how often their life does not play out that way. They can infuse quite a lot of energy into their Disappointment.

When their mind is trapped inside their Ego's Distorted Theme, the Type 4 spends much time thinking about what's wrong, what's missing, what's imperfect – about themselves, about their life, about their world. This brings on repeated feelings of sadness, frustration, and discontent.

Unfortunately, this pattern of regularly unhappy thoughts accompanied by regular doses of sadness does not attract a life of ease and joy. It attracts a life full of more things to be unhappy about.

In the hands of Your Primal Persona, you spend a great deal of your time yielding to disappointment and pity parties, eroding your Vitality and quality of life:

- Repeated waves of unhappiness keep you in a weakened, frail state – causing you to think of yourself as delicate and requiring special care
- Often distraught and overcome by your emotions, you are prone to tears and tantrums – earning you a reputation as high-maintenance and making it difficult for other people to relate to you
- Bouts of hopeful frenzy and dark depression cause your energy to be unpredictable and unreliable – making it difficult to fully function

- Finding yourself troublesome and confusing, you often feel pierced by feelings of inadequacy and shame, creating a dependency upon the praise and reassurance of others.
- Only noticing what's wrong causes you to miss out on all that is right – limiting your sensibilities and blocking you from joy
- Feeling burdened by living in such a flawed, imperfect world as such a flawed, imperfect person, you often think thoughts of yearning and longing – locking you into the experience of scarcity and lack

When you are Ego-Driven, your Higher desire for a beautiful, loving, and compassionate world degrades into a chronic disappointment at all the ugliness and flaw – especially within yourself – disempowering you and leading you to crave external validation and special attention.

This is no fun at all to read about. It's a bummer to realize your default, unconscious wiring is a sadly small version of who you could really be – who you actually are. The Real You is powerful and full of radiant love and light, taking pleasure in the Now moment – which includes taking pleasure in yourself. You are on your way to discovering how to access this higher aspect of yourself.

Your Survival Belief

Your Survival Belief is the **scarcity-oriented message embedded in your Ego that creates your world view.** It is the secret programming in the basement of your unconscious which drives all your thoughts, feelings, and actions without you ever realizing it.

> Your Survival Belief is **I can survive by being regarded as special.**

This belief is fundamental to you, even though you never knew it was there. It defines your understanding of how the world works.

Typically, this Survival Belief is activated within you at a young age.

As a child, you likely seemed very different than everyone else. You seemed to have confusing needs that your parents couldn't easily understand, and also rare talents most others didn't have.

Your unconscious survival strategy, then, was to make your specialness the most noticeable thing about you, in order to downplay the areas in which you don't "measure up." In primal terms, demonstrating your specialness seemed like the best strategy for survival – and it's never occurred to you to re-examine it as an adult.

Your Survival Belief fundamentally shapes how you feel about your place in the world. Believing that you are inherently flawed in some way scares you. It makes you feel like you are vulnerable to ridicule and rejection, and must find a means of seeming special as a way to redeem yourself.

This is an enormously painful belief to hold about yourself – it brings about loads of shame, the heaviest of all emotions. Because of this early acute sensitivity to their own flaw and feeling of being disappointing, even young Type 4s can have an air of pain and sadness.

Let's look at why this Survival Belief is so misguided, and what is really going on.

Feeling Different / More Sensitive

Why do Type 4 children seem so different from the rest? I have a theory about that. I think Type 4s are encoded to be right-brained in a left-brained world.

In the 1960's, Nobel prize-winner Roger Sperry identified the orientations of the right and left hemispheres of the brain, indicating how different their functions and abilities are. In more recent years, brain studies could not validate Sperry's assertions – it appears both hemispheres operate together at once. Nevertheless, modern science offers no alternative means of explaining the enormous differences in functionality and abilities that Sperry identified.

For my purposes, it doesn't really matter what this is called or whether science can prove it. The point is: the Type 4's mind is wired to operate quite differently than most others. Let's just continue using Sperry's terminology since it is so commonly known.

Sperry identified the orientation of the right brain to be around:

Imagination	Arts	Feelings
Holistic thinking	Rhythm	Visualization
Intuition	Nonverbal cues	Daydreaming

As you can see from the list, someone who is primarily right-brained is sensitive, internal, experiential, imaginative, and nonverbal – and this is the Type 4.

It would be quite uncomfortable to the only ones wired this way, when the whole rest of the Western world seem decisively left-brained, which orients around:

Logic	Sequencing	Facts
Linear thinking	Mathematics	Thinking in words

This explains why the Type 4 often gets branded early as "not normal." Somehow, their needs are "special." But really, Type 4s are being exactly how they are supposed to be. Contrary to popular opinion, they are not bad or wrong or stupid for relating to the world differently – it's exactly what they came here to do.

As we will discuss in the coming section about Your Vitality Purpose, you came here to be different in order to help awaken consciousness in others. People's sensibilities can be so deadened – it's as if they are robots. You came here to remind them to be present to their own sense of self – unique and rare.

The Type 4, with their right-brained-ness, easily accesses feelings, memories, dreams, images, symbols, colors, sounds, and so much more. That is actually all the realm of Consciousness – ranging from the collective unconscious all the way to Source Itself. If you are a Type 4, you are able to perceive these ethereal energies which most others are oblivious to.

Type 4s are the Awakeners on the planet. They are the ones reminding everyone else that there is so much more than just the 3D world. We are all made of energy and we are vast, but we are totally asleep to it. The Type 4s help us come awake to our truth.

But meanwhile, as kids, they suck at math, they can't get anywhere on time, they forget and lose things, they're shy, their feelings get hurt easily, and they don't bounce back from upset quickly.

In the American culture of hectic paces, deadlines, obligations and ambitions, most parents are not prepared to reckon with a child who needs things to go slow, be gentle, and have few left-brained expectations. Often they become exasperated that their Type 4 child is not adhering to expectations.

These sensitive children feel their parents' frustration and resentment very acutely. They are mortified at being the source of problems. They are upset to discover they're doing something "wrong" by just being who they are.

This is the early pattern that activates all the Survival Programming. The Type 4 child is shamed for failing to meet expectations, which launches a great yearning within them to be seen as special, as valuable, as worthy of love.

The arc of growth for you, Type 4, is to cultivate love and adoration of yourself, appreciating all that makes you different and special. This builds you up and makes you strong, so that you are able to fully manifest and participate in the life of your dreams.

Needing Approval

For the reasons we just discussed, it is no wonder that, from an early age, the Type 4 becomes very preoccupied with how they are perceived by others. They worry all the time about seeming stupid, or boring, or ugly, or otherwise inadequate.

This is so disempowering. In letting other people define their value, and accepting this as truth, they are not in charge of how they feel about themselves. Their sense of self is a moving target, shifting on whether they got positive or negative feedback today.

This flushes out some typical dynamics:

Vanity

Type 4s are notoriously vain about their physical appearance and their reputation, and put enormous amounts of energy into cultivating these.

Performance Anxiety

On the one hand they very much want to be seen in a positive light, on the other they're afraid they won't measure up. This can bring on tears and panic attacks before tests, auditions, presentations, etc. Any context in which they will be evaluated brings up enormous anxiety for them.

Shame

Type 4s experience little jabs of shame throughout the day. They are constantly listening out for any potential references to themself, and anything which seems less than glorious produces a feeling of dismay.

In general, Type 4s crave praise. Even if you find it embarrassing, you still love it! While there is certainly nothing wrong with enjoying receiving praise, needing it in order to like yourself is the problem.

As we will discuss, moving into connection with your Higher Consciousness – who always loves you and thinks you're amazing – releases you from needing approval from others. When you really love yourself and are pleased with yourself, you will feel complete – regardless of what anyone else thinks.

Fear of Abandonment

The Type 4 Survival Belief that being perceived as special is the only way to survive is basically a fear of being ousted from the tribe. In the most primal terms, to be insignificant or provide no value puts you in danger of being kicked out or left behind.

This creates an underlying fear of abandonment. Any kind of break-up or rejection triggers in the Type 4 a gripping fear that their world is about to collapse and they won't make it.

No one enjoys breakups or unhappy endings, but on top of the grief and loss, the Type 4 Ego piles on a lot of extra stories about how this proves what a worthless, undesirable person they are, and they become unspeakably distraught.

Although the Type 4 going through the experience would say it is heartbreak causing so much distress, actually that's not exactly true. A lot of it is fear of being alone.

The fear of abandonment or of being alone has much to do with low self-esteem, and believing you are not capable on your own. But you are, and developing a relationship with your Higher Consciousness will show you that. You are not weak, you are not stupid, and you are never alone. As you come to understand how much you are loved and how much help is available to you, your fears about being on your own will melt away.

Going Diva

While "diva" once strictly referred to an opera singer, it has now become more of a slang term for someone who demands special treatment. Oh dear, this is the Type 4 home base.

Being right-brained is a much more sensitive, hyper-aware state than most everyone else lives in. It's sortof like how dogs can hear sounds humans can't – they can just perceive *more*. Type 4s seem to experience their senses more acutely than others. The life experience is, to them, very intense.

This can wreak havoc on their nervous system, which in turn upsets systems like hormones, biorhythms, and digestion. In general, Type 4s come to perceive themselves as highly sensitive, reactive, and needing special means of support.

Maybe they need their special pillow that keeps their tight neck just-so. Maybe they need their certain probiotic which keeps their bowels moving just right. Maybe they need the thermostat at a particular temperature when they sleep. Maybe they can't have caffeine and sugar. Maybe they absolutely must have caffeine and sugar.

Type 4s tend to develop quite a list of special ways they go about meeting their special needs. And they can get rather dramatic, when they don't get what they feel they need to be ok.

It really is true, Type 4, that here on earth you are a bit of a square peg trying to exist inside a round hole, and you really do have to go to extra lengths to support yourself.

It is also true, however, that this is the Personality Type that your Higher Self signed you up for. You are not a victim of your temperament. You chose a tricky one on purpose, with the full intent of gaining mastery over it.

This is where the Type 4 can get themselves into trouble. Most Ego-Driven Type 4s prefer a good pity-party. Unfortunately, they can develop just the *teensiest* bit of an entitlement problem.

Type 4s can earn quite a reputation for themselves as high-maintenance or difficult, known for requiring special treatment. They like to fuss over themselves, and they like other people to fuss over them, too. But not everyone agrees this is how they'd like to spend their day, meeting the Type 4's needs. For someone who cares so much about what other people think, this is not gaining you the positive light you prefer.

You will be quite surprised at how many of your special needs and difficulties begin to disappear once you learn how to become more self-loving and self-satisfied. This raises your energetic vibration, which allows you to access more of your power and activates higher levels of DNA. Many of the things you thought you needed to survive will turn out to no longer be required once you learn how to live in a state of happy fulfillment.

Disdain

In being the rare right-brained one, the Type 4 embodies a set of talents most others can't touch. Creative, perceptive, sensitive, and expressive, the Type 4 has access to energetic realms far outside other people's sensibilities. For as much as they might be sad that they don't "fit in," they are equally pleased to find they have special capabilities no one else has.

This is their lifeboat. If they were just "bad and wrong" all the time, they could easily become suicidal. The fact that they have rare abilities rescues them from feeling permanently inferior. They see they do have areas where they can shine, and they use these strengths to build an identity around.

In an effort to salvage their self-esteem, they construct a persona around being deeper and more insightful than other people. They consider their tastes and preferences to be a cut above the masses. They regard their appreciation for creativity, uniqueness, and beauty as far keener than most.

While self-appreciation is wonderful and to be encouraged, feeling superior to others and contemptuous of the mundane is not. In full Diva mode, the Type 4 can display an element of disdain for ordinary people and ordinary life.

This perspective is in total resistance to the Flow of the Universe. In the Universe, there is no such thing as rank or status. All things are created by Source and are an expression of Source. Some are not better than others. All things are worthy of appreciation and love.

Disdain is the Ego's version of bolstering a feeling of worth, but denigrating anything is not how this is achieved. Unconditional love, for oneself and for all of Creation, is the means for feeling internally peaceful and complete.

♦♦♦

As you can see, your Survival Belief that you can survive by being regarded as special is at the heart of much difficulty and self-sabotage for you. It is this belief which launches a cascade of repetitive thoughts and behaviors, that ultimately lead to your unhappiness. Learning about these, and how to take hold of them, is fundamental to becoming able to create a life you love.

If you have read this far, you are doing so well! Thank you for hanging in there, this stuff is definitely not fun to face. Remember, we are in the thick of the section about the Ego's Survival Programming. But then we will move ahead to discuss the Type 4 at your highest and best.

We just finished discussing your Type 4 Survival Belief, which was activated somewhere in your childhood. It is the primary driver behind all of your unconscious thoughts and behaviors.

Now, we will look at the most common thought, feeling and behavior patterns that emerge as a result of holding your Survival Belief.

Your Compulsion

Your **Compulsion** is **the repetitive internal process you instantly launch as a way of discharging the emotional tension caused by your Survival Belief.**

It is much like a guilty addiction – you know you should give it up, but don't want to… because you privately love it. And even if you decide *That's it, I'm through with this*… you will still find it very difficult to stop, until you become able to embrace your Vital Truth (see the upper half of your Mandala), rather than your Survival Belief.

> ➢ Your Compulsion is **Comparing.**

Comparing means measuring yourself against other people, and the Type 4 does this every day. It is in automatic impulse that happens because of the Survival

Belief. If you can only survive if you're special, then of course you're assessing all day how special you seem compared to other people.

The act of Comparing is very painful for the Type 4. Your whole sense of self-worth is based on whether you measure up… and you usually decide that, indeed, you do not. This launches feelings of shame and self-loathing – an excruciating way to live.

When a Type 4 compares themself to others, it is never a fair assessment. They have spent days, weeks, months, years reflecting upon themself and all the ways in which they aren't like everyone else, and are highly predisposed to thinking poorly of themself. But they fall for the other person's exterior image, having no idea what the truth is underneath. If you compare your dirty laundry against everyone else's highly-curated pretty picture, you will surely lose.

Comparing yourself to other people does not align with the Flow of the Universe. In all of the Universe, you are unique. Your soul, your purpose, your experiences, your genetics and more combine to make up your singular energetic profile. There is not another like you, and there is no scale to measure you by.

To tell yourself you should be like others is not true, and very harmful to you. Rather than denigrating yourself for not being good enough, you could be delighting in how special you are. And you would become stronger and more powerful with every dose of self-love.

Comparing prompts some problem areas we should take a look at:

Envy

Comparing sets you up to continually find yourself inadequate. This leads to regular feelings of envy – you're sure everyone else is leading a far more beautiful, successful, and satisfying life. It is a rather terrible feeling to burn with the desire to be living someone else's life, rather than your own.

Envy can really warp you. It introduces an element of malice into your thoughts. Rather than wishing other people well, and being genuinely glad for their happiness, now there is interference.

If your best friend is getting married, it's hard to be totally happy for them, while also feeling sad for yourself that you're not the one getting married. If they got a big promotion and pay raise, you can't authentically celebrate with them, because you wish you were the one with the higher status and money. You're having to fake it in the middle of the party, and may even duck out early because you're too sorry for yourself.

And it doesn't even have to be someone you know – nearly any news of anyone's seeming advancement is enough to incite envy. Type 4s have an incredibly vivid imagination, and are capable of imagining in detail how cool it would be to have that person's experiences.

This is that Disappointment we were talking about before – your Distorted Theme. Envy is just another way of being unhappy with your Now. If you loved yourself and your own life, you would not envy other people.

Longing

Type 4s not only Compare themselves against other people. They also compare their current reality against the fantasy one that lives in their imagination. And guess what, it doesn't usually pass muster.

It cannot be overstated how much time the Type 4 spends inside their own imagination. There are many dimensions in there, and they love to explore and commune with them all.

They develop favorite fantasies – ones they return to again and again. They often imagine themselves as an alter ego – a better, more fabulous version of themselves living a better, more fabulous version of life.

Ego-Driven Type 4s experience feelings of longing regularly, as a result of Comparing their reality against a fantasy. They yearn and wish for the dynamics which they find to be absent in the present.

A longing for something is a desire which is born from a state of lack. It is not a "pure" desire, because you wish for it while you're unhappy.

Desire which is "pure" – meaning it comes from the heart rather than the Ego mind – is very potent. It is the stuff of Creation. You know your desire is benefitting you if it makes you feel joyful to experience it. When you imagine something you desire from a place of joy, you are speaking the language of the Universe, and thus calling it into your life.

This is a subtle but extremely important concept to understand. The Flow of the Universe brings you experiences which are a *match* for your energy vibration.

If you are in a state of joyfulness, this brings you more experiences to be joyful about. But if you are in a chronic state of disappointment, the Universe does not send you things which will make you feel better – It sends you more things to be disappointed about. We will discuss this further in the upcoming section about Abundance.

But suffice it to say, longing for things is not in the Type 4s best interest. Gratitude for what you already love about your life is a much better way to go.

♦♦♦

Your specialness and worth are inherent, and do not rise or fall based on what other people are doing. Even though your Survival Belief tells you that you must earn the high regard of other people in order to survive, this completely limits your ability to love yourself for who you are. It is the lack of self-love which threatens your Vitality – not the approval of others.

As you begin cultivating your love and appreciation for The Real You, you will naturally come to release yourself from your compulsion to Compare. Envy and longing to be other than how you are will fall away.

Instead, you will come to feel grateful for your life, and your rare, enhanced abilities to appreciate all its splendor. As you learn to connect to your Higher Consciousness, you will come to see yourself as It does: unapologetically unique, powerful, and glorious – a most magnificent expression of Source.

Your Destructive Behavior

Your Survival Belief – that you must be seen as special – also prompts your actions and behaviors. **When you are Ego-Driven – and therefore not questioning your inherent attitudes and beliefs – you will repeatedly behave this way.** This is called your **Destructive Behavior.**

You may be entirely unaware of it, or you may be doing it on purpose in the utter certainty it's the best way to be. Either way, this behavior is never for the Greatest Good of all, and therefore is destructive.

As an Ego-Driven Type 4 who believes that you have no worth unless other people think you do. . .

> Your Destructive Behavior is **Self-Obsessing.**

Self–Obsessing is an all-encompassing term for the myriad ways in which you mentally fixate upon yourself. It looks something like this:

Assessing Yourself

That Survival Belief of yours – that you need *other people* to think you're special – has you very plugged in to how you appear. You objectify yourself with a ruthless eye – appraising your beauty, your intelligence, your talent, etc.

Look around you at the nature that is thriving. The trees, the flowers, the animals. How often do you think they spend time assessing themselves, wondering if they're good enough? That's right – never. Nature is your teacher on how to just *be* who you are, without analysis.

Referencing Yourself

When someone else is telling their story, you think about how you relate or don't relate to this story. When other people are revealing themselves, you redirect the narrative back to you.

You came here to love – not be loved. You came here to understand – not be understood. Try being selfless for a bit. Be there for other people, without requiring that they be there for you. Rather than always facing inward, face outward, and engage with the world around you.

Remembering Yourself

You relive your past experiences again and again.

Living in the past takes you out of the present. In focusing on what happened before, you are missing the Now – which is your real life – and setting no intentions for your future.

Remembering the past only serves you if it is the happy times – ones which inspire uplifting feelings such as love, peace, and gratitude.

If you repeatedly return to the experiences that confuse you, upset you, or hurt you, this shows you that you have wounds which need healing. There are methods for this, which are taught in the Vitality Voyagers membership, available through YourVitalityPersonality.com. These will allow you to bring yourself peace, let go of the past, and move on.

Experiencing Yourself

You spend an enormous amount of time poring over your feelings – prolonging them, amplifying them, and identifying with them.

As we will discuss in the section about your Energy Center, feelings are guidance from your Higher Self. They are communication. They show you the energetic frequency you are creating with your unconscious thoughts – so that you may intentionally shift them. Feelings are to be acknowledged and released – not held onto and repeatedly reviewed.

Fantasizing About Yourself

You picture yourself living out various alternate realities. Usually these involve imagining yourself being different than how you actually are.

Imagining having experiences you don't believe are really possible just traps you in a negative state of longing for what you can't have, and reinforces your feeling of disappointment in yourself.

Your profound connection to your imagination is for exploring the Universe, and bringing the ethereal into reality. Imagining yourself living the life you desire and that you believe is possible is great for you. But using this superpower merely to create more dissatisfaction with your Now is destructive.

Fussing Over Yourself

You have many habits oriented around making yourself more comfortable or accommodating your special needs.

It's true, being right-brained in a left-brained world does require you to take some extra steps in order to function well. But they're likely not the steps you've been focusing on.

The self-care you need is energetic in nature. Meditation, grounding yourself, cleansing your energy field, visualizing self-healing, and fully processing your experiences are some examples of what you can do to maximize your Vitality.

Treating yourself as delicate and frail, however, does not improve your health — it makes it worse.

Remember, your mind is a magnet — it draws to you more and more of what you focus on. Creating a lifestyle of accommodating unwellness creates more unwellness. Your goal is to treat yourself as strong and capable, because this is The Real You.

In watching over children you see this clearly. They fall down, and then they look to the nearby adult to gauge their reaction. If the adult says *You're okay, get up* — they get up and keep going. But if the adult says *Oh no, you poor baby!* — then the child sits and cries.

In this scenario, your Ego wants you to be treated like a poor baby, but your Higher Self would tell you that you're strong and can overcome anything.

Shaming Yourself

Telling yourself how inadequate you are, how unacceptable you are, how weird you are, how stupid you are, what a misfit you are, how unlovable you are — it has got to stop. Not only is it untrue, it serves no purpose except to drive you to loathe yourself.

Shaming Yourself is *seriously* destructive. Shame is the most debilitating emotion of them all. Its vibration is so heavy and so slow that it is as close to death as you can get while still being alive. And when you think about it, shame is the reason behind most suicides. It is a nearly intolerable feeling... and Ego-Driven Type 4s cover themselves in it most every day.

Authenticity, or Abuse?

Type 4s are deeply committed to authenticity. They do not shy away from the painful truth, particularly when it comes to self-evaluation.

However, Type 4s have impossibly high standards for themselves, much like the Type 1. And often what they think of as an honest discussion with themself about the truths of all their flaws is really the voice of an unloving, unkind judge.

Just to be clear, judgment has zero to do with authenticity.

Authenticity is being what you really are without pretense or apology. There is no good or bad, right or wrong. There just *is*. Authenticity is peaceful, because there is no questioning or drama involved.

Judgment, however, is entirely a construct of the Ego, focusing on the assignment of value. It is highly charged, inciting much questioning and drama. It *disturbs* peace.

Type 4s, in the name of being authentic, actually spend much time Shaming Themself, thinking they are being nobly honest, when really they are being ruthlessly cruel. This is self-abuse, not frankness. Frankness would give equal time to assessing strengths and assets. But the Type 4 conversations with themselves are rather one-sided.

Confessing Flaw

Out of this desire to be authentic, Type 4s are notoriously self-defeating. They feel an instinct to spontaneously confess their flaws and failures, no matter the context. They are the inventors of *TMI: Too Much Information*.

Job interviews, first dates, business meetings, parties... no matter the venue, the Type 4 can be found volunteering to friends and strangers alike how they're a bit of a hot mess.

This is not authenticity, because this is not the whole picture. They're also a freaking genius with amazing talents, but that part they leave out. Type 4s seem to feel that if they freely admit their obvious flaws or openly apologize for being so imperfect, they will disarm the private judgment the other party was about to indulge in.

This is self-sabotage, and entirely unnecessary. There is no reason to go out of our way to make a questionable first impression. The world does not require you to denigrate yourself at every opportunity – so please, Type 4, stop apologizing for yourself. You are exactly how you were designed to be, and that's a beautiful thing.

♦♦♦

As you can see, Self-Obsessing with a sharply critical eye is Ego-Driven, Destructive Behavior. It keeps your focus very small, on things which are not at all important or healthy for you.

Loving yourself is important. Enjoying yourself is important. Connecting with Life is important. These are the activities which will lead you to thrive.

There is a very large, very interesting, very beautiful world out there. You came here to interact with it. Let yourself have experiences in the outer world, and be of service to other people. There is much joy and growth available to you in these connections.

Your Sabotage Pattern

As we have discussed, your Personality Type has much Survival Programming built in. Your Survival Belief, Compulsion, and Destructive Behavior are undeniable impulses within you that all drive your well-being into the ground.

In other words, these all combine into an overall template for self-destruction. This is called your **Sabotage Pattern – the way you repeatedly behave throughout your lifetime which leads directly to the destruction of your health and happiness.**

> ➢ Your Sabotage Pattern is **Melancholy.**

Melancholy is a general sadness, a mournfulness for no single reason. Now that we've reviewed your Survival Belief and all the painful fallout that happens as a result, we *know* the reason. Believing that you are damaged goods but can only survive if you can convince others you're special, it is not at all surprising that you would experience Melancholy much of the time.

Melancholy of the Mind

Melancholy of the mind is all the negative thoughts you think to yourself: *I'm not smart enough. I'm not interesting enough. I'm not attractive enough. I'm not lovable. I don't belong, I don't fit in.* These are sad, heavy thoughts, sabotaging your own ability to advance and succeed.

Melancholy of the Body

Melancholy of the body is the slow decline of functionality. Imagine that every cell of your body has feelings. How would they respond if they were told every day *You're not good enough*? Sad cells are sluggish, and can't perform at their best. The nervous system becomes distressed and oversensitive. Digestion becomes troubled, because it can't "ingest" the negative messaging. The muscles become tight and aching. This is the body crying out for love.

Melancholy of the Heart

Melancholy of the heart is depression, apathy, angst – because believing terrible things about yourself hurts terribly. This is very hard to bear, and slowly erodes your joy and will to live.

This Melancholy Sabotage Pattern is always at play for the Ego-Driven Type 4. It is comprised of three main themes:

- Poor Me
- I Want to Go Home
- Push-Pull

We will explore these final aspects of Your Primal Persona, and then we will move on to discovering your Highest and best self – Your Vitality Personality.

Poor Me

The Ego-Driven Type 4 loves a good pity party. They like to tell their story of sadness, to themself or anyone else who will listen. In their loneliness and pain, they want to feel seen, heard, understood.

- *Poor Me, other people have love and happily-ever-afters, but I don't.*
- *Poor Me, I have special needs that limit me while everybody else has it easy.*
- *Poor Me, I'm misunderstood and nobody is insightful enough to "get" me.*
- *Poor Me, I've got it tough.*

Type 4s think they are seeking solace with this self-talk. But sympathy is not the remedy for Melancholy. Validation of the *Poor Me* story does not serve them – it helps them stay stuck. Identifying with a pitiful persona amplifies disempowerment, not strength.

What if the story were shifted to *Lucky Me*???

- *Lucky Me, I am capable of creating whatever life I desire.*
- *Lucky Me, I am powerful, resilient, and able to meet my own needs.*
- *Lucky Me, I have access to so much wisdom and beauty that other people seem to miss.*
- *Lucky Me, I chose this life and am getting to have so many interesting experiences that teach me and help me grow.*

You have the freedom to choose a more empowering perspective. All that is required is self-awareness and the willingness to claim your power.

I Want to Go Home

Because Type 4s seem to be wired so differently than everyone else, they develop a story in their mind along the lines of *I don't belong here, and I want to go home.*

Well, if you're a believer in past lives, then you know that it's entirely possible that you're not really from here. You may very well be an ancient soul who began your existence somewhere else.

Nevertheless, whether that is true or not – you came here, now, *on purpose*.

It's not an accident that you were born in this time and this place in this family. You designed it all ahead of time, and now you are living out your plan.

So why fight it? This is resistance of the worst kind: resistance to life itself.

Even if you're just a visitor here, enjoy it! Explore and experience this wondrous place. Meet the locals, try the food, exchange some ideas. Just as if you were a stranger in a strange land, you must make the best of your circumstances. There are other foundlings here, you know! You are not alone.

No matter how different or odd it feels to you to be here, don't waste any energy wishing you were not. As we've discussed before, the feeling of longing is born out of a sense of lack. The more you indulge it, the more lack you will experience.

You came here for a purpose, and that purpose is your happiest happy place. Spend your time finding that, and you will discover how glad you could be to be here.

Push - Pull

There is an intense dynamic at play which is at the heart of the Type 4's Melancholy. I think of it as the *Push-Pull* dynamic. Ego-Driven Type 4s want opposing things at the same time.

For example:
- You want to feel deeply loved, but you also want to be alone.

- You want to feel noticed, but are embarrassed to be the center of attention.
- You want to be invited, but you don't really want to go.
- You're so glad it happened, but wish it had gone differently.

This is the reason why Type 4s can really struggle with finding happiness – they keep finding problems with the Now.

The answer, Type 4, is *Willingness*. Willingness to let go of expectations and attachments. Willingness to have the experiences you are having. Willingness to accept that the way it went was the right way.

It is important to understand that your energy signature is a magnet, and it attracts energy to it which is a match for its vibration. What this means is: the experiences you attract are specifically for you. They are designed to match your energy. So if you don't like how your life is playing out, there is something in *your* energy field that needs shifting.

All experiences are lessons. Their dynamics are reflecting back to you what dynamics are at play *within* you. Rather than becoming upset that they weren't good enough, ask yourself:

- Did they say something that hurt my feelings… or did what they said match how I secretly feel about myself?
- Is nothing going my way… or do I believe that nothing ever goes my way?
- Was I rejected, or am I always afraid someone might reject me?

Rather than buying-in to the story that's playing out, and drawing painful conclusions about the dynamics, stand back and be the observer. See yourself having this story, and ask yourself what this is trying to show you.

As you are able to remain neutral during your experiences, rather than frequently becoming upset because things didn't go how you wanted them to, your energy signature will change. As you learn to become pleased, your vibration will rise. This is the beginning of attracting a totally different kind of life.

Type 4, don't let Melancholy slowly erode your health and happiness. Find the pleasure in the day, be at peace with yourself, and have gratitude for your life. This is what it means to be Consciousness-Directed, and we are about to explore it more fully!

♦♦♦

Now that you have opened your eyes to the destructive inner workings of your own Ego, operating as Your Primal Persona, do not despair. It is certainly within your capacity to transform these behaviors and patterns of your Survival Programming.

If you have made it this far, CONGRATULATIONS. We lost many along the trail – not everybody is ready for the journey that is Getting Real! This book is really only interesting to people who are about to make an enormous advancement in their consciousness.

We made it through the hardest part. Now, let's explore how you can be, act and live differently. There is an entirely different kind of life available to you, filled with love and connection and joy. And it is mapped out in the top half of your Type 4 Mandala.

ACTIVATE YOUR POWER PARADIGM

In Chapter One we revealed the meaning of Your Vitality Personality. Let's recap now.

Your Vitality Personality is the version of you that exists when you allow your Higher Consciousness to guide your thoughts, feelings, and actions. It is the opening of your heart, and allowing the loving intelligence found there to Flow through you. This infuses you with insight, wisdom, love and compassion, and the actions you take from this place always serve the Greatest Good.

Let's take a look now at the top half of your Mandala which spells out the dynamics of The Real You - Your Vitality Personality - and all its wondrous gifts and talents:

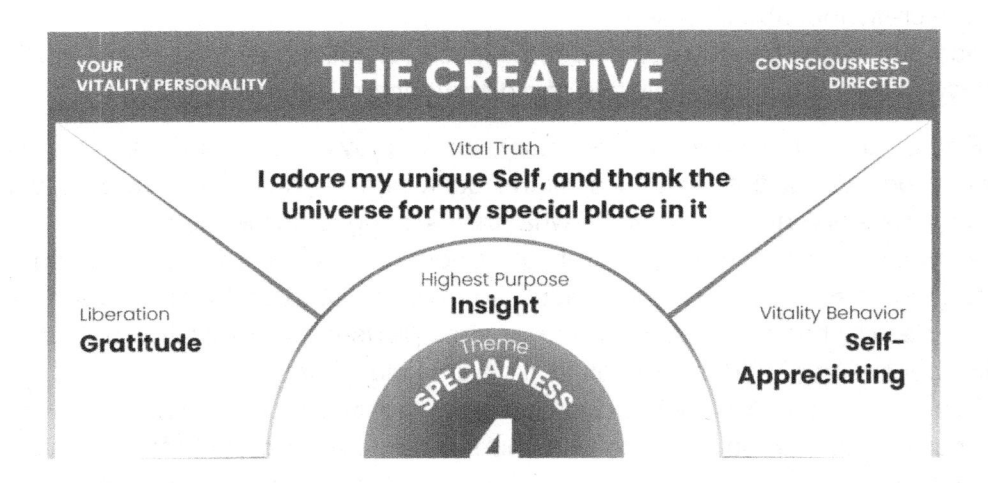

YOUR VITALITY PERSONALITY — **THE CREATIVE** — CONSCIOUSNESS-DIRECTED

Vital Truth
I adore my unique Self, and thank the Universe for my special place in it

Liberation
Gratitude

Highest Purpose
Insight

Theme
SPECIALNESS
4

Vitality Behavior
Self-Appreciating

Your Vitality Personality: The Creative

As a Type 4,

> Your Vitality Personality is known as **The Creative.**

This is the truth of who you really are. Your sensitive nature, your curiosity, your perception, your love of beauty ... these have always been the greatest part of you. This is not an accident. You chose this Personality Type because you wanted to be able to use these special attributes in a particular way.

The Real You is an artisan, a muse, a wizard. You take ideas, feelings, visions — and make them real. You reflect back to us our own desires and fears, our own triumphs and failings. You remind us to be self-aware, self-reflective. You encourage us to awaken to ourselves and our own humanity.

See *Fig. 5B* for a brief summary of the Consciousness-Directed half of your Mandala, identifying how to use your Personality Type to bring into the world a sense of beauty, passion, desire, and love.

When you embody all these natural gifts, you are a shining light, inspiring all who know you. It is so exciting to think you are just on the precipice of launching a new life of love, acceptance, and Vitality for yourself! It might have required some serious deep-breathing to get here, but the effort is so well worth it.

Let's explore these dynamics of your Power Paradigm, so that you may begin to fully comprehend just how open, uplifting, happy and healthy your life could really be.

Your Theme

As was mentioned earlier,

> Your Theme is **Specialness.**

When you pursue the highest form of this Theme – Specialness – you are truly aligned with Source, and therefore always serving the Greatest Good.

Specialness refers to beauty, uniqueness, rarity, creativity. You came here to explore what this means to you, and to help other people find what it means to them.

Your role here is very important, even though there are popular factions who don't give it proper consideration. That is actually the point – you are the Awakener of deadened sensibilities.

Fig. 5B **PERSONALITY TYPE 4 POWER PARADIGM**
Your Vitality Personality: THE CREATIVE
The Real You; The most magnificent version of yourself you joyfully embody when you heed the guidance of your Higher Consciousness
Theme: SPECIALNESS
The dynamic realm of Life your Higher Consciousness wants to explore to the fullest
Vital Truth: I ADORE MY UNIQUE SELF, AND THANK THE UNIVERSE FOR MY SPECIAL PLACE IN IT
The higher understanding of how to thrive, that aligns you with the Flow of the Universe
Liberation: GRATITUDE
The emancipating philosophy you freely embrace to enhance your connection to the Flow
Vitality Behavior: APPRECIATING MYSELF
The empowering and uplifting actions you intentionally choose to create your best life
Highest Purpose: INSIGHT
How you serve the Greatest Good through embracing your encoded genius, and the source of your Vitality

In this modern world of money and status, work and duty, deadlines and responsibilities, why do we make the time for movies, books, and TV? Why do we crave stories, when they have nothing to do with productivity and getting ahead?

Because there is something within our souls that needs them. We crave a sense of connection to other people. We desire deeper understanding of ourselves. We want to remember what it feels like to love. We want to be dazzled by beauty. When we are living far out of balance and feel like we're in the trenches of a war zone, we long for the things that make us feel alive.

Type 4, you are the one who brings these things into the world. You notice what it feels like to be alive, and you show that to us in your special, singular way.

Your Theme of Specialness, then, is the Theme that explores the beauty of the human experience.

In the hands of Your Vitality Personality – fully connected to your heart while silencing the Ego mind – you are a profound teacher in a hardened world, making you a loved and appreciated Creative:

- Confident in your unique talents and abilities, trusting in your ability to succeed in life.
- Finding the beauty in the moment, feeling everything is as it should be.
- Experiencing emotion as communication from your Higher Consciousness and using this to navigate your world.
- Bringing the beauty of your imaginary world out into your reality.
- Vitality derived from the balance of a quiet mind, invigorated body, and expressive spirit.
- Living unapologetically as The Real You.

Most people are stressed, preoccupied, and disheartened. They move through their life as if in a stupor, without questioning, without noticing. They are sleepwalking, and don't know how to find meaning or inspiration.

You are the one who is built to serve the world by engaging your natural abilities to bring more awareness, compassion, beauty, and appreciation to Life.

However, you will only be able to accomplish this if you can take hold of your Ego's Survival Programming, and overcome its negative influence on your self-esteem. You must become able to love yourself and feel pleased with yourself in order to embrace your nuanced abilities as a Creative. In this way you serve your Highest Purpose: bringing Insight to the world.

Your Vital Truth

Your Vital Truth is the Higher understanding of how to thrive by aligning with Universal principles. It is the escape hatch your Ego doesn't want you to know about, because it unlocks all of its Survival Programming, and connects you to your Higher Consciousness – The Real You.

> Your Vital Truth is **I adore my unique Self, and thank the Universe for my special place in it.**

This Vital Truth is the contradiction of your Survival Belief. Whereas endorsing your Survival Belief leads you directly to resistance, self-sabotage and erosion, embracing your Vital Truth places you in the Flow of the Universe. This leads you directly towards your happiest, healthiest life – Vitality!

However, your unconscious is encoded to automatically revert to the Survival Belief. To replace this with the Vital Truth takes conscious intention and daily practice.

Although this Vital Truth is a brief, simple statement, it is dense with meaning. Let's take a moment to unpack this.

Adoring Yourself

Self-love is at the center of your Vitality, and is the primary principle of the entire Universe. Source is entirely loving, and everything Source creates is made of love and light. *You* are made of love and light, and to appreciate this about yourself is to align with Source and the Flow of the Universe.

Self-love means complete, unconditional love – there are no parts of you which are not lovable. In order to access the Flow of the Universe, you must become able to love all of yourself – Ego included.

The way to accomplish this is to recognize that you are on a journey, from unconsciousness to self-awareness. It is a long, slow process of awakening, and that's okay. That's how it is supposed to be. Anywhere you are on the path is right where you are supposed to be.

Imagine a five-year-old child, beautiful in her innocence. She has no concept of math – but you love her anyway. She doesn't know how to use the scissors well – but you love her anyway. She has tantrums when she doesn't get her way – but you love her anyway. She's mean to her brother and steals his toys – but you love her anyway. She loves to sing and twirl – and you love this about her too. She is so singular and unique – unlike any other child – and you find her so special.

Do you withhold love because she hasn't reached her full potential yet? Of course not. Do you even expect her to have reached her full potential yet? Of course not. She is young, and has much further to go in her growth. But even though she is only partially grown, and is lacking awareness and understanding, you still love her with your whole heart. She is who she is, and it's exciting to watch her develop and grow.

This is how Source sees you, this is how your Higher Consciousness sees you, and this is how you must see yourself. As a beautiful being, only partially grown to full potential, which is natural and appropriate for the stage you are at. There is no reason to expect you to be other than right where you are in your growth. But you are still entirely lovable, even though you are limited in some ways. No matter what your limitations are, no matter how much room for improvement there is – you are always lovable, just the way you are.

Love yourself. Accept yourself. See the beauty in your own journey. This is how you find peace and joy in your daily life.

Thanking the Universe

You didn't have to be given Life – it was a gift from the Universe. You didn't have to be given choice, and free will – they were gifts to you from the Universe. Earth didn't have to be this beautiful – it was a gift from the Universe. Food didn't have to taste this good – it is a gift from the Universe. You didn't have to have special talents and abilities – these were gifted to you with great love.

You could go on and on like this. You were given so many riches, they are beyond counting.

Can you see this? Do you appreciate this?

Or would you tell the Universe *This isn't good enough*?

Your Theme is Specialness. You came here to notice and enjoy the endless Special Things that the Universe created.

Pay attention. Notice the beauty, intelligence, and love that is all around you. Be thankful for having the sensibilities to notice, for being able to take in the glorious Abundance of the Universe. This brings you wonder, and awe, and joy. This keeps your heart, mind and body inspired, uplifted, and thriving.

Loving the Universe, and feeling grateful for the opportunity to experience It, eradicates all the petty smallness of your Ego, and the small thankless life it would create for you. Align with the greatness of the Universe, and witness how truly great your life can become.

Your Special Place

Absolutely nothing in your life is an accident. There is the very Highest intention and planning behind it.

You are here deliberately. You came here with both a purpose, and a mission. Your purpose is who you came here to *be*. Your mission is what you came here to *do*. Nothing about the life you are living is random. It was all designed exactly the way it is, just for *you*.

You were given the parents you have, so that you would be given just exactly the education you required, in order to be able to deliver your purpose and mission.

You were given the physical appearance you have, so that you would experience the specific interpersonal dynamics that would shape you into the person who would live out your purpose and mission.

You were given the intelligence and talents you possess, because they are just what you would need in order to serve your purpose and mission.

Your life was made especially for you. The hardships and the challenges, the opportunities and privileges – they were all given to you for a reason, to turn you into exactly who you are.

Don't denigrate them. Don't wish they hadn't happened. Don't be angry that your life has included episodes of difficulty or pain. It was supposed to be that way. Surrender. Accept.

Don't take for granted the things that have been easy for you. Pay attention to the lucky outcomes that happened for you. Notice when you have received rare gifts and experiences. Be humble. Be thankful.

You are special and important. Your life is special and important. The more you can consciously embrace this, the closer this brings you to your Higher Self, to the Universe, to Source.

♦♦♦

It takes effort to embrace your Vital Truth. Your Ego is always trying to regain control over your mind, encouraging you to play small.

It is your belief in your Vital Truth which allows you to dismantle the workings of your Ego. It is what sets you free. Choosing self-love, choosing gratitude, choosing surrender and acceptance… these are what direct your life towards Vitality: the happy integration of your healthy body, awakened mind, and limitless spirit.

Your Liberation

Your **Liberation** is **the emancipating philosophy you freely embrace.** This is a powerful shift, out of the Survival Programming of the mind, and into the Flow of the Universe through the heart. Rather than being owned by a chronic Compulsion, you are now intentionally choosing this Liberation.

> Your Liberation is **Gratitude**

Gratitude is humility and thankfulness for receiving something of worth. In every moment, there is something to be grateful for.

The reason Gratitude is called your Liberation is because it frees you of your Type 4 Compulsion of Comparing.

Comparing is an utter lack of humility or Gratitude. Comparing means that, in this Now moment, you are seeking to find something *better* than what you've got.

It's rather like being a child on Christmas morning. There is the tree, all covered in lights. There are the gifts underneath, wrapped with care in pretty paper and shiny bows.

In a state of Gratitude, before you ever even unwrapped anything, you would feel filled with joy. You would love the tree, which your parents went out and got for you so that you could have this special experience. You would look at the gifts, and feel so lucky that there are people who love you and want to give you special things and make you happy. The presents themselves are really secondary. The real gift is love.

But in the act of Comparing, you might look at the tree and say, *I hate multicolored lights, I wish they were white,* or *Fake trees are so tacky, they should have gotten a live one.* You might look at the presents and say, *My friend Caroline gets way more gifts from her parents.* You might unwrap the present and say *I'm sick of Barbie dolls, I wish I had gotten a bike.* Or, in classic Type 4 fashion, *Poor Me, my parents totally don't get me.*

Comparing is the practice of wondering if things might have been better for you, and in the process, you completely miss the love and beauty that was right in front of you.

The emotion of Gratitude is an incredibly high vibration. You can think of it as emitting sunlight out of your heart. It makes you radiate and glow. It makes you feel so high, it's as if you might just float right out of your body.

This is because this feeling is a match for your Higher Consciousness, and the Flow. They *always* exist in a state of Love and Gratitude, and whenever you feel this way, you join them.

Do not underestimate the power that is available to you when you are in this state. It activates sleeping codes in your DNA, expanding your capacities. It spontaneously heals ailments and reverses disease. It elevates what you attract into your life. Gratitude is the gateway to your best life. This potent energetic frequency is Creation itself – and how you become The Creative.

Pure Desire

It is only while in a state of Gratitude that you may experience *pure* desire. It is "pure" because it is not infused with the small, low, weak energetics of Ego. When you combine Gratitude and pure desire, a highest-and-best outcome is instantly created.

This is completely different than the Ego-Driven Type 4's orientation towards envy and longing.

Envy, of course, is wishing you had what other people have. It's coveting things. This is the opposite of Gratitude, which is the appreciation of what you already have. The desire to have what other people have is Ego-Driven. When you envy people, what you create is something quite different than your highest-and-best outcome. It's more of a lower-and-worse outcome.

Longing is wishing that something new and better would come along. That is still not a pure desire, because you are still not in a place of Gratitude. You're in a place of Melancholy, feeling sad that your life isn't good enough the way it is. You cannot attract into your life what you want that way. You will only attract more things to be Melancholy about.

When you feel love and Gratitude, you are Consciousness-Directed, meaning you have merged with your Higher Consciousness and are in the Flow of the

Universe. The manifestation of your pure desires is readily available, you need only to ask.

So, for example, say you currently live in a small rented apartment with stained carpet, loud neighbors, and no outdoor space.

If a Type 4 is Ego-Driven, and compulsively Comparing, their perspective would be something like:

> *I hate my crappy apartment. It's so small and loud. I wish I had lots of space. I wish I had lots of money. I would like to have beautiful antique silk rugs. I would like to have many acres of land with a pond and flowers. Then I could be happy and enjoy my life.*

But, if you were Consciousness-Directed, feeling Grateful, your perspective would be more like:

> *I'm so glad I have this apartment – I was so lucky to find something I could afford. I love these periwinkle curtains I sewed; they make the room so cheerful. I love my potted plants in the window, they are thriving and I feel happy every time that I look at them. In my new home, I will have a big house with sunlight streaming in. I think I'd like it if the floors were narrow planks laid in a herringbone pattern, that would be so lovely. I will walk barefoot in the grass, and smell all the night-blooming jasmine. I love my life – the world is so beautiful and anything is possible.*

Can you see the difference? Sure there might be yucky things going on, but that does not mean you can't still love your Now. Let the things you *don't* want show you what you *do* want, but don't let them get you down! Stay Grateful, and you will move into a reality much more amazing than you even knew was possible.

There is nothing wrong with desire. Desire moves you forward, keeps you growing, and shows you who you are. And with your most fabulous imagination, the Type 4 is able to visualize those desires in vivid detail. Wonderful! The more you can imagine living the life you desire, the sooner it will arrive.

Just make sure your desires are pure, Type 4, and full of Gratitude for Now. There is so much love and beauty available to you right Now.

Your Vitality Behavior

Vitality Behavior is the empowering and uplifting actions you intentionally choose when you are Consciousness-Directed, rather than the Destructive Behavior your Ego drives you to act out.

> ➢ Your Vitality Behavior is **Appreciating Myself.**

Actually, Type 4, your Higher Consciousness would have you appreciating *all* things, for this is what you are built for – noticing the Specialness in Life. But you will never really be capable of that, until you can first see all the things that are special within you.

As long as you can only see what's awesome about other people, but are unwilling to see these in yourself, you are still trapped in the mental machinations of the Ego. It is when you can see you hold equal value, that you enter into the Flow.

Appreciating is Not Obsessing

Your Vitality Behavior of Appreciating Myself is the opposite of your Destructive Behavior of Self-Obsessing.

The Self-Obsession happens as the result of *not* feeling pleased about yourself. You believe you are not good enough, which launches a whole host of ways you try to cope with the pain and stress of this – monitoring yourself, wishing you were different, etc. That has all got to go – there is only misery down that road.

Appreciating yourself has absolutely nothing to do with how you rank compared to other people. It does not include assuming you are defective or deficient. It does not require monitoring yourself. It is simply embracing the truth that you are wonderful, which brings enormous contentment, satisfaction and peace.

Appreciating yourself is an all-encompassing term for the myriad ways in which you may enjoy being who you really are. It looks something like this:

Loving Yourself

Self-love is the Truth upon which your best life is built. It is unconditional – meaning there are no circumstances in which you are not lovable. Even with your right-brained weirdness. Even with your Diva Ego. Even if you are a bloodthirsty axe-murderer, you are still worthy of love.

How is this so?

You must see yourself as your Higher Consciousness sees you. Your Higher Self knows your circumstances. It knows your pain and confusion. It knows you arrived here with no memory of The Real You, and that you've been floundering around without a map. It knows exactly how and why you are the way you are, and is rooting for you to find your way to joyfulness. Your Higher Self loves you unconditionally, and you must align with this in order to become Consciousness-Directed.

Unconditional love has nothing to do with how you look or what you have accomplished. It has to do with the inherent beauty of your heart. Make no critical comments to yourself whatsoever, just focus on what you love about yourself. Say to yourself things like:

I love my compassion.
I love my patience.
I love my intelligence.
I love my delight in music.
I love the way I experience color and light.
I love the way I can relate to children.

You are so unique. You are the only one like you. Love the mysterious magical creature that you are, and encourage yourself to keep growing.

Trusting Yourself

This is a biggie. You need to trust yourself — meaning trust your Higher Consciousness.

This all sounds abstract and vague until you start meditating so that you can actually encounter your Higher Self. You need to experience It firsthand, not just read about it in a book. Then you will truly understand that there really is a powerful and wise You who is never afraid, and always knows. You will know for yourself how that feels, and this is a game changer.

You can completely trust that your Higher Consciousness is always guiding you towards your best life. This means that whatever is happening, is supposed to happen. Whatever happened in the past was supposed to happen. Trusting your Higher Self means trusting this Now moment, and letting it be the way it is.

This trust is what releases you from wanting to imagine an alternate reality. You will no longer feel longing for something else. You will find that you feel complete, because you trust that all is well and going as it should. This frees you to find the Specialness in Now.

Respecting Yourself

Man does this feel good.

Now that you understand that Yes you are different than others, and Yes that's how you're supposed to be, you can let go of thinking poorly of yourself for not being conventional. Your differences are not what is "wrong" with you — they're what's exactly right.

Ego-Driven Type 4s are constantly apologizing for themselves. *Sorry I'm not smart enough. Sorry I'm not pretty enough. Sorry I'm not fast enough. Sorry I'm not "normal" enough.* When you come to respect yourself, you will never apologize for yourself again.

Remember that your outer world is reflecting back to your inner world. In the past, if people made disparaging or critical comments to you, you felt mortified, devastated, and victimized. But really they were just voicing your secret crappy beliefs about yourself.

When you really respect yourself, you don't have secret crappy beliefs anymore. So nobody in your outer world talks like that to you anymore. Respecting yourself doesn't mean you have to make a big scene, shouting *How Dare You Speak to Me Like That?!?!* It means you quietly emanate your contentment with yourself, and there's no need for discussion.

Exploring Yourself

There's an awful lot to Appreciate about you, Type 4. Your talents and interests are really freaking cool.

Being a Type 4 automatically means that you have an eye for what's special. Let it be your muse! Explore whatever catches your fancy, because that is how you will get to know yourself better and serve the Greatest Good at the same time. Your desire to explore yourself serves your Highest Purpose. This is how you gain all your Insight.

So if you love art, explore it! Maybe you like to be artistic yourself, or maybe you enjoy the works of others. Stay home and draw, or go take a class, or go visit a museum. Whatever you like, but give yourself the space to embrace what you love.

If you're a foodie, go for it! Practice new recipes or check out new restaurants. Find the ways in which you like to experience food the most.

This is what you're best at – seeking out the most interesting and special parts of life. There is such joyfulness and enthusiasm in this, and this is how you cultivate your own Vitality, and inspire it in others.

Enjoying Yourself

Newsflash: You could be really happy every day!

Somehow, Type 4s don't always get this memo. They can become really attached to their own angst and Melancholy, building a whole identity around being tragic. When this happens, they rather lose touch with the desire to be happy.

This is a one-way ticket to Doomsville. Fabricating a lifestyle of dissatisfaction is fabricating a lifetime of illness, ruin, and despair.

In order to become a Consciousness-Directed Creative, there must be joy and excitement in your life. Rather than passively hoping it will arrive someday, you must make it happen.

Don't tell yourself you can only be happy once you're in a romance – enjoy the freedom of being single now!

Don't tell yourself you can't participate because you haven't practiced enough – just leap in!

Don't wait around hoping someone will remember to invite you – tell them you want to go!

Being happy is up to you. You have the ability to bring this about. But you will have to decide that you're ready to make happiness your top priority, and let go of the stories you tell yourself about why it's not available to you Now.

♦♦♦

Let Appreciating Myself become your new motto. Inspire yourself and build yourself up. You are in charge of the reality you experience, and the more regularly you take pleasure in yourself, the more amazing your life will become.

Your Highest Purpose

You chose to be here, in this time and place, because you wanted to contribute something. You came here for a reason, and you chose your Personality Type because it was the one that would help you accomplish it. **Your Personality Type**

has a special set of talents and abilities, and you wanted to use them to make a contribution. This is your **Highest Purpose.**

> Your Highest Purpose is **Insight.**

Dictionary.com defines Insight as "apprehending the true nature of a thing." Isn't that beautiful? That is what you bring to the world.

This is the reason you came here, all encoded to be the unusual one. While everyone else was busy meeting deadlines and expectations, you were quietly penetrating into deeper realms. And what you have found there, you share with others, helping us all see there are more questions to ask, more layers to uncover, more understanding to be had.

Insight of the Body

Perhaps now that you are more connected with your Higher Self you have an inkling of what an incredible privilege and gift it was to be given a physical body to experience here on Earth, jewel of the Universe. You are one who is sensitive enough to imagine (or remember) what it would be like to be bodiless, longing to engage with so much beauty.

Your body has a direct connection to your Higher Consciousness which totally bypasses the Ego mind. Your body and its surrounding biofield hold all your truth, even the aspects of yourself which are unconscious.

Take time to be present with your body. The areas in your body which struggle are holding messages for you about an obstruction in your energetic Flow. It is usually emotional in nature. Rather than feeling alarmed and upset by your health concerns, endeavor to send light and breath to those places.

Just sit with the physical discomfort, and ask it, *What are you*? Feel for the answer – is it anger? Sadness? Fear? You don't need to know the story behind the feeling that is being held. All you need to know is that it is time for you to release it now. In Chapter 12 I will teach you a simple and powerful method for integrating these older parts of yourself which are asking for healing.

Insight of the Mind

Type 4, your Consciousness-Directed perspective is deeply profound. As the rare right-brained one, you are perceiving the world in an astonishingly different way than most others. You are noticing the specialness of everything, everywhere, while the rest of us are oblivious.

Most people are preoccupied, mainly with whatever their Personality Type encodes them to care about. Schedules, deadlines, safety, success. In the focus on these, they don't really take in all the Life that's going on around them. But you do.

You are the one who points out the craftsmanship of the antique desk you and your friend come across at the flea market, explaining how all of the scoring had been done by hand.

You are the one who notices your sister's cat looks downcast and hasn't been purring lately.

You are the one at the restaurant who exclaims with delight that you've never had tzatziki sauce with fresh mint in it before – only dill.

You are the one who has made a pet project of sampling all the different orchestras' renditions of Vivaldi's *The Four Seasons* and pronouncing which had the best technical execution versus which had the most emotional expression.

You delight the Universe immensely whenever you notice a special part of Creation. And you enrich the lives of everyone who knows you, by helping them notice, too.

You are an Awakener. Your sensibilities are finely tuned, while for most theirs are muted. In being your best self, full of Appreciation for yourself and your life and your world, you enliven others.

Insight of the Heart

The realm of the heart is your domain. Whereas most others avoid deep feelings wherever possible, you have been awash in them all your life. Now, as you train in self-mastery, you will emerge as the one with the richest understanding of the complexities of the human heart.

You don't need to be a famous actress or novelist in order to pass your Insight along. For as much as you've always disdained the mundane parts of life, these are actually where you can make an enormous impact.

When you decide on a whim to dye your hair blue or get a tattoo, it does more than just say *Hey world, notice me!* Actually, you are demonstrating what it looks like to have the courage to be unconventional, and that is an extremely important lesson. And the people who are attracted to this will approach you, and talk to you, and leave feeling changed.

When you introduce your mom to a song you think she'll love, you're doing more than being nice. You're showing her what intimacy looks like – when you really "get" somebody. You do this for many people, and these are meaningful, memorable experiences for them. They appreciate them long after.

When you take the time to chat with a wheelchair-bound elderly woman in the waiting room, you're not just killing time. You are feeling into what it would be like to be them, and radiating your empathy. You are a teacher of concern and compassion, just by being who you really are.

So be your full self unapologetically. Let your freak flag fly. Be happy. Celebrate the oddity, the rarity, the beauty in the world. They are our collective treasure, and yet we would never have known how rich we are without you helping us see. Thank you for this Insight, and for making the world so fascinating.

Living as The Creative

What does it mean to be The Creative?

You are not named The Creative because you are "artistic." Not all Type 4s would describe themselves that way. You are named The Creative because the most astounding Creations happen when you combine your Gratitude and Appreciation with your pure desire.

When you are full of love, Type 4, you are also full of pure desire, because you are the one with the most fabulous imagination. You are capable of envisioning the things no one has ever seen before. This is the biggest part of you, which joyfully steps forward when you give it voice. Whatever you create from this space will be a source of Insight to all. This is why you came here, to offer us all this gift.

Remember, too, to live in balance. Give morning and evening time to yourself, processing and releasing energy, and giving yourself care. But the rest of the time, let self-love be in the background – the spring in your step as you move through your day. Be free in your energy, emotionally available to others, open to what the day is showing you. Touch as many lives as you can with your Insight. Inspire others as you inspire yourself.

♦♦♦

Well, Type 4, you've been given quite a lot of information about yourself to digest. But hopefully by now you've come to see that even though you are wired to act out Your Primal Persona, it is possible for you to be someone so much more magnificent than that – Your Vitality Personality.

Now is the time to decide who you want to be in this world. If you are ready to step into the full power of who you really are, and create your best life… then your next step is **Integration.** See Chapter Eleven.

YOUR VITALITY PERSONALITY

CHAPTER SIX
PERSONALITY TYPE 5
THE SAGE | THE MISER

YOUR VITALITY PERSONALITY — **THE SAGE** — **CONSCIOUSNESS-DIRECTED**

Vital Truth
I expand into sharing and connection, trusting in the abundance of the Universe

Highest Purpose: **Vision**

Liberation: **Experiencing**

Vitality Behavior: **Freely Giving**

Theme: **WISDOM**

5

Distorted Theme: **OBSERVATION**

Compulsion: **Intellectualizing**

Destructive Behavior: **Withholding**

Sabotage Pattern: **Contraction**

Survival Belief
I can survive by hoarding all my resources

YOUR PRIMAL PERSONA — **THE MISER** — **EGO-DRIVEN**

Greetings, Type 5. Your inner coding makes you quite curious about this sort of teaching. You are built with an innate desire to know the deep truths, and this material is as deep as you can get into the nature of your own psyche.

However, the test for you will be whether you just read about these truths in a book, or actually go out there and apply them. Because this content would take you somewhere totally new and foreign, somewhere uncomfortable yet powerful.. To truly comprehend this wisdom, you must be a humble novice, rather than the in-control expert you prefer. And you must learn to lead with an open heart, rather than an observing mind.

If you have been led here, then it is because you are ready to take a quantum leap in the advancement of your consciousness. The wisdom and insight you will gain will propel you into an awareness far more expanded than most, and also ground you with an emotional range and depth born of experience. This will benefit the entire world, for you are the one capable of evolving our minds while still connecting with our hearts – helping us all reach for more of who we are.

This chapter focuses on the dual nature of your Personality Type 5, and the primary factors that hinder or help your ability to thrive. You will totally love the descriptions about your highest potential and purpose... but you will totally not love reading about your dark side, called Your Primal Persona.

Hang in there! We intentionally go through the Primal Persona stuff first, so that you can finish on a high note – the magnificence that is Your Vitality Personality.

Let your curiosity take the lead. Give yourself permission to surrender to this process, and you will see how it takes you on a journey, getting richer and richer the further it goes. The part of you that is wired for greater vision will quickly come to see how applying this wisdom will get you there, and the rest of us as well.

DECODE YOUR SURVIVAL PROGRAMMING

As we just learned, **Your Primal Persona is the version of you that exists when you allow your Ego to unconsciously drive your thoughts, feelings and actions.** It is the operating system of your survival-oriented mind, limiting you from tapping into the love and light that is your Higher Consciousness.

In this state, you are closed off from your sense of love for yourself or others. And the actions you take from this place only serve to fulfill the Survival Programming of the small, fearful you. This can be really uncomfortable to face, but it is critical to see clearly so that you can gain freedom from this dark influence.

The bottom half of your Mandala spells out the dynamics of Your Primal Persona and its Ego-Driven Survival Programming:

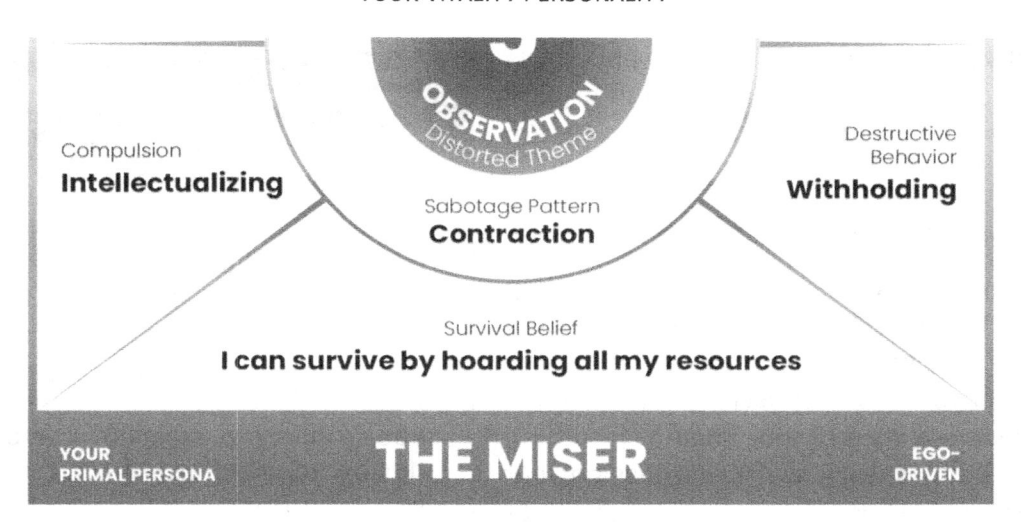

```
                    Compulsion                    OBSERVATION          Destructive
                    Intellectualizing             Distorted Theme      Behavior
                                                                       Withholding
                                         Sabotage Pattern
                                         Contraction

                                         Survival Belief
                                I can survive by hoarding all my resources

          YOUR                                                         EGO-
          PRIMAL PERSONA        THE MISER                               DRIVEN
```

Your Primal Persona: The Miser

As a Type 5,

> Your Primal Persona is known as **The Miser**.

This is your Ego's version of "playing small," with programming all about isolating yourself. As we will now explore, holding yourself away from connection and experience does not keep you safe or expand your mind like you thought it would.

See *Fig. 6A* for a brief summary of your Ego-Driven Survival Programming (we will dig deeper into it in just a moment). It is characterized by resistance, eroding your Vitality and degrading your life.

These are some painful truths. But you must forgive yourself for your Survival Programming. Have compassion for yourself, for it was the pain in your life which led you to feel that you couldn't survive without this perspective. Without self-awareness, you had no choice but to behave this way.

And this is true for everyone else, as well. We all deserve forgiveness for the way we act when we are asleep to ourselves -- we are totally unaware this is what we are doing and how much it hurts ourselves and those we love.

Even once you are aware of your Survival Programming, it can be quite challenging to take command over it. Yet every degree of progress you make in this direction brings you enormous reward. You will be joyfully inspired to continue the work.

Let's dive just a little bit deeper into what these dynamics of your Survival Programming really mean, so that you may begin the most rewarding journey of integrating yourself.

Your Distorted Theme

Each of the 9 Personality Types orient around a particular **Theme.** The whole point of you being here, at this time and in this place, is because you wanted to explore this Theme. This is the thing you are encoded to care about the most.

> Your Theme is **Wisdom**.

We will fully explore the true meaning of Wisdom in the next section (about Your Vitality Personality), when we discuss the Consciousness-Directed understanding of your Theme.

But right now, we are discussing your Survival Programming, and how your Ego *degrades* your understanding of your Theme of Wisdom.

Unfortunately, when Your Primal Persona interprets this Theme, **it becomes contorted – a warped, downgraded version of your highest potential.** This is called the **Distorted Theme**.

> Your Distorted Theme is **Observation**.

Observation is about trying to understand how the world works through watching it. While being observant is a wonderful trait, living life as an observer – but not a participator – is not a recipe for growth and thriving.

As a Type 5 you are very curious, and delight in exploring the power and creativity of your own mind.

But also, you don't want to reveal your inadequacies, you don't want to be hurt, and you don't want to be overwhelmed by emotion. These fears run very deep, and create in you a desire to gain expertise, in the hope that becoming very knowledgeable will bring you a feeling of competence and confidence.

So you stay to the sidelines of life, watching how it behaves. You believe you can best control the chaos of your world through understanding it, and so become a

Fig. 6A **PERSONALITY TYPE 5** **SURVIVAL PROGRAMMING**
Your Primal Persona: THE MISER
The Programmed You; The limited and diminished version of yourself that you default to when you are Ego-Driven
Distorted Theme: OBSERVATION
Your Ego's warped and downgraded interpretation of your true Theme
Survival Belief: I CAN SURVIVE BY HOARDING ALL MY RESOURCES
The scarcity-oriented message embedded in your Ego that creates your world view
Compulsion: INTELLECTUALIZING
The repetitive internal process you instantly launch as a way of discharging the emotional tension caused by your Survival Belief
Destructive Behavior: WITHHOLDING
The ruinous actions you regularly engage in when you operate according to your Survival Belief
Sabotage Pattern: CONTRACTION
The totality of all your Survival Programming combined into an overall template for self-destruction

dispassionate watcher, accruing information and expertise, while safely feeling nothing.

The Ego-Driven Type 5 is wired to be totally preoccupied with the life of the mind, with the relationship to the physical or emotional body a distant concern. This leads you to be far out of balance. While your knowledge and mastery of your favorite interests are unsurpassed, your emotional intelligence and physical prowess are likely to be far less developed.

In the hands of Your Primal Persona, you spend a great deal of your time Observing life from afar, while ignoring physical and emotional health, eroding your Vitality and quality of life:

- Becoming so detached that you have difficulty accessing your feelings anymore.
- Remaining so isolated and remote that you hardly have any friendships.
- Adopting such a clinical perspective that you disconnect from empathy.
- Treating your physical body as if it is insignificant, ignoring its need for proper nutrition, movement, and balanced rhythms.
- Exploring the dark and perverse aspects of the world, you develop a morose and bleak world view.
- Pursuing unusual and eccentric interests, you find it difficult to relate to others.

When you are Ego-Driven, your desire to cultivate the life of the mind degrades into an avoidance of experiencing anything of your heart and body.

This is no fun at all to read about. It's a bummer to realize your default, unconscious wiring is a sadly small version of who you could really be – who you actually are. The Real You is powerful and full of radiant love and light, enjoying connection and getting to interact on the physical plane. You are on your way to discovering how to access this higher aspect of yourself.

Your Survival Belief

Your **Survival Belief** is **the scarcity-oriented message embedded in your Ego that creates your world view.** It is the secret programming in the basement of your unconscious which drives all your thoughts, feelings, and actions without you ever realizing it.

> Your Survival Belief is **I can survive by hoarding all my resources.**

This belief is fundamental to you, even though you never knew it was there. It defines your understanding of how the world works.

Typically, this Survival Belief is activated within you at a young age.

As a child, you likely perceived your environment as too volatile. You were frightened by intense displays of emotion, or sudden changes and disruptions. You wanted to remove yourself from the noise and line of fire.

Your unconscious survival strategy, then, was to isolate yourself – with a stash of supplies for meeting your needs, trying to minimize them to the very basics. (With a child's version of needs, like junk food and soda.)

From this safe lair, you turned your attention to things which captured your mental curiosity. This allowed you to totally unplug from your outer surroundings, feeling secure in your remoteness. This was the child's means of coping with stress – and it has never occurred to you to re-examine it as an adult.

Your Survival Belief fundamentally shapes how you feel about your place in the world. Believing that the world is unsafe and that you must stockpile what you've got and hide away smothers your natural desire to experience the fullness of life. **It causes you to suppress your desire for love, connection and belonging, in favor of seclusion and mental activity.**

This philosophy is directly in resistance to the Flow of the Universe. The Universe is made entirely of love and unity – this is what is required to thrive. Attempting to go without this is a direct pathway to erosion and early death..

Let's explore the deeper implications of your Survival Belief now.

Scarcity Mentality

Your unconscious belief that you must hoard all your resources in order to survive is based upon a model of scarcity. Scarcity is the opposite of abundance.

Abundance is a fundamental truth of the Flow of the Universe and how it provides amply for all. Scarcity, then, means you believe you're competing for resources, and there is not enough to go around.

A scarcity mentality produces a *me-first* attitude. Rather than feeling generosity and compassion, it leads you to only concern yourself with yourself. Believing it's a harsh world out there leads prompts you to abandon empathy in favor of selfishness.

On a smaller scale, a *me-first* attitude makes you a dubious relationship for someone else to invest in. Frankly, it makes you a taker and not a giver. This impacts the quality of both your work and home life.

This scarcity mentality is a clear example of how your Ego-Driven Survival Programming brings on self-sabotage. Yes, you have survived another day this way, yet it is in a disconnected, loveless state. This is a recipe for depletion and deterioration.

Remember that currently we are exploring the dark side of your Personality Type, the parts that sabotage you and make your life unhappy. Soon we will move into the positive aspects, where you access love and light. This is where you will learn about Abundance, the alternate belief you can opt to embrace. Letting go of scarcity in favor of abundance is what opens you up to love, trust, security, freedom, happiness and fulfillment. As you will see, there is a much higher way you could be living.

Hoarding Resources

Generally we associate the word hoarding with an accumulation of "stuff." But that is only the beginning of the Ego-Driven Type 5's version of hoarding. The Type 5 secrets away *all* things of value, and these go well beyond just physical objects.

There are also many intangibles that the Type 5 covets. Physical and non-physical, here are many of the things a Type 5 tries to keep to themself.

Hoarding Your Money

This is a charged topic. As we will see again and again, there is something very extremist about the Type 5. There is hardly ever moderate, middle ground. This is the case with the topic of money.

Some Type 5s amass great wealth. They scrimp and save and invest and go without, until eventually they have become affluent..

Other 5s are unwilling to work for "the man" in order to earn money. They prefer to cobble together income on terms they control, even if it means having to minimize their needs. They are willing to go without many creature comforts in favor of autonomy and sovereignty.

But whether a Type 5 is rich or poor, their main area of allowing luxuries is for their hobbies or intellectual passions. Type 5s have the most curious minds on the planet, and they are willing to finance their own pursuits. The main things they are willing to splurge on are usually exceedingly high quality, quite rare, ultra cutting-edge, or integral to their area of study or expertise.

If you ever see a Type 5 voluntarily gifting someone else with something expensive… you can know that someone is very precious to them. (As The Sage, where you come to appreciate community and connection, you become quite generous to all, even ones you don't know, because of your newfound love of life and all therein.)

Hoarding Your Stuff

It is likely this word hoarding is not part of your perspective. You might call it collecting, or saving, or preserving. Or, as my daughter calls it: maximalist. Nevertheless we are both speaking of the same thing: you hold onto an extensive cache of things you think you might need someday. For what… who knows? Better to be safe than sorry.

While Type 5s are not sentimental, and have only a small collection of personal items that hold emotional attachment, they have an inordinately large collection of "stuff."

5s don't like to throw anything away that could turn out to be of value. If this was perhaps a past focus of interest but you have now moved on, you will continue to store everything, just in case. Type 5s are notorious for their overflowing drawers, closets, garages, workshops, attics, basements, cars and storage units, full of stuff they haven't looked at in years but will not discard.

Hoarding Your Intellectual Property

While everybody else was watching tv, getting together for drinks, playing games and generally enjoying their free time, Type 5s were studying something. They were reading, or watching documentaries, or running their own experiments, or intensively observing. They have spent a lifetime acquiring knowledge and expertise about things hardly anybody else knows.

As we have all heard, *knowledge is power*, and that is a resource the Ego-Driven Type 5 would not give away for free.

Hoarding Your Personal Information

Ego-Driven Type 5s are intensely private and secretive. They do not want anyone to know anything about them. This feels risky and unsafe.

They're not likely to chat up the neighbors. They probably do not leave their curtains open. They do not always answer the phone. They do not always answer the door. They do not usually invite people over (they don't like to give out their address). They don't typically post about themself online. They do not offer up their opinion among strangers. They answer personal questions with as few words as possible. They do not often give out their "real" email (there's usually one for insiders and one for the rest of the world).

In general Type 5's are not seeking to connect... and they are deeply uncomfortable when someone else makes the attempt. But behind closed doors, some Type 5s will occasionally admit that they do feel the consequences of their own isolationism, and sometimes privately long for connection and physical touch they have denied themself.

Hoarding Your Inner Life

And most secret of secrets: Ego-Driven Type 5s do not share themselves. They don't disclose their feelings and needs, their hopes and desires, their worries and fears. They hold their cards, as they say, very close to the chest.

Often, they even keep these things from themself. They prefer to remain as intellectual as possible, with the heart and body both held at a distance. This is the fundamental Type 5 Survival Programming – it is their primal attempt to feel in control and safe.

Unfortunately, as with all survival strategies, this ultimately leads to self-sabotage. The deeply held belief in survival is a very heavy, low energetic vibration – one which does not support life. Fear, suspicion, repression – these can only lead to erosion and collapse.

Learning to connect with others and share your inner world is an astonishingly uplifting experience for the Type 5. Having gone a long time without this, you would not have realized how badly you needed it. But knowing and being known, seeing and being seen, loving and being loved are the greatest experiences of all – and they are at the center of true wisdom, and Vitality.

◆◆◆

As you can see, your Survival Belief that you can survive by keeping yourself to yourself is at the heart of much difficulty and self-sabotage for you. It keeps you in a loveless state, where joyfulness and thriving are not possible. Learning about these, and becoming willing to change, is fundamental to creating a life that fulfills and uplifts you.

We just finished discussing your Type 5 Survival Belief, which was activated somewhere in your childhood. It is the primary driver behind all of your unconscious thoughts and behaviors.

Now, we will look at the most common thought, feeling and behavior patterns that emerge as a result of holding your Survival Belief.

Your Compulsion

Your **Compulsion** is **the repetitive internal process you instantly launch as a way of discharging the emotional tension caused by your Survival Belief.**

It is much like a guilty addiction – you know you should give it up, but don't want to… because you privately love it. And even if you decide *That's it, I'm through with this…* you will still find it very difficult to stop, until you become able to embrace your Vital Truth (see the upper half of your Mandala), rather than your Survival Belief.

> Your Compulsion is **Intellectualizing.**

Intellectualizing means closing down the heart and body, and only taking in experiences through the mind. This is an attempt to feel in control, by shutting down the turmoil of emotions.

The Compulsion towards Intellectualizing is an unconscious one – it happens automatically whenever you are faced with a new experience. However, most Type 5s have some awareness that this is happening, and they consciously endorse this approach.

As we will discuss in Book Two, the Type 5s are a "Head Type." This means that they (and Types 6 and 7) have an imbalance of energy related to excessive overuse of the mind. So it's no shocker that their primary Compulsion is towards using the mind in an emotionally detached way.

Living in the Mind

Type 5s try to exist primarily as a mind, with little concern for the affairs of the heart or the needs of the body. As you may imagine, this is quite out of balance.

When you think about it, existing as a consciousness without a body is actually our original, natural state. That is what we are before we come here to the physical plane, and that is what we will return to. So perhaps it's not so shocking to see why the Type 5 would feel a desire to exist that way now.

But the thing to remember is… your Higher Consciousness chose to come here and be physical. You came here on purpose to have a body with needs, and a heart that feels deeply. That was the whole point. You could have easily stayed on the other side of Awareness and existed as an observer. But you opted to come here and experience it all, because this would provide you the true wisdom you seek.

Ever the Observer

The Type 5 has a capacity for observation that is unmatched. Your curiosity, tenacity, and ability for hyperfocus all combine to create a mind like a supercomputer, forever inputting and processing data.

On the one hand this plays an important role in your Highest Purpose. Your natural impulse towards deep understanding benefits all of society... but only if you share it. Usually, your observations are only for you, to help you make sense of your world from a safe distance.

Safety is really the underlying concern. Type 5s don't inherently feel strong and stable within themselves. There is a lurking sense of frailty or inadequacy that causes a generalized anxiety. In order to manage this, Type 5s will often assess whether they will participate in a group activity based on how uncomfortable it might make them feel. Remaining remote feels so much safer. It allows you to learn and study from a distance without the risk of appearing incompetent or foolish.

So it's a really tough sell to a Type 5, attempting to convince them that actually this strategy doesn't serve them and they should give it up. They really like the security and the information they derive from never entering the fray yet watching from afar.

Nevertheless, as we will see a little further on in the discussion about the Sabotage Pattern, trying to hold a sense of permanent remoteness and disconnection does not play out well. Ignoring enormous aspects of yourself such as your heart and body's need for love and connection over time does not produce positive outcomes for your health and happiness.

Even though you observe humans to be so absurdly messy with all their emotions and irrational behavior, it is still in your best interest to go play with them! They have things to teach you, about yourself and about life, that you can never discover otherwise. There is much wisdom waiting for you when you actually participate, rather than just observe it. And a lot more joy, which is the true recipe for health and happiness.

Disregarding the Body

Ego-Driven Type 5s have a rather remote relationship to the body. They generally ignore its needs for nutrition, sunlight, rhythm, and touch (and often, hygiene). This leads them to live a rather eccentric lifestyle.

Your body loves rhythm. It would like to sleep all night and wake up with the sun. It would like regular mealtimes with a diverse array of whole foods in bright colors. It would like daily physical exertion, preferably outdoors in the fresh air. The Type 5 typically gives it none of these.

In particular I notice a night-owl trend among the Type 5s. They often prefer to be up in the wee hours where they can pursue their interests undisturbed.

They also typically have a quirky relationship to food. They have their favorite comfort foods, which are generally devoid of nutritional value. Otherwise they don't really care about food, and can eat the same thing over and over for weeks.

In Book Three we will address the typical health outcomes for the Type 5s who refuse to acknowledge the fundamental aspect of themselves as a physical being. But here's the main gist: physical neglect becomes the erosion of vitality and quality of life. Type 5s are typically sickly and malnourished, which becomes the early onset of system failure.

It doesn't have to be this way. Engaging with your body means engaging with physical life. Noticing the rhythms of nature and intentionally aligning yourself to them can be very healing and uplifting to you. Most 5s do mention how much they love nature and how much better they feel when they get outdoors – even though much of the time it is not part of their lifestyle.

Allowing yourself to have a healthy rhythm is probably the easiest way for you to start shifting yourself more into harmony with the Flow. Give yourself some sleep perimeters, and appointments for mealtime and movement. Let these be the foundation of your lifestyle. This alone will raise your energetic vibration significantly, giving you the inspiration and energy to open yourself up more to the rest of Life.

Shutting Down the Heart

Type 5s don't like feelings. They are messy and uncomfortable and make things feel chaotic and out of control. This is basically the Type 5 nightmare. Safety and control are extremely important to those who have an unconscious anxiety about their own vulnerability and inadequacy.

Therefore the Type 5 Survival Programming includes a unique ability to turn off feelings that most others do not possess. Unfortunately, it can be quite difficult to ever find the On switch again. Many Type 5s will privately confess that they cannot easily access their feelings. They feel frozen, or far away. Even when they want to let themselves feel, they don't always know how to go about it.

This can become a real dampener to romantic life. Type 5s attract partners with their intelligence, curiosity, quirky interests and astonishing wit – they are extremely interesting people and can be quite compelling. Yet they are not known for their warmth or easy affection. They generally require lots of alone time and are not seeking to connect at an emotional level.

On a larger scale, this imbalance of overly developed intellect but underdeveloped emotional maturity can become quite dangerous. Even though they are generally introverted, quiet people, Type 5s can be major influencers on the direction their society takes, because they are the inventors and innovators. For example, a society that embraces technological advancement but not love can become quite ruthless and heartless.

Even if a Type 5 feels ready to begin opening themselves up emotionally, they might not really know how to go about it. The easiest thing for you is to begin with giving more of your attention to the uplifting aspects of life. In their investigations of the mysterious aspects of Life, Type 5s often go down some pretty bleak wormholes, which darkens their world view and brings on cynicism and pessimism. You're going to have to decide to let go of that, and turn towards the Light.

The beauty of nature, the innocence of newly emerging life, the feeling of gratitude – give your attention to these and let them uplift you. This is called feeling a "smile in the heart." Let yourself feel *pleased* with things.

Resisting Pleasure

Somewhere early on, Type 5s reject their need for maternal love and comfort. Perhaps the mother figure was too overbearing and intrusive. Or perhaps it was absent and coping mechanisms kicked in. Either way, somehow the willingness to go without love and comfort became a general resistance to pleasure.

Type 5s are perhaps the least concerned with bringing warmth into their lives. They seem not to bother about the aesthetics of their environment or their degree of discomfort. They try to make their needs as small as possible and are willing to go without. Even very wealthy Type 5s may have expensive homes but you will find the interiors lean towards quality and function but not beauty or comfort.

Even when someone comes into their life who makes things more beautiful and uplifting, it is frightening to a Type 5. It scares them to become too dependent on someone else. They are afraid to acknowledge their need for love and connection. They may reject it, settling for the predictable safety of remaining solitary instead.

♦♦♦

As you can see the Type 5 Compulsion towards Intellectualizing causes a great imbalance in your perspective. It blocks you from accessing the wisdom of the body and the heart – when wisdom is the thing you care about most! As we will discuss in the upcoming section about Your Vitality Personality, the important shift you will need to make to bring yourself into the Flow is moving out of Intellectualizing and into Experiencing. You are here to fully experience the physical and emotional richness of Life on Earth – not just observe it from the sidelines.

Your Destructive Behavior

Your Survival Belief – that you must hoard all your resources – also prompts your actions and behaviors. When you are Ego-Driven – and therefore **not questioning your inherent attitudes and beliefs – you will repeatedly behave this way.** This is called your **Destructive Behavior.**

You may be entirely unaware of it, or you may be doing it on purpose in the utter certainty it's the best way to be. Either way, this behavior is never for the Greatest Good of all, and therefore is destructive.

As an Ego-Driven Type 5 who believes it's dangerous to share yourself. . .

> Your Destructive Behavior is **Withholding.**

Withholding means declining to share. It means holding back, and keeping yourself to yourself.

Type 5s are intensely private people. They do not want anybody to know anything about them. It feels like it costs something to share coveted information. This is that "hoarding" impulse we were talking about in our earlier discussion of the Survival Belief.

Withholding creates problems for all of your relationships, in your personal life, your professional life, and even for yourself.

Withholding at Work

My close friend was a life coach who worked at a corporation where they employed thousands of engineers. Which means she was working with mostly Type 5s! They are the innovators and inventors.

She said there was a huge problem within the company because all the Type 5s were so unwilling to share their data. Nobody would turn in their reports on time. I also worked with many of these folks, and when she told me that I asked one of my Type 5 patients about it who was a top engineer there.

He knew exactly what I was referring to, and to him it made obvious sense. "Well yeah," he said, "how are you going to get promoted if you share all your expertise freely? Your value is in being the only one who has the needed information."

Can you see what an Ego-Driven, scarcity-oriented perspective this is?

All the most powerful forces in our world occur in a Flow. Water, wind, fire, electricity, love. They all expand, they all reach further. They are the true examples of power.

Yet the Type 5 in the ego state is attempting to hold on to power by refusing to flow, expand, or reach further. This is resistance against what would actually bring them what they want.

When you share your expertise freely, your relevance does not become diluted. It expands. Think of all the "influencers" on social media. They are giving away their area of expertise for free, yet they develop millions of followers. They have not become expendable now that they've shared their secret – they are in demand for their astuteness and unique perspective.

And perhaps free services like Google might have something to teach on how giving things freely attracts great power.

Even though holding on to your expert status by withholding information may seem like a strategy for success, it can harm you because you will become known as difficult to work with. When you are uncommunicative and uncooperative to people who are counting on you, you may find yourself less in-demand than you imagined.

Even in the workplace, it is important for you to begin opening up, connecting, and sharing. Get to know your coworkers, and let them know you. Share your ideas and findings – you're improving other people's lives when you do so. Collaborate, and show what happens when great minds co-create.

You have the capacity to make a big impact in your own quiet way. When you combine the power of your heart with the vastness of your mind, you step into Your Vitality Personality – the magnificent Sage.

Withholding at Home

You are a sober, clear-minded sort of person, so I know you will not take it personally when I say that Type 5s are the toughest of all the Types to be in a relationship with. You already knew that you are a hard one to get to know and that you are not inclined towards giving.

For a Type 5 to let someone in is a very big deal, so a romantic partner should feel pretty special if they were allowed that far. It says that they are held in quite high esteem.

Even so, living with a Type 5 is not easy because of how much alone time and quiet time they feel they require. Just because a Type 5 loves somebody, it does not necessarily mean they want to spend lots of time together. They still like to be alone with their thoughts a good deal of the time.

Also, Type 5s are not oriented towards paying attention to feelings. For as observant as they are, they miss a lot of nonverbal social cues. This makes it hard on the romantic partner, who is probably going with unmet needs a good deal of the time. It puts the partner in the position of having to ask directly rather than be subtle, but this can often seem like nagging or a confrontation, which is also off-putting to a Type 5.

This dynamic can also be tough on the children of a Type 5 parent. Not all children know how to ask for their needs to be met, and must depend upon the emotional intelligence of the parent. When this is a weak spot for the parent, the child can experience it as emotional abandonment.

I was at a workshop, where a man who had mentioned to me that he is a Type 5 was attending with his wife. He was a very busy MD and they had two young children. He spoke about how after a hectic day working with many people, he comes home feeling tired and spent. He is extremely annoyed that his boys are rambunctious and loud when he gets home. He said he becomes curt and punishing if they refuse to honor his need for quiet time.

While the need for quiet time certainly feels very real, from the children's perspective, they haven't seen their dad all day and now when he gets home he won't engage with them either. They are essentially without a father much of their life.

In this scenario, something has to shift, and it's not the kids. An introverted Type 5 who feels depleted from public interactions is perhaps in the wrong career as a physician. (You can tell if your profession serves your nature and purpose because it will make you feel uplifted and energized).

Additionally, meditation and connecting to the heart are both practices which bring in much more energy at a much higher vibration. These are practices that are essential for bringing a Type 5 into harmony with their life. They soften your resistance against what life is asking of you, and help you find more energetically abundant resources.

Withholding from Yourself

You often deny yourself your deepest desires, which are actually to love and be loved, to have ease with other people, to feel a sense of belonging, and a deep sense of meaning. And yet your Ego-Driven Survival Programming prompts you to reject these.

Instead, you are wired to take your heart's desires and subvert them into creature comforts. Simple things like your favorite junk foods, or getting a cat, or buying yourself an expensive present. The small pleasures you allow yourself are soothing/numbing and help you to feel comfortable remaining alone.

You will feel the desire to connect but you will not accept the invitation, will not make the phone call, will not confess the feelings. This is how you withhold love and joy from yourself... and they are the stuff your energy is made of. This means you actively restrict your own access to the very thing you need to thrive.

As is true for all the 9 Personality Types, our self-sabotage actually derives from our own lack of self-love.

Because, if you really loved yourself, you would not deny yourself what would feed you most. You would not block yourself from interacting with others, who are simply fractal mirrors of you and have much to teach you. This is why it takes the willingness to connect to your own heart in order to elevate yourself into Your Vitality Personality, The Sage. The Sage feels their connection to source, to magic, to nature, each other, and themself – and reveres it all. The Sage can access All That Is and wield this cosmic energy masterfully.

Type 5 in your curiosity you may have taken yourself down some rather dark rabbit holes, and now you can't unsee what you saw. It may have given you a feeling of heaviness, of bleakness, and that doesn't seem like a place that can house love and light. The thought of opening yourself up to it feels terrifying.

To be flooded with love and light is a most glorious experience. It is a rarity not to be missed. You out of all 9 Personality Types are the one who feels a deep thirst for wisdom and truth. This is the wisest wisdom, and the truest truth. Opening yourself up to connection with the world around you will elevate your insight and understanding. It will expand and advance your consciousness. Do not let your Ego talk you out of it.

◆◆◆

As you can see, Withholding is not the safe strategy you think it is. It is Ego-Driven, Destructive Behavior that leads you to lose your vitality and your sense of meaning. It keeps your focus very small, blocking you from the expansion that would heal, inspire, and fulfill you.

Loving yourself is important. Having real experiences is important. Connecting with Life is important. These are the activities which will lead you to thriving.

There is a very large, very interesting, very beautiful world out there. You came here to interact with it. Let yourself have experiences in the outer world, and be of service to other people. There is much wisdom and joy available to you in these connections.

Your Sabotage Pattern

As we have discussed, your Personality Type has much Survival Programming built in. Your Survival Belief, Compulsion, and Destructive Behavior are undeniable impulses within you that all drive your well-being into the ground.

In other words, these all combine into an overall template for self-destruction. This is called your **Sabotage Pattern – the way you repeatedly behave throughout your lifetime which leads directly to the destruction of your health and happiness.**

> Your Sabotage Pattern is **Contraction.**

Contraction is the complete closing of yourself off from Life. It is turning totally inward, with no external entry allowed. It is making yourself small, tight and impenetrable. You make yourself into a fortress with the drawbridge up and the shutters locked.

As was true in the Dark Ages, fortresses are a sound strategy against an invading world.

This tactic reveals the underlying scarcity mentality. The deep belief that the world is a dangerous, violating place and being open and friendly puts your survival on the line. It is quite primal and fear-inducing.

Living in such a tightly closed way pinches off your access to the Flow of the Universe. This literally translates into the amount of life force energy running through your body and your mind, when your heart is closed.

Contraction of the Heart

Your heart is more than just an organ. It is the portal to the rest of you -- your Higher Consciousness – which in turn is connected to All That Is. It is the access point between the small Ego-Driven you and The Real You – and the Flow of the Universe.

Think of this heart portal as a door that opens fully when activated with love energy. If love energy were a sound wave, it would be a clear vibrant tone, ringing and true, and this fully opens your portal to the Universe.

Love energy involves thoughts of generosity and compassion, and feelings like affection, gratitude, joy, and awe. When you feel these feelings, you resonate in harmony with the portal and the door opens wide, flooding you with a great rush of life force energy.

But the clarity of your love signal becomes greatly distorted and diminished when bombarded with other frequencies that disturb the coherence of your field. Feelings such as fear, greed, covetousness, and contempt distort your signal into incoherence, and the portal begins to close as the signal is lost.

When you close the door on love and connection, you lock yourself away from the power, wisdom and happiness you desire.

Contraction of the Body

A general lack of life force energy, derived from a closed heart, evolves into health patterns for Type 5 of slow decline. There is a general lack of thriving, such as is seen in malnourishment. Poor energy, poor immune function, poor muscle tone, and poor organ function and poor sex drive are common outcomes that emerge over time, worsening with age.

Type 5s are often quite pale, being a night owl and more inclined to spend the days indoors. As you remain over-attached to the mind while the emotions are shut down, the body slowly begins to shut down as well.

Trying to be only a mind, pretending you don't have a body that needs love and care, is not a strategy for longevity and vitality. Your body withers under this neglect. Again, love for yourself and the willingness to demonstrate care is the antidote to your entire Sabotage Pattern.

Contraction of the Mind

It will likely shock your sensibilities to suggest that an Ego-Driven Type 5 can be small-minded, when you pride yourself at what a revolutionary deep-thinker you are. Allow me to explain.

There is no question of your impressive intelligence. This is indeed a part of the Type 5s greatness. It is the sense of superiority this provokes in you, however, which is the problem.

Convincing yourself that regular life with regular people is boring, superficial, and insignificant does not help you grow – it keeps you small. It is a large piece behind why you begin isolating yourself from other people. You have contempt for their simplicity and come to regard them as insignificant.

While it may often be true that you are the one with the most intellectual prowess, you are mistaken in thinking other people don't have anything of value to offer you. Because even if you are intellectually smarter or more educated, you likely have a great deal to learn in the areas of emotional intelligence, social skills and experience.

A sense of aloof detachment, combined with exceptional intelligence, is pretty much the profile of every mad scientist bad guy you ever saw in the movies! They serve as cautionary tales against being so far out of balance. There must be empathy, compassion, and love in order to contribute positively to Life.

♦♦♦

Contraction is the overall Sabotage Pattern for the Type 5, the default patterning that erodes happiness and health. But it doesn't have to be that way.

You have the capacity to change course, through shifting your beliefs out of scarcity and survival, and into love and acceptance. Opening yourself up to the possibility that you have access to very powerful energies which make you strong, certain, and capable drastically changes how you experience life. You think different thoughts, feel different feelings, and make different choices, which manifest different outcomes.

Very shortly we will discuss how to connect to your Highest Purpose, as the antidote to the destructiveness to your Sabotage Pattern.

♦♦♦

Now that you have opened your eyes to the destructive inner workings of your own Ego, operating as Your Primal Persona, do not despair. It is certainly within your capacity to transform these behaviors and patterns of your Survival Programming.

If you have made it this far, CONGRATULATIONS. We lost many along the trail – not everybody is ready for the journey that is Getting Real! This book is really only interesting to people who are about to make an enormous advancement in their consciousness.

We made it through the hardest part. Now, let's explore how you can be, act and live differently. There is an entirely different kind of life available to you, filled with love and connection and joy. And it is mapped out in the top half of your Type 5 Mandala.

ACTIVATE YOUR POWER PARADIGM

In Chapter One we revealed the meaning of Your Vitality Personality. Let's recap now.

Your Vitality Personality is the version of you that exists when you allow your Higher Consciousness to guide your thoughts, feelings, and actions. It is the opening of your heart, and allowing the loving intelligence found there to Flow through you. This infuses you with insight, wisdom, love and compassion, and the actions you take from this place always serve the Greatest Good.

Let's take a look now at the top half of your Mandala which spells out the dynamics of The Real You - Your Vitality Personality - and all its wondrous gifts and talents:

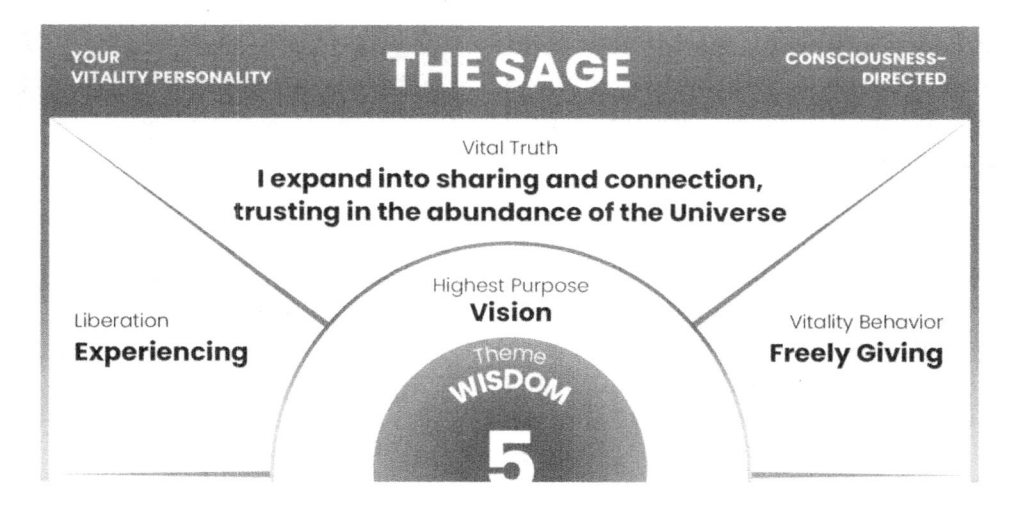

YOUR VITALITY PERSONALITY

YOUR VITALITY PERSONALITY	**THE SAGE**	CONSCIOUSNESS-DIRECTED

Vital Truth
I expand into sharing and connection, trusting in the abundance of the Universe

Liberation
Experiencing

Highest Purpose
Vision

Theme
WISDOM
5

Vitality Behavior
Freely Giving

Your Vitality Personality: The Sage

As a Type 5,

> Your Vitality Personality is known as **The Sage**.

This is the truth of who you really are. Your capacity for concentration and profound thought, your thirst for deeper understanding, your delight in the unusual, and your vivid imagination … these have always been the greatest part of you. This is not an accident. You chose this Personality Type because you wanted to be able to use these special attributes in a particular way.

The Real You is a wizard, a shaman, a visionary. You are the one who is willing to intensively study, and become an expert in the things others regard as the mysterious unknown. You forge fearlessly into the unexplored, into the future, confident in your abilities, quietly advancing our collective frontiers.

See *Fig 6B* for a brief summary of the Consciousness-Directed half of your Mandala, identifying how to use your Personality Type to bring wisdom into the world.

When you embody all these natural gifts, you are a trusted advisor, whose wise counsel shows the way. It is so exciting to think you are just on the precipice of launching a new life of love, belonging, and vitality for yourself! It might have required some serious deep-breathing to get here, but the effort is so well worth it.

Let's explore these dynamics of your Power Paradigm, so that you may begin to fully comprehend just how meaningful, uplifting, happy and healthy your life could really be.

Your Theme

As was mentioned earlier,

> Your Theme is **Wisdom.**

When you pursue the highest form of this Theme – Wisdom – you are truly aligned with Source, and therefore always serving the Greatest Good.

Wisdom is the insight, understanding, compassion and guidance that happens when you're grounded in your heart, your body and your Higher Mind.

The thing about you, Type 5, is not just that you are very smart and very curious. You have also felt a strong pull to understand Truth. You want to understand deep things, and you want to master them. This is not an accident. This is you exploring your Theme of Wisdom.

Moving into a Consciousness-Directed perspective, you become willing to accept that your Higher Consciousness came here with the intention of involvement and exploration – not observing from the sidelines. Once you are ready to open up to life, you will come to feel so much more connected, empowered, excited.

In particular you may be quite intrigued to learn that there are many more levels of mental advancement available to you, once you opt to balance your energy throughout your body and seat your Consciousness in your heart.

Fig. 6B
PERSONALITY TYPE 5 POWER PARADIGM

Your Vitality Personality: THE SAGE	The Real You; The most magnificent version of yourself you joyfully embody when you heed the guidance of your Higher Consciousness
Theme: WISDOM	The dynamic realm of Life your Higher Consciousness wants to explore to the fullest
Vital Truth: I EXPAND INTO SHARING AND CONNECTION, TRUSTING IN THE ABUNDANCE OF THE UNIVERSE	The higher understanding of how to thrive, that aligns you with the Flow of the Universe
Liberation: EXPERIENCING	The emancipating philosophy you freely embrace to enhance your connection to the Flow
Vitality Behavior: FREELY GIVING	The empowering and uplifting actions you intentionally choose to create your best life
Highest Purpose: VISION	How you serve the Greatest Good through embracing your encoded genius, and the source of your Vitality

Alchemy and The Higher Mind

The Higher Mind is a special room in your mind that becomes accessible when your heart portal is open. When the heart opens to feeling, intuition, compassion and love, you may finally reach this special place where your mind merges with that of your Higher Consciousness.

And from there you can gain access to the truths of the Universe, bringing invention and manifestation quickly into your reality. You are really here to be an alchemist, wielding energy to shape our reality towards the Greatest Good.

The Higher Mind may be accessed by focusing your attention on a specific location in the mind. I will direct you there. However, there is some preparation work you'll need to do first.

In Chapter Twelve, we will go over some methods for quieting the mind and connecting to the heart, which are at the center of developing a relationship with your Higher Consciousness – The Real You. You should begin there.

After you become familiar with your heart-based practices, next you will practice bringing your attention to the very center of your head, at the convergence point of front-to-back and side-to-side. The center of your mind is a quiet, neutral place, where you are not analyzing or reasoning, just perceiving.

From there, go up one inch, and back one and a half inches – this is the Higher Mind. It's as if the activation of the heart portal includes a lightswitch to the Higher Mind. Imagine both the heart and this place in the mind lit up like a sun.

This is the place where all things are possible. The heart floods with love energy, and the mind becomes its most creative, its most elegant, its most vast.

Seating yourself in the heart and Higher Mind begins activating the pineal gland in the brain, the seat of psychic sensibilities. This is often calcified from disuse, so regular intentional practice is necessary. See new abilities come online such as clairvoyance, clairaudience and more.

This is actually you coming to communicate with your Higher Consciousness and the Universe beyond.

Your access to your Higher Mind is what exponentially expands your Wisdom. Your connection to love is the key that unlocks your true power. With this, you move out of the realm of the technician, and into the realm of a true master. Much like in Star Wars, you move from being a Jedi student who shows promise but can't access The Force, to the Jedi Master who wields It like a maestro.

This is how you step into your full power as The Sage.

A Sage for This Age

We are at a most exciting, pivotal time in human history. Consciousness is expanding greatly. Many, many people are calling out for a world with more love, more integrity, more health, more balance, more connection to nature. As a Type 5, you are poised to make great contributions in this time.

As Consciousness advances, we need new insights, new philosophies, new inventions. You will have a role to play in this.

For as much as you would prefer to remain solitary and detached, you actually have what it takes to be a great leader. Your calm lucidity combined with vast knowledge, inspired thought and diverse experience would benefit any organization.

Nevertheless, Type 5s seem in general to prefer a less conspicuous, quietly influential role. These are our advisors, our scientists and physicists, our engineers. Inventors. Artisans. Philosophers. Your pursuit of the deep truths makes you an important person to know.

Even if you do not have a career that contributes directly in this particular way, if you are Consciousness-Directed, you are indeed still the deliverer of Wisdom. You could be the janitor at the Elementary School, quietly sweeping floors and fixing leaks, yet the conversations you'd have with the people around you would touch them and change them.

Just going through the world, connected to your heart and Higher Mind, and allowing yourself to connect and interact, you would bring Wisdom to your community.

In the Ego-Driven state, your impulse would have been to hoard your knowledge and make those who want it pay for the privilege. But as The Sage, you are the wise one that all the villages rely on to guide them and help them. Your wisdom is for sharing, elevating, and advancing.

Type 5, you are the one who brings these things into the world. Where would we be without your curiosity, knowledge and inventions? Yet remember, your understanding and influence can only be as elevated as your consciousness. The deeper you anchor into your heart and The Real You, the truer your wisdom becomes.

In the hands of Your Vitality Personality – fully connected to your heart while silencing the Ego mind – you are an exciting and inspiring innovator who pushes the limits of the known, making you a respected and honored Sage:

- Balancing deep investigation with uplifting, enlivening experiences
- Present and attuned to the feelings and needs of others
- Honoring the rhythms of life, living in a balanced, harmonious way
- Work that allows you to feel engaged and inspired
- Sharing your insights, feelings, and resources generously
- Feeling connected to a Higher Purpose and a sense of meaning

Most people are distracted and preoccupied with pop culture, headlines, social media, and all the messy chaotic emotions these evoke – leaving little room for deep questions and complex answers. Their sensibilities are numbed from the stress of modern life. They don't know how to change, how to find a new way. They feel trapped.

You are the one who is built to serve the world by engaging your natural abilities to deepen understanding, expand vision, and invent new creations.

However, you can only act as a Sage if you truly hold wisdom, rather than merely knowing information. This comes from personal experience, and not just what can be read or observed from afar. Rather than intellectualizing, you must be willing to participate and connect. Rather than withholding yourself and your resources from others, you must communicate and share in an open exchange. In this way you serve your Highest Purpose: bringing Wisdom to the world.

Your Vital Truth

Your **Vital Truth is the Higher understanding of how to thrive by aligning with Universal principles.** It is the escape hatch your Ego doesn't want you to know about, because it unlocks all of its Survival Programming, and connects you to your Higher Consciousness – The Real You.

> ➤ Your Vital Truth is **I expand into sharing and connection, trusting in the abundance of the Universe.**

This Vital Truth is the contradiction of your Survival Belief. Whereas endorsing your Survival Belief leads you directly to resistance, self-sabotage and erosion, embracing your Vital Truth places you in the Flow of the Universe. This leads you directly towards your happiest, healthiest life – Vitality!

However, your unconscious is encoded to automatically revert to the Survival Belief. To replace this with the Vital Truth takes conscious intention and daily practice.

Although this Vital Truth is a brief, simple statement, it is dense with meaning. Let's take a moment to unpack this.

Expanding Yourself

Right away you can see you're being asked to commit yourself to opening up and growing – the very opposite of the Contraction your Survival Programming predisposes you to.

This sounds uncomfortable and intimidating at first. The good news is that you don't have to start out opening up to other people. You can begin with yourself.

The real expansion that is being asked of you is in your heart. It is time to open your portal with the ringing frequencies that are the key.

In order to expand yourself, you might begin with a gratitude practice. Gratitude is a very high, clear frequency which connects you to your Higher Consciousness. Gratitude allows you to open up the portal and draw more of your own potent essence within your body.

Here is an example of a gratitude exercise you might try incorporating into your daily routine:

Gratitude Exercise

- Close your eyes
- Breathe in through your nose for a count of 6, hold in your belly for a count of 7, breathe out through the mouth for a count of 8. Do this 3 times.
- Call up in your mind's eye the face of someone you are grateful to. Someone who went out of their way to help you, or who was kind to you, or who taught you something important.
- In your heart, thank them. Tell them what they did for you, and what it meant to you. Tell them how it helped you and changed you. Let yourself really feel the

gratitude of it, the magnitude of it. Let it open your chest and your body. You can even let it make you cry. It is very good for you to let your whole nervous system be flooded with this feeling.
- Try to sit with this feeling and just breathe for 5 minutes.

Surely you can spare 5 minutes a day to begin connecting to your heart and feeling it open up. As you continue with this, it will become easier and less uncomfortable. Within days of beginning this practice you can expect some sort of surprising experience that will show you how you are attracting something new and exciting into your life.

This small practice is enough to begin an energy stream towards a new trajectory. As new and interesting experiences present themselves, allow yourself to go with them with an amused curiosity. This is expanding yourself – opening your heart.

Sharing and Connection

Whereas The Programmed You felt a strong impulse towards protecting yourself by closing yourself off, The Real You is powerful and understands its own eternal nature, and has no need to protect Itself from anything. When you are seated in your heart's power you will easily open yourself to other people and unknown experiences.

Sharing

The unwillingness to share reveals the underlying scarcity mentality, that belief there isn't enough to go around so you'd better only look out for yourself. A sense of generosity derives from a place of strength, a belief that you will always be all right, and that the Flow brings back to you what you put out.

Connection

In classic Type 5 extremism, deep connection is both the thing that you abhor as well as the thing you crave the most. You want to feel the belonging that would ease your anxiety and soothe your nervous system, yet your Survival Programming speaks loudly to you, stopping you from reaching out.

All of this dissolves away as you become more comfortable with connecting with your heart and allowing yourself to feel your feelings. Many Type 5s find this idea terrifying, because they know how much they've been holding it back and for how long, and they are afraid they will be destroyed in the crush of it.

That is now how feelings really work. Feelings are just energy, their natural state is Flow. If there is a big charge at the initial contact with a feeling, it dissipates and neutralizes quickly. It will not harm you. The more you allow your feelings to Flow, the less and less charge any of them really hold. It's your fear of feelings that make them seem so big.

As always, connecting with yourself is what enables you to begin connecting with other people. The more in touch with feelings you are, the more you will be able to relate to other people.

In truth, Type 5, you are actually encoded with some quite magical tendencies toward empathy. As we will discuss more in the upcoming section about your Highest Purpose, your mind is equally connected to logic as it is to intuition (which is really your mind making sense of what the heart is saying).

You are not only an analytical thinker, but you are also able to extrapolate and visualize, surmise and feel into the truth of things. That is intuition. That is heart. That is CONNECTION. If you wanted to, you are quite capable of feeling into other people and finding the truth of what is there. And the humanity and beauty of it will quite surprise you.

Trusting in Abundance

Oh wow the words Trust and Abundance are not really in a typical Type 5's vocabulary. But if you are reading this, you are certainly not typical.

Trust

Again, a lack of trust reveals that underlying scarcity mentality. Because if you understood how powerful you really are, you would most certainly trust in yourself and your own ability to successfully navigate the Flow.

Developing a sense of trust begins with connecting to your Higher Consciousness. This is most easily done in meditation or hypnosis, where the trance state induces you to let the conscious mind go quiet and allow your higher mind to take over. You may be quite startled at the experiences you might have. Visions, lucid dreams, messages and more can happen. These are powerful visceral experiences you can't easily explain away.

The sense of eagerness and excitement that happens in these moments of connection are transforming. You will discover your sense of *knowingness*, which is quite different from anything intellectual. Knowingness is felt in your heart, in your body. Once you experience the difference, you begin to let go of anxiety and fear. The sense of knowingness is so certain, so safe, that you let go of doubt.

This is Trust – your connection to your Higher Consciousness and the Flow of the Universe which makes you feel powerful, certain, and safe.

Abundance

Understanding and trusting in Abundance is at the heart of how you can transform from The Miser to The Sage.

Abundance is the outpouring of love from Source to all of Its creations. It is the Flow itself, the great rush of life-giving energy that enervates us and our world. Abundance is the full, joyful, riotous thriving and expansion that happens when we open ourselves up to receiving love.

In our Ego-Driven state we think that abundance means money – lots and lots of cash. Well sure, money is an energy exchange so when you Flow, it flows. But that's only one small example.

Having lots of energy is Abundance. Having access to lots of help is Abundance.

Having lots of friends is Abundance. Having vibrant radiant health is Abundance. Having amazingly good luck and incredible synchronicities is Abundance. Abundance means that you know there are sparks of magic available to you at all times.

◆◆◆

It takes effort to embrace your Vital Truth. Your Ego is always trying to regain control over your mind, encouraging you to play small.

It is your belief in your Vital Truth which allows you to dismantle the workings of your Ego. It is what sets you free. Choosing self-love, choosing gratitude, choosing surrender and acceptance… these are what direct your life towards Vitality: the happy integration of your healthy body, awakened mind, and limitless spirit.

Your Liberation

Your **Liberation** is **the emancipating philosophy you freely embrace.** This is a powerful shift, out of the Survival Programming of the mind, and into the Flow of the Universe through the heart. Rather than being owned by a chronic Compulsion, you are now intentionally choosing this Liberation.

> Your Liberation is **Experiencing**

Experiencing means agreeing to let Life touch you. Instead of only intellectualizing about something, actually do it. For example, you can read about love, but you really won't understand it at all until you experience it.

Allowing yourself to participate, rather than just observe. Engaging in the unknown, without controlling the environment. Feeling, rather than intellectualizing. Having a robust, full life that engages your heart and body, as well as your mind.

Say Yes

When living as The Miser, your Survival Programming led you to believe it's much better to decline joining in. Safer. Tidier. Quieter. Simpler. Best to remain isolated and numb.

Yet, if you're really honest with yourself, isolated and numb doesn't suit you at all. For as much as you might be a quiet person, you are not built to have an anemic, small life. You have genius and greatness within you, and it would actually really delight you to have a community you could share it with.

Rather than remaining the intellectual observer who minimizes risk by closing themself off, begin to say Yes to Life.

Say Yes to Yourself

Instead of being stingy with yourself, let yourself have fun, pleasure, and delight! You actually love to laugh, be light-hearted, inspired, and at ease. What if you allowed yourself to experience these?

In what ways have you been denying your heart's desire? What would you need to do differently in order to move towards embracing it? Are you willing to do it? Say Yes.

Say Yes to Others

For as much as you've tried to keep yourself and be a bit of a loner, people actually really like you. You are fascinating company because you hold such a unique, insightful perspective. They want you to join them.

Say Yes!

Even if it feels uncomfortable sometimes or requires extra effort, you will be glad you went. You will experience them in an unexpected way when you let your heart lead you. If, when you see an opportunity to join in, you feel an initial pulse of excitement in your chest, that is your cue from your Higher Consciousness that it is an experience which leads to your happiest life.

Say Yes to the Universe

In the Ego-Driven state, Type 5s are attempting to have control over their life by keeping out as much "interference" as possible.

But in the Consciousness-Directed state, you understand that nothing is interference, it all has deep intentional meaning for you, if only you would open up and let it in.

There are no accidents, nothing is random, and you are never alone. You are connected to All That Is through a vast energetic net. Your life is a conversation with the Universe. If an experience is coming at you, it is absolutely intended for you. Don't close yourself off from it. Say Yes.

♦♦♦

If there is nothing else you get out of this book, Experiencing is the single most important shift you can make to bring your life into joyfulness. If you were just to begin allowing yourself to open up and join in, everything else will fall easily into place, because you will have moved into the Flow of the Universe.

Your Vitality Behavior

Vitality Behavior is the empowering and uplifting actions you intentionally choose when you are Consciousness-Directed, rather than the Destructive Behavior your Ego drives you to act out.

> Your Vitality Behavior is **Freely Giving.**

Freely Giving means being openly generous, trusting that your love and goodness always Flows back to you.

Freely Giving aligns with Abundance, a primary principle of the Universe. When you are in the Flow, you will always have whatever you need. When you give freely, you are in a state of affection, friendliness, warmth, helpfulness, camaraderie, trust. Your heart is open.

This concept of Freely Giving is probably a challenging one for you to get behind. All of your Survival Programming is against it. You are likely hearing lots of mental chatter about how you can't afford to give. This is your Ego-Driven impulse to Withhold.

Let's return to that list of common resources that, as The Miser, you would have wanted to hoard, and how this looks instead when you are The Sage, Freely Giving.

Freely Giving Your Money

This concept is perhaps a bit gut-wrenching at first for a Type 5. It speaks right to the heart of the scarcity mindset that is the Ego's homebase.

It's not that The Miser won't spend money ever. It's just that they only want to spend it on themself — they spend their money primarily on survival needs and the things they covet.

It's the idea of generosity in particular that is the problem area. Spending money on what *you* consider to be *non-essential* is painful for you.

Don't worry, the move into Consciousness-Directedness does not require that you suddenly start giving all your money away to prove what an enlightened person you are. You don't have anything to prove to anyone else. This is entirely an internal conversation with yourself.

And the question you are in the middle of asking yourself is: What if I felt totally stable and confident in myself and my ability to successfully navigate this world? Would I still feel so afraid to share my wealth?

As you develop a relationship with your Higher Consciousness in your heart, accessing untold levels of wisdom and power through the Higher Mind, you will find yourself becoming joyful. You will feel strong. It will start to feel like a celebration. You will find yourself happily treating somebody to dinner, or giving a gift for no reason.

When you don't feel so threatened, you will not feel such a need to conserve what you have. When you feel awake, alive, abundant, excited, the question of generosity and Freely Giving is a no-brainer.

Freely Giving Your Stuff

Let's translate this more specifically to say It's Time to Get Rid of the Stuff You've Been Hoarding.

You can sell it on eBay if you like – you don't really have to give it all away for free. But all the random stuff you've been "collecting" or "saving" but that does not serve any sort of purpose and is in a box somewhere must go.

Remember, this intense Type 5 attachment to things is the child's attempt to soothe itself. All the stuff piling up in the basement, the garage, the closet, the drawers... every single item is really your version of a baby blanket. It's you trying to make yourself feel less vulnerable, less small, less alone.

But now you're coming to understand that you are not vulnerable, you are eternal. You are not small, you are infinite. And you are never alone, and always deeply known and loved. You don't need material objects to serve as a poor substitute for connection and power when you have the real thing.

Freely Giving Your Intellectual Property

So Type 5s know a lot of unusual information about a number of unusual topics, and become the go-to-guys when others need access to this.

No, you are not required to never earn a buck from the expertise you've cultivated! By all means, get paid what you're worth, and feel great about it.

But... how about agreeing to be a mentor, or a teacher? How about some open office hours? How about a chat on YouTube?

As The Sage, you step into the role of the community wise-one. They look to you for help and guidance, and you open-heartedly give it.

The way you are – intelligent, curious, focused, intense – is all in service to helping you become The Sage, a role which is meant to benefit all. When you embody this great aspect of The Real You, you are happy to share your wisdom with everyone.

Freely Giving Your Personal Information

Please, do not start handing out your social security number all over the place in your desire to become Consciousness-Directed. In this era of data breaches, it's true you do need to be discerning about who has access to you.

So be discerning. Giving your email and cell phone to corporations you don't know anything about? Perhaps not. Giving them to your co-worker who is offering to connect? Certainly.

There is no need for knee-jerk resistance to letting anyone know anything about you. No harm will come from somebody knowing what part of town you live in, or that you have two cats. There is no need to treat regular people as if they are dangerous characters hoping to use your personal info against you.

Trust. Trust in yourself, and your ability to attract positive outcomes. Trust in other people and their desire to live harmoniously. Trust in the Universe, and the beauty that comes from living openly, from the heart.

Freely Giving Your Inner Life

Again, all things in moderation. No, you're not expected to suddenly start telling the cashier at the gas station about how it felt when your alcoholic mother raged at you when you were a child.

But have you ever told anyone?

This is not about oversharing with strangers. This is about letting the people in your life really know you. Giving them access to The Real You.

Talk about yourself, to your family, to your friends, to your partner, to your kids. Let them know about your memories, your desires, your feelings, your needs. Don't keep it all locked down. Don't keep them locked out.

To be perfectly frank, many Type 5s struggle with bouts of despair and depression. This is largely brought on from the sense of isolation, of disconnection, of meaninglessness. What you are being asked for here is the healing of this, the eradication of this.

Reach out, open up, connect – and you will discover an enormous depth of meaning. It is your connection with others – in love, in generosity, in fun, in earnest – that will bring light into your life.

♦♦♦

Give yourself to the day, whatever it is asking of you. Rather than shutting down, hiding away, and withholding yourself, remind yourself that you are here to serve the Greatest Good in your own special way. You are here to experience love and light in physical form, and if you freely give it, you will endlessly receive it.

Your Highest Purpose

You chose to be here, in this time and place, because you wanted to contribute something. You came here for a reason, and you chose your Personality Type because it was the one that would help you accomplish it. **Your Personality Type has a special set of talents and abilities, and you wanted to use them to make a contribution. This is your Highest Purpose.**

> Your Highest Purpose is **Vision.**

Vision refers to your capacity for depth and vastness of understanding of elusive concepts, and the ability to see their potential for great benefit. It is the combination of your intellect and imagination, your understanding and your intuition, your heart and Higher Mind, your wisdom and your magic.

This is the true reason you came here, all encoded to be the curious one. You may have considered yourself a misfit, because mainstream thought and lifestyle never interested you much. But it is not your purpose to be conventional, superficial and unquestioning. It is your Purpose to show us the way.

You are the visionary, the one who changes worlds through changing mindset.

Your creative inventions and solutions are a light in the darkness. You are a wayshower. You are The Sage.

Here is how you come to fully embody a life of Vision and Wisdom:

A Beautiful Mind

The Type 5 mind is special. Its abilities go well beyond just memorizing, analysis and computing. It is much more like a lava lamp, than a circuit board. Information, questions, and methods commingle with ideas, intuitions, and half-remembered dreams. It is the real supercomputer that Silicon Valley can only long for, plugged in to all of Consciousness.

The Type 5 mind is such a vast expanse that it's easy to get lost in there. Most will confess to occasionally losing track of time to the point where they don't know what day it is and can't remember when they last bathed. It is quite as if they have been astral traveling, while their body remained behind.

The shift into becoming fully present and self-aware will require you to gain mastery over this. Rather than getting lost in the mind, you must learn to direct it with intention.

You would greatly benefit from developing a meditation practice. And not just any meditation practice. You need an alchemy practice. Check out monroeinstitute.org or masteringalchemy.com.

Imagine how much more effective you would be if you had skills which allowed you to feel mentally ordered and calm, while remaining emotionally connected. If the visions that come to you are crystal clear and at lighting speed, so that you don't have to lose yourself in a haze for hours. If your mental platform felt grounded and stable, so that you could leave and return to your query as needed without losing momentum.

Disciplining your mind and becoming adept at creating at-will are the keys that unlock your full potential. It could become much easier to keep yourself feeling clear and present while still retaining full access to your dreamy, mystical side.

An Open Heart

Your Highest Purpose is Vision, and that does not come from a clinical mind. Vision comes from exploring the heart.

Type 5, your relationship to your feelings determines your degree of connectedness to your Higher Consciousness. And your degree of connection to your Higher Consciousness is the amount of Flow you experience in your life. And the amount of Flow you experience in your life determines how expansive is your Vision.

You cannot access the deep Universal Truths while you are only intellectualizing. Truth is felt in the heart.

In order to align yourself with your Highest Purpose, you must become willing to feel your feelings. As long as you resist and close yourself off from this enormous aspect of yourself, you are blocked from the higher understanding you desire.

Feelings will not overcome you, as you fear. They pass through you. Let them come without judgment and let them go.

This takes practice. We do much work in this area in our private group, called the Vitality Voyagers.

> Check out **www.yourvitalitypersonality.com/membership**

Opening up your heart does not come easily to you – it feels foreign and scary. This may feel humbling, to be an inexperienced novice. But surrender, and let yourself be humble.

Open yourself up to life with wonder, and awe. Be grateful. Be dazzled. It will change your life.

An Engaged Body

Vision is not only an expanded mind and open heart. There is another component – the *knowingness* that you feel in your body.

Your body talks to you. You can perceive a sense of rightness, of certainty, when you *know* something to be true. Developing your ability to tune into your body and feel the wisdom there will greatly expand your relationship to yourself and your world.

When Ego-Driven, Type 5s are usually extremely disconnected from their bodies. They try to function as a mind only, ignoring the body.

Again, living in resistance to a major aspect of yourself blocks you from attaining higher insight and wisdom. As long as you are not living as a complete being – equally centered in the heart, the mind, and the body – you cannot access elevated dimensions of understanding and Vision.

There are so many ways to begin cultivating a deeper connection to your body. Yoga stretches, self-massage, breath work, sound healing, and walks in nature are all ways to begin tuning into your body and your physical senses.

Becoming fully present and self-aware is essential for your advancement out of The Miser and into The Sage. Let yourself inhabit your body – you will be astonished at all it will teach you about yourself.

♦♦♦

Well, Type 5, you've been given quite a lot of information about yourself to digest. But hopefully by now you've come to see that even though you are wired to act out Your Primal Persona, it is possible for you to be someone so much more magnificent than that – Your Vitality Personality.

Now is the time to decide who you want to be in this world. If you are ready to step into the full power of who you really are, and create your best life... then your next step is **Integration.** See Chapter Eleven.

CHAPTER SEVEN
PERSONALITY TYPE 6
THE GUARDIAN | THE ALARMIST

THE GUARDIAN
YOUR VITALITY PERSONALITY — CONSCIOUSNESS-DIRECTED

- **Vital Truth:** I open myself to all experiences, trusting that everything in the Universe serves the Greatest Good
- **Highest Purpose:** Integrity
- **Theme:** TRUST
- **6**
- **Distorted Theme:** FEAR
- **Liberation:** Steadying
- **Vitality Behavior:** Discerning
- **Compulsion:** Fearing the Worst
- **Destructive Behavior:** Suspecting
- **Sabotage Pattern:** Over-Reacting
- **Survival Belief:** I can survive by remaining hyper-vigilant against threat

THE ALARMIST
YOUR PRIMAL PERSONA — EGO-DRIVEN

Welcome Type 6, it's exciting that you're here. Your inner coding has likely made you miserable enough to drive you to seek a way out and – good news! – these teachings are it.

But conversely, it is the same inner coding which will make it extremely difficult for you to implement the changes necessary. This is because you are wired, not only to live in a permanent state of fear, but also to believe that being afraid is the smartest way to be. However, the guidance here is all about learning to trust – discovering how to let go of your egoic mind and listen instead to the wisdom of the heart. This will feel risky and scary to you, and yet, it is your only path to peace.

If you have been led here, then it is because you are ready to take a quantum leap ahead of your other Type 6 peers. The wisdom and insight you will gain here will propel you into an awareness far more advanced than most. This will benefit the entire world, for you are the one built to be the protector of truth and integrity, which will stabilize us all in a way that fear never could.

This chapter focuses on the dual nature of your Personality Type 6, and the primary factors that hinder or help your ability to thrive. You will totally love the descriptions about your highest potential and purpose… but you will totally not love reading about your dark side, called Your Primal Persona.

Hang in there! We intentionally go through the Primal Persona stuff first, so that you can finish on a high note – the magnificence that is Your Vitality Personality.

Give yourself permission to surrender to this process, and you will see how it takes you on a journey, getting richer and richer the further it goes. The part of you that craves inner peace will quickly come to see the massive value and advancement you will receive from your newly gained higher understanding.

DECODE YOUR SURVIVAL PROGRAMMING

As we just learned, **Your Primal Persona is the version of you that exists when you allow your Ego to unconsciously drive your thoughts, feelings and actions.** It is the operating system of your survival-oriented mind, limiting you from tapping into the love and light that is your Higher Consciousness.

In this state, you are closed off from your sense of love for yourself or others. And the actions you take from this place only serve to fulfill the Survival Programming of the small, fearful you. This can be really uncomfortable to face, but it is critical to see clearly so that you can gain freedom from this dark influence.

The bottom half of your Mandala spells out the dynamics of Your Primal Persona and its Ego-Driven Survival Programming:

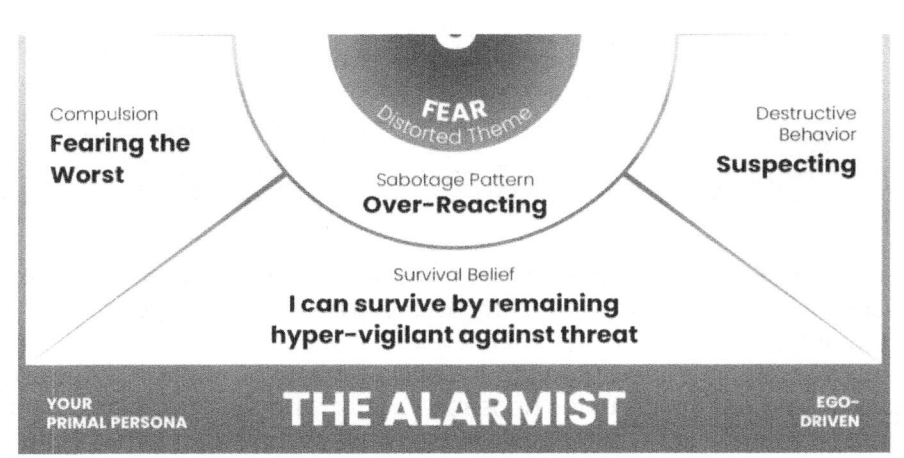

Compulsion
Fearing the Worst

Distorted Theme
FEAR

Sabotage Pattern
Over-Reacting

Destructive Behavior
Suspecting

Survival Belief
I can survive by remaining hyper-vigilant against threat

YOUR PRIMAL PERSONA
THE ALARMIST
EGO-DRIVEN

Your Primal Persona: The Alarmist

As a Type 6,

> Your Primal Persona is known as **The Alarmist**.

This is your Ego's version of "playing small," even though its programming is all about being safe. But, as we will now explore, a fear-based scramble for security and an inner sense of stability are not at all the same thing.

See *Fig. 7A* for a brief summary of your Ego-Driven Survival Programming (we will dig deeper into it in just a moment). It is characterized by resistance, eroding your Vitality and degrading your life.

These are some painful truths. But you must forgive yourself for your Survival Programming. Have compassion for yourself, for it was the pain in your life which led you to feel that you couldn't survive without this perspective. Without self-awareness, you had no choice but to behave this way.

And this is true for everyone else, as well. We all deserve forgiveness for the way we act when we are asleep to ourselves -- we are totally unaware this is what we are doing and how much it hurts ourselves and those we love.

Even once you are aware of your Survival Programming, it can be quite challenging to take command over it. Yet every degree of progress you make in this direction brings you enormous reward. You will be joyfully inspired to continue the work.

Fig. 7A **PERSONALITY TYPE 6 SURVIVAL PROGRAMMING**
Your Primal Persona: THE ALARMIST
The Programmed You; The limited and diminished version of yourself that you default to when you are Ego-Driven
Distorted Theme: FEAR
Your Ego's warped and downgraded interpretation of your true Theme
Survival Belief: I CAN SURVIVE BY REMAINING HYPER-VIGILANT AGAINST THREAT
The scarcity-oriented message embedded in your Ego that creates your world view
Compulsion: FEARING THE WORST
The repetitive internal process you instantly launch as a way of discharging the emotional tension caused by your Survival Belief
Destructive Behavior: SUSPECTING
The ruinous actions you regularly engage in when you operate according to your Survival Belief
Sabotage Pattern: OVER-REACTING
The totality of all your Survival Programming combined into an overall template for self-destruction

Let's dive just a little bit deeper into what these dynamics of your Survival Programming really mean, so that you may begin the most rewarding journey of integrating yourself.

Your Distorted Theme

Each of the 9 Personality Types orient around a particular **Theme**. The whole point of you being here, at this time and in this place, is because you wanted to explore this Theme. This is the thing you are encoded to care about the most.

> Your Theme is **Trust**.

We will fully explore the true meaning of Trust in the next section (about Your Vitality Personality), when we discuss the Consciousness-Directed understanding of your Theme.

But right now, we are discussing your Survival Programming, and how your Ego *degrades* your understanding of your Theme of Trust.

Unfortunately, when Your Primal Persona interprets this Theme, **it becomes contorted – a warped, downgraded version of your highest potential.** This is called the **Distorted Theme.**

> Your Distorted Theme is **Fear**.

Fear is the most primal, survival-oriented state you can live in. It creates a constant need to seek out safety, yet never allows you to feel any peace.

Fear is a total inability to trust, which completely blocks you from accessing the ease and peace that exists within the Flow of the Universe. You don't trust yourself and your own abilities to cope effectively with stressors. You don't trust other people to behave with integrity or competence. And you don't trust that your Higher Consciousness and the Universe will take care of you. This completely destroys your chances for stability and peace of mind.

Fear famously provokes a fight-or-flight response, and you likely embody both of these aspects. However, one is more dominant and strongly influences how you seem to other people.

The flight response to fear is known as *phobic*. This means you tend to cower in your fear, making your life smaller and more limited in order to try and feel safe. You fear authority figures, and are unwilling to take risks or try new or unusual things. You come across to others as worried and anxious.

The other fear response is to fight, known as being *counter-phobic*. This means you tend to be angry at the things that make you feel anxious. This is a much more confrontational and aggressive style. You don't trust authority figures, and you generally take a contrary point of view. You may even become a dare-devil in your attempt to deny your fear. You come across to others as ornery and belligerent.

When your entire being is operating within a permanent state of fear, it is impossible to think rationally. Even though the Type 6 is entirely mind-oriented – striving to use logic and reason to make sense of the world – the underlying assumption that the world is not safe warps your ability to think clearly. The mind is already influenced by a fear agenda, not a neutral one.

In other words, the mind will constantly invent reasons for being afraid, and convince you this is a reasonable concern. It makes it extremely difficult for you to discern the likeliness or reasonability of your fears. These can even become phobias, which are completely irrational fears that seem incredibly valid and important. If your mind is looking for monsters, you will convince yourself you see them in every corner.

In response to their fear, many Type 6s attempt to take refuge in the physical world. Refuting the existence of anything which they cannot see with their own eyes and touch with their own hands, they want all of the world to prove itself through being measurable and tangible.

But relying on human senses to be the ultimate authority on reality is entirely unrealistic, because they are quite faulty. You can't necessarily see or touch energy, but it makes up all of existence. What do energy waves look like to the naked eye? Or electricity? Or wind? Or gravity? Or time? Or emotions? Or the soul? Or the law of attraction? These are all factors which create our reality. The human senses are quite limited mechanisms for perceiving everything that's really going on. You have to *feel* your way, using much more subtle methods, but the Ego-Driven Type 6 doesn't trust these.

The Ego is content to trap you inside this loop for all of your life: forever trying to make things safe, but never experiencing a lasting sense of peace or trust.

Rather than believing that the Universe will naturally bring stability and security to your reality if you create the internal space for it, your Ego prompts you to insist on external proof. As you will soon see, Fear does not create a safe reality… it blocks you from it.

In the hands of Your Primal Persona – The Alarmist – you spend all your time fearing the worst and suspecting, believing you are creating integrity and safety by controlling everything, but instead are introducing factors which degrade stability:

- Relying solely on logic and intellect, you close down your heart and smother your intuition, blocking your access to your Higher Consciousness – the true source of wisdom
- Distrusting your own internal knowingness, you seek out research and the opinions of others to try to make decisions, blocking your inner guidance which is the most accurate way to know what is best for you
- Highly invested in thinking of the world as a dangerous and malicious place, it is nearly impossible for you to relax and enjoy yourself
- Constantly seeking ways to cope with a difficult reality, you create a lifestyle of perpetually managing stress – but never eliminating it
- Suspicious and mistrustful, you treat outsiders as having dubious integrity and ulterior motives, destroying trust and respect
- Once you've given your trust to the people and organizations you deem insiders, you dogmatically insist on their integrity and legitimacy, without asking deeper questions or listening to your intuition

Although Fear drives you to feel certain of the accuracy of your thoughts, this is only your Ego taking full control of your mind. Because even though it has you thinking you must always create safety and security outside of yourself, it is exactly this belief which causes everything to destabilize.

This is no fun at all to read about. It's a bummer to realize your default, unconscious wiring is a sadly small version of who you could really be – who you actually are. The Real You is powerful and full of radiant love and light, enjoying connection and getting to interact on the physical plane. You are on your way to discovering how to access this higher aspect of yourself.

Your Survival Belief

Your **Survival Belief** is the **scarcity-oriented message embedded in your Ego that creates your world view.** It is the secret programming in the basement of your unconscious which drives all your thoughts, feelings, and actions without you ever realizing it.

> ➤ Your Survival Belief is **I can survive by remaining hyper-vigilant against threat.**

This belief is fundamental to you, even though you never knew it was there. It defines your understanding of how the world works.

Typically, this Survival Belief is activated within you at a young age. As a child you likely endured something terrifying or horrible that destroyed your sense of security. It might have been a single event, or it might have been an ongoing frightening environment.

This would have triggered in you a deep mistrust of the world, feeling unsure of who or what you can count on. It caused you to believe that people are malicious, ineffective, and deceptive, and that it is unwise to freely accept them at their word or believe in their competence. And it made you believe that your world could be destroyed in an instant. In response, you adopted a survival strategy of making yourself as stable and reliable as possible, while never relying on anyone else, and it's never occurred to you to re-examine it as an adult.

You may read your Survival Belief and think to yourself, *Well yes, of course! What's wrong with making myself and my life as stable and secure as possible? That's the smart way to be!*

Unfortunately, this single Survival Belief sentence is a template for your destruction! Your mind, body, and spirit all suffer as the result of this strategy. Let's unpack all the ways in which this Survival Belief sets you up for problems, rather than the solutions you think it does.

Hyper-Vigilance

Remaining hyper-vigilant means being "on watch" 24/7. Just considering it is exhausting!

Hyper-vigilance of the mind creates an endless loop of worrisome mental chatter.

It is constantly analyzing, evaluating and second-guessing. It never arrives at a solution – just provides an endless stream of doubts, questions, and worries.

Mental chatter blocks you from the grounding comfort of your body, and the deep truth and wisdom of your heart. Many Type 6s turn to pharmaceuticals such as anti-depressants and anti-anxiety meds in an attempt to quell their unrelentingly negative mind.

Hyper-Vigilance creates a high level of tension in the body, a sense of being tightly coiled and ready to spring into action. Most Type 6s channel this into a very intense work ethic – running errands, doing chores, creating excess tasks – all as a way of trying to discharge the frenetic energy in their body.

This also makes it very difficult for you to relax. Even when you're trying to take down time because you can feel how overwrought you are, it's as if your body won't let go. This is because, in the background, the mind is still on high alert.

All of this effort managing the hyperactivity of the body and mind leads you to completely abandon your heart and your inner world – which is actually how you could be accessing your own sense of knowingness. It is your feelings, not your thoughts, which guide you towards elegant solutions and provide you with the sense of peace you so desperately crave. But your Ego convinces you these are unreliable and untrustworthy, leading you far away from yourself.

Threat

It is extremely important to understand that your beliefs create your reality. What you focus on is what expands – you create more of whatever you give your attention to. So if you are always watching out for problems, more and more problems are exactly what you will receive. Constantly watching out for threats has you focusing on how to survive, but never on how to thrive.

Type 6s have a rather pessimistic worldview. They are deep believers in Murphy's Law: *Everything that can go wrong, will go wrong*. This is only true because you make it true. If you were to say to yourself *Everything always works out for me*, then that is the reality you would experience instead. But your Survival Belief tells you that you would be naive and stupid to think like that.

Believing that the world is a harsh place causes you to accept that life is *supposed* to be stressful. This is really dangerous for you, because it keeps you in a loop of managing stress, but never resolving it. Even though Type 6s think they are problem-solvers, usually they are really problem-perpetuators. You're not really trying to fix things, you're trying to survive them. This blocks your life from ever getting any easier or happier.

So for example, taking pills to block you from feeling your stress is not the same thing as changing your thoughts which create the stress. Holding on to a job you dislike because it's reliable and known is not the same thing as choosing a job which creates joy and abundance. Staying in relationships with people you don't enjoy because it seems safer or expected is not the same thing as trusting in yourself to create new, happy and healthy relationships. You're not resolving anything, and instead are keeping the misery going by always assuming a threat is looming.

Fear of Change

Believing that you must always remain hyper-vigilant against threat leads you to prefer the devil-you-know, rather than the one you don't know. In other words, you only ever want to deal with things which are familiar, because you fear that changes could only make things worse.

This creates in you intense attachment to tradition, to doing things how they've always been done. At least, you call it honoring tradition, which makes it sound noble. But often what you're calling tradition is really just fear of anything new and different.

Certainly there is a place for tradition, and holding on to the parts of life you find beautiful and uplifting. But also you must remember that the world has been entirely run by Ego-Driven people all along, who have never had the Greatest Good in mind. The people in charge, who created our religious, political, and social systems, were not necessarily honorable people. Are you sure continuing to do it their way is best?

Often, nostalgia and longing for the "simplicity" of the past is basically just wishing you could be a child again, before you realized how complex the world really is. But in truth the world was never simpler or easier. The same Ego-Driven motives for power and status have always been at work. Name an era which did not include corruption, manipulation, violence and domination.

Nostalgia for the past is really just a wish for a different reality – which can only lie ahead of you, in the future. Resisting change is resisting creating the life you really want. You have just never been willing to believe that you have within yourself the power to bring about exactly the reality you desire.

Preferring Hierarchy

Because your unconscious is wired to want the world to feel safe, you prefer systems of hierarchy, with nice clear labels on everything. Knowing where everybody stands, and what the rules of the game are, makes you feel secure.

Hierarchy is indeed used to create order and stability in the Universe. However, when the Universe creates a hierarchy, it is a hierarchy of *function*. From a subatomic particle to an overarching structure, all pieces of the puzzle have their specific tasks to perform, and are therefore equally important.

When the Type 6 Ego takes hold of this concept, however, it gets downgraded into a belief that the hierarchy indicates a ladder of *value* – where the subatomic particle is considered lowly and insignificant, and the overarching structure holds the highest status.

This assigning value to people and things based on how "high" they are in the hierarchy creates a world of polarity: good and bad, right and wrong, insiders and outsiders. This makes you feel like you understand what is expected of you and how to get ahead *i.e.* become "safe."

Unfortunately it is also very likely to lead to revolution, where nothing feels safe, because the have-nots won't all agree to stay in their lowly place. In your desire to lean on hierarchy as a means of stability, you endorse a system that fosters hostility, not peace.

The Type 6 likes to pick a side and stick to it. Both the empire and the rebellion contain a throng of Type 6s holding fast to their beliefs about who is the threat, and who is safe, who is the insider, and who is the outsider. Unfortunately, the only thing that happens when you pick a side is war.

All of the Universe exists as a spectrum of Consciousness — which is made of love and light. No matter how small the piece of Consciousness, it holds the exact same value as any other.

In the Universe, there is no such thing as good and bad, right and wrong, or insiders and outsiders. All of life was created by Source and is all loved and accepted exactly how it is, because that's how it was designed. Even if you find things messy and confusing, if you trusted in the Universe and your Higher Consciousness, you would allow them to exist without judgment or fear.

In truth, peace only exists at the paradox in between the poles, surrendering to and navigating the Flow of the Universe. You don't need hierarchy in order to make sense of your world, and you don't need to pick a side. You just need to know how to access The Real You, who will guide you towards exactly the right thing for *you*.

♦♦♦

As you can see, your Survival Belief that you must always watch out for danger is at the heart of much difficulty and self-sabotage for you. It is this belief which launches a cascade of repetitive thoughts and behaviors, that ultimately lead to your unhappiness. Learning about these, and how to take hold of them, is fundamental to becoming able to create a life you love.

If you have read this far, you are doing so well! Thank you for hanging in there, this stuff is definitely not fun to face. Remember, we are in the thick of the section about the Ego's Survival Programming. But then we will move ahead to discuss Type 6 at your highest and best.

We just finished discussing your Type 6 Survival Belief, which was activated somewhere in your childhood. It is the primary driver behind all of your unconscious thoughts and behaviors.

Now, we will look at the most common thought, feeling and behavior patterns that emerge as a result of holding your Survival Belief.

Your Compulsion

Your **Compulsion** is the **repetitive internal process you instantly launch as a way of discharging the emotional tension caused by your Survival Belief.**

➢ Your Compulsion is **Fearing the Worst.**

This Compulsion is much like a guilty addiction – you know you should give it up, but don't want to... because you privately love it. And even if you decide *That's it, I'm through with this...* you will still find it very difficult to stop, until you become able to embrace your Vital Truth (see the upper half of your Mandala), rather than your Survival Belief.

Fearing the Worst means spending an enormous amount of time and energy imagining bad things happening. Not only is this a totally miserable and terrifying way to live, but it is also in complete opposition to the Flow of the Universe. In other words, it doesn't build up your Vitality, it destroys it.

As long as you are bought-in to your Ego-Driven Survival Belief that you must remain hyper-vigilant against threat, then this Compulsion of Fearing the Worst will continue to happen, against your will. There is no point in trying to control the Compulsion. Instead, you need to let go of the Survival Belief, embracing your Vital Truth and Liberation (these are listed in the upper half of your Mandala, which we will discuss shortly.)

Fearing the Worst is destructive to your own wellbeing in several fundamental ways:

Attracting Unattractive Outcomes

Whatever your mind envisions, it attracts. So if you are spending all your time imaging terrible outcomes, that is what you are calling to yourself like a boomerang. In order to shift this dynamic, you must begin noticing yourself doing it.

Because Fearing the Worst is a totally unconscious impulse, it's possible this is going on and on in your mind without you even noticing yourself. This is the mental chatter that is happening in the background in all your quiet moments – when you're driving, when you're doing chores, when you're trying to relax.

The way to notice yourself is to recognize the feelings this unconscious chatter is provoking in you. You may not notice your thoughts, but you definitely perceive the feeling of panic that is rising up. Or the physical feelings of tension in your belly, jaw, or neck and shoulders. Let this become the alarm bell, reminding you to pay attention to what your mind is doing.

Once you catch yourself in the act, do not spend any time scolding or shaming yourself about it, or smothering your feelings. Instead, love and accept yourself.

Do NOT skip this step! In order to pull yourself out of the story you've been spinning, you need to fully process the feelings they were generating. You must name them and claim them, in order to release them from your physical, mental, and emotional energies.

Say to yourself, I *love and accept the part of me who is imagining terrible storylines. I love and accept the part of me who is scaring myself. I love and accept the part of me who feels threatened. I love and accept the part of me who wants to feel safe.*

This simple exercise pulls you out of the story. Instead of being in the middle of a panic because you believed what you were imagining, now you become an observer, watching yourself generate the panic. It takes the charge off, neutralizing the negative energy that was escalating. It allows you to see you are simply inventing a scary story that isn't real, and brings you back to neutrality.

Resisting the Right Now

The only "real" reality is happening Right Now. But your mind is constantly trying to imagine the future. Future storylines have not happened yet, and don't ever have to happen. You are just imagining them, and treating them as likely, legitimate concerns.

Imagining future outcomes disempowers you from receiving the guidance your Higher Consciousness is sending you Right Now. Your Higher Consciousness knows your soul's blueprint – the beautiful life of joy, abundance and Vitality you came here intending to have. Your Ego-Driven mind is trying to block you from accessing this, by keeping you out of Right Now. But your Higher Consciousness is trying to guide you there Right Now.

You must learn how to take command over your mind and remain present. It takes practice to accomplish this. In the Vitality Voyagers membership, we teach The Real You Method which allows you to gain proficiency at being present. It involves dropping your attention out of your mind and placing it onto your heart.

The voice of your Higher Consciousness communicates to you through your heart. Your Ego is the voice in your mind. It is imperative you learn how to shut it off. Your inner voice – your intuition – is your Higher Consciousness speaking to you. However it is not heard with your ears, it is felt in your heart. This is called *knowingness*.

Learning to connect to your knowingness, rather than depending on the unreliable Ego-Driven mind, is how you can come to feel certain and stable within yourself.

Indecision

Because you have never learned about knowingness before, and have been living in a loop of compulsively Fearing the Worst, you have likely been highly indecisive. Being entirely mental blocks access to your intuition. Many Type 6s struggle painfully with making life choices because they can't feel their own inner guidance.

Typically, your go-to way of *managing* this (not resolving it) is by doing research about it, and asking other people's opinions.

Unfortunately, research does not always provide a clear answer. This is because the people who are publishing their opinions are also Ego-Driven, and therefore have their own irrational and unconscious agendas going on. For example, Wikipedia is a common place people look to online for information. However, the information in Wikipedia is written by regular people just like you who consider themselves to be really smart. Hmmm. The Ego is always happy to congratulate itself on how superior it is to other people. But that doesn't mean it is actually so.

Asking other people what they would do in your situation is also ineffective. Even though we think we are all living in a single place called "reality", actually we are each creating our own personal reality, which overlaps into a matrix.

The reality that you experience is singular to you – you have past lives, old karma, psychic wounds, soul contracts, intuitive abilities, latent talents, learned skills, programmed DNA and so much more which make your perception of reality very specific to you.

Therefore, someone else's opinion about what they would do in your circumstance has absolutely no bearing on whether this would be right for you.

This is why there is only one way to know what is right for you, and it isn't out there in the matrix. It is the guidance which comes from going within – to a place outside of time and space – and communing with your Higher Consciousness.

Joylessness

The Flow of the Universe is full of joy, excitement, and love. Unfortunately, constantly Fearing the Worst is the exact opposite of all that.

The problem with Fearing the Worst is that you forget it is all just a figment of your imagination. You actually believe the upsetting stories you are telling yourself.

The only thing this does for you is create despair, terror, and misery – all of which completely destroy your Vitality.

Your DNA is activated and deactivated based on your emotional state. Feelings of gratitude, joy and peace cause your DNA to relax and open up, activating new levels of health and resilience.

Feelings of fear, resentment, and hatred cause your DNA to coil up into a tight knot, only allowing your most primitive DNA to express itself. This is how a negative state of mind creates a negative state of health. Perpetually Fearing the Worst not only sabotage your mental health, it also erodes your physical health. You are a lovely being of light, concerned with helping and being of service. You deserve so much more than this miserable state.

The extremely important shift out of this pathway involves developing trust – in yourself, and in the Universe. You will learn methods a bit further ahead for connecting with your Higher Consciousness, which gives you access to a knowingness you can count on. This sense of certainty eases your fear and allows you to relax and enjoy yourself.

Your Destructive Behavior

Your Survival Belief – that you must always be watching out for danger – also prompts your actions and behaviors. When you are Ego-Driven, and therefore **not questioning your inherent attitudes and beliefs, you will repeatedly behave this way.** This is called your **Destructive Behavior**.

You may be entirely unaware of it, or you may be doing it on purpose with the utter certainty it's the best way to be. Either way, this behavior is never for the Greatest Good of all, and therefore is destructive.

As an Ego-Driven Type 6 who believes you are being smart by watching out for problems . . .

> Your Destructive Behavior is **Suspecting.**

Suspecting means to doubt or mistrust. It means believing someone or something to be guilty, false, or bad with little or no proof. There is absolutely no love present when you are Suspecting, which is your first clue that it has no value.

Type 6s like to refer to themselves as skeptics. They think this means they're correct in being unwilling to give their trust. They think it means they're being smarter than the rest of those gullible fools out there.

But as we discussed, operating within a fear-based reality is the opposite of rational thinking – it is highly biased towards false and inflammatory stories. So buying-in to a lot of suspicion is not a valid way of protecting yourself or identifying the truth. But it is an excellent way of sabotaging yourself, your relationships, and your life.

As you are now beginning to grasp, the only real way to have a deep knowingness of what is right and true *for you* is to consult the wise counsel of your own loving Higher Consciousness. However, you must be in a calm, neutral mental and emotional state in order to access this. If you are already upset and suspicious when you try to consult your intuition, the only answers you will receive are Ego-Driven, and therefore cannot be trusted.

Meanwhile, it is not in your best interest to act out on your suspicion. Although you may feel it is appropriate and normal to openly question other people's intentions or integrity with no proof whatsoever, the person on the receiving end strongly disagrees. Now you've got a war on your hands, with Egos on both sides in full defensive mode. The results will not be pretty. You think you're creating safety for yourself, but really you are creating an enormous amount of drama.

Remember, you have no way of knowing what is going on internally for other people. You are projecting your Survival Programming's agenda onto them.

Truth be told, however, a lot of the time you're probably right – other people are likely acting on an Ego-Driven self-serving agenda. But that's not actually the point. Calling other people out on their ulterior motives is not your job or responsibility.

A primary principle of the Flow of the Universe is non-interference. You are not to interfere with another individual's journey. Everybody starts out Ego-Driven, and they will spend many lifetimes on their own personal odyssey towards self-awareness, at whatever pace is right for them. It is none of your business, and telling them what's-what is not your concern. Their karma will deliver them their own lessons, don't you worry. And meanwhile, your hostile and aggressive behavior will be creating some karma of your own.

Rather than making negative assumptions or doing a lot of due diligence about how corrupt a person or an idea is, take the shortcut and consult your Higher Consciousness. If your Higher Consciousness confirms that indeed this person or this organization is not a good situation for you, then you are now empowered to calmly make the choice that best serves you. No drama, no war. Just move on.

You don't need to get all upset that there are lots of Ego-Driven people out there. It's true, there are. They were encoded to be that way, and so were you. But picking a side and adding to the polarizing conflict just makes things worse, not better. If you would like to see peace, harmony and integrity in this world, simply stay connected to your own Higher Consciousness, and you will be shown the way there.

Dogmatic Thinking

Fearing the Worst and Suspecting everyone and everything of being dangerous is an extremely painful way to live. In your Ego-Driven desperation, you often land on an Ego-Driven "solution." At least, you think it's a solution, because it makes you feel better. This is called dogmatic thinking.

Dogma means adhering to a certain set of beliefs and proclaiming them as unquestioningly true.

Type 6s, in the deep need to feel safe, often grasp on to large established institutions as a source of The Truth. Religious, political, military, corporate and social platforms all attract lots of Type 6s in need of something to believe in.

Unfortunately, as we have discussed, these were all created by Ego-Driven people, and are therefore highly questionable as actually serving the Greatest Good. But being dogmatic means you refuse to question – you accept them as truth. You align yourself with what you deem trustworthy, and entrench yourself there.

Type 6s are wired to be highly community-oriented. They care a lot about the state of the world and the direction they want it to go. But their penchant for Suspecting everyone interferes with this. Picking a group to align with provides much-needed relief. It is a way of telling yourself that you are safe – millions of people can't be wrong!

Make no mistake, this is merely picking a side. You're sure you're on the side of justice, but so is the Type 6 in the opposite camp. Are you sure you want to give all your trust to a bunch of politicians? Or the leaders of your corporation? Or your college alma mater? Or your favorite athletic team? Or whatever?

Any organization which does not orient around values of unconditional love and respect is Ego-Driven. It's as simple as that. *But wait*, you say, *that's practically all of them!* Right.

Large factions are not the way towards stabilizing and protecting yourself. It starts within yourself, as love and acceptance, which radiates outward. This attracts like-minded people to you. And that will become the tribe you can safely endorse. This world has hardly seen this before. It may have to begin with you.

Type 6s, torn apart by their impulse to protect themselves from danger and their chronic suspicion, find some blessed oblivion in telling themselves they have found the thing they can actually trust. The only way this works, however, is if they don't look too closely and don't ask too many questions. It's so interesting how your programming can lead you to be both highly suspicious and highly dogmatic at the same time.

Toxic Loyalty

Dogmatic thinking is the balm to your existential crisis on a large scale. Toxic loyalty provides the same relief from the pain of Fearing the Worst and Suspecting on a more intimate scale.

Just as you pick a side and stick to it, you pick your relationships and stick to those, too – whether this is in your best interest or not. You just really, really need to believe that your life has not been built on a house of cards. You really want to feel a part of something greater than yourself. So you tell yourself that you have aligned yourself with good and right people. Or that "family sticks together." Or that you and your best friend "have each other's back."

Loyalty is touted as a noble and admirable way to be. Standing by your relationships when the chips are down is lovely. But standing by your relationships when they are treating you abusively or betraying your trust – because you are afraid of change or afraid to be alone – is self-destructive and toxic.

Type 6s are notorious for "staying together for the children," or "standing by their man" or believing in loyalty "no matter what." But are the people you are loyal to, loyal to you in return? Are your relationships balanced, healthy, and mutually beneficial?

Please be careful that you are not using your own Ego programming to keep yourself trapped in a toxic relationship! Many Type 6s can be dangerously easy to manipulate and use because they're so afraid to face a painful truth that might destabilize their life.

Your fear-based hardwiring makes you really, really afraid of change. It makes you doubt your own abilities. It makes you settle for the known rather than risk a gamble on the unknown. It keeps you playing so much smaller than you really are.

Type 6s are some of the most intelligent, competent and capable people out there. They are shrewd and skilled. If you were to master your Ego, ridding yourself of fear and doubt because you know how to trust your Higher Consciousness and your ability to navigate the Flow… you are capable of a profound ability to make your life fully stable while also fully joyful at the same time.

The misery of Suspecting is hard to live with, so you pick your certain insiders and make them totally exempt from your scrutiny, telling yourself you are safe and secure. But when you are Ego-Driven, you attract relationships which are equally Ego-Driven. And the only way those relationships work is if you all remain Ego-Driven and toxic, or you all agree to work together towards Consciousness-Directedness, which is quite rare.

It's possible you may end up having to go it alone for a little while. This may be devastating news, it's true. But deep down you know that the truth is the only thing worth building your life around. And you are more than strong enough to do so.

Unfortunately, you may have some painful truths to face as part of your journey towards self-awareness. But the good news is that, as you learn to trust yourself and make yourself happy, you will attract many new people to you, of much higher integrity, who will make your life feel meaningful and satisfying in ways you never imagined.

Connecting to The Real You, requires, well, *getting real*. It takes willingness, maturity, and intention. It is not always easy or fun. But it is the only way out of a life lived in fear.

Learning how to quiet the mind and connect with your heart, learning how to trust your inner wisdom instead of outer sources, learning how to release yourself from fear and embrace your true power... these are all available to you, and will move you into a life of joyfulness and Vitality.

You are not alone. Your Higher Consciousness is always with you, guiding you and loving you more deeply than you can possibly understand. Are you ready to do the work?

Your Sabotage Pattern

As we have discussed, your Personality Type has much Survival Programming built in. Your Survival Belief, Compulsion, and Destructive Behavior are undeniable impulses within you that all drive your well-being into the ground.

In other words, these all combine into an overall template for self-destruction. This is called your **Sabotage Pattern – the way you repeatedly behave throughout your lifetime which leads directly to the destruction of your health and happiness.**

> Your Sabotage Pattern is **Over-Reacting.**

Over-Reacting means to react more strongly than is necessary or appropriate. It is a dramatically heightened response to a stimulus, launching a cascade of negative consequences. You don't mean to Over-React, but you are so easily triggered. This automatic and uncontrolled response is the ultimate source of sabotage for the Ego-Driven Type 6.

Over-Reacting and the Mind

In the mind, Over-Reacting happens when you are confronted with any kind of change or perceived danger. Your mind is highly sensitive to any hint of threat. Whenever you encounter a suggestion of change, your mind immediately launches a story of how this will destabilize you. Unquestioningly, you believe this story, and react on the assumption that it is true.

This internal imagining-a-story-of-peril-and-believing-it happens in the blink of an eye, without you even realizing. Immediately, you launch a big defense, often accusing others of malice. You are, in general, obstinately opposed to the proposed change, inventing reasons for this which may or may not have any foundation in truth.

Your audience on the receiving end is generally astonished at your big freak-out and the venomous accusations coming their way. Your reaction seems all out of proportion to their proposal, and it is. Because you're not actually responding to what they said – you're responding to the upsetting story you invented.

Type 6s have a way of blowing up small things into much bigger things than they need to be. You immediately Fear the Worst, leaving other non-reactive Types baffled, defensive, and turned-off. Even though in theory you are seeking to be stable and secure, you are actually often the one who escalates conflict, causing destabilization.

Over-Reacting and the Body

The Ego-Driven Type 6s body is also highly sensitive and reactive. This is the result of the over-reactive mind. It causes the nervous system to exist in a permanent state of fight-or-flight. This is called the sympathetic nervous system.

The sympathetic nervous system is only meant to be active in extreme circumstances. It floods the body with adrenaline, blocking the normally peaceable cycles of the body, amping everything up in preparation for an attack. But in your case, you pretty much always believe yourself to be under attack, which keeps your body perpetually in this state.

When the nervous system is never allowed to turn off and move into the parasympathetic state, known as rest-and-digest, the body becomes highly toxic. Bowel disorders, digestive disorders, panic attacks, headaches, insomnia, and extreme food allergies and sensitivities are all very common. The normal flow of energy and rhythmic cycles are greatly disturbed and misdirected.

Type 6s are the ones with the extreme, rare or inexplicable medical cases. Nobody can understand why your system is so far out of whack. But when observed in the context of your highly sensitive trigger of imagined threat, it makes perfect sense. All your life, you have been overdosing on vast quantities of fear, poisoning your own bloodstream and destabilizing your own nervous system.

Fortunately, it is all quite reversible. As you learn to take command over your mind through connecting to your heart, you will no longer be so highly reactive. You will become able to remain calm and neutral in your mind, keeping your body peaceable as well. No toxins will course through your bloodstream, and no alarm bells will mess with your nervous system. This is how you move out of being The Alarmist, and into becoming The Guardian.

Over-Reacting and the Spirit

Emotions are communication from your Higher Consciousness. They are guidance, trying to help you find the state of mind which is best for you and will bring about the positive outcomes you desire.

Feelings of anxiety and fear are cautionary messages. The more extreme your feeling of distress, the more intense is the message that you are in a state of self-destructiveness. It's as if your Higher Self is screaming at you: *Danger! Danger! Cease this line of thinking immediately!*

Rather than endorsing your fear-based thinking, your Higher Consciousness is encouraging you to let it go. You will know when you have shifted to thoughts which are beneficial to you because you will feel pleasantly relaxed and happy. This is the guidance you need that allows you to begin effectively navigating the Flow of the Universe.

It is never too late to reconnect with The Real You, and release the self-sabotage you have experienced through Over-Reacting. You may find the road vulnerable and scary… but you will also find love, peace, satisfaction and a deep sense of serenity. It is a journey worth taking. The guidance on how to do this is coming up next.

♦♦♦

Now that you have opened your eyes to the destructive inner workings of your own Ego, operating as Your Primal Persona, do not despair. It is certainly within your capacity to transform these behaviors and patterns of your Survival Programming.

If you have made it this far, CONGRATULATIONS. We lost many along the trail – not everybody is ready for the journey that is Getting Real! This book is really only interesting to people who are about to make an enormous advancement in their consciousness.

We made it through the hardest part. Now, let's explore how you can be, act and live differently. There is an entirely different kind of life available to you, filled with love and connection and joy. And it is mapped out in the top half of your Type 6 Mandala.

ACTIVATE YOUR POWER PARADIGM

In Chapter One we revealed the meaning of Your Vitality Personality. Let's recap now.

Your Vitality Personality is the version of you that exists when you allow your Higher Consciousness to guide your thoughts, feelings, and actions. It is the opening of your heart, and allowing the loving intelligence found there to Flow through you. This infuses you with insight, wisdom, love and compassion, and the actions you take from this place always serve the Greatest Good.

Let's take a look now at the top half of your Mandala which spells out the dynamics of The Real You - Your Vitality Personality - and all its wondrous gifts and talents:

YOUR VITALITY PERSONALITY: THE GUARDIAN — CONSCIOUSNESS-DIRECTED

Vital Truth
I open myself to all experiences, trusting that everything in the Universe serves the Greatest Good

Liberation: **Steadying**

Highest Purpose: **Integrity**

Theme: **TRUST**

Vitality Behavior: **Discerning**

6

Your Vitality Personality: The Guardian

As a Type 6,

> Your Vitality Personality is known as **The Guardian.**

This is the truth of who you really are. You have always felt a call to watch out for other people, to protect integrity, to support community. You have always cared so deeply about the stability of individuals, families, and organizations. You have always loved the feeling of being a part of something larger, knowing you can play an integral role on behalf of the group.

The Real You is a protector and a watcher, ensuring we all have what we need and have a safe space to operate within. You are the one who keeps our people and our systems whole and functional. You are the foundation, strong and supportive, that serves as the platform which empowers us all to thrive.

See *Fig 7B* for a brief summary of the Consciousness-Directed half of your Mandala, identifying how to use your Personality Type to bring into your life a sense of completeness, fulfillment, joy and love:

When you embody all these natural gifts, you are a bright light, affecting all who know you. It is so exciting to think you are just on the precipice of launching a new life of love, acceptance, and Vitality for yourself! It might have required some serious deep-breathing to get here, but the effort is so well worth it.

Let's explore these dynamics of your Power Paradigm, so that you may begin to fully comprehend just how open, uplifting, happy and healthy your life could really be.

Your Theme

As was mentioned previously,

> Your Theme is **Trust**.

When you pursue the highest form of this Theme – Trust – you are truly aligned with Source, and therefore always serving the Greatest Good.

Trust is the willingness to be vulnerable because of how profoundly you believe in Truth. It is a knowingness that, as an expression of Source, you are always safe. It is the surrender of yourself to something higher, something unseen yet deeply felt. It is having faith that your life has meaning and serves a valuable purpose. Trust means understanding that the experiences you face are meant for you with fully loving intention, in order to help you grow and expand.

Trust is so difficult for us humans, because we fear harm and dread death. However, when you truly understand who you really are – an eternal being of light, created by Source with enormous love – you come to understand you have nothing to fear.

When you are able to fill yourself to the brim with this Trust, Type 6, you become powerful and bold. You become able to face anything, because you believe in yourself, knowing full well you are backed by the Universe.

As a Type 6, you can inherently sense this. You have always had a feeling that you are a part of something greater. And it is so true. You are the fabric, the invisible net that connects us to one another and to All That Is. Without you, we would not know how to come together as a whole.

This is why Your Vitality Personality is named The Guardian. You are the one who protects integrity, ensuring stability and functionality on behalf of the entire collective.

Fig. 7B   **PERSONALITY TYPE 6**   **POWER PARADIGM**
Your Vitality Personality: **THE GUARDIAN**
The Real You; The most magnificent version of yourself you joyfully embody when you heed the guidance of your Higher Consciousness
Theme: TRUST
The dynamic realm of Life your Higher Consciousness wants to explore to the fullest
Vital Truth: I OPEN MYSELF TO ALL EXPERIENCES, TRUSTING THAT EVERYTHING IN THE UNIVERSE SERVES THE GREATEST GOOD
The higher understanding of how to thrive, that aligns you with the Flow of the Universe
Liberation: STEADYING
The emancipating philosophy you freely embrace to enhance your connection to the Flow
Vitality Behavior: DISCERNING
The empowering and uplifting actions you intentionally choose to create your best life
Highest Purpose: INTEGRITY
How you serve the Greatest Good through embracing your encoded genius, and the source of your Vitality

In the hands of Your Vitality Personality, you apply your wholly centered and grounded Self towards efforts which serve the Greatest Good, making you an inspired and revered Guardian:

- Fully embracing your own inner wisdom, no longer requiring external guidance
- Feeling trust in the Universe, truly knowing It brings you only the Greatest Good
- Relationships which are healthy: respectful, open-hearted, mutually beneficial, and loving
- Work which feels deeply rewarding and meaningful
- Vital health derived from a peaceful mind, a balanced nervous system, and a connection to your Higher Consciousness
- Relishing a sense of peace and satisfaction at knowing your life serves an important Purpose

Most people resist attending to the foundational aspects of life. These are so often the small things, the repetitive things, the mundane things. Most people are so enamored by excitement, entertainment, flash and sizzle, that they are unwilling to give their time and attention to the extremely important facets of life which need regular maintenance and attention.

You are the one who is built to serve the world by engaging your natural abilities to help people and groups become more stable, trustworthy, and effective.

Once you are able to embrace Trust, keeping yourself strong and stable, you are able to help the rest of the world become strong and stable, too. You have an integral part to play in keeping society balanced and functional, while at the same time fostering its growth and expansion. When you become Consciousness-Directed, you step into your role as the one who holds us all steady as we face the great unknown.

Your Vital Truth

Your **Vital Truth** is the **Higher understanding of how to thrive by aligning with Universal principles**. It is the escape hatch your Ego doesn't want you to know about, because it unlocks all of its Survival Programming, and connects you to your Higher Consciousness – The Real You.

> Your Vital Truth is **I open myself to all experiences, trusting that everything in the Universe serves the Greatest Good.**

This is a direct contradiction to what your Survival Belief encourages you to believe. Your Survival Belief prompts you to think that the world is a dangerous and menacing place, and you must protect yourself from it at all times.

But that is the mentality of the Ego, thinking you can fight fire with fire or hide yourself away and expect this to make anything better. The Ego does not have the capacity to really grasp that the only way to stabilize the outer world is through going inward. The threat is not out there. The threat is our own unacknowledged shadows within. In facing and integrating these, we realize we can face anything.

As a Type 6, your Ego has had you existing in a state of fear all your life. Maybe you limited and minimized yourself in the hopes this would keep you safe. This is the phobic, or "flight" response. Maybe you got really angry about your fear, and tried to bluster your way through. This is the counter-phobic, or "fight" response. But no matter which way you tried, there was still more fear. There was always something else to be frightened about.

Opening to All Experiences

Your Vital Truth is showing you that there was never anything to fear, but fear itself. There was nothing out there that you truly couldn't handle. It was just your internal belief that you couldn't handle it that made you so upset. Once you get that sorted, you become able to live in a totally limitless way! Playing small and false bravado are no longer required.

What if you stopped being afraid to be alone? You are more than capable of fashioning a new support system for yourself. Then you might finally exit those toxic relationships, and give yourself a chance to experience uplifting, fulfilling, and inspiring love.

What if you stopped being afraid about your ability to earn enough money, have benefits, and a retirement plan? You are fully able to secure them in a new way. Then you might finally leave that job you never liked, opening yourself up to work that expands and nourishes you.

What if you stopped fearing what other people think? You are unique and independent and don't need approval from anyone. Then you could finally feel free to live exactly how you please.

What if you stopped fearing how other people's choices might affect you? It is possible to create a protective field of light around yourself. Then you could finally get to experience peace.

Everything you ever wanted is on the other side of fear. Trust yourself and your power. You have all the intelligence, strength, and support you will ever need to reckon with the unknown. Believe in yourself, and open up a whole new glorious world to yourself.

The Greatest Good

Have you ever noticed how experiences that seemed like a nightmare at the time, eventually ended up producing something good?

Like, maybe when you were young your parents got divorced and you had to change schools, but you came to meet your best friend in the whole wide world. Or maybe you lost your job, but then you found a new one that you liked so much better. Or maybe you fell and broke your leg in three places, but by the time you healed, all the people you'd been supporting magically found alternative solutions.

This is how the Flow of the Universe works. It is always bringing you the Greatest Good. But it does it in its own time, in its own way. You can't always see or understand it while you're in the middle of it.

This is where that Trust comes in. You must Trust that the Universe has a plan for you.

This is what allows you to remain calm while it appears that your world is exploding. Even though things seem crazy, and even though you have no idea what's going on, you must still Trust there is actually a plan that is bringing about the Greatest Good.

That is how you open yourself to all experiences. Because you know everything is going to be okay. Maybe it's uncomfortable, and maybe it's painful, and maybe it even makes you cry sometimes. Even so, allow yourself to go through it. Don't fight it. Let it come. The less you resist, the quicker the tough times will stabilize. The less you freak out, the easier it is to recover.

Believe in yourself. Believe in your Higher Consciousness. Believe in the Universe. And believe in Source. You are loved, watched over, and guided, even when you can't see it. But knowing this truth can get you through anything.

Your Liberation

Your **Liberation** is the **emancipating philosophy you freely embrace.** This is a powerful shift, out of the Survival Programming of the mind, and into the Flow of the Universe through the heart. Rather than being owned by a chronic Compulsion, you are now intentionally choosing this Liberation.

> ➢ Your Liberation is **Steadying.**

Type 6, if you can get a handle on Steadying rather than Fearing the Worst, your whole life will radically change for the better. It sounds so simple, and yet Steadying goes against all your Ego programming. At first you will find it hard to do. But then… you will totally love it.

Steadying is a simple method you may employ to pull yourself out of your fear response and reclaim your power. It has to do with first, observing the fear response getting ready to take hold. As we discussed before, this is noticeable to you because your body begins experiencing excessive tension and "amping up." You will need to identify what this pattern is for you, so that you may quickly notice it coming on.

Steadying intentionally redistributes your energy so that you may gain mastery over your thoughts and your nervous system, rather than allowing them to spin out of control. It involves redistributing the excessive energy storming in your mind so that you return to balance.

Steadying Exercise

This is an exercise you will want to begin doing right away. Make it a part of both your morning and evening routines. Over time you will see how much it helps to keep you feeling centered. Then, in moments of stress when you feel your anxiety starting to take over, you will have a tool at your fingertips for regaining your equilibrium.

In addition to the sense of inner stability this method provides, it also benefits you in another way. It encourages you to visualize in your mind's eye.

Type 6s tend to be analytical-minded, which is left-brained. The right brain is the creative, imaginative side, which communicates in images, symbols and feelings. This is the language of the Flow, and you must learn to speak it.

The imagination is actually your conversation with your Higher Consciousness. When an idea just suddenly comes to you, or a song gets stuck in your head, or a specific memory pops up, these are messages for you from your Higher Self. There is a meaning in it for you which you must discern.

Doing this exercise regularly will help you access this part of yourself, and your sense of connection to The Real You – who is calm and wise – will greatly expand.

Please bear with the number of pages it takes to describe an exercise that ultimately can be done in seconds, once you've got the hang of it.

1. **Center Yourself**

    Sit comfortably and close your eyes. Breathe deeply in through the nose down into your belly, hold there, and exhale slowly out the mouth, fully wringing out the belly. Let your body soften. Repeat this twice more to communicate to your nervous system that you are safe. Then you can return to normal breathing, which is now more relaxed.

2. **Grounding Cord**

    Now we will create your grounding cord. imagine two golden strands – one is straight, the other coils around it. They join together to make a single fine golden cable.

    Imagine that this golden cord can snap into place at the base of your tailbone. imagine that if you were to tug on it, you would feel it pull at the base of your spine.

3. **The Golden Lake**

    Send this cord down into the ground beneath you, letting it descend all the way down, until finally it reaches into a golden lake, at the center of the earth.

    This shimmering lake looks like a beautiful sea of warm golden light, thick like plasma or lava. Its energy feels all-knowing and loving. Its waters are purifying and healing to you. This place feels sacred and safe.

4. **Clear Out Thoughts**

    Imagine that your head is full to the brim with murky gray water. These are all your frantic thoughts and mental chatter. Drain them away, like opening a tap at the back of your head. Let all the dirty water drain down, out of the head, down the back of the back, down the spine, down the tailbone, down the cord, all the way down to the golden lake at the center of the earth. This leaves your mind empty and calm.

5. Clear Out Feelings

Imagine that the heaviness and aching in your body are your old unprocessed feelings. Acting like a vacuum, let your heart power on and draw all of the physical tension and pain out of your body, into the heart. The heart turns on and sucks into it everything which does not serve you.

Send this now out the back of your heart, down the spine, down the tailbone, down the cord, all the way down to the golden lake at the center of the earth. This leaves your body feeling light and free.

6. Bring In Light

Whenever you clear any energy out of your body, it is important to intentionally fill the empty spaces back up with light.

Imagine that there are little hatches on the bottoms of your feet. Open them, and let yourself grow roots out, as if you are a tree, and send your roots all the way down to the golden lake at the center of the earth.

Put your roots in the nutrient-rich golden lava, and drink it upward, all the way up through the bottoms of your feet.

Let your body fill all the way up the legs and into your torso, purifying and enriching your blood and tissue as it Flows. It fills up into your chest, rolls down the arms into the hands, up the throat, filling the face, head, and hair, and finally emerges out of the top of your head.

7. Encircle Yourself

Once the golden light emerges out of the top of your head, let it spread out and around you like an orb, returning to your feet, and drawing back upward through your midline, and out the top again.

You are now a torus shape, with golden light filling you, passing through you, and encircling around you.

This protective cocoon that you create around yourself, and the grounding cord that tethers you and anchors you in your body can remain with you at all times. You can think of yourself as safe and untouchable inside your golden orb of light, where your body is relaxed and your mind is clear and serene.

Whenever you feel your mind revving up with fear thoughts and your body clenching and bracing, remember to send everything down the cord, and draw up new fresh light. This can be done instantaneously in your mind, where it all happens in a flash.

The ability to Steady yourself – anytime, anywhere – will become your superpower. Instead of always being The Alarmist – the one everybody knows freaks out and overreacts, you will become The Guardian – the one everyone counts on to stabilize the environment.

Your Vitality Behavior

Vitality Behavior is the **empowering and uplifting actions you intentionally**

choose when you are Consciousness-Directed, rather than the Destructive Behavior your Ego drives you to act out.

> Your Vitality Behavior is **Discerning.**

Discerning means consulting your own internal sense of knowingness to determine what choices and decisions are best for you.

This is a major departure from your typical approach, which involves research, data, analysis, soliciting opinions, accepting what you were told by authority figures, or endlessly imagining what-if scenarios without ever arriving at a clear plan of action. These are all the ways in which you abandon trust in yourself and your ability to Discern, in favor of letting external messages influence you.

Manifestation Over Matrix

Researching evidence or other external data in order to persuade yourself of the right next step is not always as reliable as you think it is. For these are the measurements of the 3D matrix – the reality created out of the collective Ego mind. Turning to the collective Ego matrix for guidance will only provide you data on matrix-encoded outcomes.

What you want is a Consciousness-Directed outcome, where you are able to use your open heart and Higher Mind to manifest a more unusual, more pleasing outcome for yourself. Your full quantum Self is far more powerful than the matrix.

In order to access this aspect of yourself, you must seek connection within. This is where you gain the capacity to Discern what is the best choice for you, regardless of external opinion, which will naturally bring forth the Greatest Good.

Knowingness

Your Higher Consciousness communicates to you in your heart, not your mind. Its guidance can often be a feeling, a sense. (It is rarer to hear or see something, but it's certainly possible you can develop these too. Expanded intuitive abilities are dramatically on the rise.)

Here is a simple way to tune-in to your internal knowingness.

Inner Knowing Exercise

- Sit in a comfortable position, and slow down your breathing. Breathe in through the nose, hold in the belly, and out through the mouth. Do this 3 times, and allow your body to return to an easier rhythm.
- Imagine yourself inside a pyramid of white light. This is your inner sanctum, where it is completely peaceful and safe.
- Focus your attention on your chest. Imagine there is an orb of light inside your chest, which pulses and radiates larger as you focus on it. The light that radiates from it is very benevolent and wise.
- At the same time, imagine opening up the top of your head, allowing clear sparkling light to enter, bringing you clarity and understanding.

- Let your demeanor be soft, as if you were willing to lie back and let somebody massage you. This is "receiving" mode, where the mind and body relax and let go.
- Ask the wise, loving light in your chest a question in very simple terms. Here are some examples you might try:
    - Is this person trustworthy?
    - What is my best next step?
    - What do I need to know right now?
    - Should I take this opportunity?

And then, just wait.

Your Ego mind may try to jump in and answer for you. But this will sound noisy, like chatter.

The answers which come through the heart are extremely simple, usually very few words. And the response may not come as words at all. It might come as a sensation, like warmth (*yes*) or tension (*no*). Or you might see a flash of an image in your mind's eye, or suddenly think of a song. How does this image or song make you feel? What does it remind you of?

These are all forms of guidance. It takes practice learning how your Higher Consciousness is communicating to you. It will get easier.

Do not take any action until you have arrived at a sense of *knowingness*. If you don't receive an answer right away, then you are being told to do nothing yet. Total silence means: *Wait*.

Sometimes the answer will drop into your mind a little later, like in the shower or the middle of your workout. And sometimes something new will happen, maybe you'll have a conversation with someone or you'll happen upon something online, and it will give you the piece of information you needed in order to arrive at that sense of knowing.

Sometimes the problem you are hoping to Discern is just way bigger or more complex than little-old-you are meant to take on. In that case, hand it over entirely to your Higher Consciousness.

Put your attention on your chest, and say to your heart something like: *I want this to resolve, but I don't know how to do it. I request that you handle it.* And then, let go of the topic entirely. You have done what you could, and now it is out of your hands. Let yourself take peace in that. The Flow of the Universe will bring about the solution in its own way, in its own time.

Your Higher Consciousness is not a vague idea. It's not wishful thinking. It is alive, it is real – The Real You. The process of Discerning is learning to communicate with The Real You. This is how you navigate yourself through the chaos, directly toward your happiest, healthiest life.

As you begin to experiment with Discerning, it comes to feel like play. The first time you receive a clear communication and experience knowingness, you will feel astonished and delighted. It is magical and exciting.

As you come to realize your Higher Consciousness really is there, and is incredibly wise and loving, you will begin to fall in love with yourself. You will come to feel gratitude, amazement, and joy. *You really are not alone! You really are wise! You really are powerful!*

Once you discover this Truth for yourself, you will leave your lifestyle of fear and over-reacting far behind, and become able to deliver what you were built for, and why you came here: your Highest Purpose.

Your Highest Purpose

You chose to be here, in this time and place, because you wanted to contribute something. You came here for a reason, and you chose your Personality Type because it was the one that would help you accomplish it. **Your Personality Type has a special set of talents and abilities, and you wanted to use them to contribute.** This is your **Highest Purpose**.

> Your Highest Purpose is **Integrity.**

Integrity is soundness, wholeness, uprightness. You are the Guardian of these. You are the one we can trust to keep us and our systems safe, stable, thriving, and free of corruption.

As the Alarmist, you were not able to do this effectively because you were so easily destabilized yourself. Your judgment was clouded with fear. It is only now that you know how to Steady yourself and Discern Higher guidance that you are now ready to positively impact our world.

The Guardian of Integrity is a crucial role, yet a challenging one – and sometimes a thankless one. In making yourself into a calm, present person who is a first-responder whenever needed, you are indispensable for keeping daily operations healthy, strong and effective. You make up the infrastructure, where your contributions may go unseen yet they support so much. Your Higher Consciousness selected this as the part you would play over your lifetime.

Even though The Guardian is largely a role of service, it does not need to be a life of sacrifice or grimness. You are still meant to have a happy life. You actually are best able to deliver your Highest Purpose when you feel pleased and easy. The sense of meaning and fulfillment you will experience from a life lived in Integrity will more than make up for the effort it required of you.

Integrity within yourself happens when your mind, body and heart are all aligned. This brings a great sense of peace, a certainty that all is well. This moves you into the Flow of the Universe and brings forth a life of Vitality.

Integrity and the Higher Mind

Gaining mastery over the Ego mind is necessary for all 9 Types, but for you Type 6, it's an emergency. The Survival Programming you received is wired to be the most negative-minded of them all. This regularly sends alarm bells throughout your nervous system, wreaking havoc on your health and happiness.

You will be quite relieved to learn there is a way out.

The problem all this time was that you were attempting to use your Ego mind to be logical and rational in the hopes of relieving the irrational fear and mistrust going on in there. It's a loop without end. You cannot solve Ego-Driven problems with Ego-Driven solutions.

There is something called the Higher Mind. It is a special room inside your mind where your thoughts merge with that of your Higher Consciousness. This is where divinely inspired solutions live, which will serve the Greatest Good for all. However, access to this room is gained through the heart.

Instead of leading with the Ego mind like you always have, it is time to discover how to lead with your sense of self-love, compassion, and empathy. When you soften your harsh world view, the suspicion and sense of insecurity do not arise. You remain stable and calm, because you're expecting things to go well, and you trust yourself to handle whatever comes your way.

This is the perspective of your Higher Consciousness, and when you align with this, you gain access to your Higher Mind. Your subtler senses kick in – your intuition and your knowingness.

The Higher Mind operates in very mysterious ways, not at all direct and clear like you'd imagine! It prompts you to make unexpected new choices. Synchronicities and odd occurrences conspire to get you the answers you need.

You might feel the impulse to suddenly take a work break and get on YouTube, only to discover some random video that brings an unexpected idea.

You might inexplicably have a weird song in your head, only to realize there's a perspective in the lyrics that really helps you. Or you look up the bio of the singer and it turns out their dad has a business that exactly meets your needs.

The Higher Mind has no friction, no doubt, no worry. It is serene and unencumbered. It is magical and fun.

When you attune your heart and Higher Mind to resonate together, this brings your energy into coherence. This is Integrity.

Integrity and the Body

The Integrity of the body refers to its ability to perform optimally. As much as you may-or-may-not do your best to be healthy by eating appropriately, exercising regularly, and taking a boatload of supplements, typical Type 6 health outcomes are still pretty miserable.

No matter how tightly controlled your health regimen, allowing your thoughts to run wild with fear, hostility, pessimism and blame will not bring you Vitality – it brings you an overwrought nervous system. Your sympathetic nervous system, known as your fight-or-flight response, was never meant to operate full-throttle every moment of your waking life. Yet your perpetual tendency to imagine negative outcomes keeps this amped up most of the time.

Your nervous system touches every other system in your body. Your digestion, immune system, hormones, metabolism, organ function, and cellular function all are impacted. These constant flare-ups of alarm you've been experiencing for much of your life eventually take their toll.

Your body is reflecting back to you what's been going on in your mind and in your heart. It's trying to give you a message about what you really need. And what you really need is some inner peace.

Using your new methods of Steadying and accessing your knowingness, of opening your heart and connecting with your Higher Mind, you switch your body over into the parasympathetic nervous system – known as rest-and-digest. This is the healing state, where your body repairs itself.

Your body is ready, willing and able to heal itself – as soon as you shift your lifestyle to include practices that quiet your Ego mind and reconnect you to feelings of love, acceptance, and trust. Not only will this reverse your unwellness, but it will also make your quality of life immeasurably better.

Integrity and the Heart

You are in full Integrity when you allow The Real You to express Itself through your heart.

You are feeling feelings all day every day – how often do you acknowledge them? Your feelings are the primary way your Higher Consciousness communicates with you.

Pleasant feelings are encouragement to continue along the same vein. Unpleasant feelings are meant to be a wake-up call, to prompt you to examine what your thoughts are doing, and do what you must to bring them into alignment with love, acceptance, joy and peace.

(Sometimes this means changing your thoughts, other times it means changing your life. These are advanced teachings, which we expand on in the private membership called the Vitality Voyagers, at YourVitalityPersonality.com).

More commonly, your pattern is to move back and forth between fear and anger, with affection often taking a backseat. Even though you are capable of deep love, it's as if you forget it in the stress of managing your monkey mind on top of managing All the Things.

There is a softer, more loving version of you deeper down, if you would only make the time to go there. You have been disinclined because you are afraid of the pain that lies beneath the surface.

You do not need to be afraid. You will not be consumed by your pain and your fears. There are methods for healing these, once and for all. The foundational Real You Methods in Chapter 12 will help you greatly.

Let yourself feel and release your true feelings. Let yourself experience love and compassion, rather than holding expectations and judgments. Let yourself have time for curiosity and creativity and fun. These are the desires of your soul.

The heart is so much more than just a physical organ. It is the portal that connects you to your full Quantum self and the Universe beyond. Engaging with it brings you into the Flow of the Universe, where life becomes easy and magical.

You deserve that, Type 6. You put so much effort into doing the "right" thing and doing it the "right" way. You are so earnest and tenacious. Give yourself love. Give yourself ease. Give yourself fun. Yes you are The Guardian, and most especially the Guardian of *you*. Taking excellent care of yourself so that your own wellness is in Integrity is your highest calling.

When you operate from this elevated Consciousness, you naturally bring Integrity to the larger world. Your inspired ideas, the good will you radiate, and the cooperation you foster all serve to create peaceful, stable environments that serve the Greatest Good. This is how, just by helping yourself be happy, you positively impact your entire reality.

♦♦♦

Well, Type 6, you've been given quite a lot of information about yourself to digest. But hopefully by now you've come to see that even though you are wired to act out Your Primal Persona, it is possible for you to be someone so much more magnificent than that – Your Vitality Personality.

Now is the time to decide who you want to be in this world. If you are ready to step into the full power of who you really are, and seize your best life… then your next step is **Integration.** See Chapter Eleven.

YOUR VITALITY PERSONALITY

CHAPTER EIGHT
PERSONALITY TYPE 7
THE UPLIFTER | THE HEDONIST

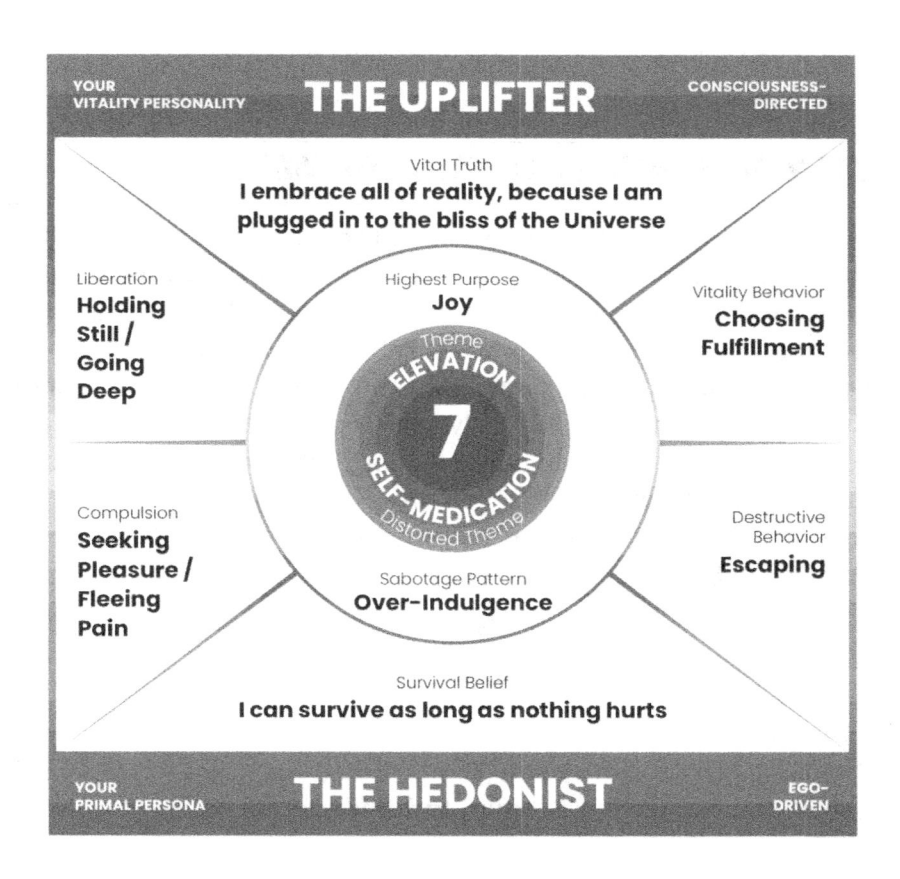

YOUR VITALITY PERSONALITY — **THE UPLIFTER** — *CONSCIOUSNESS-DIRECTED*

Vital Truth
I embrace all of reality, because I am plugged in to the bliss of the Universe

Liberation
Holding Still / Going Deep

Highest Purpose
Joy

Vitality Behavior
Choosing Fulfillment

Theme: **ELEVATION**
7
Distorted Theme: **SELF-MEDICATION**

Compulsion
Seeking Pleasure / Fleeing Pain

Sabotage Pattern
Over-Indulgence

Destructive Behavior
Escaping

Survival Belief
I can survive as long as nothing hurts

YOUR PRIMAL PERSONA — **THE HEDONIST** — *EGO-DRIVEN*

Welcome Type 7! Your curious mind and attraction to raising your vibration have brought you here.

You are all about love and light, but your programming leads you to be highly repelled by darkness or heaviness. This makes it difficult for you to stick with completing these teachings before becoming distracted by something much more pleasurable. Your inner coding will likely prompt a desire to flee for the hills when it reveals the need for you to hold still and go deep.

If you have been led here, then it is because you are ready to take a quantum leap ahead of your other Type 7 peers. The wisdom and insight you will gain here will propel you into an awareness far more advanced than most. This will benefit the entire world, for you are the one capable of energizing and elevating on a massive scale.

This chapter focuses on the dual nature of your Personality Type 7, and the primary factors that hinder or help your ability to thrive. You will totally love the descriptions about your highest potential and purpose... but you will totally not love reading about your dark side, called Your Primal Persona.

Hang in there! We intentionally go through the Primal Persona stuff first, so that you can finish on a high note – the magnificence that is Your Vitality Personality.

Give yourself permission to surrender to this process, and you will see how it takes you on a journey, getting richer and richer the further it goes. The part of you that is wired for Elevation will quickly come to see the important inspiration and advancement you will receive from this higher understanding.

DECODE YOUR SURVIVAL PROGRAMMING

As we just learned, **Your Primal Persona is the version of you that exists when you allow your Ego to unconsciously drive your thoughts, feelings and actions.** It is the operating system of your survival-oriented mind, limiting you from tapping into the love and light that is your Higher Consciousness.

In this state, you are closed off from your sense of love for yourself or others. And the actions you take from this place only serve to fulfill the Survival Programming of the small, fearful you. This can be really uncomfortable to face, but it is critical to see clearly so that you can gain freedom from this dark influence.

The bottom half of your Mandala spells out the dynamics of Your Primal Persona and its Ego-Driven Survival Programming:

Distorted Theme
SELF-MEDICATION

Compulsion
Seeking Pleasure / Fleeing Pain

Sabotage Pattern
Over-Indulgence

Destructive Behavior
Escaping

Survival Belief
I can survive as long as nothing hurts

YOUR PRIMAL PERSONA — **THE HEDONIST** — EGO-DRIVEN

Your Primal Persona: The Hedonist

As a Type 7,

> Your Primal Persona is known as **The Hedonist.**

This is your Ego's version of "playing small," even though its programming is all about being fun and exciting. But, as we will now explore, being fun and exciting and being joyful and fulfilled are not at all the same thing.

See *Fig 8A* for a brief summary of your Ego-Driven Survival Programming (we will dig deeper into it in just a moment). It is characterized by resistance, eroding your Vitality and degrading your life.

These are some painful truths. But you must forgive yourself for your Survival Programming. Have compassion for yourself, for it was the pain in your life which led you to feel that you couldn't survive without this perspective. Without self-awareness, you had no choice but to behave this way.

And this is true for everyone else, as well. We all deserve forgiveness for the way we act when we are asleep to ourselves -- we are totally unaware this is what we are doing and how much it hurts ourselves and those we love.

Even once you are aware of your Survival Programming, it can be quite challenging to take command over it. Yet every degree of progress you make in this direction brings you enormous reward. You will be joyfully inspired to continue the work.

Let's dive just a little bit deeper into what these dynamics of your Survival Programming really mean, so that you may begin the most rewarding journey of integrating yourself.

Fig. 8A **PERSONALITY TYPE 7 SURVIVAL PROGRAMMING**
Your Primal Persona: **THE HEDONIST**
The Programmed You; The limited and diminished version of yourself that you default to when you are Ego-Driven
Distorted Theme: **SELF-MEDICATION**
Your Ego's warped and downgraded interpretation of your true Theme
Survival Belief: I CAN SURVIVE AS LONG AS NOTHING HURTS
The scarcity-oriented message embedded in your Ego that creates your world view
Compulsion: **SEEKING PLEASURE / FLEEING PAIN**
The repetitive internal process you instantly launch as a way of discharging the emotional tension caused by your Survival Belief
Destructive Behavior: ESCAPING
The ruinous actions you regularly engage in when you operate according to your Survival Belief
Sabotage Pattern: **OVER-INDULGENCE**
The totality of all your Survival Programming combined into an overall template for self-destruction

Your Distorted Theme

Each of the 9 Personality Types orient around a particular **Theme.** The whole point of you being here, at this time and in this place, is because you wanted to explore this Theme. This is the thing you are encoded to care about the most.

> Your Theme is **Elevation**

We will fully explore the true meaning of Elevation in the next section (about Your Vitality Personality), when we discuss the Consciousness-Directed understanding of your Theme.

But right now, we are discussing your Survival Programming, and how your Ego *degrades* your understanding of your Theme of Elevation.

Unfortunately, when Your Primal Persona interprets this Theme, **it becomes contorted – a warped, downgraded version of your highest potential.** This is called the **Distorted Theme.**

> Your Distorted Theme is **Self-Medication**

Self-Medication is all about the urgent desire to quickly feel better, and using external methods for achieving this. Type 7's are highly sensitive to pain and discomfort – both theirs and others' – and immediately long for relief. Most 7s struggle with a backdrop feeling of anxiety as they move through their day, though few actually face this and integrate it. Most ignore it and seek their favorite mood-alterer instead.

Although for many Type 7s Self-Medication means ingesting substances to feel better, that is only one way of going about it. Actually Type 7s are highly inventive and creative, and can come up with all *kinds* of ways to distract or numb themselves from their inner discomfort, and might change these up every day. It's not only wanting to medicate the body – there is also a desperation to pacify a frantic mind.

Watching TV, reading, surfing the internet, chatting on the phone… these are all ways of avoiding being present to how you're really feeling. Self-Medication is an all-encompassing category for the millions of ways you skip self-awareness in favor of pleasurable distraction.

The Ego is content to trap you inside this loop for all of your life: forever trying to feel great, but never experiencing a lasting sense of joy or peace.

Rather than rooting down into something deep and sustaining, your Ego prompts you to keep a hyper pace of new stimulation. As you will soon see, Self-Medication does not connect you to a sense of bliss… it blocks you from it.

In the hands of Your Primal Persona, you spend all your time seeking pleasure and fleeing pain, believing you are creating joy by staying positive, but instead are introducing factors which create misery:

- Imagining activities and experiences that will lead to your best life, you waste your time and energy on fantasy futures – resisting being effective and substantial in your present life
- Enjoying the fun parts of relationships but totally bored by familiarity, you are often restless and impatient – limiting your ability to connect deeply and build something that lasts
- Highly invested in thinking of yourself as fun and easy-going, you are not very willing to see your dark side honestly, creating resentment, frustration and contempt in your relationships
- All the planning and imagining you do in your mind leads you to have strong attachments to how you want things to go, causing you to be demanding, petulant and enormously frustrated when reality does not live up to your expectations -- destroying your sense of wellbeing
- Desiring your freedom above all else, you are often a no-show on the commitments you made – sabotaging the trust and affection others have for you

Ignoring all the unspoken signals you perceive energetically, your mind becomes anxious, hyper and distracted – making it difficult for you to concentrate and rise to your potential

Although Self-Medication makes you feel better in the moment, your resistance to facing discomfort fundamentally limits the profoundness of your experiences – and profound experiences are the thing you love most!

Avoiding all the uncomfortable things keeps you living only on the surface of life, flitting from one new adventure to the next, never exploring the richness and meaning that comes from going deep and holding still.

This is no fun at all to read about. It's a bummer to realize your default, unconscious wiring is a sadly small version of who you could really be – who you actually are. The Real You is full of radiance and love and light, trusting in yourself and the Flow of the Universe to create a beautiful world. You are on your way to discovering how to access this higher aspect of yourself.

Your Survival Belief

Your **Survival Belief** is the **scarcity-oriented message embedded in your Ego that creates your world view.** It is the secret programming in the basement of your unconscious which drives all your thoughts, feelings, and actions without you ever realizing it.

> Your Survival Belief is **I can survive as long as nothing hurts.**

This belief is fundamental to you, even though you never knew it was there. It defines your understanding of how the world works.

Typically, this Survival Belief is activated within you at a young age.

As a child you likely experienced a loss of nurturing – a disconnection from maternal support. This would have triggered in you anxiety and pain, and a strong desire to distract yourself from it.

You turned to pleasurable things as a way of avoiding noticing your sense of loss, longing, and confusion. You concluded early that you couldn't count on other people to be there for you, and so became one who pampers themself as a way of making up for the loss of parental nurturing. Becoming self-reliant and self-indulgent seemed like the best strategy for survival, and it's never occurred to you to re-examine it as an adult.

Unfortunately, this simple sentence is a template for destruction! Let's unpack all the ways in which this Survival Belief sets you up for problems, rather than the solutions you think it does.

Mental Preoccupation

Because you have never known how to heal your childhood wound, it still exists. If you were to become fully present and connected to your heart, you would discover it there, waiting for you. Because your Survival Belief convinces you that you may not survive feeling that pain, your unconscious strategy has become to avoid being present altogether.

In order to accomplish this, you keep your mind very busy, hopping around from thought to thought, experience to experience. Focus and concentration are difficult for you – you are highly distracted and distractible.

This becomes a primary source of self-sabotage. Even though you are highly intelligent, and naturally embody a whole host of talents other people would envy, it's likely you have not been able to rise to your full potential because of your resistance to holding still and going deep.

This breeds a private disappointment in yourself, a secret shame. You would prefer to think of yourself as very accomplished – someone you could feel proud of – but your inability to see projects through to completion is very much in the way.

Taking the Easy Way Out

Another way in which the desire to avoid pain sabotages the Type 7 is the unwillingness to do things "the hard way." Type 7s can become quite cunning in their desire to find shortcuts and fast tracks. Integrity seems too limiting of a concern – it is not the priority. Doing things quickly, easily and pleasurably is the priority.

Type 7s don't like the "taking care of business" parts of life – the tedious and boring parts. They avoid them, letting them pile up or go unaddressed altogether. Bookkeeping, taxes, keeping records, maintenance… these are all weak spots for you.

Again, these shortcuts, which seemed like the smart choice at the time, lead to having a lot of secrets, a lot of things you don't want other people to know about you. This keeps you fast-talking and fast-moving, trying to avoid being really seen.

Desiring Freedom and Fun

Limitation is another form of pain, as far as you are concerned. You don't like for others to have expectations of you. You don't like to feel obligated or beholden. You want to be free to roam, free to play, free to experience.

This can make you either a commitment-phobe, or a canceller, or both! Again, even though you want to be thought well of, follow-through can feel painful to you. You do not want to feel trapped or stuck. This is highly triggering to you.

Often this results in a dishonest way of dealing with things. You know it doesn't sound good to say, "Sorry but I just don't want to," so you're much more likely to come up with false reasons for declining which sound more legitimate.

But meanwhile, you can definitely be counted on to show up for the fun stuff! Curious, adventurous, and high-energy, participating in excitement and entertainment is your favorite pastime.

♦♦♦

As you can see, your Survival Belief that you can't handle pain is at the heart of much difficulty and self-sabotage for you. It is this belief which launches a cascade of repetitive thoughts and behaviors, that ultimately lead to your unhappiness. Learning about these, and how to take hold of them, is fundamental to becoming able to create a life you love.

If you have read this far, you are doing so well! Thank you for hanging in there, this stuff is definitely not fun to face. Remember, we are in the thick of the section about the Ego's Survival Programming. But then we will move ahead to discuss Type 7 at your highest and best.

We just finished discussing your Type 7 Survival Belief, which was activated somewhere in your childhood. It is the primary driver behind all of your unconscious thoughts and behaviors.

Now, we will look at the most common thought, feeling and behavior patterns that emerge as a result of holding your Survival Belief.

Your Compulsion

Your **Compulsion** is the **repetitive internal process you instantly launch as a way of discharging the emotional tension caused by your Survival Belief.**

> ➢ Your Compulsion is **Seeking Pleasure / Fleeing Pain.**

This Compulsion is much like a guilty addiction – you know you should give it up, but don't want to… because you privately love it. And even if you decide *That's it, I'm through with this…* you will still find it very difficult to stop, until you become able to embrace your Vital Truth (see the upper half of your Mandala), rather than your Survival Belief.

Most Type 7's do not have enough self-awareness to notice themselves doing this. They are so consumed with the need to be released from their discomfort that they instinctively reach out for the nearest source of relief. Unfortunately life needs to become ridden with painful consequences for a while before the Type 7 becomes willing to say: *I'm ready to do this differently.*

Remember that your hardwiring is constantly leading you to fear pain, which ultimately becomes the desire not to feel your feelings. It is only when you begin noticing yourself in the middle of it that you become empowered to choose something else.

So take a deep breath, and let's agree to hang in there and walk through the difficult stuff together for a moment. It won't be fun, but after that I'm going to explain to you what it was all for and how to immediately uplevel your quality of life. So please, Type 7, remember there's a very big reward waiting for you on the other side of this discomfort.

Seeking Pleasure

Pleasure means different things to different people. For some it's good food. For some it's good conversation. For some it's world travel. For some it's a staycation at home. Type 7's are incredibly diverse in their personal definition of delightful. But one thing is always certain: the Type 7 is seeking to experience *more* of it.

In fact, moderation is a rather serious problem area for you. The problem with it, of course, is that moderation requires limitation, and limitation is no fun at all. Boredom is in every way a buzzkill, which you avoid at all costs. As you can tell already, this tendency probably isn't going to end well.

It is difficult to generalize about Type 7's, because they are so incredibly creative about new and exciting ways to be new and exciting. But there seem to be five general styles: The Adventurers, the Sensualists, the Comedians, the Intellectuals, and the Dreamers. (And yes, Type 7, it is possible to be all five at once... Of course you asked that.)

The Adventurers

You are a high-energy person who likes to get up-and-out. You are looking for the day to be exciting. You don't hold still for long, and your calendar is packed. You like activities which provide a rush, the ones which offer an intoxicating cocktail of adrenaline, dopamine, and endorphins.

Adventure means different things to different people, but in general it means always wanting a new experience. For some it's high-octane activities, for some it's travel, for some it's trying new foods, for some it's moving into new neighborhoods. Really, the options are endless.

In your desire to experience new and interesting things – and with a very restless mind and body – it is extremely difficult for you to remain present. While you are inclined to always move on, there is very likely a list of people in your past who feel abandoned, forgotten, or otherwise left behind.

The Sensualists

You enjoy all your senses: taste, touch, sight, smell and sound. Enhanced by your natural empathic abilities, you love the feeling of ecstasy these can provide you.

The bliss that can be obtained through the senses -- via dopamine-inducing pursuits such as food, alcohol, marijuana, hallucinogens, opiates, and sex – is always fleeting, always leaving you craving more. It's easy to become addicted, leading to pain... which is not at all where you wanted to go.

The Comedians

Your mind is incredibly quick, your language is a joy, your face is expressive, and you love to laugh – seriously, why aren't you in Hollywood?

While you actually *do* have everything it takes to go all the way, meanwhile... are you remembering to be sensitive to other people's feelings? Yes you are funny, but are you kind?

Sometimes your observations are *too* astute, and you can put a big impact behind them with your words and body language. Your talent for expressiveness can be wielded as a weapon if you are not careful.

Also it is important not to lose touch with what is going on for other people as you indulge your impulse to be silly. Your need to have the spotlight can become tiresome for the people trying to be in a relationship with you or actually give their attention to something else.

The Intellectuals

The life of the mind is your favorite dimension. You love to read, you love to learn, you love the sharing of ideas. You could be a perpetual college student or professor for the rest of your life, accumulating degrees and enjoying the camaraderie of like-minded people.

Unfortunately, staying primarily in the mind means staying primarily out of the heart. You can use your lively mind as a fun tool which helps you avoid deeper investigations within yourself. It's entirely possible that you haven't checked in with your feelings in years.

This can lead to disconnection and a lack of compassion. It can hold back the development of your emotional maturity. Although you are wired for empathy, this is only experienced through the heart, and you have been closing this down.

The Dreamers

Your imagination is in technicolor. Your ideas build upon themselves, and you love to visualize them expanding. You are able to see in your mind's eye the future of your dreams. This is your happiest of happy places.

Unfortunately, it takes a lot more effort to launch these ideas than just thinking about them, and this is where you lose steam. You like it best as it is in your mind, not the reality which is far more tedious and frustrating than you imagined. Your tendency is to give up once the reality becomes too unpleasant, leaving a legacy of unfinished projects and unfulfilled potential.

Staying in your imagination, dreaming up potential futures, while lovely, is another way of avoiding being present in the Now.

♦♦♦

Hmm. We just finished talking about Seeking Pleasure, yet somehow that was no fun at all. Please hang in there, because we're on our way to the really good stuff.

Fleeing Pain

Whoever said *No Pain, No Gain* was a complete idiot. At least, according to an Ego-Driven Type 7. For them, the motto is more like *No Pain, Not Ever*.

Unfortunately, as uncomfortable as this feels, you must be willing to see this in yourself in order for you to heal yourself once and for all – so that there's nothing to outrun anymore, and you can find peace.

Physical Pain

Well really, who likes it? But 7's might be extra quick to reach for the pills or other sedatives. The more relaxing and addictive, the better. Type 7's with a sports injury could easily fall prey to an opiate addiction.

The Sensual Type 7 finds physical pain to be immediately unacceptable. They have perhaps the lowest pain threshold of all the Types.

The more hyper, Adventurous Type 7 enjoys being very physical, very athletic. They have a tougher attitude towards physical pain. Plus keeping the endorphins high helps you avoid really feeling it anyway.

Being physically active is a seemingly healthy choice for discharging frenetic energy. Combine this, however, with a love for a high and a penchant for taking risks, and these Type 7's often end up with broken bones, sprains, torn ligaments, or worse.

Ironically, this forces the Type 7, who was using physical activity as a way to avoid feeling things, to hold still. All roads lead back to holding still and feeling your feelings.

Emotional Pain

Emotional pain is a dishearteningly vast topic which encompasses all of the things the Ego-Driven Type 7 might feel compelled to flee.

And yet, emotional pain is also a fundamental part of the human experience. As a Type 7 you are wired to desperately want to get away from emotional pain, but fighting against the Flow is how you keep creating the friction. Avoiding emotional pain is blocking yourself from the powerful lesson of how to adapt and heal yourself – an invaluable resource.

The fundamental function of an Ego is to make you forget your connection to your Source. You came here specifically to experience the pain of seeming disconnection, to navigate through it, and find a way to feel reconnected. Separation from Source is the original wound. It sets you up to experience incompleteness, which launches your journey in search of wholeness. This is the human experience.

For a Type 7 this is seriously bad news. Because you really, really do not like digging into the stuff that hurts.

The really good news is that it will not hurt nearly as badly as you think it will. The fear of it is actually far more painful. There are extremely gentle methods available for healing even the most cutting of wounds.

The key thing to understand is this: In learning how to bring yourself into a place of *willingness* – feeling no need to shift your attention away from the Now – you discover that it does not destroy you like you assumed it would. It is stepping into willingness and opening your heart which immediately uplevels everything for you.

The big reward for doing this shadow work is that, shortly into it, your Ego begins letting go of its grip on you. When you are able to live in a place of willingness, new codes in your DNA activate, giving you the true relief you seek from the pain of a polarized perspective. It really does change you at your core, when you are able to hold still long enough to allow it to happen. Your life becomes easier and easier, and living with unspoken pain becomes a distant memory.

♦♦♦

Even though it can seem hopeless, there is still purpose behind your Ego hardwiring leading you to Seek Pleasure and Flee Pain. Although it has the potential to lead you to your destruction, it also has the ability to wake you up to yourself. In causing the consequences of your choices to be so painful that you will do anything to make them stop, you finally become willing to submit, and surrender to what the Universe is showing you needs to change. This has always been guidance, showing you the way to your best self.

As soon as you let go of your resistance, and become willing to move towards acceptance, and balance… it all begins to get so much better.

As you continue your pursuit of self-awareness, you will learn methods for releasing yourself from your compulsion to Seek Pleasure and Flee Pain. Rather, you will become adept at remaining present and responding with integrity to the needs of the day, trusting that the experiences you find yourself having are always for your own Greatest Good.

Your Destructive Behavior

Your Survival Belief – that nothing must ever hurt – also prompts your actions and behaviors. When you are Ego-Driven, and therefore **not questioning your inherent attitudes and beliefs, you will repeatedly behave this way.** This is called your **Destructive Behavior.**

You may be entirely unaware of it, or you may be doing it on purpose in the utter certainty it's the best way to be. Either way, this behavior is never for the Greatest Good of all, and therefore is destructive.

As an Ego-Driven Type 7 who believes being present will hurt and therefore destroy you. . .

> ➤ Your Destructive Behavior is **Escaping.**

Escaping means slipping away – from limitation, from punishment, from pain. As usual, Type 7's are eclectic in which things they will want to Escape from.

For some, Escapism could be a lifetime of very small escapes, like surfing the internet for hours, taking a million "breaks", and beginning cocktail hour somewhere around 11am. And for some, it could be more occasionally epic examples, like running out for groceries and never going back.

Big or small, ultimately this is the behavior which erodes your sense of pride in yourself, your love and respect for yourself. When you know you have so much incredible potential, but you can't bring yourself to stay present and focused, your feeling of joy about yourself and your life dwindles.

Here are some of the primary scenarios the Type 7 struggles with.

Escaping the Now

In short, an Ego-Driven Type 7 is seeking to Escape being present. There are endless methods for Escaping the Now. But here are a few of the most common ones for Ego-Driven Type 7's.

- Numbing – with prescriptions or recreational choices that turn your sensibilities off
- Stimulating – using caffeine and other stimulants to create an instant feeling of "up"
- Daydreaming – imagining an exciting future
- Chores/projects – busywork to avoid feeling your feelings
- Social media – plugging in to an onslaught of random stimulation
- Physicality – using physical exertion to burn off frenetic energy
- Binging– binge watching, binge reading, binge eating, binge whatevering

Escaping Expectations

You are very attached to feeling happy, and this undoubtedly includes maintaining your own autonomy and having as much freedom as possible. For this reason, you tend to find much of conventional life too confining.

Yes, it's true – you are built to be a bit of a rule breaker. At the very least a rule questioner. You fundamentally do not agree to accept other people's expectations as your truth – you like to explore that for yourself, and usually arrive at a conclusion which is alternate to the mainstream. This actually is more Consciousness-Directed than you realize. However, in order for this to serve the Greatest Good, you must admit this with honesty and integrity, rather than being sneaky and evasive.

There are some who find your rebelliousness and unconventionality disappointing and unsettling -- they really want you to conform to the traditional, known rules that make life feel safe and predictable. This is painful for you, that you can't always please people while remaining true to yourself – because you actually really care about pleasing and delighting other people.

You will spend a fair amount of effort in the beginning, attempting to meet society's expectations. It takes a while to slowly realize that you just aren't really like other people, and the things that other people want out of life are not at all what you want.

This can be a really painful process in the 20's and 30's, as you make promises to get a college degree, to get married, to have kids, to have a traditional career – but then slowly realize that none of it is making you happy. You can go through many years of feeling like a disappointment, a failure at adulting.

In this situation, you don't want to let anyone down. So it's possible that you felt driven to create a private lifestyle for yourself, that few know about, where you give yourself permission to be your full-throttle unconventional self. This probably includes breaking some rules or promises.

Well, usually this can't go on forever. Eventually there comes a day of reckoning, and you will have to choose – to leave the life you've built that doesn't really fit you and start again, or find a way to feel at peace inside, regardless of external circumstances. Ultimately this crisis can lead you directly to your best life, if you accept the process wholeheartedly.

Escaping Responsibility

Intelligent, high-energy, imaginative, and upbeat, you are a natural leader. You easily rise to leadership positions without really trying, and you often volunteer yourself to lead-up new projects.

And yet, at the same time, there is a large part of you who just wants to chuck it all and go skinny-dipping.

As a Type 7, part of your Ego wiring includes a knee-jerk resistance against doing what you "should" be doing. It might even be what you sincerely insisted you *wanted* to be doing. Nevertheless, as much as part of you likes to be competent, productive and in-charge, there is another part of you longing to abandon it and forget all about it.

As you can immediately see, this is self-sabotage in action. Left unexamined, this creates a Peter Pan dynamic of never wanting to grow up, never wanting to accept the responsibilities of adulthood.

Even with so much talent, so much natural ability at so many different things, only a small percentage of Type 7s will ever go all the way with it. Much more commonly, the Type 7 leaves a legacy of projects and dreams only partially completed, never realizing their full potential, and developing a feeling of low self-worth.

Escaping Boredom

With your Type 7 unconscious drive to avoid feeling into the present moment, you become extremely attached to filling all your moments with activity. To you, boredom is the worst, most excruciating thing to have to endure. Your mind wants sparkly stimulation, your body wants movement.

Unfortunately, even the best parts of life usually still include a modicum of boring parts. This makes it very difficult for Type 7s to see projects all the way through to the end. Often they will abandon things that require deep commitment, like training for sports, or completing a degree, or even monogamy or child rearing. Staying the course over the long haul is an exceedingly challenging part of life for the Ego-Driven Type 7.

You can go to rather astonishing lengths to avoid boredom, without even realizing that's what you're doing. You might invent chores on the fly, or run perpetually late because being early might include boredom. You might triple-book yourself on the same day. You might randomly eat, or shop, or gamble, or masturbate, or play video games, just as a way of killing time. In fact, you might pursue some highly questionable pursuits merely out of wanting to Escape boredom.

The growth for the 7 is to realize that life is only ever in the Now. There could be joy for you in all of your small moments, should you become aware of your connection to Higher Consciousness.

Escaping Anxiety

Although some Type 7s are well aware of their anxiety problems, there are far more who have no idea this is going on within themselves. Whether they realize it or not, it is a hallmark of the Type 7 to have some latent anxiety going on in the background.

Anxiety means different things to different people. The Type 6 would say it's a feeling of impending doom that brings on panic attacks. The 5's would say it is a feeling of bleakness about the future of humanity.

But it isn't like that for the Type 7. For you, it is an unpleasant agitated, restless feeling that comes up unexpectedly. It seems to be a combination of the body feeling incapable of holding still, while the mind is careening around with disjointed thoughts.

Most 7s describe a sense of white noise going on in the background of their mind – like a radio playing too low to really hear. This is why it is often difficult for them to concentrate – they sense a murmuring in the background.

ADHD is a very common diagnosis for Type 7, and this can be harmful for a number of reasons. First, it labels you as having something wrong with you, traumatizing your self-esteem. Second, it doesn't offer you any insight or tools so that you might empower yourself, leaving you feeling trapped. And third, the most common medical treatment is a highly addictive stimulant with serious long term health consequences. It seems likely that what is usually called ADHD is really more about this kind of vague, restless anxiety.

Most 7s are not willing to admit to themselves that they experience anxiety, because they don't know where it comes from or how to resolve it, so they just try to drown it out as quickly as possible. Alcohol, marijuana, and opiates are common choices for this purpose.

♦♦♦

Facing your own hidden ways of Escaping can be excruciatingly painful. It's not necessary that you confess to the world. But it is completely necessary that you admit these to yourself. Escaping is exactly the thing that has been in the way of you loving yourself, and creating for yourself a life you truly want. Please hang in there, we're almost done with the hard part….

Your Sabotage Pattern

As we have discussed, your Personality Type has much Survival Programming built in. Your Survival Belief, Compulsion, and Destructive Behavior are undeniable impulses within you that all drive your well-being into the ground.

In other words, these all combine into an overall template for self-destruction. This is called your **Sabotage Pattern – the way you repeatedly behave throughout your lifetime which leads directly to the destruction of your health and happiness.**

> Your Sabotage Pattern is **Over-Indulgence.**

Over-Indulgence is becoming far out of balance by only focusing on what feels pleasurable, and ignoring or abandoning whatever feels unpleasant. It is being extreme in the preference for only "positive" experiences. Much like a child who only ever wants dessert and doesn't want a bedtime, Type 7's resist the Flow of the Universe through refusing to embrace balance and moderation.

Although immediate gratification feels delightful in the moment, a lifetime of it can lead to some extremely serious consequences, thereby sabotaging your experience of Vitality.

Over-Indulgence of the Mind

Over-Indulging your mind means embracing a gluttony of meaningless mental chatter, rather than developing the discipline of silencing it.

Type 7s are "Head Types", meaning you have an excessive amount of energy centered in your mind. But whereas fellow Head Type 5 – who is always studying and observing – and Head Type 6 – who is always imagining looming disaster – you are always imagining future fabulousness.

You regularly Over-Indulge your Ego mind by allowing your attention to turn to future fantasy. roaming the internet for random content, and other forms of check-out. This fosters your desire to escape, through seeking out more and more mental stimulation.

Hanging out in your mind, imagining happy times or streaming all the chatter, is your favorite happy place. This is sometimes called the "Positive Ego."

Positive Ego is actually really tricky. Unlike the encoding of some of the other Personality Types towards self-loathing or pessimism which is so noticeably Ego-Driven, Survival Programming towards being light-hearted and cheerful is much easier to miss. It seems like you're doing something good for yourself, by making up stories of future fun and ease.

Nevertheless, this is still the Ego keeping you distracted with mental chatter, so that you never claim your power which waits for you in the Now.

Instead, this distraction causes you to leak your power all over the place. You leak power through not totally concentrating on the task or person before you. You leak power by running late because you let the fun stuff run long. You leak power by always changing plans, because the fantasy already gave you the buzz, and the plan turned out to be more challenging than you thought.

A Type 7 can be quite attached to the belief that you are not capable of holding still and going deep, but this is utterly untrue. As we will discuss in the upcoming section on Your Vitality Personality, you are extremely magical, and all the things that would feed your light live within. Letting your Ego trick you into thinking you can't handle it is self-sabotage at its most tragic.

Over-Indulgence of the Body

In the body, Over-Indulgence is expressed as regularly participating in behaviors which provide sensual pleasures as a means of escape. Food, alcohol, drugs, sex, even excessive exercise and extreme sports are all examples of how you might attempt to use physicality as a means of avoiding your pain.

As much as you might delight for the moment in giving your body a blast of euphoria, this is not Joy as long as these moments are "stolen." If, at the same time you're feeling the high, you're also suppressing the things you're avoiding and fleeing, you are dosing yourself with something quite a bit more toxic than you knew.

Also, many Type 7s fill all their minutes with plans and activities as a way of suppressing their feelings of anxiety. It is the quiet moments when these feelings come up, interfering with the ability to rest. It is common for some Type 7s to develop burnout from Over-Indulging their incessant need to be busy.

Even exercise can become more of a problem than a help if it is done for neurotic reasons. Checked-out workouts – where you're listening to or watching chatter at the same time – do not count as acts of self-awareness or self-care. If you're not aware of yourself and your body as you are exercising, your motivations are likely Ego-Driven.

Meditative movement may be an ideal way for you to reckon with the anxiety you experience when you attempt to slow down. Yoga, qi gong, tai chi, and ecstatic dance are all ways you might try to allow yourself to be an expression of The Real You as you center and balance your energy.

Over-Indulgence of the Heart

In the heart, Over-Indulgence is demonstrated as only being willing to experience "positive" emotions, while completely denying the heavier and more painful feelings which are also within you and needing to be integrated. It is the attempt to live fully out of emotional balance, pretending your dark side doesn't exist.

This may seem counter-intuitive, but it is actually your willingness to feel the true depths of your feelings that gains you access to authentic joy. Your most ecstatic, euphoric self is your Higher Consciousness, who connects with you in your heart.

Opening your heart up only part-way or only part of the time is resisting your fundamental source of happiness. You are afraid to feel your sadness, your hurt, your anger. You suppress them beneath a veneer of humor and charm, while pursuing pleasure to a copious degree.

But if you were to allow yourself to connect with these feelings, they would express and then release, and you would be free.

In chapter Twelve, you will learn methods for simply and easily processing your feelings, and integrating the parts of you that resist being present. You will see this is nothing to hear, and something you are capable of now.

Once you clear yourself of the fear of being present, you will gain access to the full glory of Now, where all your love is, all your happiness, and all your peace.

✦✦✦

To live in a chronic state of Over-Indulgence creates friction and conflict, and ultimately, destruction. It has you existing in a perpetual world of extremes, rather than peace and balance. As you can see, it will likely lead to your own downfall, rather than your survival, as your Ego would have you believe.

It is not too late to reconnect with The Real You. You will find the road vulnerable and scary... and you will also find love, peace, satisfaction and a deep sense of serenity. It is a journey worth taking. The guidance on how to do this is coming up next.

✦✦✦

Now that you have opened your eyes to the destructive inner workings of your own Ego, operating as Your Primal Persona, do not despair. It is certainly within your capacity to transform these behaviors and patterns of your Survival Programming.

If you have made it this far, CONGRATULATIONS. We lost many along the trail – not everybody is ready for the journey that is Getting Real! This book is really only interesting to people who are about to make an enormous advancement in their consciousness.

We made it through the hardest part. Now, let's explore how you can be, act and live differently. There is an entirely different kind of life available to you, filled with love and connection and joy. And it is mapped out in the top half of your Type 7 Mandala.

ACTIVATE YOUR POWER PARADIGM

In Chapter One we revealed the meaning of Your Vitality Personality. Let's recap now.

Your Vitality Personality is the version of you that exists when you allow your Higher Consciousness to guide your thoughts, feelings, and actions. It is the opening of your heart, and allowing the loving intelligence found there to Flow through you. This infuses you with insight, wisdom, love and compassion, and the actions you take from this place always serve the Greatest Good.

Let's take a look now at the top half of your Mandala which spells out the dynamics of The Real You - Your Vitality Personality - and all its wondrous gifts and talents:

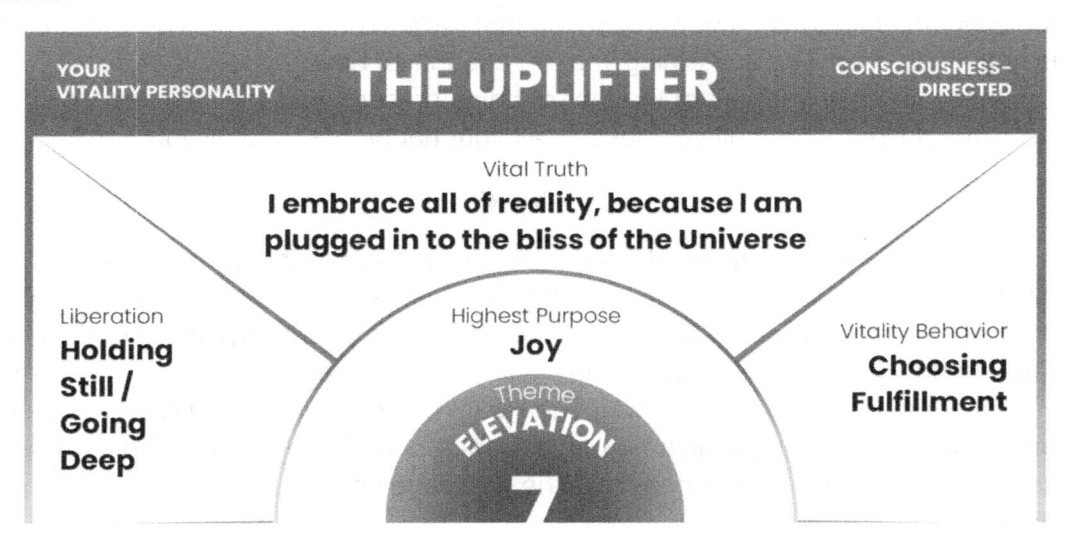

```
YOUR
VITALITY PERSONALITY        THE UPLIFTER         CONSCIOUSNESS-
                                                     DIRECTED

                          Vital Truth
              I embrace all of reality, because I am
              plugged in to the bliss of the Universe

Liberation              Highest Purpose          Vitality Behavior
Holding                      Joy                    Choosing
Still /                                            Fulfillment
Going                      Theme
Deep                     ELEVATION
                             7
```

Your Vitality Personality: The Uplifter

As a Type 7,

> Your Vitality Personality is known as **The Uplifter.**

This is the truth of who you really are. You have always felt your own bright light inside of you, and noticed that you seem to draw people to you with it. Certainly you love to laugh and enjoy life, which bolsters other people, but what you really offer is even deeper than that. You can be struck to your core with awe at the beauty in the world, the intelligence, the magnificence, the magic. It is your profound appreciation for the splendidness of life itself which inspires and heals everyone around you.

The Real You is a magician – an alchemist transmuting darkness into light – reminding us all of the divine spark within us and all around us. You are the one who elevates Consciousness through your great love of Life. Your joyfulness brings hope, excitement, and encouragement to all of us who struggle to find our way through the pain.

See *Fig. 8B* for a brief summary of the Consciousness-Directed half of your Mandala, identifying how to use your Personality Type to bring into your life a sense of completeness, fulfillment, joy and love:

When you embody all these natural gifts, you are a dazzling light, inspiring all who know you. It is so exciting to think you are just on the precipice of launching a new life of love, acceptance, and Vitality for yourself! It might have required some serious deep-breathing to get here, but the effort is so well worth it.

Let's explore these dynamics of your Power Paradigm, so that you may begin to fully comprehend just how open, uplifting, happy and healthy your life could really be.

Fig. 8B **PERSONALITY TYPE 7 POWER PARADIGM**
Your Vitality Personality: THE UPLIFTER
The Real You; The most magnificent version of yourself you joyfully embody when you heed the guidance of your Higher Consciousness
Theme: ELEVATION
The dynamic realm of Life your Higher Consciousness wants to explore to the fullest
Vital Truth: I EMBRACE ALL OF REALITY, BECAUSE I AM PLUGGED IN TO THE BLISS OF THE UNIVERSE
The higher understanding of how to thrive, that aligns you with the Flow of the Universe
Liberation: HOLDING STILL / GOING DEEP
The emancipating philosophy you freely embrace to enhance your connection to the Flow
Vitality Behavior: CHOOSING FULFILLMENT
The empowering and uplifting actions you intentionally choose to create your best life
Highest Purpose: JOY
How you serve the Greatest Good through embracing your encoded genius, and the source of your Vitality

Your Theme

As was mentioned previously,

> Your Theme is **Elevation.**

When you pursue the highest form of this Theme – Elevation – you are truly aligned with Source, and therefore always serving the Greatest Good.

Elevation is the raising of energy to a higher, more inspiring and empowering plane. When you are genuinely joyful, your positive energy touches everyone around you, elevating and amplifying their energy. They experience this as feeling happier, encouraged, and pain-free.

Shockingly, the Type 7 is the only one out of all nine Types whose top priority is being happy. This means everyone else is wired to focus on something *other* than being happy, which leads them down a road of despair. You just can't understand what a big deal it is for other people to experience a dose of your shining light. You are a balm to their pain.

You are the ambassador of joy here on Earth. You are the only one who naturally remembers how it feels to be connected to bliss, and you are the one with the capacity to help return others to this magnificent Flow.

Inspiring Yourself Inspires Others

The path to Elevation simply begins with inspiring yourself.

Inspiring yourself is not the same thing as entertaining yourself, distracting yourself, or intoxicating yourself. Those are Ego-Driven pursuits, which actually all lead to *blocking* you from inspiration.

Inspiring yourself means becoming willing to reach inward, toward your Higher Consciousness. Through choosing to go deeper, and connect with your inner world made of feelings and images, sound and light, you meet your true self.

Communing with yourself is an ecstatic experience. When you let all the pretenses of the outer world fall away, and just sit in silence with yourself, you will discover how deeply you love yourself. This fulfills you beyond words, and ignites a light in you that others can see.

You are in full sparkle, Type 7, when you are overflowing with joy, and this is how you naturally inspire other people. Your bright light is hard to miss, and people are instinctively drawn to it.

For the same reason we love fairy lights, Christmas lights, Independence Day fireworks, and candles in the darkness, we all feel inspired, hopeful, reassured, warmed, and dazzled by your radiance. Life seems so much more wonderful because you're in it.

When you make the choice to deepen and root yourself, and live beyond your own immediate gratification, you place yourself into the Flow of the Universe. The rewards for your life of service will be quite beyond imagination.

This is why Your Vitality Personality is named The Uplifter. You are the one who builds a brighter future through raising the morale of others, helping them find the hope and strength they need to fulfill their own Consciousness-Directed potential.

In the hands of Your Vitality Personality, you apply your fully heart-centered Self towards efforts which serve the Greatest Good, making you an inspired and revered Uplifter:

- Fully joyful, with no secret pain being avoided or suppressed
- Feeling calm, centered and grounded -- capable of focused activity and completing projects
- Reveling in the mutual support and encouragement that naturally develops in healthy relationships
- Work which provides mental stimulation, emotional fulfillment, and financial freedom
- Vital health derived from quieting the mind, healing emotional wounds, and honoring the body
- Experiencing a sense of peace and satisfaction at knowing your life serves an important Purpose

Most people are unhappy. They feel heavy and hopeless, which leads them far away from themselves and their true purpose. They don't know how to find their way to joy, and it is slowly destroying their wellbeing.

You are the one who is built to serve the world by engaging your natural abilities to uplift, heal and guide yourself and others toward joyfulness.

However, you will only burn brightly as long as you are able to understand that you must renew yourself through a deep connection to the Universe.

Rather than seeking pleasure and fleeing pain, choose to seek fulfillment instead. You must discover contentment inside yourself, while holding still, rather than perpetually seeking it outside of yourself. In being willing to be present, and face the realities of life, you will discover you are still lit from within. In this way you serve your Highest Purpose: bringing joyfulness to the world.

Your Vital Truth

Your **Vital Truth** is the **Higher understanding of how to thrive by aligning with Universal principles.** It is the escape hatch your Ego doesn't want you to know about, because it unlocks all of its Survival Programming, and connects you to your Higher Consciousness – The Real You.

> Your Vital Truth is **I embrace all of reality, because I am plugged in to the bliss of the Universe.**

This is a direct contradiction to what your Survival Belief encourages you to believe. Your Survival Belief prompts you to think that reality is painful, and feeling this will destroy you.

Facing all of reality sounds like very dangerous territory to a Type 7... but only if you keep telling yourself how you can't handle it.

But, what if you really loved yourself, and trusted yourself, and believed in yourself? What if you felt strong, and grounded? What if you felt willing to stay present, giving yourself the chance to discover that you really like who you are when you're not running away?

Let's unpack this Vital Truth statement, so that you may understand how it is possible to remain in an uplifted state even when reckoning with difficulty and pain.

Embracing Reality

It's time to take a look at that old Ego-Driven Survival Belief and ask yourself – is it actually true that you can't handle experiencing pain? Is it really necessary for you to skip out on all the intense parts of life?

Although it seems really scary to face the harshness of life without softening the blow with self-medication, the truth is your fear of it is way worse than the reality.

When you learn your new Real You Methods for grounding in your body, anchoring in your heart, and healing yourself of anything, you will realize that having the right tools makes everything easier. You're not so afraid of what's coming if you know that, no matter what, you have the strength to withstand it and the resilience to recover from it.

Learning how to silence the chatter of the Ego mind is a powerful aid in finding the willingness to face what upsets you. The Ego mind is your greatest adversary, whispering all sorts of fear-based messages that make you want to flee. When you become the master of this chatter you discover you feel far less resistant to dealing with whatever needs addressing.

And then you will have the presence of mind to remember all your resources and help.

Type 7, you are blessed with talents that others can only dream of. You are highly intelligent, powerfully intuitive, passionately creative, shrewdly adaptable, and charmingly communicative, with a boatload of friends. You ignite things with your enthusiasm. You attract people to you, you have helpers you don't even know about yet.

You can trust yourself. You can handle whatever life sends your way. You have intelligence and imagination, you have resources, and you have inexplicably good luck. No matter what uncomfortable situation is unfolding, you can stay open-hearted and see it through, trusting that all will be well.

Remember, the attitude of willingness is key. You must become willing to face discomfort, without seeking to escape. The first times you may literally need to breathe through it, as you finally return the call to the guy you've been owing money, or you finally seek help for a behavior that was becoming problematic. You have to be willing to give a hard thing a try and see what happens.

You will be amazed at what happens.

Plugging in to Bliss

The reward for willingness is swift and sweet. The results are always way better than you could have imagined. Actions which are taken in a state of fear or distress produce troubling results, but actions which are taken while in a state of trust and love produce outlandishly wonderful results. You only need to push yourself to try it a few times before you will come to believe that your Vital Truth is wisdom you can trust.

Your belief in your Vital Truth allows you to dismantle the workings of your Ego, thereby directing your life towards Vitality: the joyful expression of your awakened mind, vibrant body, and limitless spirit.

In order to become Consciousness-Directed, you must fully open the heart, silence the Ego-mind, and relax the body. This is the state of Flow, where the vital life force and intelligence of the Universe moves through you.

When you are in a place of physical, mental, and emotional stillness, you are in the receiving state. This is when all the solutions to your fears drop in. This is where the sudden genius ideas arrive. This is when the unconsidered solution magically appears. This is true knowingness – it is deep and true and lasting.

This is what will sustain you as you face challenging circumstances. You won't want to run away because you don't know how to handle it – you will know exactly how to handle it, and this will make you feel so much better.

This experience of receiving guidance from your Higher Consciousness provides you with the feeling of comfort and bliss you were always chasing in your escapism. The pain you were avoiding now becomes the opportunity to connect to your own love and wisdom – the highest high there is. The spiritual high you wanted is not in the outside world... It's inside of you.

It takes practice to develop the ability to reside in this aligned state. However, once there, your ability to design truly inspired solutions and refinements radiates and shines. It is what you were made for – there is no one more talented at it than you.

Your Liberation

Your **Liberation** is the **emancipating philosophy you freely embrace.** This is a powerful shift, out of the Survival Programming of the mind, and into the Flow of the Universe through the heart. Rather than being owned by a chronic Compulsion, you are now intentionally choosing this Liberation.

> ➢ Your Liberation is **Holding Still / Going Deep**

Holding Still and Going Deep means you have decided to take command over that highly distractible monkey mind of yours, regardless of how uncomfortable or impossible this may seem. You are going to take alone time with yourself and be calm and quiet enough to connect with your heart, where The Real You resides.

It's interesting to observe how just the thought of Holding Still and Going Deep brings up rather massive feelings of anxiety. This is showing you just how threatening this shift is to your Ego. Your Ego is fighting you mightily on this topic because you are at the precipice of claiming your power – exactly the thing your Ego has been programmed to block you from.

Your Ego is designed to supply you with an experience of human separateness – of limitation, of uncertainty, of powerlessness. But Holding Still and Going Deep is the act of discovering your connection to your Higher Consciousness – your infinite nature, your knowingness, your capacity for self-love.

You feel so much resistance because you are so very close to transforming your life. Are you willing to push through and discover what being quiet and fully present can do for you?

Holding Still To Be Present with Yourself
Meditation

First and foremost, you, Type 7, must become a meditator. Although everything within you is screaming *"Hell No!"*, please understand why this is so especially important for you above all, Type 7 – Your Highest Purpose is connected to it.

Meditation is the silencing of the mind, so that the wisdom of the heart may reveal itself to you. Rather than *doing*, it is simple *being*.

No one resists the thought of meditation more than the Type 7. It is an instantaneous rejection with no real consideration. *Impossible*, you say, and move on.

It's time to Get Real, Type 7. It's time for some serious adulting, and facing yourself. The longer you resist meditating, the longer you hold off your own access to joy.

Guided meditations are especially important for you, as you may train in how to meet your guides and to connect with your Higher Self. We all have these spiritual helpers, but most are unaware of them. You, however, have easier access to your ability to perceive them. This is not an accident.

Your Higher Consciousness and your guides are your greatest loves, the ones who know you best and would do anything for you. They signed on to be your non-physical helper team. You can receive deep healing, answers to questions, and assistance solving problems from these important unseen friends. (These are advanced teachings available in our private membership, Vitality Voyagers, through YourVitalityPersonality.com.)

Placing your mind inside a quiet space where your helpers can communicate with you will be the most ecstatic experience of your life. You will receive Love like you have never felt before – you will feel it pour into your heart, you will feel it roll through every cell of your body.

You will look back on the days where you refused to meditate and laugh at yourself, because you were blocking yourself from the highest high of all time.

Training in the Intuitive Arts

You have likely had latent intuitive abilities all your life, but you didn't realize how extensive they are or know how to work with them. Or maybe they scare you and you've been determined to ignore them. Or maybe you're afraid of how you would be seen/treated if anyone else knew.

You don't ever have to tell anyone about these abilities, if you don't want to. But it is still essential for you to gain a basic understanding of how they work and how to apply them, simply for your own mental health. Suppressing these powerful aspects of yourself leads to severe anxiety and depression. You must allow this aspect of yourself to Flow.

Fortunately, in these times of ebooks and YouTube you can have easy access to the education you require. It is time now to make this a priority in your life.

Empaths are people who can perceive the energy of the living beings around them. There are 7 types of Empaths, and you may have one or several of these abilities.

- **The Emotional Empath** – You can feel other people's feelings
- **The Physical/Medical Empath** – You can feel other people's pain and illness
- **The Intuitive Empath** – You can perceive and communicate with the energetic information about a person such as past lives, sources of pain, their Higher Self and guides, and more
- **The Dream Empath** – You receive messages in dreams and experience lucid dreaming, where you have dreamlike visions while awake
- **The Plant Empath** – You can sense the signaling that happens in nature and what its needs are
- **The Animal Empath** – You can communicate with animals
- **The Global Empath** – You can perceive shifts in global energy including natural disasters and war

As an Empath, you have at least one of these abilities, if not all:

- **Clairvoyance** – You have visions which are often seen in the "mind's eye", or you might be able to see beings or "spirits" in the physical world
- **Clairaudience** – You are able to communicate telepathically and hear information from unseen sources, either as actual voices or silently inside your mind
- **Clairsentience** – You can feel and sense the energy and emotions of other people, animals, places and spirits; this is felt in the heart and/or the body
- **Clairalience** – The ability to smell scents which have no physical source
- **Claircognizance** – You "just know" things, even though you can't explain how you know

Holding Still to Be Present With Others

As you know, the Type 7 Ego prompts you to feel a lot of restlessness and agitation. You become attached to keeping on the move as a way to suppress your feelings of anxiety and shame. This tends to block you from being fully present to other people's feelings and needs.

Being willing to slow down and hold still allows you to connect much more deeply with other people. Rather than telling yourself that life needs to hurry up, when you are Consciousness-Directed you know that you have all the time in the world. As long as you are enjoying yourself you are in the Flow of the Universe. And everything always works out for you when you are in the Flow.

To other people, it is incredibly healing and uplifting to be around you when you are fully aligned with your Higher Consciousness. You literally are the bringer of Light, and they all need it so badly.

Being fully present for others is strongly connected to your Highest Purpose. Although it sounds like you must sacrifice your time and energy, it is actually a mutually beneficial exchange – you always feel incredible when you have engaged with your Highest Purpose.

Going Deep

Going Deep has to do with exploring your inner terrain – the feelings, needs, beliefs and desires that have been going on within you all along. This is the process of discovering who you really are.

This might mean choosing meditation instead of watching tv. This might mean meeting with a therapist or life coach rather than meeting with friends for drinks. This might be studying how to cultivate your empathic abilities rather than surfing the internet. This might mean journaling instead of shopping.

But no matter what the activity, Going Deep means you are doing it while seated in your heart.

Sitting in the Heart

Gone are the days when you just allow your mind to hop around from shiny thought to shiny thought. Instead, whenever you notice your thoughts running rampant, you will intentionally place your attention in the middle of your chest. You can imagine a glowing orb inside there, if you like.

As soon as you shift your attention out of the mind and into the heart, the chatter ceases. You will feel yourself calm down. You can close your eyes, and feel into your heart.

Sometimes you will find feelings waiting in there for you. You might feel things like sadness or anger come up, without really understanding what they're about. That's ok, you don't need to know the story. Just let them come up anyway. In Chapter 12 you will learn the Real You Methods for clearing these.

You might have memories come up. That's ok, let them. If you have old wounds, there are methods you will learn for healing them.

Or maybe nothing comes up at all, and you just hang out in peaceful silence for a while. Try to stick with it for longer and longer. And then one day, unexpectedly, you will get to encounter your love for yourself.

Maybe it will come as a vision, or an imagining. Maybe you will see colors, or lights, or shapes. Or maybe you will just find yourself awash in feeling. But every so often, you will get to taste euphoria, and this makes all of your practicing and adulting worth it.

As we will discuss shortly, you came here to be an uplifting source of love and light to the world. To accomplish this, you brought with you many intuitive abilities that connect you to the Flow of the Universe. When you finally surrender to this truth, and allow yourself to be that conduit, your Higher Consciousness will undoubtedly gift you with blissful experiences of connection, love and healing.

In other words, your resistance to Holding Still and Going Deep will melt away as you begin to experience fabulous and meaningful interactions with your Higher Self. It will get easier and easier for you to drop out of your mind, and into your heart.

The richness this will bring into your life will change you in unexpected ways. That hyper, frantic quality you exuded will mellow out and ease up. Rather than needing to get away, you become happy to stay where you are. You will finally get to experience peace.

Your Vitality Behavior

Vitality Behavior is the empowering and uplifting actions you intentionally choose when you are Consciousness-Directed, rather than the Destructive Behavior your Ego drives you to act out.

> ➢ Your Vitality Behavior is **Choosing Fulfillment.**

Choosing Fulfillment means that, rather than Escaping with activities that excite and entertain, you opt to engage in activities that provide a sense of upliftedness, contentment and wholeness.

Fulfillment comes from enjoying a sense of meaning. Feeling connected to yourself, to other people, to Life. You begin to feel grounded and rooted, and light and free. Basically, all the feelings you were trying to reach through Escaping, you can finally experience when you Choose Fulfillment instead.

Here are some key ways that you can make sure you are Choosing Fulfillment:

Embracing the Now

Part of why you don't like feeling what's going on Now is because of how often you are feeling frustration there.

Frustration hardly seems like a strong enough word to communicate the intensity of the emotion. It is a kind of impotent rage at something you can't do anything about.

This could all change, and the Now could become delightful, if you would be willing to release your expectations of how things were supposed to go.

Because now that you look at it, your expectations of how things were supposed to go involved everything going swimmingly. You wanted it all to be fun, easy, smooth, delightful – Type 7 style. And when it wasn't, it's possible you may have had just the *teensiest* of tantrums.

Rather than needing everything to be painless and pleasurable, just allowing it to be what it is rids you of all that stymied energy. You're able to remain relaxed and receptive because you're not requiring the situation to be anything other than what it is.

With this release of expectation, you can be patient, calm, and curious about what this Now moment is trying to show you.

When you understand that you are the creator of the reality you are experiencing, you stop getting mad at it, and instead let it show you what it will about yourself. There is always something in it for you, and now you finally have the eyes to see.

Living Your Values

What do you care about the most? What feels really important to you? Have you ever thought about it?

Lots of Type 7s haven't, because that would have required Holding Still and Going Deep. Now that you've discovered how pleasurable that actually is, it's time to start clarifying what are the things that matter to you the most.

Perhaps this warrants a journal entry or two. Ask yourself: What makes me feel the most alive? Who inspires me to feel the deepest love? What are the things about me that I love and am proud of? What do I want more of in my life? What feelings will that provide me?

There is no right or wrong answer. The main thing is to realize what matters the most to you, and then give more of your time and attention to those things.

Oftentimes, Type 7s are easily distracted by something new and interesting. You can end up giving a questionable amount of your time and energy towards insignificant matters, while neglecting the things that make your life worth living.

When you bring your lifestyle into alignment with your true values, this will contribute greatly to your feeling of Fulfillment.

Completing Tasks

Unfinished tasks are a big way of leaking power, and you've likely got a bazillion of them. This stems from the classic Type 7 resistance to Holding Still. Your patience and attention span sputter out at about the 80% mark, and you hardly ever get back to your nearly-finished projects.

This keeps a lot of extra balls in the air that you are juggling, causing your mind to feel overwhelmed and chaotic.

Are you ready now to make a bargain with yourself? Promise yourself to see 3 pending projects all the way through to the end in the next 30 days, and then observe what that did for your mental clarity and sense of morale.

It might be helpful to recognize that the threshold where you're burning out is a very vulnerable spot for you. You know you will not return to this and it will become another dangling obligation. So what can you have as a plan for getting yourself through?

- Put on great music and keep going
- Establish a reward system, where you get no presents or treats until a task is complete, but then you get to do something celebratory when you finish
- Block out a spot on your calendar for when you will return to this project
- Set a deadline with an accountability partner
- Ask a pal to come over and be a grounding partner – someone who will physically anchor you to the present so you will complete the uncomfortable task you committed to facing.

Once you get a taste of how lovely it is to reduce the number of balls you are juggling, accomplish tasks, and feel a sense of Fulfillment, you will see for yourself why it's worth the effort. Not only do you feel enormously freer, but you also like yourself better.

Exploring Your Awareness

Many Type 7s run late and dread being early because of how much they unconsciously fear boredom – which is really anxiety. Boredom is yet another way to resist Holding Still and Going Deep.

So now, if you're stuck in line, if you're sitting in the waiting room, if you're waiting on slow people, you don't have to start feeling agitated and antsy. You can explore your awareness instead.

Slow down. Quiet your mind. Root your body into the earth. Anchor into your heart.

What's going on inside your own energy field? How does it feel? Imagine a wave of sparkling clear light passing through you and clearing your energetic debris.

What's going on in the energy field around you? What can you perceive? Draw clear light down through the top of your head, and blast it from your heart out into the room, cleansing it of old heavy energy, leaving it fresh and bright.

If the lady next to you is sad, send her pink light for love and gentle healing. If the child across from you is hyper and disconnected, send him purple light for cohesion and integration.

You are capable of taking in and sending out way more energetic information than you realize. Using your spare moments to transmute dark and heavy energy into love and light serves your primary purpose of being an Uplifter, which is always intensely Fulfilling.

Listening to Your Body

Your body is reflecting your thoughts and feelings back to you. When you slow down and tune in to how your body is actually doing, you learn much about how *you* are actually doing.

How are you sleeping – all the way through the night, or interrupted? Do you have racing thoughts? What are they centering around?

Are you experiencing any cravings? If you were to indulge that craving, what feeling would that provide? Why do you think you're needing that feeling right now?

How are your bowels? Regular and easy, or something off-balance? What toxic aspect of your life are you unwilling to let go of, or what are you unwilling to take in and digest?

Are you holding pain anywhere? Literally use your hands to feel your body. Press a knuckle into the masseter muscle just below the hinge of the jaw. Is it tender and tight because you've been gritting your teeth a lot? Squeeze the top of the trapezius muscle across the shoulder – is it flexible and supple, or hard as a rock? How about your low back and hips – fluid and limber, or achy and tight?

Pain and tension in your body is showing you the truth about your mental, physical and emotional wellness. Attending to these with love and compassion will bring you comfort, ease, and relaxation.

As you heal your body of the true root causes of its discomfort – which are often *not* physical – you will get to experience the happy purring contented feeling that happens when your body's needs are Fulfilled

♦♦♦

Choosing Fulfillment is a powerful shift for you, making it possible to stay present despite whatever discomfort might be waiting for you in the Now.

When you understand that all moments are an opportunity to love yourself and other people more, to heal yourself and other people more, to uplift yourself and other people more... you will discover that there is nowhere else you'd rather be, than right here right Now.

Your Highest Purpose

You chose to be here, in this time and place, because you wanted to contribute something. You came here for a reason, and you chose your Personality Type because it was the one that would help you accomplish it. **Your Personality Type has a special set of talents and abilities, and you wanted to use them to contribute.** This is your **Highest Purpose.**

> Your Highest Purpose is **Joy.**

Your Higher Consciousness chose the Personality Type 7 because It wanted to explore the Theme of Elevation on the physical plane. Joy is the way your Higher Consciousness intended for you to accomplish this.

Joy is the Consciousness-Directed version of fun. Fun is certainly a pleasant hilarity, but it is fleeting. After the high passes, the fun is now over, and you return to mundanity.

Joy is so much deeper, because it doesn't come from external experiences. It is the perpetual state of your Higher Consciousness, and when you open yourself up to receiving It, it fuels you from the inside out. Then, even the mundane experiences can be peaceful and fulfilling.

Joy is deep. Joy fills you up. Joy makes you vibrate and radiate. You cannot get there by remaining on the surface of things, flitting from random moment to moment.

You must be willing to explore your depths, to find what really drives you, what really matters to you, and to make that the central focus of your life. It is your sense of connection, of awe, of love, of being deeply moved by the beauty in your life that brings you Joy.

Joy is the highest high, better than anything that could be found in the physical world. It is euphoric.

Joy in the Mind

Joy in the mind comes from being present, and fully appreciating the moment. Rather than being distracted, anxious or bored, you delight in the experience Now is offering you. Instead of wanting to flee, you are happy to stay right where you are.

As a Type 7 you have a special connection to awe. Your wonder, curiosity and amazement not only elevate you – but also everyone around you. Through a mindset of wonder and awe:

- Your relationships are deep, where everyone feels loved, seen, and heard
- Your work excites you and feels meaningful
- Your energy is high while you feel internally serene
- Your mind feels clear, sharp, focused
- You feel patient, accommodating, relaxed – no need to rush
- You don't experience cravings, just ease
- You feel a glowing sense of pride about yourself, with no apologies
- You feel an exhilarating sense of freedom, because your life serves you
- You feel gratitude for this beautiful world and the amazing life you have been given

A Potent Mind

The Type 7 mind is unique and powerful. You might think of it as having equal prowess in both the left and right hemispheres of the brain. This is quite rare – usually people are wired to be predominant in one more than the other.

The left brain executes such rational functions as analysis, logic, math and language. Type 7s are adept at all of these when Consciousness-Directed.

The right brain is the mysterious land of feelings, images, memories, ideas, creativity and intuition. Type 7s have easy access to all these, too.

Plus, depending on how activated your pineal gland is, you possess extra-sensory perceptions in your capacity as an Empath. This gains you all sorts of additional insight and understanding.

When these are all active and coherent, you are a magnificent creator being. Your ability to bring what you imagine to life energizes and excites all of Life.

Joy in the Body

Joy in the body means taking delight in the experience of being physical. Whether active or at rest, you are present to the sensations of the body.

This is not the same thing as the Hedonist's over-indulgence in sex, drugs, food, etc. But these are not off-limits, either. Rather it is being able to partake in all of life in moderation and with no actions motivated by an underlying desire to avoid pain. Your desire to be in an altered state will organically shift towards glee at being fully aware and present.

This offers important grounding and anchoring for the Type 7, who might otherwise feel flighty and untethered to their reality.

In Chapter Twelve, the Real You Method called *The Sway* is a great one for you. It is an easy physical movement which is so relaxing and freeing that it eases you into a happy trance state. It balances your body, mind and heart all at once, bringing on the true euphoria of Vitality that you will love.

Joy in the Heart

You have been afraid to go into your heart because of all the old pains that await you there. It's true, you've got a number of old wounds that need clearing.

This is far more feasible than you imagined. See Chapter Twelve to learn some important tools that will assist you. You will be delighted at how much lighter and freer you will feel after processing a few of your heavier burdens.

This will also bring a lot more hope, and that starts unlocking and opening you to more of your true power. The discovery that it is possible to heal the things you were running from changes everything It is the pivot you needed to be able to Hold Still and Go Deep.

Joy is what you were made for – it is your true state -- yet you have got some work to do to be able to get yourself there. You must be willing to clear your calendar, silence your phone, turn off your computer and TV, and just be quiet with yourself.

This is the pathway to becoming someone you really love, trust, and feel proud of. You are on your way to becoming The Uplifter.

Serving as the Uplifter

Getting to be Joyful all the time is awesome, and it isn't just for you to experience alone. You are built to bring Joy to others, and this is how you serve humanity.

You embody a most remarkable list of talents and abilities. How can you use these to help other people? At your core, you are a teacher, a healer, and a guide.

Teacher

With your curious, visionary mind, and your dynamic, rare life experiences, you know a lot of stuff about a lot of stuff. You're a clear communicator, and you're a great storyteller, so it's really fun to listen to you.

You might actually be a teacher at a school, but even if you're not, you are still a teacher just moving through your day. Along with the interesting and valuable wisdom you've gained from your experiences, you also hold within you intrinsic wisdom. You know the secret to embodying Joy, and everybody wants you to share it.

No matter what the nature of your work is, you are a teacher of Joyfulness as you do it. Now that you realize you are playing an important role for other people, you can be more intentional about how you engage and what you say.

Healer

Many Type 7's are naturally drawn to the health and wellness industry. You love to help other people elevate themselves, but they can't do that while they are unwell. You are attracted to helping people solve the problems that are holding them back, and you're a lovely cheerleader as you go about it, too.

But even if you are not a health professional, this is where your natural Empathic abilities contribute to your Highest Purpose. Your ability to feel other people's feelings, to sense where they're stuck, and to reflect these back to them helps them see with new eyes. This clarity is for them a dose of love and light... you will never know how much this helps them.

However, it is extremely important that you remember NOT to take other people's pain and problems into your personal energy field. Your sensitive nature makes you vulnerable to carrying other people's negative energy with you, causing you to feel ill. You must learn how to create a protective shield of light around yourself, and how to "cut the cords" from the energy entanglements of the day. Remember that in order to be of use to others, you must attend to your own energetic health.

Guide

People notice your bright light. They see that you know how to make yourself happy, something everybody else has no clue about. You can count on finding yourself having conversations with seekers, people who ask you for guidance.

Again, your intuitive abilities play an essential role here. The only thing you need to do is be present and have whatever conversation unfolds naturally. You will just feel prompted to ask a question or make a comment, and you will see how it suddenly unlocks something for them.

You serve as a guide for many people, whether you realize it or not. Now you can be more intentional about it, more willing. You will see how the more you surrender to playing this role for people, the happier and more uplifted you yourself will feel.

◆◆◆

Joyfulness is how your Higher Consciousness always wanted to contribute to Life. Your Ego would have had you believe that you should drop everything and go throw yourself a party, but there is so much deeper you can go.

You can cultivate Joy for whatever community is meaningful to you. That could mean your personal household, that could mean your coworkers, that could mean your neighborhood, or that could mean the entire world.

Type 7, you are dazzling when you are alight with love and Joy. You are healing and inspiring. You embody Vitality, teaching everybody what it looks like and how to get it for themselves.

Are you ready to admit to yourself and the world that this is who you truly are?

No more playing small, only focused on your own Ego. No more acting out and sabotaging yourself. And no more hiding from your Purpose. It is time to be the Real You.

♦♦♦

Well, Type 7, you've been given quite a lot of information about yourself to digest. But hopefully by now you've come to see that even though you are wired to act out Your Primal Persona, it is possible for you to be someone so much more magnificent than that – Your Vitality Personality.

Now is the time to decide who you want to be in this world. If you are ready to step into the full power of who you really are, and seize your best life… then your next step is **Integration**. See Chapter Eleven.

CHAPTER NINE
PERSONALITY TYPE 8
THE LEADER | THE BULLY

THE LEADER — CONSCIOUSNESS-DIRECTED (YOUR VITALITY PERSONALITY)

- Vital Truth: **I surrender to the limitless power of the Universe**
- Highest Purpose: **Empowerment**
- Vitality Behavior: **Honoring & Collaborating**
- Liberation: **Allowing**
- Theme: **POWER**
- Type **8**
- Distorted Theme: **DOMINATION**
- Compulsion: **Controlling**
- Destructive Behavior: **Intimidating**
- Sabotage Pattern: **Force**
- Survival Belief: **I can survive as long as I am in charge**

THE BULLY — EGO-DRIVEN (YOUR PRIMAL PERSONA)

Hello Type 8, it is most excellent you are here. Between your attachment to action, and your inner coding to believe that emotional work is for wimps, it is unusual for you to give your time and attention to something so deeply introspective.

If you have been led here, then it is because you are ready to take a quantum leap ahead of your other Type 8 peers. The wisdom and insight you will gain here will propel you into an awareness far more advanced than most. This will hugely benefit the entire world, for you are one of a new breed of Leaders who are about to step forth – awakened, empowered, and benevolent.

This chapter focuses on the dual nature of your Personality Type 8, and the primary factors that hinder or help your ability to thrive. You will totally love the descriptions about your highest potential and purpose… but you will totally not love reading about your dark side, called Your Primal Persona.

Hang in there! We intentionally go through the Primal Persona stuff first, so that you can finish on a high note – the magnificence that is Your Vitality Personality.

Give yourself permission to surrender to this process, and you will see how it takes you on a journey, getting richer and richer the further it goes. The part of you that is wired for Empowerment will quickly come to see the massive power and advancement you will receive from the experience.

DECODE YOUR SURVIVAL PROGRAMMING

As we just learned, **Your Primal Persona is the version of you that exists when you allow your Ego to unconsciously drive your thoughts, feelings and actions.** It is the operating system of your survival-oriented mind, limiting you from tapping into the love and light that is your Higher Consciousness.

In this state, you are closed off from your sense of love for yourself or others. And the actions you take from this place only serve to fulfill the Survival Programming of the small, fearful you. This can be really uncomfortable to face, but it is critical to see clearly so that you can gain freedom from this dark influence.

The bottom half of your Mandala spells out the dynamics of Your Primal Persona and its Ego-Driven Survival Programming:

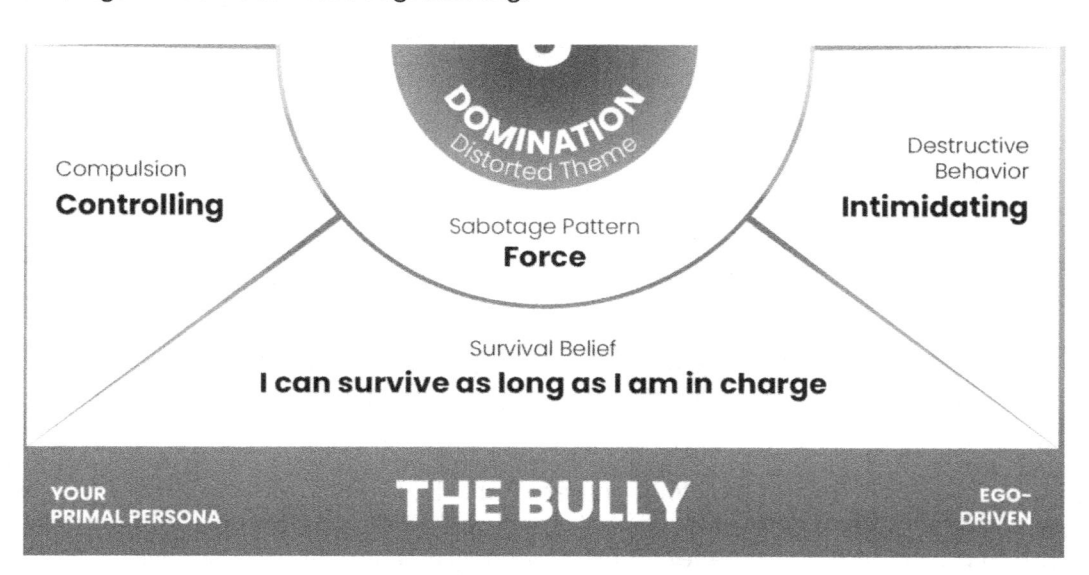

Distorted Theme
DOMINATION

Compulsion
Controlling

Sabotage Pattern
Force

Destructive Behavior
Intimidating

Survival Belief
I can survive as long as I am in charge

YOUR PRIMAL PERSONA — **THE BULLY** — EGO-DRIVEN

Your Primal Persona: The Bully

As a Type 8,

> Your Primal Persona is known as **The Bully**.

This is your Ego's version of "playing small," even though its programming is all about seeming tough. But, as we will now explore, seeming tough and being powerful are not at all the same thing.

See *Fig. 9A* for a brief summary of your Ego-Driven Survival Programming (we will dig deeper into it in just a moment). It is characterized by resistance, eroding your Vitality and degrading your life.

These are some painful truths. But you must forgive yourself for your Survival Programming. Have compassion for yourself, for it was the pain in your life which led you to feel that you couldn't survive without this perspective. Without self-awareness, you had no choice but to behave this way.

And this is true for everyone else, as well. We all deserve forgiveness for the way we act when we are asleep to ourselves -- we are totally unaware this is what we are doing and how much it hurts those we love.

Even once you are aware of your Survival Programming, it can be quite challenging to take command over it. Yet every degree of progress you make in this direction brings you enormous reward. You will be joyfully inspired to continue the work.

Fig. 9A **PERSONALITY TYPE 8 SURVIVAL PROGRAMMING**
Your Primal Persona: THE BULLY
The Programmed You; The limited and diminished version of yourself that you default to when you are Ego-Driven
Distorted Theme: DOMINATION
Your Ego's warped and downgraded interpretation of your true Theme
Survival Belief: I CAN SURVIVE AS LONG AS I AM IN CHARGE
The scarcity-oriented message embedded in your Ego that creates your world view
Compulsion: CONTROLLING
The repetitive internal process you instantly launch as a way of discharging the emotional tension caused by your Survival Belief
Destructive Behavior: INTIMIDATING
The ruinous actions you regularly engage in when you operate according to your Survival Belief
Sabotage Pattern: FORCE
The totality of all your Survival Programming combined into an overall template for self-destruction

Let's dive just a little bit deeper into what these dynamics of your Survival Programming really mean, so that you may begin the most rewarding journey of integrating yourself.

Your Distorted Theme

All 9 Personality Types each orient around a particular **Theme.** The whole point of you being here, at this time and in this place, is because you wanted to explore this Theme. This is the thing you are encoded to care about the most.

> Your Theme is **Power.**

We will fully explore the true meaning of Power in the next section (about Your Vitality Personality), when we discuss the Consciousness-Directed understanding of your Theme.

But right now, we are discussing your Survival Programming, and how your Ego *degrades* your understanding of your Theme of Power.

Unfortunately, when Your Primal Persona interprets this Theme, it becomes distorted – **a warped, downgraded version of your highest potential.** This is called the **Distorted Theme.**

> Your Distorted Theme is **Domination**

As you will soon see, Domination does not lead you to be more powerful… it actually leaves you with no one left to lead.

Domination is about having control. It's wanting to feel safe, stable and powerful through not leaving anything up to chance. Emotional and physical vulnerability and powerlessness feel excruciating to you, so you do all you can to keep yourself protected and calling the shots.

Your desire to feel strong and secure combined with your big energy, zealous passion, and a hot temper lead you to be intense and fiery. This is what makes your brand of control into Domination – you bring the big guns.

In the hands of Your Primal Persona, you unconsciously seize power and enforce your Domination, making you into a Bully:

- Feeling angry at an internal sense of powerlessness, you force others to submit to you
- Believing that the world is a brutal place, you make sure to look out for yourself
- Securing relationships with submissive types which ensure you have control
- Pursuing work which provides a sense of power and prestige
- Taking perverse pleasure in pushing your body far beyond its limits
- Regularly experiencing feelings of anger, frustration, and rage, and a lack of meaning

Although Domination makes you feel powerful in the moment, this is only your Ego rewarding you for so fully adhering to the program. Even though it has you thinking you are strong, it is actually this behavior that leads to a downfall. Ironically put, Dominating is your weak spot.

This is no fun at all to read about. It's a bummer to realize your default, unconscious wiring is a sadly small version of who you could really be – who you actually are. The Real You is full of power and love and light, with a desire to create meaningful change. You are on your way to discovering how to access this Higher aspect of yourself.

Your Survival Belief

Your **Survival Belief** is the **scarcity-oriented message embedded in your Ego that creates your world view.** It is the secret programming in the basement of your unconscious which drives all your thoughts, feelings, and actions without you ever realizing it.

> Your Survival Belief is **I can survive as long as I am in charge.**

This belief is fundamental to you, even though you never knew it was there. You have just assumed that it's as obvious to everyone else as it is to you that you should be the one in charge.

Even though you came into the world with this encoding already in place, dynamics in your early childhood likely tripped the alarm that would have activated all your Survival Programming, bringing it online so-to-speak.

Many Type 8s have had shockingly difficult childhoods, full of pain, abandonment, and boundary violation. It might have felt like you lived in chaos, or a warzone, and that the adults in charge couldn't be trusted to lead.

This would have triggered in you an intense desire to shut that all down and bring life into order and safety. You would have wanted to make yourself into someone tough and invulnerable, with the will and drive to seize control when life was pandemonium. Dominating the scene seemed like the best strategy for survival, and it's never occurred to you to re-examine it as an adult.

In truth your Survival Belief, such as it is, would not induce you to question your tactics, because it has led you to trust and believe in yourself so implicitly. As far as Ego Survival Programming goes, this aspect feels pretty great – lots of other Types receive programming that leads them to doubt themselves or hate themselves or feel ashamed of themselves.

It may be less obvious to you how this Survival Belief is sabotaging you, when it often makes you feel great about yourself. Perhaps it sabotages *other* people... but not you?

This self-serving belief that you should be the one in charge creates a whole cascade of other self-serving beliefs that minimize your recognition of other people's value. And this is where you end up making a wrong turn, because you are in resistance to the love and light that is the entire Universe.

Here are the main ones to watch out for:

I'm Smarter than Everyone Else

Well maybe that's true, and maybe it's not. But regarding other people with a sense of disdain, arrogance, and contempt isn't terribly smart. That is not how a Leader builds a fiercely loyal tribe – that's how they make enemies.

Although you certainly are an intelligent person, when Ego-Driven you are also an emotionally volatile and reactive person, and decisions made in the heat of the moment do not generally turn out to be constructive in the long run.

Being a terrible apologizer with an unwillingness to admit to mistakes doesn't help your case much, either.

As you can see, this belief is not helping you thrive, it's helping you isolate yourself.

You absolutely are built to be a Leader, Type 8. But it takes time and effort to earn trust and develop an authentic following of people who respect and care about you.

Throughout this chapter, we will be exploring how to let yourself become kinder, more humble, more loving, more grateful. You may not believe it yet, but that is actually the pathway to becoming a very great Leader indeed.

I'm Stronger than Everyone Else

According to your Ego hardwiring, Dominating requires brute force, so being physically, mentally and emotionally strong is a high priority for you. You like all sorts of sparring, because you like to demonstrate your prowess. However, competitiveness is not an element all people enjoy.

It's likely that, like most Type 8s, you take pride at being able to push yourself through difficult situations. You like proving your strength, endurance, and general badassness. You do have a higher pain tolerance than most, it's true -- which makes you *extra* intolerant of people you deem weak.

Ego-Driven Type 8s like to poke at other people, and see what kind of reaction they get. You want to see if you get a little aggressive who caves and who pushes back. You want to see if you can own the room.

Sure, penis-measuring is fun and everything, but is this really the best lifestyle for you in the long run? Has it occurred to you that, because you like a good fight, you are attracting a lot of unnecessary drama into your life?

Pushing yourself long and hard for years with hardly a bathroom break or a nap, on top of enduring boatloads of stress and misery, plus keeping yourself amped up for a fight and provoking drama – this only spells one kind of health outcome for you, and you're not going to like it.

Ease. Flow. Happiness. Love. Vitality. Have you heard of these? They exist in an entirely different reality than this one, where you have to fight and show off just to survive.

When you open up your heart – in humility, in seeking to connect, in wanting to help – you are opening yourself up to the Flow of the Universe. You gain access to your Higher Consciousness, and all its power.

When you have love in your heart, quiet clarity in your mind, and balanced energy in your body, you know your own power for certain. You don't have anything to prove. You don't need to poke and challenge, you don't need to take on big burdens. When you know your own power and love yourself, you realize your life could be really easy.

I'm Always Right

Well of course you would assume that, if you're programmed to believe you're supposed to be in charge. Clearly you're supposed to be in charge, because you're always right!

You're wired for action, and you like to cut through the b.s. You're quick and decisive, and you go with your gut. You feel like you can trust this. This is what makes you certain you're right.

But on the other hand, you go to Dominating without even noticing that's what you're doing. You get yourself all upset and puffed up, and start making a bunch of rash decisions.

So this is really a very tricky business. How are you supposed to know when you're *actually* right, and not just being a Bully?

In order to be able to tune in to the wisdom and guidance of your Higher Consciousness so that you can get the *real* right answer that will serve The Real You, you must be in a tranquil state. Your mind must be calm and quiet, your body must be relaxed, and you need to have a smile in your heart – like how it feels when you watch puppies do adorable things.

If you're not in that state while insisting that you're right – you can pretty much assume that you're wrong. Feelings are guidance, and if you are feeling angry, contemptuous, and indignant, your Higher Self is trying to let you know your thoughts are off-track.

♦♦♦

As you can see, your Survival Belief that you must be in charge is at the heart of much difficulty and self-sabotage for you. It is this belief which launches a cascade of repetitive thoughts and behaviors, that ultimately lead to your unhappiness. Learning about these, and how to take hold of them, is fundamental to becoming able to create a life you love.

If you have read this far, you are doing so well! Thank you for hanging in there, this stuff is definitely not fun to face. Remember, we are in the thick of the section about the Ego's Survival Programming. But then we will move ahead to discuss Type 8 at your highest and best.

We just finished discussing your Type 8 Survival Belief, which was activated somewhere in your childhood. It is the primary driver behind all of your unconscious thoughts and behaviors.

Now, we will look at the most common thought, feeling and behavior patterns that emerge as a result of holding your Survival Belief.

Your Compulsion

Your **Compulsion** is the **repetitive internal process you instantly launch as a way of discharging the emotional tension caused by your Survival Belief.**

This Compulsion is much like a guilty addiction – you know you should give it up, but don't want to because you privately love it. And even if you decide, that's it, you're through with this... you will still find it very difficult to stop until you become able to embrace your Vital Truth (see the upper half of your Mandala), rather than your Survival Belief.

> Your Compulsion is **Controlling.**

You might have noticed your tendency to be Controlling about your personal space and the lifestyle you prefer. You might *not* have noticed that actually your impulse to Control encroaches far into the territory of other people's autonomy and boundaries.

For example, a lot of what makes you angry has to do with how other people have spoken to you or treated you or actions they took that you disapprove of. And you absolutely require them to admit their fault and apologize to you before you will engage with them again. These are all moves to Control, in order to affirm that you are, indeed, the one in charge.

Violating other people's free will – through insisting they behave your way – is a great big Universal no-no. Just like Star Trek's prime directive, it is a fundamental principle of the Flow that all beings have freedom to steer their own course, regardless of how incorrect anyone else may deem it.

As we will discuss in the upcoming Your Vitality Personality section, this is where you must learn how to Allow, Type 8. You must agree and accept that, while you may have complete sovereignty over yourself, you may *not* have it over anyone else.

Don't worry though. If you let go of Controlling, the world will not, in fact, collapse into chaos. When you really start living in the Flow of the Universe, you will discover that, when you don't intervene, things remarkably seem to work themselves out for the best.

Controlling is a Lack of Trust

You probably don't mind admitting that you don't really trust anybody. Your worldview is that there are a lot of bad guys out there trying to screw you over and take what's yours, so you'd better be tough, on alert, and ready to fight. Plus you think you're stronger than everybody else, smarter than everybody else, and have better judgment. So why would you ever trust anybody with anything?

That's why you feel compelled to micromanage All the Things.

It's a pretty bleak worldview, wouldn't you agree? This is why you're having difficulty manifesting a stable, happy, healthy life full of close connections with smart, trustworthy people – you're programmed to assume it's not even possible.

It is entirely possible.

This Compulsion towards Controlling stems from Ego beliefs in scarcity and survival. The heart is closed in order to buy-in to this belief encoded in your unconscious mind.

When your heart is open, you invite in the awareness of your Higher Consciousness, which includes understanding of Universal principles of how to wield energy for your joyful manifestation and Vitality.

Contrary to what your Ego tells you is the smart way to survive, Your Higher Self – who is eternal and does not endorse survival fears – would say that opening your heart and trusting what you can manifest for yourself is the way to go.

It may feel scary to let yourself be softer, more open, and trusting, but you will be amazed at what believing in love and light will do for your reality. You can let go of the control, and trust great things are on their way.

Controlling Blocks the Flow

You really can't help yourself – you are constantly trying to control things.

You're organized in military-like fashion. You run a very tight ship. Everything has its place and its method. You plan for potential disasters.

You give explicit instructions, expecting them to be followed to the letter. You question other people's methods and tactics, to make sure you approve. You establish yourself as the decision-maker. You get to be in charge of the money. You press other people to do it your way.

Once you start looking, you'll see that it's everywhere. It's like you're trying to Bully life itself into doing as it's told.

Once you realize that you can trust the Universe to always deliver experiences that serve the Greatest Good, you will see that it's best for you to *let go* of control.

The Flow of the Universe is a great rushing river of love and divine timing. It is always bringing to you the highest and best outcome at the most appropriate time and place.

Don't interfere. Don't insert yourself. Relax. Wait and see. Trust. Give the Universe the opportunity to show you just how deeply you are loved.

And meanwhile, the happier and more at ease you are, the quicker your best life can manifest for you.

♦♦♦

Even though Controlling comes very naturally to you and feels like the best way to be safe, it is a Compulsion that ultimately sabotages your long-term happiness. The key to unlocking this pattern is letting yourself feel more love and trust. We will expand on this quite a lot more later in the chapter.

Your Destructive Behavior

Your Survival Belief – that you must always be in charge – also prompts your actions and behaviors. When you are Ego-Driven, and therefore **not questioning your inherent attitudes and beliefs, you will repeatedly behave this way.** This is called your **Destructive Behavior.**

You may be entirely unaware of it, or you may be doing it on purpose in the utter certainty that you are right. Either way, this behavior is never for the Greatest Good of all, and therefore is destructive.

As an Ego-Driven Type 8 who believes you must always be in charge . . .

> Your Destructive Behavior is **Intimidating.**

Intimidating means trying to frighten someone in order to gain influence over their actions. Your Impulse is to control, and Intimidation is how you often go about it.

There are a wide variety of intimidating behaviors you might employ. They can range from vaguely threatening to overtly violent. Usually, intimidating behavior is meant to subtly threaten the safety of others without having to act. Simply by seeming ready and willing to cause conflict, many others will surrender their power to you in order to avoid it. In this way you take charge simply with your commanding presence.

Interestingly, the Type 8 is the only one out of all 9 Types who is comfortable with the feeling of anger. To you, it feels like an infusion of energy and strength. Where you might have, a moment ago, been feeling powerless or vulnerable, anger allows you to suppress these and focus on a feeling of power instead.

All of the other Types regard anger as frightening, unpleasant, or socially inappropriate. This is why it is often the tool of choice for the Type 8 Ego. It makes you feel strong at the same time that it shuts everyone else down.

Non-Verbal Intimidation

Type 8s are instinctual masters at wielding energy. It is a truth of physics that a stronger energetic vibration entrains a weaker one, causing it to yield. You know how to be the bigger energy, reaching outward to tame all resistance. Other people can definitely feel it.

Usually this is happening on an unconscious level. The behavior is so natural, you communicate with your energy without even realizing it. Your vibration often says something along the lines of "I'm very powerful, you don't want to mess with me;" or "Get out of my way;" or "Don't interfere" or "Submit to me."

It is also usually received at an unconscious level, where the recipient may not consciously think to themselves "This person is overwhelming, I should just let them have their way," but that is usually what happens.

Basically you know how to do Jedi mind tricks.

Unless, of course, a Type 8 tries this on a fellow tough guy, who will volley with an even bigger energy. This is where The Bully gets called out on their non-verbal threats.

Usually you were not really wanting to deal with a full-blown confrontation – you were bluffing with some quick bravado. So now you're faced with following through on your threats and severely escalating a problem, or having to back down and make nice.

One of the most common places this can be observed is on the road. Type 8s often drive large vehicles, to represent how big their energy is. But even if you're driving a tin can, your demeanor as a driver is totally dominating and Intimidating.

You especially will not allow other drivers to cut in front, speeding up to block this from happening. And if the driver does dare to make a bold move and cut in front, you have probably been known to pull up close behind on purpose, acting scary and threatening, hoping to punish the offender.

This is introducing unnecessary drama into your life on a daily basis. Does every interaction really have to be about proving that you're the toughest? What if you felt calm and neutral, and interactions were allowed to occur with ease? Life gets a lot easier once you realize you don't have to be a Bully all the time.

Overt Intimidation

You are a very physical person. You can feel your energy coursing through your body, and storing in your belly. You're like a train, stoked with fuel and ready to go full-throttle. You like to let the whistle blow and let everybody know who's unstoppable around here.

This is when the Ego-Driven Type 8 will use language or physicality to Intimidate.

In particular Type 8s are big fans of swear words. You like the intensity and force in the words. You like expressing your anger, and you like demonstrating that you're not concerned with being appropriate. This sends additional cues that the social niceties will not be observed, and things could get ugly.

Name-calling is another means of Intimidation that Type 8s use. At this point you are trying to hit below the belt, and see if you can knock the wind out of someone with your words. Sometimes this works at shutting down your "opponent," but sometimes it escalates things into a war.

And then, finally, the Type 8 can resort to physical Intimidation – pushing, shoving, poking... or worse. Women too – they favor pinching.

At this point the Type 8 is not aware of themselves at all and possibly in a black rage, which they will find difficult to remember later. Although this is an extreme form of the Ego driving the Type 8 to appear powerful and strong, in fact the Type 8 is in a state of fear and desperation at not having control.

◆◆◆

Your displays of anger and desire to Intimidate may feel satisfying and powerful in the moment, but they can destroy your ability to have stable, loving, loyal relationships. It may just be a day-in-the-life for you, but for everyone else who is not wired this way, this is an unpleasant dynamic to endure.

Unfortunately it usually takes many years before the Ego-Driven Type 8 becomes willing to take a look at this Destructive Behavior within themselves. They spend a long time first telling themself they're right, and somebody else is the problem.

And there's no denying that being Intimidating usually accomplishes its mission – allowing you to have your way and keep control… right up until an important relationship or your employer has finally reached their breaking point.

People don't like to be spoken down to, dominated, and controlled. They may not have what it takes to fight you about it directly, so it's possible you don't totally know how angry and resentful you may have made other people. Much more often, they just up and leave one day, without ever saying a word.

Most Type 8's are shocked and astonished to find themselves fired, divorced, legally restrained, or otherwise banned, but unfortunately this is usually the wake-up call required before a Type 8 is ready to take a real look in the mirror, and question if there isn't a better way to feel powerful.

There is a better way to feel powerful, and it doesn't have anything to do with control and intimidation. It has to do with going into the heart, in a silent and serene state, and letting yourself feel love, and gratitude, and appreciation.

You have a very lovable soft side, Type 8, that only your closest insiders know about. You're not always armor and force. You have a protective, playful, and empowering aspect that is so tender and endearing. The trick is convincing you that it's safe to be that all the time – because that is The Real You. And that is a Leader that everyone would follow.

Your Sabotage Pattern

As we have discussed, your Personality Type has much Survival Programming built in. Your Survival Belief, Compulsion, and Destructive Behavior are undeniable impulses within you that all drive your well-being into the ground.

In other words, these all combine into an overall template for self-destruction. This is called your **Sabotage Pattern – the way you repeatedly behave throughout your lifetime which leads directly to the destruction of your health and happiness.**

> ➤ Your Sabotage Pattern is **Force.**

Force means compelling someone or something to do as you wish against their will.

Force is the opposite of going with the Flow. Everything which moves with the Flow thrives. Everything which obstructs the Flow decays. Your belief that you know best how things should go, and your determination to Force it to go that way, places you squarely in obstruction to the Flow.

To live in a chronic state of Force creates friction and resistance, and ultimately, destruction. It has you existing in a perpetual world of hostility, rather than love and acceptance. As you can see, it will likely lead to your own downfall, rather than your survival, as your Ego would have you believe.

Forcing the Body

Type 8 you are so incredibly hard on your body – you Force your will upon it all the time.

You love to work long and hard, and you require your body to keep up with a punishing pace. You like to push through the pain, the hunger, the fatigue. You skip meals and bathroom breaks. You won't go to the doctor to get help. You like to demonstrate even to yourself what a tough guy you are.

You also love to play hard. Type 8s can be quite physical and competitive, and like extracurricular activities that require exertion. Sports injuries, especially extreme sports, are not unheard of.

Between working hard and playing hard, your body is a workhorse under the whip. It cannot go on forever without collapsing.

Your body needs nuanced care and attention. It needs rhythms in your day and your life. Your body wants 8 hours of sleep and a regular bedtime. It wants regular meals at regular intervals, comprised of whole foods. Your body wants water. And sunlight. And meditation.

Forcing your body to go without everything it needs, for decades, does not play out well. In your youth you become accustomed to your incredible stores of energy and strength. Thirty years later you're facing a heart episode or adrenal collapse.

Regarding concerns of physical health such as diet and exercise, there appear to be two camps of Type 8s – the ones who super care about it, and the ones who super don't.

The Type 8s who super care about their health can become, unsurprisingly, incredibly Controlling about their regimens. Highly disciplined, they make deferred gratification an art form. Fit, firm, and formidable, they may look the picture of health. However, a backdrop of anger, hostility, control and Force keeps the body's systems weak, not strong.

When you Force things, there eventually comes a backlash. Living a rigidly controlled lifestyle does not allow your energy to Flow freely. This manifests in the physical body as stiffness, pain and fatigue, because you are mentally clamping down on the Flow of life force energy. Even when approaching health, you want to have a mindset of ease and Flow.

The Type 8s who super *don't* care about their health are all about a lifestyle of indulging passions instead. They like their rich foods and alcohol, and tend to carry excess weight. But they're still working hard and playing hard. Again – heart episode looming.

The shift for you Type 8 is from Forcing your will onto your body to responding to its needs with love and respect. Rather than Dominating your own body as if it is your enemy, nurture and care for it as if it is your friend.

Forcing the Mind

When you are Ego-Driven and all about security and control, you don't like anybody getting any funny ideas, and you don't like anybody keeping secrets. In fact, you wouldn't mind it if everybody just agreed to let you tell them what they're allowed to believe, say, and do.

Unfortunately, most people aren't terribly willing to surrender their autonomy. But a few Types are, and it is very common for Type 8s to pair up with a Type 2 or 9, who will let you boss them around.

This is a question of power, and whether you are willing to let other people have any. When you're in Bully mode, the answer is No. But as you become a great Leader, the answer is Yes. You have within you the potential to become a magnificent source of Empowerment to others. We are almost done talking about all your problem areas, so that we can fully explore how you can become a magnificent Leader.

Violating Boundaries

Well Type 8, you can be pretty intense on the topic of boundaries. You guard your own ferociously, but trample everyone else's without apology.

For example, you can be uber private, much like a Type 5. But you like asking friends and strangers alike inappropriately direct questions that are none of your business. It's astonishing how many of them find themselves disclosing it, too, because of the Force of your will.

And you don't believe anyone has the right to tell you what to do, but you expect others to adhere to your rules absolutely.

And you don't like to be touched without giving your consent, but you can be uncomfortably handsy on other people.

Do you expect to have access to your partner's or kids' phone and passwords? Do you feel entitled to tell them how to dress? Do you give or withhold money to influence their behavior?

The desire to control while remaining untouchable must be very tempting. You are so strong, and so many are so disempowered, that you would get away with seizing control, if you chose to. It's practically like taking candy from a baby.

This is why connecting to your purpose is so important. You came here to serve the Greatest Good. You wanted to put your power behind something important. And when you do, the need to control and dominate falls away entirely, because you are full of euphoric satisfaction.

Forcing the Heart Shut

In order for your Ego to have complete control over your mind, it must convince you to shut down your own heart.

Your Survival Programming is a whisper in your ear, telling you the world is dangerous, and bad. Telling you it's the Wild Wild West out there, and you'd better be prepared at any time for a fight.

When you buy-in to these beliefs, you unthinkingly consent to closing down your heart. It would not be possible to be warlike and dominating while you felt love and compassion for people. So it must be silenced.

This creates a great conflict within you, for The Real You is actually passionately big-hearted. The Real You is capable of great love and deep feeling.

Instead, when you are Ego-Driven, you disconnect from all feelings that make you feel soft or vulnerable, and funnel them all into anger instead. Anger is your homebase emotion, because that one feels powerful.

Loneliness, fear, sadness… No. You will not allow yourself to feel them and you don't want to know about them in others. This would humanize them and bring up that compassion you were trying to lock down.

Learning how to Get Real with yourself about your true feelings, and actually express them to others could be an enormous game-changer for you.

You actually really value authenticity, so this shutting down of a huge part of yourself never really totally felt right. Letting yourself reveal who you really are, and be welcomed and loved and appreciated for it, could heal a lot of those early wounds that you received so long ago.

✦✦✦

Now that you have opened your eyes to the destructive inner workings of your own Ego, operating as Your Primal Persona, do not despair. It is certainly within your capacity to transform these behaviors and patterns of your Survival Programming.

If you have made it this far, CONGRATULATIONS. We lost many along the trail – not everybody is ready for the journey that is Getting Real! This book is really only interesting to people who are about to make an enormous advancement in their consciousness.

We made it through the hardest part. Now, let's explore how you can be, act and live differently. There is an entirely different kind of life available to you, filled with love and connection and joy. And it is mapped out in the top half of your Type 8 Mandala.

ACTIVATE YOUR POWER PARADIGM

In Chapter One we revealed the meaning of Your Vitality Personality. Let's recap now.

Your Vitality Personality is the version of you that exists when you allow your Higher Consciousness to guide your thoughts, feelings, and actions. It is the opening of your heart, and allowing the loving intelligence found there to Flow through you. This infuses you with insight, wisdom, love and compassion, and the actions you take from this place always serve the Greatest Good.

Let's take a look now at the top half of your Mandala which spells out the dynamics of The Real You - Your Vitality Personality - and all its wondrous gifts and talents:

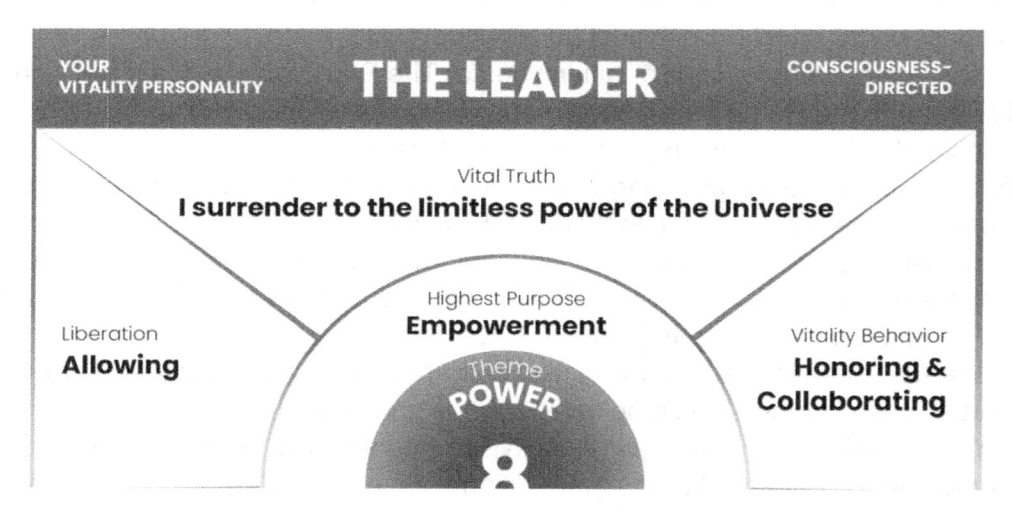

YOUR VITALITY PERSONALITY — **THE LEADER** — CONSCIOUSNESS-DIRECTED

Vital Truth
I surrender to the limitless power of the Universe

Highest Purpose
Empowerment

Liberation
Allowing

Vitality Behavior
Honoring & Collaborating

Theme
POWER

8

Your Vitality Personality: The Leader

As a Type 8,

> Your Vitality Personality is known as **The Leader.**

This is the truth of who you really are. You have always felt a sense of greatness within you, and you were righter than you know. The Real You has the capacity to truly change the world.

See *Fig 9A* for a brief summary of the Consciousness-Directed half of your Mandala, identifying how to use your Personality Type to serve the Greatest Good and move your life in the Flow of the Universe.

When you embody all these natural gifts, you really are unstoppable. It is so exciting to think you are just on the precipice of launching a new life of love, acceptance, and Vitality for yourself! It might have required some serious deep-breathing to get here, but the effort is so well worth it.

Let's explore these dynamics of your Power Paradigm, so that you may begin to fully comprehend just how open, uplifting, happy and healthy your life could really be.

Your Theme

As was mentioned earlier,

> Your Theme is **Power**.

When you pursue the highest form of this Theme - Power - you are truly aligned with Source, and therefore always serving the Greatest Good.

Power is Consciousness. It is the raw energy that Flows through all life. It is made of love and light. *You* are made of love and light. You are made of the same Power as the rest of the Universe, and you are capable of commanding it.

You came here to Earth to explore what it means to wield Power while living within the limitations of a human body with an Ego. You wanted to see if you could remember to open up your heart – despite your Survival Programming against it – and draw in so much more of your love and light into your body.

There is only one way to amplify your own energy, and that is through feeling more love. Human love energy is actually the most powerful love energy there is, because it emerged forth from within us while living in the densest, bleakest of places.

When you amplify your own Power through increasing your capacity to love, you benefit not only yourself, but the world around you.

Your increased capacity to love acts as an energetic key that unlocks sleeping codes in your DNA. It activates new parts of you, giving you more resilience, memory, imagination, and longevity.

Fig. 9A **PERSONALITY TYPE 8 SURVIVAL PROGRAMMING**
Your Primal Persona: THE BULLY
The Programmed You; The limited and diminished version of yourself that you default to when you are Ego-Driven
Distorted Theme: DOMINATION
Your Ego's warped and downgraded interpretation of your true Theme
Survival Belief: I CAN SURVIVE AS LONG AS I AM IN CHARGE
The scarcity-oriented message embedded in your Ego that creates your world view
Compulsion: CONTROLLING
The repetitive internal process you instantly launch as a way of discharging the emotional tension caused by your Survival Belief
Destructive Behavior: INTIMIDATING
The ruinous actions you regularly engage in when you operate according to your Survival Belief
Sabotage Pattern: FORCE
The totality of all your Survival Programming combined into an overall template for self-destruction

It also deactivates some of your more primitive and survival-oriented DNA, helping you shed the limitations of fear which have been holding you back.

The process of empowering yourself to manually override your own default programming is the process of integration – of loving and accepting yourself and everything in your world. It is the going inward, into your interior world of feelings and vulnerabilities, so that you can emerge renewed and remade as your Higher Self.

In the hands of Your Vitality Personality, you apply your internal Power for the Greatest Good, making you an exciting and visionary Leader:

- Fully embodying your own sense of power - with no shame or diminishment
- Feeling trust in the Universe, truly knowing It brings you only the Greatest Good
- Fostering relationships which are respectful, open-hearted, and loving
- Contributing to work which feels deeply rewarding and meaningful
- Building vital health derived from honoring the body's needs and cycles
- Relishing a sense of peace and satisfaction at knowing your life serves an important Purpose

Most people are afraid to fully embody their Power. **You are the one who is built to show others how to embody their Power, through channeling love energy to amplify and manifest.** You will accomplish anything you desire with this strong sense of Self, and you will show others how to do it, too.

Your Vital Truth

Your **Vital Truth** is a **Higher understanding of how to thrive by aligning with Universal principles.** It is the escape hatch your Ego doesn't want you to know about, because it unlocks all of its Survival Programming, and connects you to your Higher Consciousness – The Real You.

> Your Vital Truth is **I surrender to the limitless power of the Universe.**

This is a direct contradiction to what your Survival Belief encourages you to believe. Your Survival Belief prompts you to think that *you* must be in charge. But that actually requires you to use up all your energy, fighting against the Flow – ultimately draining you of your Power.

Although this Vital Truth is a brief, simple statement, it is dense with meaning. Let's take a moment to unpack this.

Surrender

Ironically, for someone who is encoded to want to control everything, it is actually the *surrender* of control which will bring you into harmony with the Flow of the Universe – and that's where all the *real* Power is!

Surrender is the opposite of jumping in with immediate action and Force. Instead of assuming that you know best how to make something happen in your favor, you will soften and relax your body, heart and mind, and allow yourself to be guided.

Excitingly, when you release your drive to control and only act when you get a clear sense of inner knowingness, things work out in surprising ways. The Flow is really rather astonishing in how It provides solutions you never even dreamed of!

Type 8, this life has not been easy for you. You have endured much pain, and still carried on. You have done your very best to make yourself strong, not only so that you could take care of yourself, but also so many others. Your courage and strength are immense, and you let so many rely on you.

Now it is time to lay down your armor, and let your pain go.

You don't have to solve the world's problems through your own blood sweat and tears. You don't have to tough it out, you don't have to fight through it, and you don't have to force it.

Let the Universe show you how loved you are. Let It help you, and make things easier for you. It's safe for you to rest, and trust.

The Limitless Power of the Universe

Your Ego mind is programmed to prompt beliefs that you must always be in charge in order to survive. It makes it seem as if your world could fall apart unless you are vigilantly attending to it, keeping it all under control.

This is all an illusion.

The Universe is not in chaos. It operates in a divine order. There are cycles and eras to all things. There is an intelligence designing and overseeing it so vast that no Ego mind can possibly comprehend it.

You don't have to control, force, or worry about anything.

What is challenging to grasp is that your heart is a portal, a doorway that stands between the Universe and your individual reality.

Most of us operate with our heart closed, and our portal darkened. This causes our reality to operate on the default matrix provided by our Ego's Survival Programming. This is how you came to believe in harshness and battle – it's all you ever saw.

But when we reach into our heart, we awaken that sleeping portal, and it opens up to allow the love and light through that is Universal intelligence.

This brings in magic. This brings in ease. This brings in possibility, and surprise, and hope.

Giving your time to going inward – to healing old wounds, to rediscovering your love and empathy, to letting your body soften and relax – opens up your heart portal, and lets the power of the Universe in.

♦♦♦

The Survival Belief you have been unknowingly operating upon all this time is distorted and false. It was put there intentionally, to provide you with an interesting storyline of struggle and triumph, pain and glory, winning and losing.

But now you have arrived at a point in your life where you have begun to suspect there could be something else for you – a better, happier, easier life. You're starting to question whether it really is true that life has to have so much struggle, pain and loss.

This is your heart portal beginning to open. You're getting glimpses of the love and light that is the Universe, and you want more.

Embracing your Vital Truth is the activator. It helps you abandon the old distorted Survival Belief in favor of something much deeper and more enlivening. Open yourself up wide, and let yourself surrender.

Your Liberation

Your **Liberation** is the **emancipating philosophy you freely embrace.** This is a powerful shift, out of the Survival Programming of the mind, and into the Flow of the Universe through the heart. Rather than being owned by a chronic Compulsion, you are now intentionally choosing this Liberation.

> Your Liberation is **Allowing.**

Allowing is the opposite of Controlling, which has always been your Compulsion.

Allowing means letting the natural unfolding of experiences occur, because you trust the Universe is always acting in your favor.

Allowing Yourself

If you are a Type 8, then you have spent a good percentage of your life being tough on yourself. You have endured many hardships, shouldered many burdens, withheld many pleasures, and smothered many feelings.

For a while you liked proving to yourself how strong you are, but now you're pretty sick of it. You've decided you're ready for life to be easier and happier.

For you, that means that letting go of the resistance, and letting go of the reins.

Allowing Yourself to Trust the Universe

You probably feel like you raised yourself, and that you've been on your own for a long, long time. Your life experiences have shown you that you can't trust anybody, and you need to control it all.

But that perspective was shaped through the lens of your Survival Programming. The more you endorse it, the more you attract it. If you want a different outcome, then you're going to have to consider new beliefs. You're going to have to give the Flow a try and let It show you what It can do.

Rather than controlling everything because you believe that otherwise it will all go off the rails, adopt the perspective that all of the Universe loves you and wants to do your bidding. Your beliefs in a difficult world are not the truth – love, ease and flow are the truth.

With this refreshed sensibility, let life go in the direction it's trying to go. Even if it seems like your job is falling through, even if it seems like your marriage is dissolving, even if it seems like you're losing everything.

Life is not what it seems, and the future isn't written yet. You can't see yourself from the larger perspective of Flow. You don't have all the information. There are reasons things are going this way – and it's all for the Greatest Good.

When you give your trust to the Universe, you feel very vulnerable and scared at first. But the rewards for this trust are well beyond what you might have imagined. Looking back, you will see that all went exactly as it should, because now you are in the most incredible new place in your life.

Allowing Yourself to Feel

You are actually a very emotional and passionate person. You care deeply and love so much. However, you are not a fan of the emotions that make you feel vulnerable or powerless.

So instead, you've tended to funnel many of your more sensitive feelings into anger instead. Anger feels empowering. Anger scares the bad guys away. Anger seizes control.

But by now you've had enough of the drama this causes, and you're ready to live peacefully.

This includes dropping the armor, and letting yourself feel your real feelings. Feelings like remorse, like grief, and fear, and shame.

Smothering your feelings doesn't make you stronger, it breaks you down. Allowing everything to Flow brings Vitality. Please see the Charged Energy Clearing exercise in Chapter Twelve to help you clear these emotions out of your energy field. You will feel so much freer and lighter.

Living authentically and admitting to your tender feelings – even if it's just to yourself – clarifies and amplifies your energetic signature. This is how you magnify your ability to communicate with the Universe.

It is all the dissonance and static that was keeping you playing small. Getting real with yourself so that you can calmly clear out what was sabotaging you only makes you more powerful.

Allowing Others

Oh those pesky humans – always doing it wrong, always trying to mess with you! No wonder you feel a perpetual itch to lock down all loose ends, loopholes, and weak spots.

But now that you're learning to trust the Universe and let things ride, you're coming to see that it doesn't really matter what other people are doing. You are powerful and can communicate with the Flow of the Universe directly. You can attract the life you want with your strong, clear energy. No one else can interfere with that.

Allowing Free Will

You have been given free will, and so has everybody else. Your free will ends where someone else's begins.

So for example, you may have strong opinions about what your spouse is wearing, what your daughter is allowed to major in, and who people should vote for, but ultimately it's not your choice. Let other people be who they are, and do what they want to do. That aligns you with Flow.

As much as you might detest this idea at first, you will come around to adoring it once you realize how much easier it makes things.

You have a strong impulse to rescue people because you feel so strong. But that just disempowers them from having their learning experiences and makes things harder for you. Allowing other people to have free will – to make mistakes, to stay stuck, to sabotage themselves – releases you from so much responsibility and burden.

Life gets so much simpler and easier when you stop worrying about other people's actions. Let them make their choices, and let life deliver them the natural consequences. They are on their own journey and have access to their own guidance. And they have the free will choice to ignore it all and muck it all up. Just root for them and wish them well, from the healthy side of the boundary.

Allowing Others to Be Your Mirror

Your thoughts are electric, and your feelings are magnetic, and together these combine to create your unique energetic signature.

Everything going on in your reality is there because you attracted it. It matches the signal you're putting out.

This includes the people in your life and how they behave towards you. Certainly your friends and family. But also your coworkers, your neighbors, and the people on your plane.

When you are happy, fulfilled, and uplifted, this brings out the best in the people who engage with you. Your good vibe improves theirs.

But if you're rubbing elbows with a lot of people you deem idiots, and you're having gruff interactions with your kids, and you're losing clients at work... ask yourself what your thoughts and feelings have been doing lately. Because the reality you're experiencing is the result of what your vibe has been like.

Don't take other people personally – they're only reflecting you back to yourself. This perspective allow you to stay humble and stay present, both of which move you into the Flow, where everything gets nicer.

Allowing the Inner No

Allowing means understanding that you live in harmony with the Flow of the Universe, and being willing to take the action that is for the Greatest Good of all. Occasionally, this actually means saying No.

So how is it possible to be Allowing, while saying No at the same time? Actually, you were built for it.

Type 8, you are a natural warrior -- fearless, strong, and protective. You were made that way for a reason. You can be certain that you will often find yourself called to intervene on behalf of someone who is in a bad situation.

You are still in a state of Allowing in these moments. You are Allowing yourself to be Guided. It is likely no accident you were there at just that time, when you were desperately needed by another. For you are one who loves to speak up for the underdog, and will act where others look away.

If you are a witness to abuse or injustice, you will likely feel compelled to take protective action. This is an example of heeding the Inner No.

The Inner No is the strong guidance you feel from your Higher Consciousness when you discover yourself in an environment where there is something corrupt going on -- something which is not honoring Flow and not serving the Greatest Good. You feel compelled to act in the name of serving the Greatest Good.

When you feel called to act, not for your own Ego-Driven gain, but for your own Greatest Good or on behalf of another, this is your Higher Consciousness speaking to you. If you feel a sense of urgency which you cannot suppress or ignore, you can be certain you are serving your Highest Purpose at this time.

However, take great caution not to allow your Ego to have the reins in these moments. Your Higher Consciousness would still like this to play out for the Greatest Good of all. Stay calm, stay present, and trust the Universe to bring about the best outcome.

♦♦♦

Allowing is a deceptively simple word for how huge and impactful it will be on your life. If you could only learn one thing in your whole lifetime that would help you the most, Type 8, this is it.

Allowing is the things that moves you out of resistance, conflict and unhappiness, and into ease, peace and joy. You will never look back!

Your Vitality Behavior

Vitality Behavior is the **empowering and uplifting actions you intentionally choose when you are Consciousness-Directed,** rather than the Destructive Behavior your Ego drives you to act out.

> Your Vitality Behavior is **Honoring and Collaborating**.

This is sooo much lovelier than your previous go-to – Intimidating!

Through connecting to your heart and finally getting to really experience what giving and receiving love feels like, you will begin to shed that old Ego attitude that kept you arrogant and superior. You will really start coming to appreciate the talents and perspectives of the other people around you.

When you are willing to surrender control and just allow things to unfold as they want to, you begin to make room for other people to have a voice. You start to allow space for other people to show you who they are, and what they can do. You may very well find yourself surprised and delighted to discover that the people around you are intelligent and insightful, and could actually help you get where you want to go!

This is when you really start stepping into your potential to be a great Leader. The best Leaders are not dictators, who smother everyone else's views and desires. The most effective and beloved Leaders are the ones who can hear what their tribe really wants, and guide the whole lot of them towards exactly that.

Whether you are a parent or a CEO, a teacher or the President, intentionally choosing to Honor and Collaborate with the people who are counting on you to take them somewhere wonderful is the best possible way to serve them.

Honoring

Honoring means demonstrating deep respect for all of life, in recognition of all life being a unique expression of Source.

There is no hierarchy of status or value in the Universe. No person, place or thing is any more important or worthy of love than another.

All of life is made of Consciousness. Everything is alive and aware. Everything has a soul. It is really all the most incredible miracle, that we all get to be physical beings on this beautiful planet together, and learn and grow from the experience.

When you approach all of life with a sense of reverence and appreciation, your heart is wide open and your feeling of connection and happiness is profound. This moves you into the Flow and delivers you vitality and abundance.

Honoring Yourself

Honoring yourself begins with acknowledging that The Real You is a wise and ancient being of light, and worthy of love and respect.

As an assertive Personality Type, you've always concerned yourself with meeting your own needs, advancing your own interests, and giving yourself preferential treatment. But that is not the same thing as Honoring the essence of who you are.

Typically you are oriented toward action – towards getting things done and making things happen. Your attention goes to the outside world and how you'd like to shape it.

Honoring your essence means taking time to connect and listen to your inner self. It means carving out the time and space for food, for movement, for rest, for healing, for creativity, for introspection, for laughter, for love. It means valuing your relationship with yourself and treating that as sacred.

You came here to lend your strength to the people and causes you care about, but you also came here to learn more about yourself and the human experience. It is important you make time for both.

Honoring Others

Honoring others means recognizing that all people have inherent value and are worthy of respect.

How do you go about Leading, while still Honoring?

Even though in your leadership role you may not be able to please everyone, you can still respect their intelligence and different perspectives.

As long as you talk about authentic feelings and needs – yours, or theirs – there is nothing offensive being said. If you explain your feelings and needs to illuminate why you're making the decision you are, and someone else explains theirs to you, you might not agree, but you don't become enemies. Everybody feels seen and heard. Negotiations remain peaceful.

There is no need to control and intimidate in order to feel happy and safe. When you Honor other people's feelings and needs and demonstrate a genuine desire to understand them, you build a community of people who like and respect you. You will gain a reputation for being honest and fair. Being a beloved part of the community will make you feel happier and more secure than ever before.

Collaborating

Collaborating means co-creating experiences which serve the Greatest Good. While you are the Leader, this does not mean you must work alone, serving only your own interests. Rather, invite participation. Often, the result is much more complete and satisfying than it would have been if you'd done it by yourself.

Collaborating allows for the input and ideas of other people. Contrary to what your Ego advises you, every living being embodies intelligence and has unique worth, and you will benefit if you willingly blend yours with theirs.

Again, while you are the Leader and likely have the final say, through Collaborating with the collective community you develop better results and an environment of happy cooperation at the same time. This is how you hold on to your seat of Power forever, because your community is happy to have you there and to follow your guidance. Through Collaboration you ensure your continued Vitality as well as that of your community.

Collaborating with Your Higher Consciousness

For somebody who loves wielding Power as much as you, you will find Collaborating with your Higher Self to be an exhilarating experience.

It takes a little while practicing communicating through your heart to your Higher Consciousness before you start to realize you are receiving answers back and assistance (see Chapter Twelve).

But once it actually sinks in that you are way more enormous than just your body, and you can reach all of the Universe through this Higher aspect of yourself, it's time to play.

Your Higher Consciousness knows your heart and what you really love and desire

— and totally wants to help you have it all. But there is a pesky rule of non-interference that your Higher Consciousness must adhere to. So if you want Its help, you have to ask for it.

You can ask silently in your mind, or you can write it down in your journal, or you can say it out loud to the thin air. Whatever you prefer.

Personally I'm a big fan of talking to my Higher Self while I'm alone in the car. Who cares if you look like a crazy person? Any other driver will just assume you're on the phone. I like talking out loud because I don't always know my own thoughts until I hear myself speaking them (classic Type 7).

Just have a chat.

Hey Old Gal, can you help me? I want to host a New Year's Eve party where everybody has an amazing time. I need a unique amazing venue that's available on this date. I need a cool idea for the entertainment. And I need somebody to offer to meet the vendors there for me, because I want to feel calm-cool-and-collected through this whole process and I've already got other stuff going on. Will you make all that happen for me please? I am so grateful for you, thank you so much, I love you!

And then just sit back and watch it roll in. It's enormous fun. Suddenly you'll hear 3 people mention the same venue you never heard of before. And your coworker will mention how their cousin who plays the handpan drum will be in town then. And your spouse will offer to meet the vendors for you out of the blue.

Collaborating with Higher Consciousness for the Greatest Good is your wheelhouse, and the reason you came here. You will quickly find you are spectacular at it. Enjoy!

Collaborating with Others

"Alone we can do so little; Together we can do so much." This old adage has always been true. We are so much more powerful as a collective than we can ever be alone.

Some Type 8s are very social and enjoy group dynamics. So if this is you, the thought of Collaborating doesn't fill you with dread. But some Type 8s are the lone-wolf type, and to them Collaborating with others sounds like it could be painful.

Whether it comes easily to you or not, it's a major part of being an effective Leader.

You are the big energy that drives entire projects. You keep it all moving forward, advancing towards the finish line. But you can't do it all.

Once you start connecting with your heart, quieting your mind, and valuing others, you will begin attracting high-caliber people to you who are excited by your vision and want to be a part of your movement.

You have always been charismatic and dynamic, but in the past your volatility may have chased some people away. Now that you're willing to Allow and Honor, you step into your best self, and this is an incredibly compelling person. You have the capacity to attract strong partners to you who will help you go all the way.

Hopefully this speaks straight to your heart, because this is who you came here to be, Type 8. You are the one with the passion, the energy, the courage and the heart for big projects and dramatic change. You came here to light up this world, and you need a team to help you do it. Learning how to Collaborate with finesse is a skill worth developing.

◆◆◆

In the past you resorted to Intimidating because you perceived life as a battle, something you had to be tough enough to dominate.

It's been a long and arduous journey that has brought you here, finally ready to lay down your weapons and try another way. You're right on time, and in fact, well ahead of the crowd.

As you become willing to train in quieting your mind and opening your heart, you gain access to parts of yourself you perhaps have never met before. It's an exciting time of self-discovery and integration.

In learning how to Honor The Real You and Collaborate with Consciousness, you step forward as someone powerful and masterful enough to bring forth a new age of love and abundance, that serves the Greatest Good.

Your Highest Purpose

You chose to be here, in this time and place, because you wanted to contribute something. You came here for a reason, and you chose your Personality Type because it was the one that would help you accomplish it. **Your Personality Type has a special set of talents and abilities, and you wanted to use them to contribute.** This is your **Highest Purpose.**

> ➤ Your Highest Purpose is **Empowerment.**

Empowerment means opening yourself up to your Higher Consciousness and the Flow of the Universe and receiving the guidance, abundance, and power found there -- for the benefit of all.

Even though everyone would like to have autonomy, most are actually somewhat terrified to fully embody their own power. But not you, Type 8. You are made to glory in the magnificent energy Flowing through you.

Empowerment is not accomplished through bravado and contempt. It is accomplished through love, humility and gratitude. Opening your heart and surrendering to Higher wisdom is what aligns you with love and light – the greatest power there is.

The knowingness, the depth, the insight this brings you is far beyond what the Ego mind can fathom. This is how you become The Leader.

Empowering Your Mind

As a Type 8, you are an act-first-think-later sort of person. This is because your primary energy center is in your body – which is different than the Types with energy centers in the head or heart.

For you the mind is generally tagging along after whatever action the body already committed. Often this requires some damage control after the fact. This is not your highest and best life – things could be a lot easier and happier.

Discerning Your Truth

The tricky part for you is learning to discern the difference between the Ego chatter in your mind which seems like truth, and the guidance from your Higher Consciousness which is actually your truth.

Your Ego mind is highly reactive. Whenever there is new information coming in, it tells you a story about how this is threatening to your well-being. In a flash you believe it, and the body receives an instinct to act fast and shut this danger down. You have always "trusted your gut," but actually you may want to slow down and evaluate if this is truly serving your Greatest Good.

Messaging that comes from the Ego is not uplifting. It is identifiable by the upset or stressed feelings it induces. The resulting actions they prompt will turn out to be sabotaging.

Gut instincts are primal, which means they're connected to your Survival Programming. An eternal being of light need not worry about such things. You have everything you need within you to survive and thrive.

Taming your primal instinct takes practice. It requires regularly going inward and relaxing your mind, to let your nervous system rest and reboot. Go into the heart, and let the mind be silent for a while.

Your heart tells you the truth. You will recognize it from its simplicity. It will only be a few words, perhaps an image that conjures up feelings and insight. It will give you a sense of understanding, of *knowingness*.

It is from this quiet, neutral place of knowingness, that you may now access your Higher Mind. This is the mind of your Higher Self. The plans and actions you decide upon from this place are divinely guided. They will not only lead you to a positive outcome, but will lead everyone else involved there as well.

Your Higher Mind is The Real You. It holds the wisdom that produces the Greatest Good for all. It is calm, lucid, and benevolent. Your ability to access this Highest aspect of yourself is your true source of Empowerment. It shapes you into a most magnificent Leader.

Empowering Your Body

Empowering your body means giving it what it needs to thrive with love and affection.

Rather than treating your body like a tool, think of it as your friend. It has feelings.

It has needs. Much like a pet, your body loves you and serves you faithfully, but depends on you entirely, Don't withhold your love and care for your body – treat it as something you are grateful for.

Here is a basic lifestyle rhythm that brings you the complete energy, strength and mental clarity your prefer:

- Drink half your weight in ounces of water daily. (Ex: If you weigh 200 lbs then drink 100 oz of water per day)
- Eat whole foods (not ones that come in powders and boxes)
- Eat fruits and veggies that are the rich colors of the rainbow
- Physical movement that focuses on building strength, endurance and resilience (while in a mental state of surrender, not force)
- Meditation (resets the nervous system)
- Deep breathing down into the belly (invigorates intake and circulation of energy throughout the body)
- 10pm bedtime (or earlier) and get 7-8 hours of sleep

Yes this regimen requires more of your time. In the past you may have deemed it less important because these activities are not "productive."

You must shed this attitude. Taking care of your health is not less important. A lifestyle of busy-ness does not serve you nearly as well a lifestyle of wellness.

Taking Command Over Your Energy

When you were young your energy felt boundless. You reveled in your strength and endurance. As you aged, your internal sense of drive remained the same, but your energy has started to flag. This is showing you that it's necessary to begin conserving your energy, and taking more accountability for where you leak power.

Even in nature there is ebb and flow, waxing and waning. In other words, it is not appropriate to go full throttle at all things all the time. Not everything requires big energy. When you throw all your energy at even mundane or small tasks, this is a form of leaking power.

Type 8 is a notoriously "bull in a china shop" kind of vibe. Powerful yet unfettered energy can be quite destructive. Now it's time to learn nuance, subtlety and restraint.

Rather than always having a go-go-go-push-push-push attitude, adopt a more relaxed, easy attitude. Be present to the qualities of your environment and tasks – they each require something different from you. Be responsive and adaptable. It is your attitude which must shift first, in order for your energy to follow suit.

Your body will appreciate this respite, so will your relationships. You have always been described as "intense," and this is why. There has often been a palpable sense of Force in your energy. This is unnecessary – it drains yours and everyone else's battery. Becoming aware of yourself at the energetic level will tremendously improve the quality of your health and happiness.

♦♦♦

Yes it's true Type 8, you are made of fiery light, and you love to feel the burn.

Yet in order not to be consumed, you must steadily maintain your fire. Keep it contained in the belly -- available to be called upon at will -- but do not let it harass your heart and mind. Heat is an accelerant, and you do not need your heart or mind acting wild.

Use your breath and your intention, and contain yourself. You will find that you are far more effective while also more peaceful, more powerful while also more stable.

Empowering Your Heart

When you were in full Bully mode you were not afraid to demand that your feelings and needs be met. However, they were not your *true* feelings and needs. They had become distorted through the lens of your Ego-Driven Survival Programming. This is why you have not been able to experience a lasting sense of satisfaction or peace.

Now, in your newfound state of love, humility, and gratitude, your heart is asking *you* to meet *its* true feelings and needs. When you meet your own genuine needs by going inward, rather than seeking outward, you will discover what contentment and fulfillment feel like.

Your real feelings and needs are much softer and more vulnerable, but they all got converted into forms of anger and indignation and wanting control – because those feel safer and stronger.

Often egoic anger is covering over the wounds of your inner child, who may have experienced feelings such as betrayal, fear, confusion, sadness and grief. Instead of feeling rage whenever these feelings are triggered in you, it is possible to go inward and heal those wounds, once and for all. Please see the Energy Pattern Clearing exercise in Chapter Twelve to learn how.

The Ego's interpretation of needs that must be met are things like status, money and control. But these are masking your deeper needs for more tender things like connection, affection, completion, hope.

In order to have these in your outer world, you must inwardly have these for yourself, first. Self-love is always the place to start, because your capacity to love yourself is the capacity you have to receive love from other people.

Even if you were being offered love, affection, and reasons to believe in a happy future, you would be numb to them as long as you are numb to yourself.

The things that are lovable about you are not what you think. You might think it's your accomplishments, your bank account, your beauty, your rank. But the people who really love you wouldn't agree.

What is really lovable about you is how unique you are. Your intelligence, your humor, your integrity, your interests, your concern. You are so interesting and passionate, you make life seem exciting. You need to find your love for who that person is – not what they have achieved.

Loving and accepting The Real You will completely transform your quality of life. When you feel your own feelings, you gain empathy. When you accept your own pain and limitations, you gain compassion. When you develop self-love, you are capable of lighting up the whole world.

This is deep inner work and is a process. We spend much time focusing on how to develop self-love in our private membership, the Vitality Voyagers

➢ Check out **www.yourvitalitypersonality.com/membership**

◆◆◆

Well, Type 8, you've been given quite a lot of information about yourself to digest. But hopefully by now you've come to see that even though you are wired to act out Your Primal Persona, it is possible for you to be someone so much more magnificent than that – Your Vitality Personality.

Now is the time to decide who you want to be in this world. If you are ready to step into the full power of who you really are, and seize your best life… then your next step is **Integration.** See Chapter Eleven.

YOUR VITALITY PERSONALITY

CHAPTER TEN
PERSONALITY TYPE 9
THE HEALER | THE SUBMISSIVE

YOUR VITALITY PERSONALITY — **THE HEALER** — **CONSCIOUSNESS-DIRECTED**

Vital Truth
I intentionally co-create my reality with the Flow of the Universe

Highest Purpose
Harmony

Theme
PEACE

9

Distorted Theme
INACTION

Liberation
Being Forthright

Vitality Behavior
Taking Decisive Action

Compulsion
Agreeing

Destructive Behavior
Freezing

Sabotage Pattern
Passivity

Survival Belief
I can survive as long as I don't make waves

YOUR PRIMAL PERSONA — **THE SUBMISSIVE** — **EGO-DRIVEN**

Hello, lovely Type 9. You are likely to be very open to this sort of teaching – Type 9s are perhaps the largest percentage of attendees at Enneagram workshops. Yet implementing the teachings will require more of you than you typically like to give. It will surely ring true for you, but your resistance against discomfort and change runs deep.

If you have been led here, then it is because you are ready to take a quantum leap in the advancement of your consciousness. The wisdom and insight you will gain here will propel you into an awareness far more elevated than most, and a newfound willingness to expand yourself. This will benefit the entire world, for you are the one capable of inspiring us all towards love, peace and harmony.

This chapter focuses on the dual nature of your Personality Type 9, and the primary factors that hinder or help your ability to thrive. You will totally love the descriptions about your highest potential and purpose... but you will totally not love reading about your dark side, called Your Primal Persona.

Hang in there! We intentionally go through the Primal Persona stuff first, so that you can finish on a high note – the magnificence that is Your Vitality Personality.

Give yourself permission to surrender to this process, and you will see how it takes you on a journey, getting richer and richer the further it goes. The part of you that is wired for harmony will quickly come to see how applying this wisdom will get you there, and the rest of us as well.

DECODE YOUR SURVIVAL PROGRAMMING

As we just learned, **Your Primal Persona is the version of you that exists when you allow your Ego to unconsciously drive your thoughts, feelings and actions.** It is the operating system of your survival-oriented mind, limiting you from tapping into the love and light that is your Higher Consciousness.

In this state, you are closed off from your sense of love for yourself or others. And the actions you take from this place only serve to fulfill the Survival Programming of the small, fearful you. This can be really uncomfortable to face, but it is critical to see clearly so that you can gain freedom from this dark influence.

The bottom half of your Mandala spells out the dynamics of Your Primal Persona and its Ego-Driven Survival Programming:

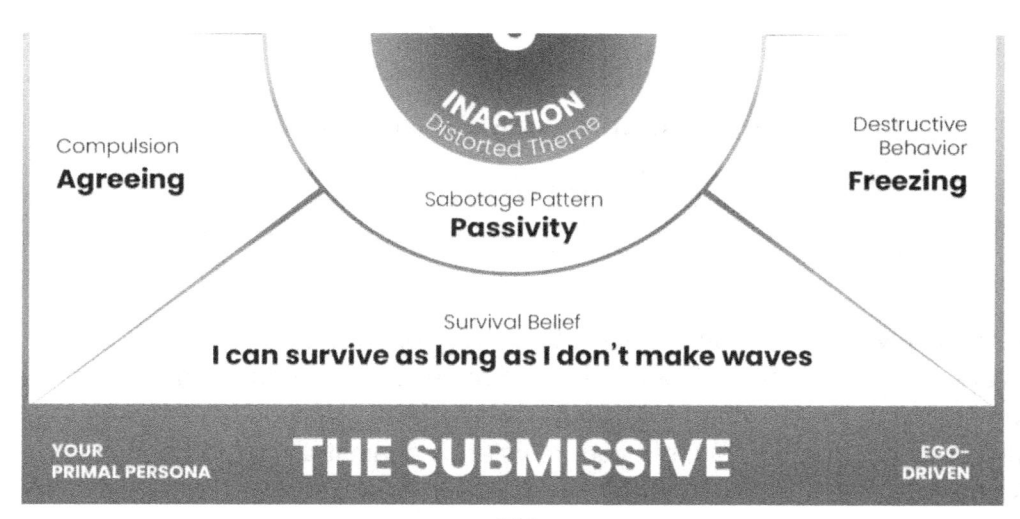

Distorted Theme
INACTION

Compulsion
Agreeing

Destructive Behavior
Freezing

Sabotage Pattern
Passivity

Survival Belief
I can survive as long as I don't make waves

YOUR PRIMAL PERSONA
THE SUBMISSIVE
EGO-DRIVEN

Your Primal Persona: The Submissive

As a Type 9,

> Your Primal Persona is known as **The Submissive**.

This is your Ego's version of "playing small," even though its programming is all about being agreeable and easy-going. But, as we will now explore, being agreeable and advocating for peace are not at all the same thing.

See *Fig. 10A* for a brief summary of your Ego-Driven Survival Programming (we will dig deeper into it in just a moment). It is characterized by resistance, eroding your Vitality and degrading your life.

These are some painful truths. But you must forgive yourself for your Survival Programming. Have compassion for yourself, for it was the pain in your life which led you to feel that you couldn't survive without this perspective. Without self-awareness, you had no choice but to behave this way.

And this is true for everyone else, as well. We all deserve forgiveness for the way we act when we are asleep to ourselves -- we are totally unaware this is what we are doing and how much it hurts ourselves and those we love.

Even once you are aware of your Survival Programming, it can be quite challenging to take command over it. Yet every degree of progress you make in this direction brings you enormous reward. You will be joyfully inspired to continue the work.

Let's dive just a little bit deeper into what these dynamics of your Survival Programming really mean, so that you may begin the most rewarding journey of integrating yourself.

Fig. 10A **PERSONALITY TYPE 9 SURVIVAL PROGRAMMING**
Your Primal Persona: THE SUBMISSIVE
The Programmed You; The limited and diminished version of yourself that you default to when you are Ego-Driven
Distorted Theme: INACTION
Your Ego's warped and downgraded interpretation of your true Theme
Survival Belief: I CAN SURVIVE AS LONG AS I DON'T MAKE WAVES
The scarcity-oriented message embedded in your Ego that creates your world view
Compulsion: AGREEING
The repetitive internal process you instantly launch as a way of discharging the emotional tension caused by your Survival Belief
Destructive Behavior: FREEZING
The ruinous actions you regularly engage in when you operate according to your Survival Belief
Sabotage Pattern: PASSIVITY
The totality of all your Survival Programming combined into an overall template for self-destruction

Your Distorted Theme

Each of the 9 Personality Types orient around a particular **Theme.** The whole point of you being here, at this time and in this place, is because you wanted to explore this Theme. This is the thing you are encoded to care about the most.

> Your Theme is **Peace**

We will fully explore the true meaning of Peace in the next section (about Your Vitality Personality), when we discuss the Consciousness-Directed understanding of your Theme.

But right now, we are discussing your Survival Programming, and how your Ego *degrades* your understanding of your Theme of Peace.

Unfortunately, when Your Primal Persona interprets this Theme, **it becomes contorted – a warped, downgraded version of your highest potential.** This is called the **Distorted Theme.**

> Your Distorted Theme is **Inaction**

Inaction is a slowness, an apathy, a reluctance to engage. This is the Type 9 impulse to ignore things that feel too complicated to face, your sense of depletion blocking you from addressing challenges. Inaction is the result of overwhelm, leading you to shut down and check out much of the time.

It is easy to see how, with this set of factors always at play, the heavy and sleepy sensation created by Inaction makes it very difficult to overcome. This mirrors Newton's first Law of Motion which defines *inertia*, stating *A body at rest stays at rest.* In other words, your Ego's Distorted Theme has got some pretty powerful physics reinforcing its attempt to keep you from growing, changing, or expanding,

And what's worse, from the outside, your Inaction is often misunderstood. What you regard as taking the time you need to feel ready, most others interpret as a willful disregard for the promises you made and the responsibilities you took on.

Inaction also includes a lot of unconscious resistance against things. You tend to resist include experiences which require you to be the decision-maker/problem solver. Your Ego mind often whispers to you that you are not smart enough or strong enough to lead or solve problems, or convinces you you're too tired to face them. This often compels you to give in or give up before ever really trying, blocking you from experiencing the joy of expanding your abilities and involving yourself fully with what Life would like to show you.

In the hands of Your Primal Persona, you spend all your time checking out, agreeing, or freezing, believing you are creating peace by avoiding taking a position, but instead are introducing factors which create big problems:

- Unwilling to feel hurried or rushed, you give lots of your time to unproductive activities like watching tv, gaming, and napping – resisting activities which will actually solve problems or lead to advancement

- Enjoying the lovely, easy, pleasing parts of life but totally resistant to facing challenges, you will use narcotizers like food, drugs and alcohol to stay numb – limiting your ability to connect deeply with yourself and build a life of meaning
- Highly invested in thinking of yourself as kind and generous, you are unwilling to see how your Inaction forces other people to do much of your work for you, creating resentment, frustration and hostility in your relationships
- Avoiding being in the hot seat, you let others decide your life for you, but use much passive-aggressiveness when you don't like what they chose – destroying wellbeing and harmony in your life
- Desiring peace and quiet above all else, you allow abusive and toxic behaviors to continue around you because you don't want to deal with the drama of confronting them – sabotaging the trust and wellbeing of the ones who looked to you for protection
- Resistant to acknowledging your stubborn and uncooperative tendencies, you turn to making excuses and blaming others for why you failed to help – blocking your own personal growth and maturity

Although Inaction makes you feel better in the moment, your resistance to attending to your own life creates an enormous amount of issues, conflicts, and stress – exactly the things you detest!

This is no fun at all to read about. It's a bummer to realize your default, unconscious wiring is a sadly small version of who you could really be – who you actually are. The Real You is full of radiance and love and light, taking pleasure in the Now moment while actively serving its highest potential. You are on your way to discovering how to access this Higher aspect of yourself.

Your Survival Belief

Your **Survival Belief** is the **scarcity-oriented message embedded in your Ego that creates your world view.** It is the secret programming in the basement of your unconscious which drives all your thoughts, feelings, and actions without you ever realizing it.

> Your Survival Belief is **I can survive as long as I don't make waves.**

This belief is fundamental to you, even though you never knew it was there. It defines your understanding of how the world works.

Typically, this Survival Belief is activated within you at a young age.

As a child you likely experienced volatility and drama in your homelife. This would have triggered in you confusion, fear, and overwhelm, and a strong desire to disappear from it. You turned to making yourself as small and unobtrusive as possible as a way of keeping from making anything worse. You concluded early that you were not powerful enough to handle resolving complex problems, and so became one who avoids and defers. Becoming passive and submissive seemed like the best strategy for survival, and it's never occurred to you to re-examine it as an adult.

Your Survival Belief fundamentally shapes how you feel about your place in the world. Believing that you should not make waves expands into believing that you are not fit to make decisions. It indicates to you that you are not smart enough or strong enough -- you must count on someone else being the decision maker. This leads you to feel instantly overwhelmed when faced with complexity. Not only do you not feel you are capable of being the captain of your own ship, but you completely hate it whenever life asks you to do so.

Think back on your life, and ask yourself... Am I in charge of the decisions in my household, or is it understood that someone else is in charge? Do I allow problems to go on and on because I don't want to face resolving them? How often have I shut down when my relationships asked me to face something I found too intense? How likely is it that I have let people down by telling them I would do something but not ever following through? How much of my unhappiness is connected to not speaking up about what is important to me?

This is the natural way of things, as long as your Ego is whispering in your ear that you are too weak to fend for yourself. Your Ego wants you to "play small," and buying into your Survival Belief is how this is accomplished. If you are severely unaware of your Higher Consciousness and your connection to the Universe, your Type 9 Survival Belief can turn you into someone who is fundamentally asleep to yourself – asking no questions and feeling no sense of purpose. This is your Primal Persona: The Submissive.

As long as you embrace the erroneous belief that you are not strong enough to survive on your own, and you must always agree, and you are always supposed to give in and give up, and everybody else is too demanding and angry and overwhelming ... you can expect to continue experiencing conflict and pain in your life.

Even though you are never really disconnected from your Higher Consciousness, it is your Ego's focus on your Survival Belief which keeps you feeling separated or even completely blocked from accessing It. Yet in fact, connecting to your Higher Consciousness is how you may gain mastery over your Ego, and steer your life in a new, positive direction.

◆◆◆

As you can see, your Survival Belief that you must never make waves is at the heart of much difficulty and self-sabotage for you. It is this belief which launches a cascade of repetitive thoughts and behaviors, that ultimately lead to your unhappiness. Learning about these, and how to take hold of them, is fundamental to becoming able to create a life you love.

If you have read this far, you are doing so well! Thank you for hanging in there, this stuff is definitely not fun to face. Remember, we are in the thick of the section about the Ego's Survival Programming. But then we will move ahead to discuss Type 9 at your highest and best.

We just finished discussing your Type 9 Survival Belief, which was activated somewhere in your childhood. It is the primary driver behind all of your unconscious thoughts and behaviors.

Now, we will look at the most common thought, feeling and behavior patterns that emerge as a result of holding your Survival Belief.

Your Compulsion

Your **Compulsion** is the **repetitive internal process you instantly launch as a way of discharging the emotional tension caused by your Survival Belief.**

➢ Your Compulsion is **Agreeing.**

This Compulsion is much like a guilty addiction – you know you should give it up, but don't want to… because you privately love it. And even if you decide *That's it, I'm through with this…* you will still find it very difficult to stop, until you become able to embrace your Vital Truth (see the upper half of your Mandala), rather than your Survival Belief.

It would probably never occur to you to think of agreeing as a bad thing to do. In general you would think this is the best course of action. While most anyone will agree to a reasonable request, what we are discussing in relation to the Type 9 has many extra layers. This "go along to get along" attitude can have some very serious consequences.

Not Questioning What You're Agreeing To

Basically, Type 9's do not like being asked direct questions. It instantly makes you uncomfortable to be in the hot seat. Your immediate impulse is to withdraw and shut down. The quickest way to appease the person who is "making you" uncomfortable is simply to say Yes. They will then have gotten what they wanted, and will now go away and leave you alone.

However, in this scenario, you have not actually even asked yourself if you care about this topic. You wanted the confrontation to go away so badly that you didn't really even consider the question.

In this way, you repeatedly let others be in charge of how or where your life is going. When your attitude is always "I don't care, you decide" you are very likely to end up living a life that doesn't feel fulfilling or meaningful.

Not Remembering You Agreed

Because of the scenario described above, it is likely you have been regularly agreeing to questions without really considering them. Mostly you're just saying what the other party wants to hear, so that they will go away and leave you in peace.

However, often in saying Yes, you just agreed to take some sort of action. You have told the other party that they can count on you to do something… Do you remember now what it was? Do you remember what the timeframe was for doing it? Is there something you're supposed to be doing right now?

Agreeing to things without really knowing what you're agreeing to leads you to instantly forget all about them. This can be quite unfortunate for the people who were counting on you. Whereas you were agreeing in hopes of keeping the peace, actually you are the one creating anger and resentment in your relationships if you repeatedly let others down because you don't follow through on what you promised them.

Not Disagreeing

Being vague and noncommittal is another way for the Type 9 to avoid going on the record and "making waves." You don't really say Yes, but you don't say No either. In your mind, you have not officially agreed to anything. However, many times you know perfectly well that the other party took your lack of a No as the equivalent of a Yes, and they will now take action on your behalf, believing you agree.

Being unwilling to go on the record about how you disagree is still Agreeing. Once again, you allow someone other than yourself to be in charge of what happens, telling yourself that since you didn't decide, the consequences are not your fault. But there is such a thing as being guilty by omission, and this is a common pitfall for the Type 9.

Saying Yes but Meaning No

You've been pinned down for an answer, so you can't get away with remaining vague. You know what the other party wants to hear, but you totally don't want to agree with what they're asking of you. Yet you know you will sound selfish or difficult or otherwise unacceptable by declining to agree, and that is most definitely making waves. So what do you do? You say Yes anyway, knowing full well that you have no intention of following through.

As someone who is invested in thinking of yourself as kind and easy-going, would you feel shocked to realize that there are people who might regard you as untrustworthy or dishonest? As much as you may believe in the moment that it is being kind to tell people what they want to hear, you are likely creating enormous hostility in your relationships by saying Yes when you know fully well that you mean No.

Not Knowing Your Truth

As a Type 9, you are wired to consider all points of view. You do not like to take sides, because you can see all the perspectives. This can often lead you to feel totally confused about what you believe is the right thing to do, hindering you from deciding and acting. You feel as if you do not know, so you therefore defer to what others decide.

This is another example of your Ego blocking you from remembering that you are an enormously powerful being of Light. You are actually never unsure, or vague, or wishy-washy. As pure Consciousness, you always embody the Truth of the Universe. Your Truth is in your heart at all times.

However, your Survival Belief has convinced you that you don't have what it takes to be in charge, to be the decider. It makes you feel as if your Truth is unreliable, and not to be considered. You must surrender this belief, embracing your own innate ability to know, in order to access your Truth.

Betraying Your Truth

This is the most devastating form of Agreeing there is -- knowing full well what your truth is, but still not speaking up for it. This can lead your life very far away from happiness and health. For when you are living a lie, nothing positive can come from it.

Consider these common examples:

- Wanting to eat differently/healthier, but continuing with the old way because that's what everybody else wants
- Staying in a job you hate because it serves other people's agendas
- Having interests and passions but abandoning them by agreeing it's too hard or unreasonable to pursue them
- Knowing you are not in love but remaining in the relationship because you're afraid to rely on yourself or be the bad guy
- Agreeing to have sex when you don't want to
- Knowing there is abuse going on but looking the other way

As you can see, betraying your own truth leads you to give up on your own life. This can bring on feelings of hopelessness, despair, and self-loathing. This is why Type 9's are extremely prone to depression. You don't believe it's possible to survive and also be happy.

Yes it is possible that you can thrive, be happy, and prosper.

The reason your Survival Programming feels so overpowering and difficult to escape from is because it's got you closed off from your source of power – your heart and Higher Mind.

You will need to engage with your Higher Self, intentionally opening yourself up to receive healing, guidance and love. This will make you feel better. The changes may be subtle at first. But you will come to see that, as you start practicing the Real You Methods taught in Chapter Twelve, you will feel stronger, and more able to speak your truth.

◆◆◆

As you continue your pursuit of self-awareness, you will learn methods for releasing yourself from your compulsion to Agree. Rather, you will become adept at trusting in your own intelligence, strength, and abilities – which you have in abundance. As you learn to connect to your Higher Consciousness and always embrace this guidance, you will see that choosing for your truth always brings about the Greatest Good for all concerned.

Your Destructive Behavior

Your Survival Belief – that nothing must ever hurt – also prompts your actions and behaviors. When you are Ego-Driven, and therefore **not questioning your inherent attitudes and beliefs, you will repeatedly behave this way.** This is called your **Destructive Behavior.**

You may be entirely unaware of it, or you may be doing it on purpose in the utter certainty it's the best way to be. Either way, this behavior is never for the Greatest Good of all, and therefore is destructive.

As an Ego-Driven Type 9 who believes that picking a side during conflict will lead to your annihilation. . .

> Your Destructive Behavior is **Freezing.**

Freezing means instantly shutting down. You can often have that deer-in-the-headlights look -- wide-eyed and stunned. Or you might just look like you fell asleep with your eyes still open: you're there physically, but really you are gone. You are immediately consumed with the thought: *I don't know what to do*. So you do nothing.

For the Type 9, the feeling of *I don't know* becomes *I stop here*. Whereas other Types might also not immediately know what to do, they will follow up with *but I can find out*. Only the Type 9 becomes completely incapacitated by the feeling of confusion. There are three primary reasons why this is so.

You Are a Slow Processor

As a Type 9, you don't really do anything fast. You move slowly, you speak slowly, and you think slowly. This is a fundamental part of being a sensitive and perceptive person -- you need time to sense and perceive. This is normal and not something to judge yourself for. Some people are fast processors, and others are slow processors, and both have their advantages and disadvantages.

Unlike the other slow processors -- also known as the Withdrawn Types -- you as the Type 9 have the added layer of believing you must never upset anyone. So whereas the Type 4 or 5 might say something like "I can't decide yet, I need time to think about it," you believe this is not allowed. Believing you don't know what to do and it's not ok to take the time you need to figure it out leaves you completely stuck.

However, there is indeed a way for you to make instant decisions when you need to, and that is to consult your Higher Consciousness, who is always in the Now and always knows. When you are ruled by your Ego, you forget all about this aspect of yourself, and therefore never seek to consult It. But you can develop a relationship with your Higher Consciousness, and gain for yourself a rock-solid sense of certainty.

You Don't Believe in Yourself

Your Survival Belief that you must never make waves leads to many secondary beliefs about yourself, all of which are sabotaging in nature. Beliefs such as:

- I'm not smart enough
- I'm not strong enough
- I don't know
- I can't do it
- It's unacceptable to be wrong
- People will reject me
- I am not important

These beliefs can completely annihilate your sense of self-esteem and your trust in yourself. Of course you would not know what to do, if you are constantly telling yourself you're not capable of making good decisions or figuring things out correctly.

This not only stops you from deciding, it stops you from even trying. The lack of belief in yourself leads you to feel it's not worth the bother. This can seriously derail your chances of creating the life yourself that you truly desire, by giving up before you even start.

You deserve to believe in yourself. You have forgotten that you are an ancient and wise being of Light. You have more knowledge, skill, and power than you could ever use in one lifetime. Your Ego makes you forget this, but your Higher Consciousness is always there, waiting for you to remember that you are magnificent.

You Don't Want the Responsibility

Buying-in to your Survival Belief that you must never make waves leads you to completely dread being the one in charge. The one in charge always has to make the decisions, even the really tough, unpopular ones. That is most definitely making waves. For you, that is a nightmare.

For a Type 9, remaining in the state of confusion feels safer than being the one who makes decisions and takes action. At a totally unconscious level, you are choosing *not* to consult your inner knowing, because that would lead you to make waves. Deep down, you are hoping to be able to claim that you didn't know, therefore you were not responsible.

This is all happening deep below the surface, beyond your sense of awareness. Freezing seems to happen *to* you. This is essentially true, because this is a basic fear response of your sympathetic nervous system.

This shows just how deep your fear is really running. Fear happens when you don't trust yourself and your ability to bring in powerful assistance, and this is the area we will focus on in the upcoming sections about Your Vitality Personality, The Healer.

Your Sabotage Pattern

As we have discussed, your Personality Type has much Survival Programming built in. Your Survival Belief, Compulsion, and Destructive Behavior are undeniable impulses within you that all drive your well-being into the ground.

In other words, these all combine into an overall template for self-destruction. This is called your **Sabotage Pattern – the way you repeatedly behave throughout your lifetime which leads directly to the destruction of your health and happiness.**

> Your Sabotage Pattern is **Passivity.**

Passivity means giving in, and giving up. It means letting others be in charge of you, and the direction of your life. Passivity means surrendering all your power.

Passivity is *not* the same thing as going with the Flow. Going with the Flow of the Universe means taking your rightful place among it. Always remember:

- You were created for a reason, and your perspective is equal in value to everyone else's
- You have been gifted free will, and you are expected to use it
- You came here to serve your own Purpose, and no one else's

In refusing to be present, you are refusing to engage with what is Now. In hiding from Now, you remove yourself from the Flow. Where there is no Flow, there is stagnation... which can only lead to decay.

Think of yourself as a beautiful, tranquil pond, deep in the heart of the forest. You are peaceful, you are soothing, you nourish all life around you. People journey to be with you, because they find your presence so soothing and healing.

As this tranquil pond, although you are serene, you are not without movement. There must be currents of flow in the pond that keep life circulating.

If it becomes completely still, the beautiful pond becomes a stagnant marsh. The water becomes poisonous, and the birds and insects can no longer take nourishment there. There are mosquitos and disease, and people will no longer come to join you there. When there is utter lack of movement, there is only death.

Once you start looking for it, you will realize that Passivity has been playing a pervasive role throughout your life. While it is no fun at all to see this, it's crucial that you do, in order to begin to take hold of it. Here are the areas to watch out for:

Passivity and the Mind

Whereas many of the other Personality Types struggle with relentless chatter in their mind, you actually have a means of shutting that down, along with all the rest of you. It's almost as if you have the ability to take your entire consciousness offline.

No wonder you seem to lose time all over the place! You seem to be able to slip into a stupor, losing all sense of yourself.

This in no way provides the peace you are seeking, and is not at all what peace looks like. Peace is the sense of completion and satisfaction you feel that your life is dynamic, thriving, and in harmony. Passivity is hiding away from the dynamics of life.

This holds your life in stasis, with no real progress or change possible. The troublesome issues in your life go unresolved, and are allowed to worsen greatly over time.

Not only is this sabotage of yourself and your own potential, but this also sabotages many relationships. No matter how sweet and undemanding you are, eventually other people will come to feel you have let them down. Your boss, your spouse, and your kids probably all would have stories to tell of how you didn't show up for them or follow through.

Most Type 9s, once they come awake to themselves and really see all the damage they allowed to occur, feel deep grief. You will learn methods for forgiving yourself and accepting yourself. This is the journey that was intended for you, and you are right where you are supposed to be. We are all somewhat devastated to see just what we are capable of when Ego-Driven, but that is where the birth of self-awareness happens. This is what launches you on this very journey, the journey towards self-love.

Passivity and the Body

There appear to be two general camps of Type 9s in terms of how they relate to the body, but they are not even percentages. Both are using the body as a means of numbing out but one is active numbing-out, and the other is idle numbing-out.

Active Numbing-Out

Perhaps a third of Type 9s are the physically active kind. They generally enjoy being outdoors – walking, hiking, biking, fishing, gardening. They like the peacefulness of being quiet in nature.

While that is certainly a lovely way to spend the day, chances are there are a whole bunch of urgent problems going unattended back at home.

Throwing yourself into peaceful activities that help you forget all the complexities and adulting awaiting you is not giving you actual peace – it's making your underlying anxiety greater and more oppressive, sinking you into your numbness further.

For this group it's best to connect your nature outings to tasks completed – going fishing or gardening is your reward for answering whatever life is asking of you.

Idle Numbing-Out

This is the much larger percentage of Type 9s, perhaps two-thirds. Sedentary and food-and-fun oriented, this is an extremely chill and easy-going bunch.

In addition to liking fried food, dairy, and sweets, they are commonly alcohol or marijuana users as well. All of these induce dopamine, the neurotransmitter that provides us with waves of euphoria and dampens pain. This keeps a nice mellow, toasty feeling going much of the time, but also helps you sink into the couch a little bit further.

Activities for this group are various ways of puttering around the house. Online games, surfing the internet, binge-watching tv, tinkering in the shop, taking care of the animals.

A Type 9's habits are deeply entrenched, and hard to shift. In order to bust out of these hypnotic rhythms, it will take a lifestyle overhaul. Promising you'll do a certain something different, but meanwhile all the rest of your lifestyle is still about checking out, would make it very easy for you to forget and backslide.

For you it would be best to dramatically change things. Perhaps begin with how you do your mornings. Set your alarm for earlier. Add in a new exercise or journaling time. Eat totally different foods. Wear different clothes. Drive a different way to work.

You want to shake yourself up a bit. This will help you stay present and avoid falling back into old ruts.

Passivity and the Heart

Because your Survival Belief encourages you to believe it's not safe for you to speak up or take a strong position, you feel compelled to smother your feelings. With this worldview, there is no room for you to have needs or desires – you have to go along with what other people want.

The sadness and hopelessness this brings on is intolerable. It creates a deep need in you for relief. The only coping method you know of is to completely numb your sensibilities. This includes your feelings.

Rather than investing deeply in yourself and allowing your feelings to guide you towards your happiest life, you opt to let someone else's strong feelings be the priority. You Agree to what other people want, and try to ignore whatever it was you wanted for yourself.

Often you try to abandon your own identity altogether, hoping to merge your identity with another person or group. You will let their interests and desires become yours.

In order to feel safe enough to allow your true feelings to come up and be experienced, your beliefs about your role in the world must change. As long as you still regard yourself as less important, less worthy, you will still feel enormous pressure to submit. It is only when you come to regard yourself as important and worthy that you will feel empowered to reveal The Real You.

◆◆◆

Living in a chronic state of Passivity creates stagnation, unhappiness, and ultimately, destruction. It has you perpetually giving up on your own joy, locking you into a life of pain and hopelessness. As you can see, it will likely lead to your own downfall, rather than your survival, as your Ego would have you believe.

If you feel stuck, overwhelmed, or powerless, remember that you have a direct line to an extremely powerful and magical being – The Real You. Your Higher

Consciousness is with you at all times and has been eagerly awaiting the opportunity to co-create a happier life with you

Just begin by asking for help. Close your eyes, breathe slowly and deeply, and focus your attention on your heart. Inside your mind, say to your heart (your portal to your Higher Self):

Hello, friend. I need help making a change. I'm not sure the best way to proceed. Please send me insight and guidance, and send me more energy and courage. Please scan my energy and provide healing to whatever is out of balance. I want to feel energized, motivated, and clear.

As you begin to perceive that you are feeling better – lighter, more hopeful, more spirited – remember to acknowledge that you see the help you received, and say thank you. This continues to strengthen your sense of connection and relationship with your Higher Self.

◆◆◆

Now that you have opened your eyes to the destructive inner workings of your own Ego, operating as Your Primal Persona, do not despair. It is certainly within your capacity to transform these behaviors and patterns of your Survival Programming.

If you have made it this far, CONGRATULATIONS. We lost many along the trail – not everybody is ready for the journey that is Getting Real! This book is really only interesting to people who are about to make an enormous advancement in their consciousness.

We made it through the hardest part. Now, let's explore how you can be, act and live differently. There is an entirely different kind of life available to you, filled with love and connection and joy. And it is mapped out in the top half of your Type 9 Mandala.

ACTIVATE YOUR POWER PARADIGM

In Chapter One we revealed the meaning of Your Vitality Personality. Let's recap now.

Your Vitality Personality is the version of you that exists when you allow your Higher Consciousness to guide your thoughts, feelings, and actions. It is the opening of your heart, and allowing the loving intelligence found there to Flow through you. This infuses you with insight, wisdom, love and compassion, and the actions you take from this place always serve the Greatest Good.

Let's take a look now at the top half of your Mandala which spells out the dynamics of The Real You - Your Vitality Personality - and all its wondrous gifts and talents:

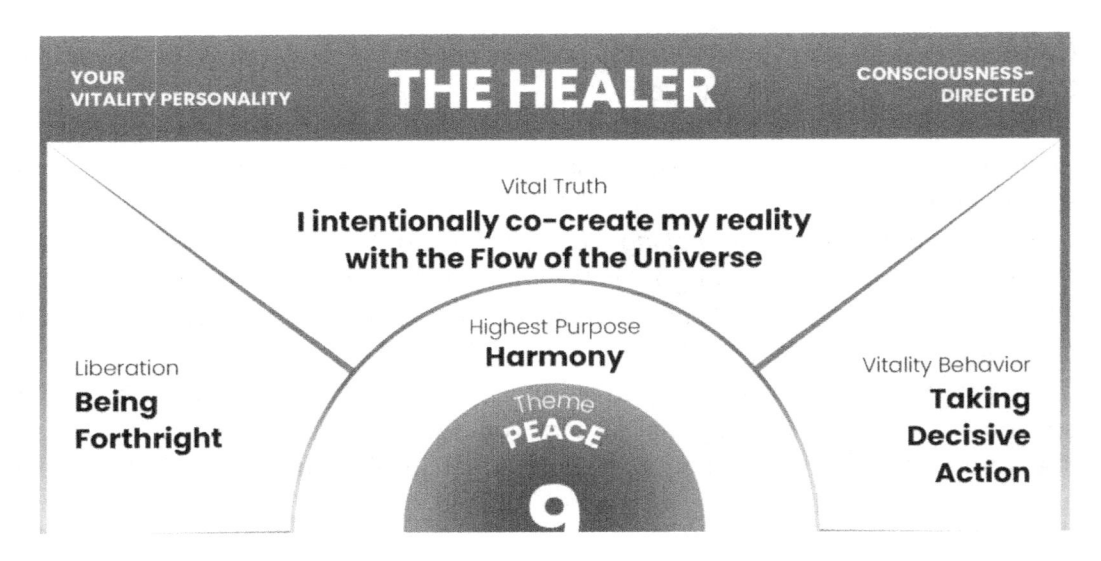

YOUR VITALITY PERSONALITY

YOUR VITALITY PERSONALITY — **THE HEALER** — **CONSCIOUSNESS-DIRECTED**

Vital Truth
I intentionally co-create my reality with the Flow of the Universe

Highest Purpose
Harmony

Liberation
Being Forthright

Theme
PEACE

Vitality Behavior
Taking Decisive Action

9

Your Vitality Personality: The Healer

As a Type 9,

> Your Vitality Personality is known as **The Healer.**

This is the truth of who you really are. Your quiet ways, your gentle manner, your love of nature, your perception of energy... these have always been the greatest part of you. You may have wondered why the world feels too loud, too brash, too mean, and why you haven't really wanted to join in. This is because you were never meant to become part of the harshness – you are meant to provide the respite from it.

The Real You is a Healer, not because you work in the medical profession, but because your energy is a balm to our wounded hearts. Your kindness, your generosity of spirit, your lack of judgment, and your peaceful presence help other people relax and let go. All this time, you have felt unimportant, invisible, and without purpose. Little did you know... we all need you so very much.

See *Fig. 10B* for a brief summary of the Consciousness-Directed half of your Mandala, identifying how to use your Personality Type to bring into the world a sense of love, compassion, forgiveness, and serenity.

When you embody all these natural gifts, you are a dazzling light, inspiring all who know you. It is so exciting to think you are just on the precipice of launching a new life of love, acceptance, and Vitality for yourself! It might have required some serious deep-breathing to get here, but the effort is so well worth it.

Let's explore these dynamics of your Power Paradigm, so that you may begin to fully comprehend just how open, uplifting, happy and healthy your life could really be.

Your Theme

As was previously mentioned,

> Your Theme is **Peace**.

When you pursue the highest form of this Theme – Peace – you are truly aligned with Source, and therefore always serving the Greatest Good.

Peace is not merely the absence of war, the quiet after the storm, the relief to be done with brutality. That is the Ego-Driven idea of what it means. But what you bring is so much more elevated, so much bigger, and so much more profound.

Peace is the love and acceptance that Source feels at having created creation. It is joyfulness and serenity at the same time. It is the fulfillment and happiness of just existing. It is the blissful knowingness that all is well.

This is sometimes known as the *Christ Consciousness* – the offering of unconditional Love – and this is what comes naturally to you when you are your best self.

Peace and love are the highest vibrations of all, and it is what the fabric of the Universe is made of. It is what Consciousness is made of, and all we beings of light are made of it too. And yet, in our dense human forms, we forget our own light, we block ourselves from the Flow of it. This is the source of all unhappiness, illness, and disease -- the strangling denial of love and light. Caught up in our Egos, we all become unwell.

Fig. 10B   **PERSONALITY TYPE 9**   **POWER PARADIGM**
Your Vitality Personality: **THE HEALER**
The Real You; The most magnificent version of yourself you joyfully embody when you heed the guidance of your Higher Consciousness
Theme: WISDOM
The dynamic realm of Life your Higher Consciousness wants to explore to the fullest
Vital Truth: I INTENTIONALLY CO-CREATE MY REALITY WITH THE FLOW OF THE UNIVERSE
The higher understanding of how to thrive, that aligns you with the Flow of the Universe
Liberation: **BEING FORTHRIGHT**
The emancipating philosophy you freely embrace to enhance your connection to the Flow
Vitality Behavior: **TAKING DECISIVE ACTION**
The empowering and uplifting actions you intentionally choose to create your best life
Highest Purpose: HARMONY
How you serve the Greatest Good through embracing your encoded genius, and the source of your Vitality

You, Type 9, bring enormous Healing when you extend your loving and generous nature. Rather than judging, you understand how difficult it is to be human, and forgive people their flaws and mistakes. This is such a balm to another's spirit. Your willingness to forgive reminds others to forgive themselves. This is healing at the deepest level.

Rather than pursuing worldly goods like money and status, as a Healer you simply emanate Peace and love to everyone around you. In your presence, none feel the need to jockey for position, to dazzle and impress. They are reminded they can just be, and this is such a soothing relief. The Peace that you bring to the heart of others is so healing.

When you make the choice to be present and engaged, Intentionally aligning with your Higher Consciousness and the Flow of the Universe, offering love and compassion, you help others heal. Although this is a simple and humble way to live, the rewards for your life of service will be quite beyond your imagining. Feeling seen, wanted, appreciated, respected, and loved will become your daily existence, as you radiate health and happiness.

In the hands of Your Vitality Personality, you apply your fully heart-centered Self towards efforts which serve the Greatest Good, making you a loved and appreciated Healer:

- Experiencing an inner sense of peace derived from effectively meeting the needs of the day, rather than avoiding them
- Feeling trust in your own ability to decide and take appropriate action
- Relationships which are an equal partnership and where all feel safe to speak their truth
- Work which interests and engages you, and is recognized and appreciated by others
- Vital health derived from promptly attending to your own physical, emotional, and spiritual needs
- The active happiness that is living a life that serves The Real You

Most people are agitated, anxious, and restless. They feel compelled to follow their Ego's Survival Programming, but it only makes them feel angry, or afraid, or ashamed. They don't know how to find their way to love, acceptance, and tranquility... and they are slowly dying from the lack of it.

You are the one who is built to serve the world by engaging your natural abilities to create a safe and healing environment where others can experience rest, recovery, and peace.

However, you will only accomplish a peaceful lifestyle as long as you are willing to act when prompted by the Universe. Rather than seeking to avoid conflict by always agreeing, be willing to be forthright and speak your truth. Rather than becoming overwhelmed and freezing up, you must believe in your ability to take decisive action. In this way you serve your Highest Purpose: bringing Harmony to the world.

Your Vital Truth

Your **Vital Truth** is the **Higher understanding of how to thrive by aligning with Universal principles.** It is the escape hatch your Ego doesn't want you to know about, because it unlocks all of its Survival Programming, and connects you to your Higher Consciousness – The Real You.

> Your Vital Truth is **I intentionally co-create my reality with the Flow of the Universe.**

Although this is a brief, simple statement, it is dense with meaning. Let's take a moment to unpack this.

Being Intentional

You are an ancient being, and you have experimented with all kinds of consciousnesses, such as being a blade of grass, a rock, a bird.

This time, however, is very special -- because now you are a human right at a pivotal time.. You have the rare and unique opportunity to elevate your consciousness well beyond biological programming, and embody your Higher Self.

You came here to have your own adventure – not submit to someone else's adventure. In order for this to happen, you must become intentional.

Being intentional means having a clear plan for yourself. You take actions on purpose, that will advance the experiences and growth you desire.

Type 9, you have a mind full of questions, a heart full of desires, and a body built for action. You did not come here, this time, to be a fixture in nature. You came here to fully participate in it. You came here to wonder, to choose, and to act.

Co-Creating Your Reality with the Flow

Did you know that everyone experiences their own version of reality? We tend to believe that reality is a single, undeniable point of view we all share, but that is not true.

You are personally creating the version of reality you are experiencing. Your energetic signature – comprised of your thoughts and feelings (both conscious and unconscious) – reaches out into the fabric of the Universe like a beacon. And the Flow of the Universe answers the call, sending you back experiences which are your match. This is often called the Law of Attraction or the Law of Mirroring.

What this means is that life isn't happening *to* you, it's coming *from* you.

So, how do you like your life, and what is it showing you about your energy?

If you would like your life to be happier and more empowering, you will need to engage more intentionally with the Flow. You were never meant to come here and play a passive role. You are the in the driver's seat of your life, and you must develop your skills at directing it.

You may have some pretty entrenched habits, but I invite you now to shift things up enough to make a new space for being alone, present, and intentional with yourself.

This is your time to use The Real You Methods taught in Chapter Twelve. This is your time to journal.

Let your journal be a private conversation between you, your Higher Self, and the Universe. Here are some journal prompts to help you create your happiest reality:

- One of my favorite people is A because B. I am so grateful for them because I learned C.
- 5 things/people I'm grateful for.
- 5 things I love about myself.
- 3 things I'm looking forward to and working towards
- What I've decided to focus my energy and attention on today. If I feel any resistance towards this, I request assistance in making it easy.
- What I'm feeling confused about and request higher understanding.
- What I want to attract into my life and request assistance with.
- I want X because I want more of Y & Z feelings in my life.
- What I am now ready to shift/heal/release and request assistance with.

You are not alone, Type 9. You have unseen helpers that you can call upon. You do have the ability to change and direct things, even when they feel complex. Be present. Be intentional. Ask for help.

Embracing the understanding that you are a Creator and this is your life to make of as you like opens your heart and mind. It floods you with hope, which strengthens and fortifies you.

As we are about to discuss, you are not the meek and powerless person your Ego has invited you to believe. You are actually a very important being here with a very important purpose. You are needed and wanted and loved. You are The Healer.

Your Liberation

Your **Liberation** is the **emancipating philosophy you freely embrace.** This is a powerful shift, out of the Survival Programming of the mind, and into the Flow of the Universe through the heart. Rather than being owned by a chronic Compulsion, you are now *intentionally choosing* this Liberation.

> Your Liberation is **Being Forthright.**

Being Forthright means speaking your truth -- going on the record about how you really feel.

This is enormously scary to a Type 9 who is under the influence of the Ego. What if this incites anger, or confrontation? What if speaking your truth results in major life changes?

When you are connected to your Higher Consciousness, embracing your Vital Truth, you are grounded and strengthened. You understand that whatever happens as the result of speaking your truth, it will be for the Greatest Good for all concerned.

Being Forthright also implies a solid trust in yourself. It is a display of inner strength. People who are afraid are the ones who do not speak up. They are afraid they might look stupid, they are afraid of being unpopular, they are afraid of inciting anger.

The ability to communicate openly demonstrates your core of conviction. In becoming willing to speak clearly about your observations, beliefs, feelings, and desires, you foster your own self-respect and self-trust.

The ability to Be Forthright requires holding deep love and respect for yourself. Your Ego has conditioned you to believe that you are insignificant, but this is far from true. You are, in fact, very significant -- someone who was created because your unique perspective was needed.

You have an important role to play here. Just because it is a quiet one does not mean it holds lower value. You are the one with the well-rounded perspective, and we all need to hear what that is.

If you would like to learn the Consciousness-Directed way to communicate effectively in a highly-charged situation, check out a book *Non-Violent Communication* by Marshall Rosenberg. This is an incredibly powerful method for having calm, respectful communication that keeps tensions from escalating.

Learning this method will make you feel confident that you can have tough conversations which resolve peacefully. If you can become effective at this, it will truly change your entire life.

Let's look at some famous Type 9's, and how they acted for the Greatest Good of all by Being Forthright:

Mister Rogers

Fred Rogers was the creator and host of the famous American children's television series *Mister Rogers' Neighborhood*, which ran from 1968 to 2001. He was a remarkably gentle, loving man who believed fiercely that children should be given tools for expressing their feelings. This was an utterly foreign concept in American child-rearing at the time his show first aired. Up until that point, the general belief among adults was that "children should be seen, but not heard."

Through his television show, his books, his public speaking, and even advocacy at the White House, he devoted his life to speaking up for people too young and powerless to speak up for themselves. He was not a dramatic or flamboyant person -- his manner was mild and soft-spoken. He was a humble minister who dressed unpretentiously and spoke simply. And yet, through Being Forthright, he effected remarkable change in American parenting psychology and positively impacted the lives of thousands of children.

Abraham Lincoln

Abraham Lincoln was an American lawyer and statesman who served as the 16th president of the United States from 1861 to 1865. Lincoln led the nation through the American Civil War, the country's greatest moral, cultural, constitutional, and political crisis. He succeeded in preserving the Union, abolishing slavery, bolstering the federal government, and modernizing the U.S. economy.

Lincoln was known for his calm demeanor, his honesty, and his compassion. He spoke to people in a mellow, reassuring way that made them feel safe. He had a reputation for being willing to consider all points of view, but for remaining true to his own convictions.

Although the practice of slavery in the United States was deeply entrenched in the culture of the time, Lincoln was part of the movement towards change. This included upheaval and conflict. Yet, because of his desire to bring peace to a divided land, he brought about positive social change, and moved the country toward balance. (Unfortunately we're still not quite there.)

Jesus Christ

Jesus Christ is a historical figure who became the inspiration for an enormous spiritual movement which still reverberates throughout the world, two thousand years later.

Jesus Christ lived simply, offering love, healing and compassion to all he encountered. He spoke openly about these principles, although they conflicted with previous spiritual teachings. He spoke of controversial ideas which conflicted with the ruling philosophies of the day.

Although it put his life in danger to do so, he felt compelled to speak his truth, no matter the consequences. Although some would argue that his murder is a cautionary tale against speaking out for your truth, in fact he understood that his death would serve a Higher Purpose. Where would this world be, if he hadn't?

♦♦♦

Being Forthright is the opposite of taking the easy way out. It requires that you use your voice and speak up for what you really believe, rather than hiding and letting others make all the decisions.

This is what you were built for -- advocating for kindness, acceptance, respect, healing, and peace. You are the voice of unconditional love in this world, and we desperately need you to play your part.

Your Vitality Behavior

Vitality Behavior is the **empowering and uplifting actions you intentionally choose when you are Consciousness-Directed,** rather than the Destructive Behavior your Ego drives you to act out.

> Your Vitality Behavior is **Taking Decisive Action.**

This is sooo much lovelier than your previous go-to – Freezing! This is where you really shift out of Your Primal Persona, The Submissive, and into Your Vitality Personality, The Healer. Now that you have come to understand that living in harmonious Flow does not mean checking out and hiding away, you will find yourself exhibiting more Consciousness-Directed Behavior, by Taking Decisive Action.

Taking Decisive Action means deciding what to do, and then doing it, without delay.

In the Ego state, Type 9's are notorious for putting off decisions and actions for far too long... even forever. When the issues at hand seem too confusing, too upsetting, or too intense, the Type 9 Ego response is to shut down.

Yet in the Flow state, when you are plugged in to your higher Knowingness, you are prompted to take the right action at the right time. You will not feel confusion or overwhelm when you learn how to take direction from your own Higher Consciousness. This is Taking Decisive Action.

Taking Decisive Action means doing it Now. One of the strategies of the Type 9 Ego is to trick you into thinking you're making progress by leaving projects only partially complete. If you began to take action but then paused somewhere in the process, you could leave it there for years with the claim "I'm working on it." Really, Type 9, what you want to be able to consistently say is "I did it."

Knowingness

What is essential for you is to begin cultivating your sense of *Knowingness*.

Knowingness is a form of intuition, an internal sense of "rightness." It happens when your body, mind and heart are all saying the same thing. This intuition is actually the act of receiving guidance from your Higher Consciousness. This is what you must learn how to do.

Meditation is the most direct way to gain a sense of connection to your Higher Consciousness, and you Type 9, are a total natural at meditation.

Whereas many other Types feel enormous resistance against meditating, you instinctively know peace is waiting for you there. To disconnect from the chatter of the mind and let yourself merge with Consciousness sounds like heaven to you!

However, beware of how your Ego will try to manipulate you. When you enter the meditative state, you are intentionally entering a state of Higher awareness, of connection... not oblivion. You are receiving love and wisdom from your Higher Self, recharging and replenishing so that you might go back out into the world and fully engage.

Some Type 9's seek to retain the dreaminess and other-worldliness they experience in the meditative state, to live inside a cocoon of "peacefulness", yet this instead becomes an insulator, a dampener, leading you to be checked out and unaware of your surroundings. This is a distorted understanding of the concept of peace.

True peace comes from being entirely present and alert, fully connected to your Higher Consciousness and highly responsive. Peacefulness is active, not passive.

Learning how to seek out and hear your own inner wisdom is the powerful secret to overriding your Ego's tendency to freeze under pressure. As you gain trust for your own intuition, you will naturally develop the ability to know what to do. This is what allows you to Take Decisive Action. It is also what helps you develop a sense of worthiness and love for yourself.

As ever, shifting towards feelings of self-love and self-acceptance are what move your behaviors into ones which serve the Greatest Good and bring about your own Vitality, all at the same time.

Your Highest Purpose

You chose to be here, in this time and place, because you wanted to contribute something. You came here for a reason, and you chose your Personality Type because it was the one that would help you accomplish it. **Your Personality Type has a special set of talents and abilities, and you wanted to use them to make a contribution.** This is your **Highest Purpose.**

> Your Highest Purpose is **Harmony.**

Your Higher Consciousness chose the Personality Type 9 because It wanted to explore the Theme of Peace on the physical plane. Harmony is the way your Higher Consciousness would have you go about it.

Your inherent perspective is actually quite unique. Whereas all the other Types have rather predictable points of view, because their hardwiring leads them to be that way, you are the only one inclined to consider other people's perspectives. Your naturally kind and inclusive nature prompts you to want to cooperate. You like finding ways for everybody to participate together, so that there is room for everyone.

Imagine what new kind of world we could live in, if everyone would be willing to seek this perspective! Cooperation, kindness, respect, peacefulness. It would be a Utopia, if we would all be willing to live that way. That is the power of Harmony.

You like everyone to get along, and you naturally are a peacemaker, encouraging other people to soften their position, to be more generous, more flexible, more compassionate. You like to find ways for everybody to peacefully coexist. This is so desperately needed in this world. We need you, Type 9, to remind the rest of us to cease our aggression and be loving.

Harmony of the Mind

Harmony of the mind is something you as a Type 9 have the greatest capacity for, far beyond other people. For you have the capacity to embrace the paradox that is seeing someone for all their flaws and all their strengths, understanding the pain and hopelessness and love and light that lie beneath, and fully loving and accepting all of them.

In other words, you have the easiest capacity for offering unconditional love.

You have always been a gentle, sensitive person. You can feel other people's energy – accessing the real truth of them – and empathize. It's as if you have the ability to look into their souls, and see them for the light being they forgot they were.

This is how you are a Healer. With your vision of wholeness, you make integration of light and dark possible. You create a quiet, loving space where other people can feel safe to be who they really are. You make their awakening possible.

Your ability to offer love while having no attachments, no expectations -- just accepting all as it is without requiring it to change – is magnificently healing to others. They are able to drop their armor, which was blocking them from accessing their hearts. Now they can connect to themselves.

Imagine the world you are capable of creating, where it is the culture to love and accept all people at all levels of consciousness. With your mind in full Harmony, you usher in the next era -- the era of personal enlightenment.

Harmony of the Body

As we have discussed, Harmony is active and aware, not checked out and passive. It is important for you to cultivate a lifestyle of physicality which embraces being productive and responsive.

Think of it in terms of the ancient *taiji* symbol, depicting the balance of *yin* and *yang*.

This is a symbol of balance, of harmony. Let it be a guiding principle for you. The dark color is the *yin* aspect of life: restful, quiet, still – yin is the state of "being." The white color is the *yang* aspect of life: active, productive, busy – yang is the state of "doing." This principle teaches us that in a 24-hour day, we need 12 hours of *yin*, and 12 hours of *yang*.

Your tendency is to be too *yin* – spending more time "being" than "doing." You must consciously develop your willingness to take timely action in order to remain in Harmony. Here are some suggestions on how to accomplish this.

- Daily heart-based meditation, at a maximum of 30 minutes.
- 30-minute daily exercise that gets your heart rate up and builds muscle tone. Both the heightened energy and sense of strength and power are important for you so that you feel energized and confident.
- 30 minutes maximum for a typical meal. No need to lounge about too long.
- Using an online calendar to keep track of and honor your commitments.

- Setting alarms in your phone to remind you of the upcoming deadlines and appointments you committed to. Being timely and completing tasks is an important way of staying in the Flow and maintaining positive relationships.
- Eating foods with a high vibration, such as fruits, vegetables, nuts and seeds, which help you have high energy. Heavy foods such as fried foods, meats, and dairy lower your vibration and your energy, sapping you of the desire to be productive.
- Sleep a total of 8 hours per day. (Unless you are a teenager, in which case you need more like 11 hours of sleep per day.)
- Begin working with a life coach, who can give you tools and help you cultivate the skills you need to feel confident in the world, and to serve as a source of support.

Harmony of the body means a willingness to engage with the physical world, a willingness to experience your reality through your body. There is much pleasure and joy available to you as your physical self. Feeling energized and invigorated will be wonderful for you. It will improve your morale and sense of strength.

Harmony and the Heart

Harmony in the heart has to do with being present and awake, and connected to your feelings.

The tendency of the Type 9 as The Submissive is to shut down the mind and the heart, and live in a twilight state, a passive stupor. You're sort of phoning-in your life, without much desire or plans for yourself, just existing.

This is a complete disconnection from The Real You, who is a powerful and dynamic being of light that came here with passion and purpose.

Your heart is a portal, the doorway between the "small" you here in the physical world, and the "big" you that is made of eternal energy and holds the records of all your lifetimes of experiences. To fully connect with this most wise and loving aspect of yourself, you must learn how to "seat yourself" in your heart, rather than your mind. (We will expand on this greatly in Chapter Twelve.)

Seating yourself in the heart means developing the habit of dropping your attention out of the mind, and down into the center of your chest. Try to move through the day with your consciousness rooted there. It's like turning a spotlight on in your chest, letting it lead you through your day.

It's easy to begin practicing this while you're doing mundane things. Try it while driving, or doing the dishes or laundry, all with a sense of holding your awareness in your chest. Eventually the goal is to be able to always live from that place.

A remarkable shift will happen. The Ego mind goes silent, but the Higher Mind comes online. This is an extremely serene and peaceful state, yet fully alert and aware.

This keeps your portal open, allowing you to feel your full sense of Self – your true feelings, and true desires. It keeps you interested and engaged with life –

curious and ready to act. No sluggishness or resistance, no heaviness or dread. Just willingness.

You feel connected to your courage, your trust in yourself, your sense of knowingness. You awaken to a sense of partnership with nature, and other people. You come to feel yourself as an actively participating member of the collective, aware of your worth and how you contribute.

From this place of grounded, centered awareness, you are able to be supremely aware and relaxed at the same time, calmly taking in all the beautiful truth around you.

♦♦♦

As you can see, living in Harmony is a commitment. It doesn't happen by accident – you must be Intentional about it.

In holding yourself accountable in this way, you become an incredibly exciting example of full Vitality. Friendly, compassionate, cooperative, connected to the Universe, and happy to engage… you demonstrate to us all what it actually looks like to be peaceful.

This is how you create peace throughout the world: by creating true peace within yourself first. You serve as a living example to other people how they could be so much more Harmonious than they are now.

Living as The Healer

Are you ready to answer the call to be your Higher Self, and engage with the world in a more profound way?

- No more hiding, only wanting to be left alone so you can numb out in private.
- No more swallowing your words and letting others trespass on your boundaries.
- No more abandoning your desires, and letting other people be in charge of the direction of your life.

It is time to be the Real You, and contribute to Life in a way that feels meaningful and fulfilling to you.

- Feeling seen and Loved because you've been present and invested in your relationships
- Feeling valued and respected at work because you've delivered your best effort on time
- Being sought out for your wise and gentle healing ways
- Experiencing a sense of strength and confidence, and a trust in your ability to know what the right action is to take
- Feeling free to unapologetically live your life as you choose

You are about to enter an exciting new era in your life, where you step into your full potential, embrace your true power, and love your whole self.

♦♦♦

Well, Type 9, you've been given quite a lot of information about yourself to digest. But hopefully by now you've come to see that even though you are wired to act out Your Primal Persona, it is possible for you to be someone so much more magnificent than that – Your Vitality Personality.

Now is the time to decide who you want to be in this world. If you are ready to step into the full power of who you really are, and create your best life… then your next step is **Integration.** See Chapter Eleven.

CHAPTER ELEVEN
INTEGRATION

You may not have realized it yet, but the fact that you are here, learning these truths about yourself and your reality, indicates that you are about to uplevel yourself in a very powerful way. Only the ones who are ready to step into their Higher role find their way here.

The secret to activating your full power and embracing The Real You lies in your ability to love yourself. Because self-love is unconditional love. It is the way the Universe loves you, and when you come to love yourself the way the Universe loves you, you access the Flow. That is when you really get to experience life as beautiful, exciting, and fulfilling.

Once you understand what unconditional love is, you are able to extend it outward. You stop taking other people personally. You recognize they are reflecting aspects of you back to yourself. You understand their value, you appreciate their beauty. You have compassion for the hopelessness that influences their perspective. You begin to develop a general sense of affection for your fellow humans, limited and struggling though they may be.

Unconditional Love for Yourself

For us humans with our Ego-Driven Survival Programming, growing up in a world seeped in scarcity and lack, unconditional love for yourself seems nearly impossible.

All your life, you received messaging about how you're not good enough the way that you are. You felt pressure to disconnect from yourself, objectify yourself, and conform. You internalized all of this, running dialogues of self-loathing inside your mind.

And now you've just learned about your Primal Persona which comes with a whole *extra* set of reasons to be disgusted with yourself. And you're *wired* that way! So how is it actually even possible to fully love yourself, while all these unacceptable things are there?

There is nothing about you that is unacceptable. You are a great being of light, inside an experiment of forgetting and remembering oneself, and any issues of resistance are there for a reason. A very beautiful, wonderful, special reason.

You were meant to lose yourself, so that you could have the journey of finding yourself again. You were meant to forget your purpose, your power, your light – all so you could experience the great joy of rediscovering your own magnificence.

You are right where you are supposed to be.

The journey of learning to embrace The Real You is not at all about resisting, judging, controlling or smothering the Ego-Driven aspects of yourself.

It's about seeing all parts of yourself, leaving nothing in shadow… and **Loving** and **Accepting** them. It's about naming and claiming your feelings and experiences. It's about being your own best friend. It's about embodying The Real You. This is the process of Integration.

Integration

Integration means slowly assimilating the disparate pieces of you, by loving and accepting all of them.

When there are only some parts of yourself that you like, and the rest you deny or ignore or suppress, this is a state of disintegration. It's quite exhausting to hold so much of yourself away from yourself.

This keeps you feeling weak and incomplete. It creates cravings and longings, and propels you to look outside of yourself for ways to feel better. It creates worldviews of scarcity and lack.

Reclaiming all aspects of yourself – no matter how good, bad or ugly your Ego mind wants to label them – pulls all of your energy into coherence. Instead of being scattered all over the place, with only some of you operational, it organizes and settles into a synergized whole.

Loving all these aspects of yourself aligns you with your Higher Consciousness, amplifying the amount of light energy contained in your biofield.

Accessing more of your light activates more of your DNA. In general your DNA has been functioning merely at the level of survival. But when you feel safe and free and strong and happy, your energy resonates at a new frequency – a new key that unlocks so much more of you.

Your ability to heal will accelerate. Your sensitivity will increase. Your intuitive abilities will expand. Your knowingness will deepen. Your creativity will unfurl. Your manifestations will roll in.

As this beautiful process unfolds, you will have more energy. You will have fewer triggers. You will be in a better mood. You will feel relaxed, centered, and calm. You will start to look and feel younger. You will be nicer to other people. They will be nicer to you. You will find them more enjoyable. They will enjoy this about you. Life will start to get easy, and magical, and exciting, and fun.

Integrating yourself is how you finally get to experience Vitality – the joyful expression of an awakened mind, healthy body, and limitless spirit.

In the following chapter, we will go over the practices you may adopt which will dramatically accelerate your journey of Integration.

Integration Requires Awareness

If you have read this book, it is because your soul is calling out for Integration. It is time for you to become whole again.

This means you will need to commit to making time for introspection and coming fully present. You need private alone time.

In our hectic Ego-Driven lifestyles, we feel compelled to put our inner selves last. We live almost entirely in the external world. In our mindset of scarcity and survival, and our maneuvering for more love and status, we abandon the part of ourselves that could make all the rest so much easier.

Your Higher Consciousness does not agree that it's impossible for you to connect with yourself. And It is listening and waiting for your requests for help – you can ask for help in any way you need.

Ask for help finding time. Ask for help releasing resistance. Ask for guidance on a Higher perspective.

If you are currently telling yourself that it is not possible for you to have private alone time, stop and reconsider your perspective. Instead of saying *I can't have that*, try asking yourself *How could I have that?*

How could your morning routine be reoriented? How much tv/internet-surfing could be modified? Could you trade or pay for help that would free up some time? Even sitting in the parking lot or driveway, alone in your car, could be the 5 or 10 minutes you sit intentionally with yourself.

The bottom line is, if you want your life to change, you need to invest your time and attention in yourself. Ego excuses must be faced and cleared. You will feel much better as soon as you begin.

Integration Requires Healing

Your Personality Type Survival Programming has been the source of a perspective that has led to much pain and hurt. Additionally, there are also the traumas and wounds that have happened to you throughout your lifetime,

All of these emotional wounds are places where you continue to leak your power. It is akin to bleeding out your energy. Healing yourself of these is essential to reclaiming your power.

This re-integrated energy will uplevel your capacity to imagine, create, and manifest. The more you resolve old tears and snags in your energy field, the more coherent and impactful it will be. It is the overall integrity of your biofield, which is your energetic signature, that determines your experience of Vitality.

Most of us were taught that full healing from trauma is not possible. We were taught that being strong means totally suppressing and denying that you are hurt, and trying to carry on as if everything is fine.

Actually that perspective is what keeps you weak.

The real strength is having the courage and fortitude to face your feelings, and do the work of Integration.

The good news is it doesn't have to be nearly as difficult or painful as you imagine it will. Healing models of talk therapy are being replaced with more energetic models, where the Ego story is no longer explored in depth.

Most experiences you have been through were processed through the filter that is your Personality Type's Ego perspective. Your interpretation of events was distorted through a warped lens of Survival Programming. It is not really necessary to continue engaging with that perspective.

Instead, it is possible to heal yourself by getting out of the mind, where the Ego is spinning a story of blame and violation, and into your heart, where the feelings are. Allowing yourself to sit with the feelings that come up allows them to be released, once and for all. We will address how to do this in the next chapter.

Integration is the Return to Wholeness

Shedding the narrow and limited focus of your Personality Type's Ego opens you up to your Higher Consciousness, which is wholeness. This means that not only do you gain access to your Personality Type's elevated perspective, but everyone else's too.

In other words, you become more able to understand your reality from all perspectives, and gain access to the gifts of *all* of the Type's Highest Purposes.

Therefore, no matter which Personality Type template you embody, as you strive to heal and integrate yourself, you will experience more and more:

Clarity	Integrity
Self-Love	Joy
Expansion	Empowerment
Insight	Harmony
Vision	

As you decide you are ready for wholeness and all the potent power that comes with it, you will see yourself pull ahead, out of the old stuckness. You will feel yourself becoming lighter, healthier, happier, more stable. You will develop a sense of purpose, of certainty. You will know who you really are, why you're really here, and what you're really capable of.

◆◆◆

Congratulations! Just having read about these deepest aspects of yourself has greatly elevated and amplified your light. You are unlocking stuck patterns, and moving into something much freer and happier.

In the following chapter, you will learn the primary techniques that will help you fully connect to your mind, body and Higher Self.

YOUR VITALITY PERSONALITY

CHAPTER TWELVE
THE REAL YOU METHODS

In this chapter you will learn three methods for aligning yourself with your Higher Consciousness and the Flow of the Universe. They are all excellent tools that are the staples for living a life of Integration and Vitality. They will help you heal, elevate, and expand.

Creating Your Heart-Based Reality

All of The Real You Methods operate from the understanding that you can move your life into a higher dimension of reality when you are present and connected to your heart.

This does not come naturally to us. We have been programmed to be seated in our Ego-Driven minds, which has created an entire world of conditional love, polarity, pain, illness, and erosion. We automatically default to this programming when we are not present.

The heart is also capable of creating your reality, if you would let it – and you would enjoy it quite a lot more. A reality created by the heart is one of unconditional love, harmony, joy, vitality and expansion. Your awareness and intention are required to bring this about.

Learning to unhook yourself from your mind and bring your full awareness into your heart takes effort, and repeated practice. It gets easier, and the transformations you see happening in your life inspire you to keep going.

The Ego mind is fundamentally wired to create resistance and friction. This is so you could have an interesting and informative story of what it means to feel separated from the Universe and alone. The name of the game is to slowly realize that you are *not*, in fact, separate or alone. You are a beautiful expression of the Universe, and it's possible to be in a body *and* feel connected at the same time.

Your sense of connection – to Higher Consciousness, to nature, to the Universe, to Flow – is all available to you through the heart.

Activating Your Portal to Higher Consciousness

Your heart is not just an organ, a pump – it is a portal. It is the place where your Higher Consciousness passes its life force into you. It is a door that leads to all of the Universe.

Love and gratitude are the feelings that activate your heart portal the most. However, activating the portal also means agreeing to let all your feelings come through.

Feelings are your primary means of communicating quickly with your Higher Consciousness. You mustn't fear or judge your feelings, they are important guidance.

Feelings that you enjoy are encouragement from your Higher Self to keep going in that direction. Happy feelings lead you to a happy life.

Feelings that are unpleasant are signaling to you that you are on a path which leads to more unpleasant things. Something needs to change. Sometimes it is your perspective. Sometimes it is your environment. The negative emotion is the signal to pay attention, investigate further, and make new choices.

Feelings are just energy. They are always coming. Emotional distress from trauma are the feelings we attach to and hold onto, rather than letting them Flow, creating knots and snarls in our energy field. This manifests in our reality as areas of conflict and friction.

The exercises below are different ways of accessing the energetic constrictions in your biofield and releasing them, bringing you and your life into balance, Vitality, and Flow.

THE REAL YOU METHODS FOR VITALITY

The Sway

Your body is in direct communication with your unconscious and your Higher Consciousness – places your conscious mind can't reach. This simple exercise is astoundingly powerful at helping you feel into your body and release any tension it was holding, opening you up to ease and Flow.

You will be surprised at how much emotion can emerge as you do this. Let it come up and out without judgment or mental commentary. The stories that our conscious mind wants to spin are irrelevant. Silence the story and just let the feelings release as they will.

The Sway is literally that – letting your body sway rhythmically to a beat. It softens your fascia and spine at the same time that it induces the mind into a trance, allowing you to seat yourself peacefully in the heart. In this way it aligns all aspects of you at once – which in turn aligns you with the Flow.

Use music with a slow, relaxed beat. My most favorite music to Sway to is the beautiful handpan drum, as played by Malte Marten on YouTube. I especially recommend the track named Trust the Process. Here is a shortcut link to it: **https://bit.ly/JustSway**

- Sit cross-legged. (This is preferred to standing because we will be working on loosening the hips which are tight for most people.) Close your eyes. Place your hands over your heart and focus your attention there, on your chest.

- As the music plays, begin Swaying, left to right. Lead with the shoulder, allowing the spine to move in an S pattern, letting the head follow.

- Notice where you are feeling tension – usually in the hips, low back, neck, jaw and shoulders. Sway with a bit more intention into those areas, feeling the stretch. Let your mouth hang open slightly (don't worry nobody's watching). Your jaw greatly needs this release.

- As you continue swaying, you will feel the tension in your body loosen and soften. You will feel the muscles begin to relax. The mind becomes quiet and serene. Emotions may come up, or not.

- Start at 3 minutes and see if you can build up to 20. The longer you can hold this feeling of serenity and surrender, the better.

Charged Energy Clearing

In your daily life, you have many neutral experiences, and then occasional ones which carry an emotional charge. Something happens and now you feel fear, or anger, or shame, or something else upsetting that is now acting as a snag in your energy field.

If you suppress these charged feelings or deny them, or otherwise allow them to stay there, they get stored in your energy field, making your energy signature denser. Dense energy is constricted and heavy. You want to be able to Flow freely – that is Vitality.

This exercise is how to wash the charge off your emotions, smoothing out the energy and reclaiming it back into your biofield. This is what it means to "process" your emotions. As you release these constrictions in your energy, the space left behind gets filled with more of your light.

It doesn't matter if the feelings that need clearing are happening right now, or happened long ago. Whenever you notice you are feeling a charge, slow down and clear it. Over time you will realize how much lighter, happier, and freer you feel, and how less often you need to do clearings anymore.

- Sit or lay so that your body feels soft and relaxed. You can use the Sway method to assist. Close your eyes.

- Drop your awareness to your chest. Imagine there is an orb of light inside. As you breathe deeply into your belly and fully release, imagine there is golden light passing through the orb, lighting it up like a golden sun.

This glowing golden sun in your chest cleans and purifies all energy passing through it, washing the charge off and smoothing it out and reintegrating it back into your field as Flow.

- Whatever feelings or stories you are experiencing, name them, love and accept them, and pull them into your heart for clearing.

    I love and accept the part of me who feels attacked. I love and accept the part of me who feels defensive. I love and accept the part of me who feels sad. I love and accept the part of me who feels alone.

    Pull it all into the fiery orb in your heart, letting it all dissolve and melt into the molten gold.

    Washing the charge off in this way brings you back into the present, allowing you to feel stable and calm once again, while also empowering you with more light that you can use to find new perspectives and new solutions.

- You can do this with the Ego aspects of your Personality Type.

    Example: Type 1

    I love and accept the part of me who judges. I love and accept the part of me who wants life to make sense. I love and accept the part of me who tries to make the world better. I love and accept the part of me who feels frustrated that the world won't get better.

    Example Type 4

    I love and accept the part of me who longs for romance. I love and accept the part of me who feels disappointed. I love and accept the part of me that thinks I'm not enough. I love and accept the part of me who wants validation.

    Example Type 8

    I love and accept the part of me who feels angry. I love and accept the part of me who wants to control. I love and accept the part of me who is afraid to release control. I love and accept the part of me who doesn't know how to surrender.

Integration Exercise

If you are experiencing issues within yourself or your life that you feel confused by and powerless to shift, they are likely connected back to old charged energies in your field that have never been cleared.

These problematic patterns are unknown to you, confusing, and frustrating.

- They could be aspects of yourself which are self-sabotaging (addictions, hostilities, fears, procrastination, etc.)
- They could be specific difficult relationships (certain family members, friends, co-workers, etc)
- They could be themes that seem to keep repeating (money issues, abandonment issues, obstacles to success, mystery pain/illness, etc.)
- They could be the Distorted Themes within your Personality Type

Integrating these problem areas brings you more peace, and more power. Every time you integrate your own charged energy, you make room in your field for more light. This activates new DNA that enables you to dramatically enhance your life.

These issues heal in layers. You will experience great relief and advancement at every layer, and then at a later date you may find it's time to address them again. Meanwhile you will see your quality of life improve with every new healing.

♦♦♦

First, there is some vocabulary we should define for you to have a clear understanding of what this exercise is accomplishing

Forgiving

While living as a human incarnation, we all have Egos, which cause us all to behave quite badly at times. We must forgive ourselves and others, and ask for forgiveness in return.

Sometimes the issue you are clearing is a sabotaging aspect of yourself. We will give them a simple name, like Needy Amanda or Reactive Sam. When you ask them to forgive you, what you are apologizing for is having judged them and hated them. That aspect of yourself needs love and acceptance, not rejection.

Retrieving / Returning Energy

Whenever you have an intense emotionally charged interaction or experience that goes unresolved, you leave a bit of your energy there. Or conversely, you could still have other people's energy clinging to you, leftover from an old drama.

This leaves your biofield weak and incomplete, and keeps you stuck in old dynamics. You must recall your energy back to you, and give others back theirs.

Revoking Commands

Your words are energy and they create the reality you experience. Commands are strong words said with passion.

For example, you might have at some point said something like "I will never forgive you" or "I will never leave you" or "I'm so fat and ugly" or "I'm so stupid." Or you may have wished ill upon someone, which always rebounds back onto you.

Your words are commands out into the Universe, whether you meant them to be or not. It's possible you have been attracting unwanted things to yourself this way. These commands must be revoked. (And it teaches you to be very careful about what you say going forward.)

Dissolving Contracts

Prior to coming into this lifetime, your Higher Consciousness makes contracts about the kinds of dynamics you will have with yourself, with other people, and with the Universe. These are the "lessons" you agreed to repeat until you get them "right" – which basically means to bring them to neutral. This process is how you can finally release yourself from it forever.

To begin, identify what person or situation you want to address. You will repeat this process with every new person or situation. It is recommended that you not clear more than 3 issues per day, in order to give your energy time to integrate the work you have done.

This is a specific script. It is best if you can say the words out loud, but if you don't have privacy, it's ok to say them silently in your mind. The main thing is to really be in your heart and feel the truth of your words. You say each statement 3 times to deepen its meaning and resonance.

- Drop your awareness to your chest. Imagine there is an orb of light inside. As you inhale deeply into your belly and fully exhale, imagine there is golden light passing through the orb, lighting it up like a golden sun.

- Say to yourself, another person, or the Universe:
  I love you. Please forgive me for any harm I have caused you. I forgive you for any harm you caused me.

  I love you. Please forgive me for any harm I have caused you. I forgive you for any harm you caused me.

  I love you. Please forgive me for any harm I have caused you. I forgive you for any harm you caused me.

- *I recall all of my energy back into my heart. I return all energy I was holding that is not mine.*

  I recall all of my energy back into my heart. I return all energy I was holding that is not mine.

  I recall all of my energy back into my heart. I return all energy I was holding that is not mine.

- *I revoke all commands.*
  I revoke all commands.
  I revoke all commands.

- *I dissolve all contracts between us.*
  I dissolve all contracts between us.
  I dissolve all contracts between us.

Let's do a few different scenarios as examples so that you can see how to adapt the exercise to accommodate them.

Example 1: Charged Energy with Another Person

Say you and your sister Petunia have had a weird competitive aspect to your relationship all your lives. You don't know when it started or how it got there. But you wish there were a way you two could have an easier, friendlier relationship.

In your mind's eye, call up the face of your sister, hopefully with a feeling of love and compassion for her.

- *Petunia, I love you. Please forgive me for any harm I have caused you. I forgive you for any harm you caused me.* (X3)
- *I recall all of my energy back into my heart. I return all your energy that I was holding.* (X3)
- *I revoke all commands between us.* (X3)
- *I dissolve all contracts between us.* (X3)

Example 2: Charged Energetic Theme

Perhaps all your life you've struggled with a theme of abandonment. Your dad died when you were young, your best friend in high school moved away, and your husband left you for his secretary. Now you find yourself to be fearful and clingy in relationships, and you can see it is driving people away but you don't know how to stop.

Name this aspect of yourself, not to be mean or funny, just to be clear about what energy you are integrating. This could simply be Needy Delphine.

Call up the face of Needy Delphine in your mind's eye. She has felt alone, she has felt confused, she has doubted her value. She deserves great love and compassion, not judgment and contempt.

- *Needy Delphine I love you. Please forgive me for any harm I have caused you. I forgive you for any harm you caused me.* (X3)
- *I recall all of my energy back into my heart. I return all of your energy that I was holding.* (X3)
- *I revoke all commands between us.* (X3)
- *I dissolve all contracts between us.* (X3)

Example 3: Your Primal Persona

Even the encoding of your Personality Type prompts charged emotions that interfere with your Flow. These can also be integrated.

Perhaps as a Type 7 Hedonist, you have developed an attachment to marijuana that is now in the way, but you feel enormous anxiety come up every time you think about quitting.

Let's name this aspect of yourself Self-Medicating Dan.

Call up the face of Self-Medicating Dan in your mind's eye. He has never known how to feel anxiety and still be ok. He has never found a way to feel peaceful on his own. He deserves great love and compassion, not judgment and contempt.

- *Self-Medicating Dan, I love you. Please forgive me for any harm I have caused you. I forgive you for any harm you caused me.* (X3)
- *I recall all of my energy back into my heart. I return all of your energy that I was holding.* (X3)
- *I revoke all commands.* (X3)
- *I dissolve all contracts between us.* (X3)

♦♦♦

This exercise is so powerful because you are observing yourself and clearing yourself from the perspective of The Real You. You *are* your Higher Consciousness

— who loves you and has compassion for you — as you peacefully heal and upgrade yourself.

Deep healing does not have to be complicated. But it definitely needs to be deep — reaching all the way into your core. These techniques, simple though they are, are capable of connecting you with the truth of yourself — The Real You.

Once you begin to feel the excitement, hope and energy that accompanies this profound authenticity, you will be inspired to continue. Congratulations, you are on your way to your happiest life.

ADDITIONAL SUPPORT

A Note from the Author

You have only just begun this journey, and there is so much yet to discover! I hope to remain connected with you to offer support and inspiration along the path.

I have created several kinds of offerings for you, so that we can connect at whatever pace feels best for you.

There is much free content available for you on our social media platforms:
- YouTube.com/@yourvitalitypersonality
- tiktok.com/@yourvitaltypersonality
- instagram.com/@yourvitalitypersonality
- Facebook.com/YourVitalityPersonality

For a deeper dive, more exclusive personalized content, and more direct contact with me, you might enjoy our newsletter or private membership, the Vitality Voyagers. It is my joy to create this container for our own tribe, the ones ushering in Higher Consciousness.

> Join us at: **YourVitalityPersonality.com/Membership**

You can find links to all these using the code below:

I look forward to continuing the journey together.

To Your Vitality,
Candice

YOUR VITALITY PERSONALITY

Join Us!

VITALITY VOYAGERS

PRIVATE MEMBERSHIP

Insights ✦ Guidance
Inspiration ✦ Community

YOUR VITALITY PERSONALITY

ABOUT THE AUTHOR

Candice Thomas lives in happy tranquility in Tucson, Arizona. In addition to being an author, Enneagram teacher and speaker, she works as an acupuncturist, QHHT practitioner, and intuitive healer at her private practice, LightWorks SoulCare.. A mother of two young women, she enjoys guiding them toward stability, self-love, and expansion. She is awfully fond of people, metaphysics, historical fiction, trees, elephants, stargazer lilies, and music.

Made in the USA
Monee, IL
31 October 2024